Emerging Technologies of Augmented Reality:
Interfaces and Design

Michael Haller
Upper Austria University of Applied Sciences, Austria

Mark Billinghurst
Human Interface Technology Laboratory, New Zealand

Bruce H. Thomas
Wearable Computer Laboratory, University of South Australia, Australia

T0321800

IDEA GROUP PUBLISHING
Hershey • London • Melbourne • Singapore

Acquisition Editor:	Kristin Klinger
Senior Managing Editor:	Jennifer Neidig
Managing Editor:	Sara Reed
Assistant Managing Editor:	Sharon Berger
Development Editor:	Kristin Roth
Copy Editor:	Larissa Vinci
Typesetter:	Marko Primorac
Cover Design:	Lisa Tosheff
Printed at:	Yurchak Printing Inc.

Published in the United States of America by
Idea Group Publishing (an imprint of Idea Group Inc.)
701 E. Chocolate Avenue
Hershey PA 17033
Tel: 717-533-8845
Fax: 717-533-8661
E-mail: cust@idea-group.com
Web site: http://www.idea-group.com

and in the United Kingdom by
Idea Group Publishing (an imprint of Idea Group Inc.)
3 Henrietta Street
Covent Garden
London WC2E 8LU
Tel: 44 20 7240 0856
Fax: 44 20 7379 0609
Web site: http://www.eurospanonline.com

Library of Congress Cataloging-in-Publication Data

Emerging technologies of augmented reality : interfaces and design / Michael Haller, Mark Billinghurst, and Bruce Thomas, editors.
    p. cm.
  Summary: "This book provides a good grounding of the main concepts and terminology for Augmented Reality (AR), with an emphasis on practical AR techniques (from tracking-algorithms to design principles for AR interfaces). The targeted audience is computer-literate readers who wish to gain an initial understanding of this exciting and emerging technology"--Provided by publisher.
  Includes bibliographical references and index.
  ISBN 1-59904-066-2 (hardcover) -- ISBN 1-59904-067-0 (softcover) -- ISBN 1-59904-068-9 (ebook)
  1. Human-computer interaction--Congresses. 2. Virtual reality--Congresses. 3. User interfaces (Computer systems) I. Haller, Michael, 1974- II. Billinghurst, Mark, 1967- III. Thomas, Bruce (Bruce H.)
  QA76.9.H85E48 2007
  004.01'9--dc22
                            2006027724

British Cataloguing in Publication Data
A Cataloguing in Publication record for this book is available from the British Library.

All work contributed to this book is new, previously-unpublished material. The views expressed in this book are those of the authors, but not necessarily of the publisher.

Emerging Technologies of Augmented Reality:

Interfaces and Design

Table of Contents

Preface

Motivation

Augmented reality (AR) research aims to develop technologies that allow the real-time fusion of computer-generated digital content with the real world. Unlike virtual reality (VR) technology, which completely immerses users inside a synthetic environment, augmented reality allows the user to see three-dimensional virtual objects superimposed upon the real world. Both AR and VR are part of a broader reality–virtuality continuum termed "mixed reality" (MR) by Milgram and Kishino (1994) (see Figure 1). In their view, a mixed reality environment is "one in which real world and virtual world objects are presented together within a single display anywhere between the extrema of the virtuality continuum."

Figure 1. Reality-virtuality continuum (Milgram & Kishino, 1994)

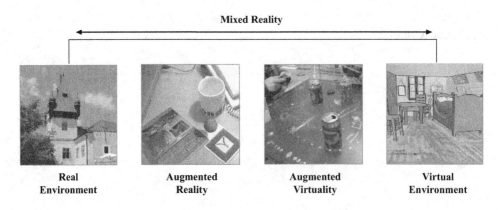

State of the Art

Mixed reality technology can enhance users' perception and interaction with the real world (Azuma et al., 2001), particularly through the use of augmented reality. Using Azuma's (1997) definition, an AR system has to fulfill the following three characteristics:

- It combines both the real and virtual content,
- The system is interactive and performs in real-time, and
- The virtual content is registered with the real world.

Previous research has shown that AR technology can be applied in a wide range of areas including education, medicine, engineering, military, and entertainment. For example, virtual maps can be overlaid on the real world to help people navigate through the real world, medical imagery can appear on a real patient body, and architects can see virtual buildings in place before they are built.

Analyzing the proceedings of the leading AR/MR research symposium (The International Symposium on Mixed and Augmented Reality), we can identify several significant research directions, including:

- **Tracking techniques:** How to achieve robust and accurate overlay of virtual imagery on the real world
- **Display technologies:** Head mounted, handheld, and projection displays for AR
- **Mobile augmented reality:** Using mobile computers to develop AR applications that can be used in outdoor settings
- **Interaction techniques:** Methods for interacting with AR content
- Novel **augmented reality applications**

Overview

Although the field of mixed reality has grown significantly over the last decade, there have been few published books about augmented reality, particularly the interface design aspects. *Emerging Technologies of Augmented Reality: Interfaces and Design* is written to address this need. It provides a good grounding of the main concepts of augmented reality with a particular emphasis on user interfaces and design and practical AR techniques (from tracking-algorithms to design principles for AR interfaces).

A wide range of experts from around the world have provided fully peer reviewed chapters for this book. The targeted audience is computer-literate readers who wish to gain an initial understanding of this exciting and emerging technology. This book may be used as the basis for a graduate class or as an introduction to researchers who want to explore the field of user interfaces and design techniques for augmented reality.

Book Structure and Use

This book is structured around the following four key topics:

- Technologies that support augmented reality
- Augmented reality development environments
- Interface design and evaluation of augmented reality applications
- Case studies of augmented reality applications

The first section, **Introduction to Technologies that Support Augmented Reality**, provides a concise overview of important AR technologies. These chapters examine a wide range of technologies, balanced between established and emerging new technologies. This insight provides the reader with a good grounding of the key technical concepts and challenges developers face when building AR systems. The major focus of these chapters is on tracking, display, and presentation technologies.

In **Chapter I**, mixed reality applications require accurate knowledge of the relative positions of the camera and the scene. Many technologies have tried to achieve this goal and computer vision seems to be the only one that has the potential to yield non-invasive, accurate, and low-cost solutions to this problem. In this chapter, the authors discuss some of the most promising computer vision approaches, their strengths, and their weaknesses.

Chapter II introduces spatially adaptive augmented reality as an approach to dealing with the registration errors introduced by spatial uncertainty. The authors argue that if programmers are given simple estimates of registration error, they can create systems that adapt to dynamically changing amounts of spatial uncertainty, and that it is this ability to adapt to spatial uncertainty that will be the key to creating augmented reality systems that work in real-world environments.

Chapter III discusses design and principles of head mounted displays (HMDs), as well as their state-of-the-art examples, for augmented reality. After a brief history of head mounted displays, human vision system, and application examples of see-through HMDs, the author describes the design and principles for HMDs, such as typical configurations of optics, typical display elements, and major categories of HMDs. For researchers, students, and HMD developers, this chapter is a good starting point for learning the basics, state of the art technologies, and future research directions for HMDs.

Chapter IV shows how, in contrast to HMD-based systems, projector-based augmentation approaches combine the advantages of well-established spatial virtual reality with those of spatial augmented reality. Immersive, semi-immersive, and augmented visualizations can be realized in everyday environments—without the need for special projection screens and dedicated display configurations. This chapter describes projector-camera methods and multi-projector techniques that aim at correcting geometric aberrations, compensating local and global radiometric effects, and improving focus properties of images projected onto everyday surfaces.

Mobile phones are evolving into the ideal platform for portable augmented reality. In **Chapter V**, the authors describe how augmented reality applications can be developed for mobile phones and the interaction metaphors that are ideally suited for this platform.

Several sample applications are described which explore different interaction techniques. The authors also present a user study showing that moving the phone to interact with virtual content is an intuitive way to select and position virtual objects.

In **Chapter VI**, the authors describe how to compute a 2D screen-space representation that corresponds to the visible portions of the projections of 3D AR-objects on the screen. They describe in detail two visible surface determination algorithms that are used to generate these representations. They compare the performance and accuracy tradeoffs of these algorithms, and present examples of how to use our representation to satisfy visibility constraints that avoid unwanted occlusions, making it possible to label and annotate objects in 3D environments.

The second section, **Augmented Reality Development Environments**, examines frameworks, toolkits, and authoring tools that are the current state-of-the-art for the development of AR applications. As it has been stated from many disciplines, "Content is King!" For AR, this is indeed very true and these chapters provide the reader with an insight into this emerging important area. The concepts covered vary from staging complete AR experiences to modeling 3D content for AR.

AR application development is still lacking advanced authoring tools—even the simple presentation of information, which should not require any programming, is not systematically addressed by development tools. In **Chapter VII**, the authors present APRIL, the augmented presentation and interaction language. APRIL is an authoring platform for AR applications that provides concepts and techniques that are independent of specific applications or target hardware platforms, and should be suitable for raising the level of abstraction at which AR content creators can operate.

Chapter VIII presents DART, The designer's augmented reality toolkit which is an authoring environment for rapidly prototyping augmented reality experiences. The authors summarize the most significant problems faced by designers working with AR in the real world and use DART as the example to guide a discussion of the AR design process. DART is significant because it is one of the first tools designed to allow non-programmers to rapidly develop AR applications. If AR applications are to become mainstream then there will need to be more tools like this.

Augmented reality techniques can be used to construct virtual models in an outdoor environment. **Chapter IX** presents a series of new AR user interaction techniques to support the capture and creation of 3D geometry of large outdoor structures. Current scanning technologies can be used to capture existing physical objects, while construction at a distance also allows the creation of new models that exist only in the mind of the user. Using a single AR interface, users can enter geometry and verify its accuracy in real-time. This chapter presents a number of different construction-at-a-distance techniques, which are demonstrated with examples of real objects that have been modeled in the real world.

Chapter X describes the evolution of a software system specifically designed to support the creation and delivery of mixed reality experiences. The authors first describe some of the attributes required of such a system. They then present a series of MR experiences that they have developed over the last four years, with companion sections on lessons learned and lessons applied. The authors' goals are to show the readers the unique challenges in developing an MR system for multimodal, multi-sensory experiences, and to demonstrate how developing MR applications informs the evolution of such a framework.

The next section, **Interface Design and Evaluation of Augmented Reality Applications,** describes current AR user interface technologies with a focus on the design issues. AR is an emerging technology; as such, it does not have a set of agreed design methodologies or evaluation techniques. These chapters present the opinions of experts in the areas of design and evaluation of AR technology, and provide a good starting point for the development of your next AR system.

Ubiquitous augmented reality (UAR) is an emerging human-computer interaction technique, arising from the convergence of augmented reality and ubiquitous computing. In UAR, visualizations can augment the real world with digital information, and interaction with the digital content can follow a tangible metaphor. Both the visualization and interaction should adapt according to the user's context and are distributed on a possibly changing set of devices. Current research problems for user interfaces in UAR are software infrastructures, authoring tools, and a supporting design process. The authors in **Chapter XI** present case studies of how they have used a systematic design space analysis to carefully narrow the amount of available design options. The next step is to use interactive, possibly immersive tools to support interdisciplinary brainstorming sessions and several tools for UAR are presented.

The main goal of **Chapter XII** is to give characteristics, evaluation methodologies, and research examples of collaborative augmented reality systems from a perspective of human-to-human communication. Starting with a classification of conventional and 3D collaborative systems, the author discusses design considerations of collaborative AR systems from a perspective of human communication. Moreover, he presents different evaluation methodologies of human communication behaviors and shows a variety of collaborative AR systems with regard to display devices used. will be a good starting point for learning about existing collaborative AR systems; their advantages and limitations. This chapter will also contribute to the selection of appropriate hardware configurations and software designs of a collaborative AR system for given conditions.

Chapter XIII describes the design of interaction methods for tangible augmented reality applications. First, the authors describe the general concept of a tangible augmented reality interface and review its various successful applications, focusing on their interaction designs. Next, they classify and consolidate these interaction methods into common tasks and interaction schemes. Finally, they present general design guidelines for interaction methods in tangible AR applications. The principles presented in this chapter will help developers design interaction methods for tangible AR applications in a more structured and efficient way, and bring tangible AR interfaces into more widespread use.

The final section, **Case Studies of Augmented Reality Applications**, provides an explanation of AR through one or more closely related real case studies. Through the examination of a number of successful AR experiences, these chapters answer the question, "What makes AR work?" The case studies cover a range of applications from industrial to entertainment, and provide the reader with a rich understand of the process of developing successful AR environments.

Chapter XIV explains and illustrates the different types of industrial augmented reality (IAR) applications and shows how they can be classified according to their purpose and degree of maturity. The information presented here provides valuable insights into the underlying principles and issues associated with bringing Augmented Reality applications from the laboratory and into an industrial context.

Augmented reality typically fuses computer graphics onto images or direct views of a scene. In **Chapter XV**, an alternative augmentation approach is described as a real scene that is captured as video imagery from one or more cameras, and these images are inserted into a corresponding 3D scene model or virtual environment. This arrangement is termed an augmented virtual environment (AVE) and it produces a powerful visualization of the dynamic activities observed by cameras. This chapter describes the AVE concept and the major technologies needed to realize such systems. AVEs could be used in security and command and control type applications to create an intuitive way to monitor remote environments.

Chapter XVI explores how mixed reality (MR) allows the magic of virtuality to escape the confines of the computer and enter our lives to potentially change the way we play, work, train, learn, and even shop. Case studies demonstrate how emerging functional capabilities will depend upon new artistic conventions to spark the imagination, enhance human experience, and lead to subsequent commercial success.

In **Chapter XVII** the author explores the applications of mixed reality technology for future social and physical entertainment systems. A variety of case studies show the very broad and significant impacts of mixed reality technology on human interactivity with regards to entertainment. The MR entertainment systems described incorporate different technologies ranging from the current mainstream ones such as GPS tracking, Bluetooth, and RFID tags to pioneering researches of vision based tracking, augmented reality, tangible interaction techniques, and 3D live mixed reality capture system.

Entertainment systems are one of the more successful uses of augmented reality technologies in real world applications. **Chapter XVIII** provides insights into the future directions of the use of augmented reality with gaming applications. This chapter explores a number of advances in technologies that may enhance augmented reality gaming. The features for both indoor and outdoor augmented reality are examined in context of their desired attributes for the gaming community. A set of concept games for outdoor augmented reality are presented to highlight novel features of this technology.

As can be seen within the four key focus areas, a number of different topics have been presented. Augmented reality encompasses many aspects so it is impossible to cover all of the research and development activity occurring in one book. This book is intended to support readers with different interests in augmented reality and to give them the foundation that will enable them to design the next generation of AR applications. It is not a traditional textbook that should be read from front to back, rather the reader can pick and choose the topics of interest and use the material presented here as a springboard to further their knowledge in this fast growing field.

As editors is it our hope that this work will be the first of a number of books in the field that will help capture the existing knowledge and train new researchers in this exciting area.

References

Azuma, R. (1997). A survey of augmented reality. *Presence: Teleoperation and Virtual Environments*, *6*(4), 355-385.

Azuma, R., Baillot, Y., Behringer, R., Feiner, S., Julier, S., & MacIntyre, B. (2001). Recent advances in augmented reality. *IEEE Computer Graphics and Applications*, *21*(6), 34-47.

Milgram, P., & Kishino, F. (1994, December). A taxonomy of mixed reality visual displays. *IEICE Transactions on Information Systems*, *E77-D*(12).

Acknowledgments

First of all, we would like to thank our authors. It always takes more time than expected to write a chapter and all authors did a great job. Special thanks to all the staff at Idea Group Inc. that were always there to help in the production process. Special thanks to our development editor, Kristin Roth! The different chapters benefited from the patient attention of the anonymous reviewers. They include Blaine Bell, Oliver Bimber, Peter Brandl, Wilhelm Burger, Adrian D. Cheok, Ralf Dörner, Steven Feiner, Maribeth Gandy, Christian Geiger, Raphael Grasset, Tobias Höllerer, Hirokazu Kato, Kiyoshi Kiyokawa, Gudrun Klinker, Gun A. Lee, Ulrich Neumann, Volker Paelke, Wayne Piekarski, Holger Regenbrecht, Christian Sandor, Dieter Schmalstieg, and Jürgen Zauner. Thanks to them for providing constructive and comprehensive reviews.

Michael Haller, Austria
Mark Billinghurst, New Zealand
Bruce H. Thomas, Australia

June 2006

Section I:

Introduction to Technologies that Support Augmented Reality

Chapter I

Vision Based 3D Tracking and Pose Estimation for Mixed Reality

Pascal Fua, Ecole Polytechnique Fédérale de Laussane (EPFL), Switzerland

Vincent Lepetit, Ecole Polytechnique Fédérale de Laussane (EPFL), Switzerland

Abstract

Mixed reality applications require accurate knowledge of the relative positions of the camera and the scene. When either of them moves, this means keeping track in real-time of all six degrees of freedom that define the camera position and orientation relative to the scene, or equivalently, the 3D displacement of an object relative to the camera. Many technologies have tried to achieve this goal. However, computer vision is the only one that has the potential to yield non-invasive, accurate, and low-cost solutions to this problem, provided that one is willing to invest the effort required to develop sufficiently robust algorithms. In this chapter, we therefore discuss some of the most promising approaches, their strengths, and their weaknesses.

Introduction

Tracking an object in a video sequence means continuously identifying its location when either the object or the camera are moving. More specifically, 3D tracking aims at continuously recovering all six degrees of freedom that define the camera position and orientation relative to the scene, or equivalently, the 3D displacement of an object relative to the camera.

Many other technologies besides vision have been tried to achieve this goal, but they all have their weaknesses. Mechanical trackers are accurate enough, although they tether the user to a limited working volume. Magnetic trackers are vulnerable to distortions by metal in the environment which are a common occurrence, and also limit the range of displacements. Ultrasonic trackers suffer from noise and tend to be inaccurate at long ranges because of variations in the ambient temperature. Inertial trackers drift with time.

By contrast, vision has the potential to yield non-invasive, accurate, and low-cost solutions to this problem, provided that one is willing to invest the effort required to develop sufficiently robust algorithms. In some cases, it is acceptable to add fiducials, such as LEDs or special markers, to the scene or target object to ease the registration task. Of course, this assumes that one or more fiducials are visible at all times, otherwise, the registration falls apart. Moreover, it is not always possible to place fiducials. For example, augmented reality end-users do not like markers because they are visible in the scene and it is not always possible to modify the environment before the application has to run.

It is therefore much more desirable to rely on naturally present features, such as edges, corners, or texture. Of course, this makes tracking far more difficult. Finding and following feature points or edges on many everyday objects is sometimes difficult because there may only be a few of them. Total, or even partial occlusion of the tracked objects typically results in tracking failure. The camera can easily move too fast so that the images are motion blurred; the lighting during a shot can change significantly; reflections and specularities may confuse the tracker. Even more importantly, an object may drastically change its aspect very quickly due to displacement. For example, this happens when a camera films a building and goes around the corner, causing one wall to disappear and a new one to appear. In such cases, the features to be followed always change and the tracker must deal with features coming in and out of the picture. Next, we focus on solutions to these difficult problems and show how planar, non-planar, and even deformable objects can be handled.

For the sake of completeness, we provide a brief description of the camera models that all these techniques rely on, as well as pointers to useful implementations and more extensive descriptions in the appendix at the end of this chapter.

Fiducials-Based Tracking

Vision-based 3D tracking can be decomposed into two main steps; First image processing to extract some information from the images, and second pose estimation itself. The addition in the scene of *fiducials*, also called *landmarks* or *markers*, greatly helps both steps.

They constitute image features easy to extract, and they provide reliable, easy to exploit measurements for pose estimation.

Point-Like Fiducials

Fiducials have been used for many years by close-range photogrammetrists. They can be designed in such a way that they can be easily detected and identified with an *ad hoc* method. Their image locations can also be measured to a much higher accuracy than natural features. In particular, circular fiducials work best, because the appearance of circular patterns is relatively invariant to perspective distortion, and because their centroid provides a stable 2D position, which can easily be determined with sub-pixel accuracy. The 3D positions of the fiducials in the world coordinate system are assumed to be precisely known. This can be achieved by hand, with a laser, or with a structure-from-motion algorithm. To facilitate their identification, the fiducials can be arranged in a distinctive geometric pattern. Once the fiducials are identified in the image, they provide a set of correspondences that can be used to retrieve the camera pose.

For high-end applications, companies such as Geodetic Services, Inc., Advanced Real-time Tracking GmbH, Metronor, ViconPeak, and AICON 3D Systems GmbH propose commercial products based on this approach. Lower-cost and lower-accuracy solutions have also been proposed by the computer vision community. For example, the concentric contrasting circle (CCC) fiducial (Hoff, Nguyen & Lyon, 1996) is formed by placing a black ring on a white background, or vice-versa. To detect these fiducials, the image is first thresholded, morphological operations are then applied to eliminate too small regions, and a connected component labeling operation is performed to find white and black regions, as well as their centroids. Along the same lines, State, Hirota, David, Garett, and Livingston (1996) use color-coded fiducials for a more reliable identification. Each fiducial consists of an inner dot and a surrounding outer ring, four different colors are used, and thus 12 unique fiducials can be created and identified based on their two colors. Because the tracking range is constrained by the detectability of fiducials in input images, Cho, Lee, and Neumann (1998) introduce a system that uses several sizes for the fiducials. They are composed of several colored concentric rings where large fiducials have more rings than smaller ones, and diameters of the rings are proportional to their distance to the fiducial center to facilitate their identification. When the camera is close to fiducials, only small size fiducials are detected. When it is far from them, only large size fiducials are detected.

While all the previous methods for fiducial detection use *ad hoc* schemes, Claus and Fitzigibbon (2004) use a machine learning approach which delivers significant improvements in reliability. The fiducials are made of black disks on white background, and sample fiducial images are collected under varying perspective, scale, and lighting conditions, as well as negative training images. A cascade of classifiers is then trained on these data. The first step is a fast Bayes decision rule classification, the second one a powerful but slower nearest neighbor classifier on the subset passed by the first stage. At run-time, all the possible sub-windows in the image are classified using this cascade. This results in a remarkably reliable fiducial detection method.

Extended Fiducials

The fiducials previously presented were all circular and only their center was used. By contrast, Koller et al. (1997) introduce squared, black on white fiducials, which contain small red squares for their identification. The corners are found by fitting straight line segments to the maximum gradient points on the border of the fiducial. Each of the four corners of such fiducials provides one correspondence and the pose is estimated using an Extended Kalman filter.

Planar rectangular fiducials are also used in Kato and Billinghurst (1999), Kato, Poupyrev, Imamoto, and Tachibana (2000), and Rekimoto (1998) and it is shown that a single fiducial is enough to estimate the pose. Figure 1 depicts their approach. It has become popular because it yields a robust, low-cost solution for real-time 3D tracking, and a software library called ARToolKit is publicly available (ARtoolkit).

The whole process, the detection of the fiducials and the pose estimation runs in real-time, and therefore can be applied in every frame. The 3D tracking system does not require any initialization by hand, and is robust to fiducial occlusion. In practice, under good lighting conditions, the recovered pose is also accurate enough for augmented reality applications. These characteristics make ARToolKit a good solution to 3D tracking, whenever the engineering of the scene is possible.

Using Natural Features

Using markers to simplify the 3D tracking task requires engineering of the environment which end-users of tracking technology do not like or is sometimes even impossible, for

Figure 1. Processing flow of ARToolKit: The marker is detected in the thresholded image, and then used to estimate the camera pose (Reproduced from Kato et al., 2000, © 2000 IEEE, used with permission)

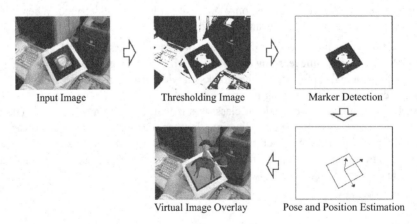

example, in outdoor environments. Whenever possible, it is therefore much better to be able to rely on features naturally present in the images. Of course, this approach makes tracking much more challenging and some 3D knowledge is often required to make things easier. For MR applications, this is not an issue since 3D scene models are typically available and we therefore focus here on model-based approaches.

Here we distinguish two families of approaches depending on the nature of the image features being used. The first one is formed by edge-based methods that match the projections of the target object 3D edges to area of high image gradient. The second family includes all the techniques that rely on information provided by pixels inside the object's projection.

Edge-Based Methods

Historically, the early approaches to tracking were all edge-based mostly because these methods are both computationally efficient, and relatively easy to implement. They are also naturally stable to lighting changes, even for specular materials, which is not necessarily true of methods that consider the internal pixels as will be discussed later. The most popular approach is to look for strong gradients in the image around a first estimation of the object pose, without explicitly extracting the contours (Armstrong & Zisseman, 1995; Comport, Marchand, & Chaumette, 2003; Drummond & Cipolla, 2002; Harris, 1992; Marchand, Bouthemy, & Chaumette, 2001; Vacchetti, Lepetit, & Fua, 2004a), which is fast and general.

RAPiD

Even though RAPiD (Harris, 1992) was one of the first 3D trackers to successfully run in real-time and many improvements have been proposed since, many of its basic components have been retained in more recent systems. The key idea is to consider a set of 3D points on the object, called control points, which lie on high contrast edges in the images. As shown in Figure 2, the control points can be sampled along the 3D model edges and in the areas of rapid albedo change. They can also be generated on the fly as points on the occluding

Figure 2. In RAPiD-like approaches, control points are sampled along the model edges; the small white segments in the left image join the control points in the previous image to their found position in the new image, the pose can be inferred from these matches, even in presence of occlusions by introducing robust estimators (Reproduced from Drummond & Cipolla, 2002, © 2002 IEEE, used with permission)

contours of the object. The 3D motion of the object between two consecutive frames can be recovered from the 2D displacement of the control points.

Once initialized, the system performs a simple loop. For each frame, the predicted pose, which can simply be the pose estimated for the previous frame, is used to predict which control points will be visible and what their new locations should be. The control points are matched to the image contours, and the new pose estimated from these correspondences via least-squares minimization.

In Harris (1992), some enhancements to this basic approach are proposed. When the edge response at a control point becomes too weak, it is not taken into account into the motion computation, as it may subsequently incorrectly latch on to a stronger nearby edge. As we will see next, this can also be handled using a robust estimator. An additional clue that can be used to reject incorrect edges is their polarity, that is whether they correspond to a transition from dark to light or from light to dark. A way to use occluding contours of the object is also given.

Making RAPiD Robust

The main drawback of the original RAPiD formulation is its lack of robustness. The weak contours heuristics is not enough to prevent incorrectly detected edges from disturbing the pose computation. In practice, such errors are frequent. They arise from occlusions, shadows, texture on the object itself, or background clutter.

Several methods have been proposed to make the RAPiD computation more robust. Drummond and Cipolla (2002) use a robust estimator and replace the least-squares estimation by an iterative re-weighted least-squares to solve the new problem. Similarly, Marchand et al. (2001) uses a framework similar to RAPiD to estimate a 2D affine transformation between consecutive frames, but also replaces standard least-squares by robust estimation.

In the approaches previously described, the control points were treated individually, without taking into account that several control points are often placed on the same edge, and hence their measurements are correlated. By contrast, in Armstrong and Zisserman (1995) and Simon and Berger (1998), control points lying on the same object edge are grouped into primitives, and a whole primitive can be rejected from the pose estimation. In Armstrong and Zisseman (1995), a RANSAC methodology (Fischler & Bolles, 1981) is used to detect outliers among the control points forming a primitive. If the number of remaining control points falls below a threshold after elimination of the outliers, the primitive is ignored in the pose update. Using RANSAC implies that the primitives have an analytic expression, and precludes tracking free-form curves. By contrast, Simon and Berger (1998) use a robust estimator to compute a local residual for each primitive. The pose estimator then takes into account all the primitives using a robust estimation on the above residuals.

When the tracker finds multiple edges within its search range, it may end up choosing the wrong one. To overcome this problem, in Drummond and Cipolla (2002) the influence of a control point is inversely proportional to the number of edge strength maxima visible within the search path. Vacchetti et al. (2004a) introduce another robust estimator to handle multiple hypotheses and retain all the maxima as possible correspondents in the pose estimation.

Texture-Based Methods

If the object is sufficiently textured, information can be derived from optical flow (Basu, Essa, & Pentland, 1996; DeCarlo & Metaxas, 2000; Li, Roivainen, & Forchheimer, 1993), template matching (Cascia, Sclaroff, & Athitsos, 2000; Hager & Belhumeur, 1998; Jurie & Dhome, 2001, 2002), or interest-point correspondences. However the latter is probably the most effective for MR applications because they rely on matching local features. Given such correspondences, the pose can be estimated by least-square minimization, or even better, by robust estimation. They are therefore relatively insensitive to partial occlusions or matching errors. Illumination invariance is also simple to achieve. And, unlike edge-based methods, they do not get confused by background clutter and exploit more of the image information, which tends to make them more dependable.

Interest Point Detection and 2D Matching

In interest point methods, instead of matching all pixels in an image, only some pixels are first selected with an "interest operator" before matching. This reduces the computation time while increasing the reliability if the pixels are correctly chosen. Förstner (1986) presents the desired properties for such an interest operator. Selected points should be different from their neighbors, which eliminates edge-points; the selection should be repeatable, that is the same points should be selected in several images of the same scene, despite perspective distortion or image noise. In particular, the precision and the reliability of the matching directly depends on the invariance of the selected position. Pixels on repetitive patterns should also be rejected or at least given less importance to avoid confusion during matching.

Such an operator was already used in the 1970s for tracking purposes (Moravec, 1977, 1981). Numerous other methods have been proposed since and Deriche and Giraudon (1993) and Smith and Brady (1995) give good surveys of them. Most of them involve second order derivatives, and results can be strongly affected by noise. Several successful interest point detectors (Förstner, 1986; Harris & Stephens, 1988; Shi & Tomasi, 1994) rely on the auto-correlation matrix computed at each pixel location. It is a 2×2 matrix, whose coefficients are sums over a window of the first derivatives of the image intensity with respect to the pixel coordinates, and its measures the local variations of the image. As discussed in Förstner (1986), the pixels can be classified from the behavior of the eigenvalues of the auto-correlation matrix. Pixels with two large, approximately equal eigenvalues are good candidates for selection. Shi and Tomasi (1994) show that locations with two large eigenvalues can be reliably tracked, especially under affine deformations, and considers locations where the smallest eigen value is higher than a threshold. Interest points can then be taken to the locations that are local maxima of the chosen measure above a predefined threshold. The derivatives involved in the auto-correlation matrix can be weighted using a Gaussian kernel to increase robustness to noise (Schmid & Mohr, 1997). The derivatives should also be computed using a first order Gaussian kernel. This comes at a price since it tends to degrade both the localization accuracy and the performance of the image patch correlation procedure used for matching purposes.

For tracking purpose, it is then useful to match two sets of interest points and extract from two images taken from similar viewpoints. A classical procedure (Zhang, Deriche, Faugeras, & Luong, 1995) runs as follows: For each point in the first image, search in a region of the second image around its location for a corresponding point. The search is based on the similarity of the local image windows centered on the points, which strongly characterize the points when the images are sufficiently close. The similarity can be measured using the zero-normalized cross-correlation that is invariant to affine changes of the local image intensities, and make the procedure robust to illumination changes. To obtain a more reliable set of matches, one can reverse the role of the two images, and repeat the previous procedure. Only the correspondences between points that chose each other are kept.

Eliminating Drift

In the absence of points whose coordinates are known *a priori*, all methods are subject to error accumulation, which eventually results in tracking failure and precludes of truly long sequences.

A solution to this problem is to introduce one or more *keyframes* such as the one in the upper left corner of Figure 3, that is images of the target object or scene for which the camera has been registered *beforehand*. At runtime, incoming images can be matched against the keyframes to provide a position estimate that is drift-free (Genc, Riedel, Souvannavong, & Navab, 2002; Ravela, Draper, Lim, & Weiss, 1995; Tordoff, Mayol, de Campos, & Murray, 2002). This, however, is more difficult than matching against immediately preceding frames as the difference in viewpoint is likely to be much larger. The algorithm used to establish point correspondences must therefore both be fast and relatively insensitive to large perspective distortions, which is not usually the case for those used by the algorithms that need only handle small distortions between consecutive frames.

Figure 3. Face tracking using interest points, and one reference image shown (top left) (Reproduced from Vacchetti et al., 2004b, © 2004 IEEE, used with permission)

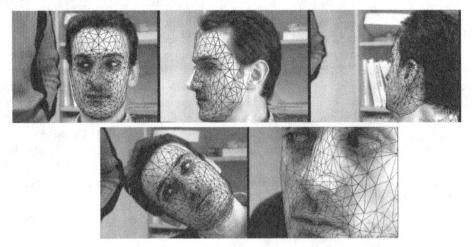

In Vacchetti, Lepetit, and Fua (2004b), this is handled as follows. During a training stage, the system extracts interest points from each keyframe, back-projects them to the object surface to compute their 3D position, and stores image patches centered around their location. During tracking, for each new incoming image, the system picks the keyframe whose viewpoint is closest to that of the last known viewpoint. It synthesizes an *intermediate image* from that keyframe by warping the stored image patches to the last known viewpoint, which is typically the one corresponding to the previous image. The intermediate and the incoming images are now close enough that matching can be performed using simple, conventional, and fast correlation methods. Since the 3D position in the keyframe has been precomputed, the pose can then be estimated by robustly minimizing the reprojection error. This approach handles perspective distortion, complex aspect changes, and self-occlusion. Furthermore, it is very efficient because it takes advantage of the large graphics capabilities of modern CPUs and GPUs.

However, as noticed by several authors (Chia, Cheok, & Prince, 2002; Ravela et al., 1995; Tordoff et al., 2002; Vacchetti et al., 2004b), matching only against keyframes does not, by itself, yield directly exploitable results. This has two main causes. First, wide-baseline matching as described in the previous paragraph is inherently less accurate than the short-baseline matching involved in frame-to-frame tracking, which is compounded by the fact that the number of correspondences that can be established is usually less. Second, if the pose is computed for each frame independently, no temporal consistency is enforced and the recovered motion can appear to be jerky. If it were used as is by an MR application, the virtual objects inserted in the scene would appear to *jitter*, or to tremble, as opposed to remaining solidly attached to the scene.

Temporal consistency can be enforced by some dynamical smoothing using a motion model. Another way proposed in Vacchetti et al. (2004b) is to combine the information provided by the keyframes which provides robustness with that coming from preceding frames, which enforces temporal consistency. This does not make assumptions on the camera motion and improves the accuracy of the recovered pose. It is still compatible with the use of dynamical smoothing that can be useful in cases where the pose estimation remains unstable, for example when the object is essentially fronto-parallel.

Tracking by Detection

The recursive nature of traditional 3D tracking approaches provides a strong prior on the pose for each new frame and makes image feature identifications relatively easy. However, it comes at a price. First, the system must either be initialized by hand or require the camera to be very close to a specified position. Second, it makes the system very fragile. If something goes wrong between two consecutive frames, for example due to a complete occlusion of the target object or a very fast motion, the system can be lost and must be re-initialized in the same fashion. In practice, such weaknesses make purely recursive systems nearly unusable, and the popularity of ARToolKit (Kato et al., 2000) in the augmented reality community should come as no surprise. It is the first vision-based system to really overcome these limitations by being able to detect the markers in every frame without constraints on the camera pose.

However, achieving the same level of performance *without* having to engineer the environment remains a desirable goal. Since object pose and appearance are highly correlated, estimating both simultaneously increases the performances of object detection algorithms. Therefore, 3D pose estimation from natural features without *a priori* knowledge of the position and object detection are closely related problems. Detection has a long history in Computer Vision. It has often relied on 2D detection even for 3D objects (Nayar, Nene, & Murase, 1996; Viola & Jones, 2001). However, there has been sustained interest in simultaneous object detection and 3D pose estimation. Early approaches were edge-based (Lowe, 1991; Jurie, 1998), but methods based on feature points matching have become popular since local invariants were shown to work better for that purpose (Schmid & Mohr, 1997).

Feature point-based approaches to be the most robust to scale, viewpoint, and illumination changes, as well as partial occlusions. They typically operate on the following principle. During an offline training stage, one builds a database of interest points lying on the object and whose position on the object surface can be computed. A few images in which the object has been manually registered are often used for this purpose. At runtime, feature points are first extracted from individual images and matched against the database. The object pose can then be estimated from such correspondences. RANSAC-like algorithms (Fischler & Bolles, 1981) or the Hough transform are very convenient for this task since they eliminate spurious correspondences while avoiding combinatorial issues.

The difficulty in implementing such approaches comes from the fact that the database images and the input ones may have been acquired from very different viewpoints. As discussed in this chapter, unless the motion is very quick, this problem does not arise in conventional recursive tracking approaches because the images are close to each other. However, for tracking-by-detection purposes, the so-called *wide baseline* matching problem becomes a critical issue that must be addressed.

In the remainder of this section, we discuss in more detail the extraction and matching of feature points in this context. We conclude by discussing the relative merits of tracking-by-detection and recursive tracking.

Feature Point Extraction

To handle as wide as possible a range of viewing conditions, feature point extraction should be insensitive to scale, viewpoint, and illumination changes. Note that the stability of the extracted features is much more crucial here than for the techniques described in this chapter where only close frames were matched. Different techniques are therefore required and we discuss them next.

As proposed in Lindeberg (1994), scale-invariant extraction can be achieved by taking feature points to be local extrema of a Laplacian-of-Gaussian pyramid in scale-space. To increase computational efficiency, the Laplacian can be approximated by a Difference-of-Gaussians (Lowe, 1999). Research has then focused on affine invariant region detection to handle more perspective changes. Baumberg (2000), Schaffalitzky and Zisserman (2002), and Mikolajczyk and Schmid (2002) used an affine invariant point detector based on the Harris detector, where the affine transformation that makes equal the two eigen values of the auto correlation matrix is evaluated to rectify the patch appearance. Tuytelaars and Van-Gool (2000) achieve such invariance by fitting an ellipse to the local texture. Matas, Chum, Martin, and Pajdla (2002) propose a fast algorithm to extract Maximally Stable Extremal Regions demonstrated in a live demo. Mikolajczyk et al. (2005) give a good summary and comparisons of the existing affine invariant regions detectors.

Wide Baseline Matching

Once a feature point has been extracted, the most popular approach to matching it is first to characterize it in terms of its image neighborhood and then to compare this characterization to those present in the database. Such characterization, or *local descriptor*, should not only be invariant to viewpoint and illumination changes, but also highly distinctive. We briefly review some of the most representative next.

Local Descriptors

Many such descriptors have been proposed over the years. For example, Schmid and Mohr (1997) compute rotation invariant descriptors as functions of relatively high order image derivatives to achieve orientation invariance; Tuytelaars and VanGool (2000) fit an ellipse to the texture around local intensity extrema and uses the generalized color moments (Mindru, Moons, & VanGool, 1999) as a descriptor. Lowe (2004) introduces a descriptor called SIFT based on multiple orientation histograms, which tolerates significant local deformations. This last descriptor has been shown in Mikoljaczyk and Schmid (2003) to be one of the most efficient. As illustrated by Figure 4, it has been successfully applied to 3D tracking in Se, Lowe, and Little (2002) and Skrypnyk and Lowe (2004) and we now describe it in more detail.

Figure 4. Using SIFT for tracking-by-detection: (a) Detected SIFT features; (b) (c) they have been used to track the pose of the camera and add the virtual teapot (Reproduced from Skrypnyk & Lowe, 2004, © 2004 IEEE, used with permission)

(b)

(c)

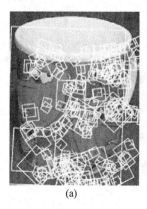

(a)

The remarkable invariance of the SIFT descriptor is achieved by a succession of carefully designed techniques. First the location and scale of the keypoints are determined precisely by interpolating the pyramid of Difference-of-Gaussians used for the detection. To achieve image rotation invariance, an orientation is also assigned to the keypoint. It is taken to be the one corresponding to a peak in the histogram of the gradient orientations within a region around the keypoint. This method is quite stable under viewpoint changes, and achieves an accuracy of a few degrees. The image neighborhood of the feature point is then corrected according to the estimated scale and orientation, and a local descriptor is computed on the resulting image region to achieve invariance to the remaining variations, such as illumination or out-of-plane variation. The point neighborhood is divided into several, typically 4×4, subregions and the contents of each subregion is summarized by an height-bin histogram of gradient orientations. The keypoint descriptor becomes a vector with 128 dimensions, built by concatenating the different histograms. Finally, this vector is normalized to unit length to reduce the effects of illumination changes.

Statistical Classification

The SIFT descriptor has been empirically shown to be both very distinctive and computationally cheaper than those based on filter banks. To shift even more of the computational burden from matching to training, which can be performed beforehand, we have proposed in our own work an alternative approach based on machine learning techniques (Lepetit, Lagger, & Fua, 2005; Lepetit & Fua, 2006). We treat wide baseline matching of keypoints as a classification problem, in which each class corresponds to the set of all possible views of such a point. Given one or more images of a target object, the system synthesizes a large number of views, or image patches, of individual keypoints to automatically build the training set. If the object can be assumed to be locally planar, this is done by simply warping image patches around the points under affine deformations, otherwise, given the 3D model, standard computer graphics texture-mapping techniques can be used. This second approach relaxes the planarity assumptions.

The classification itself is performed using randomized trees (Amit & Geman, 1997). Each non-terminal node of a tree contains a test of the type: "Is this pixel brighter than this one?" that splits the image space. Each leaf contains an estimate based on training data of the

Figure 5. Detection and computation in real-time of the 3D pose: (a) A planar object; (b) (c) a full 3D object (Reproduced from Lepetit et al., 2005, © 2005 IEEE, used with permission)

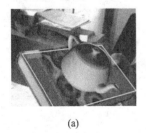 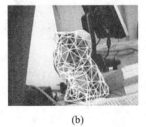 

(a)   (b)   (c)

Figure 6. Real-time detection of a deformable object. Given a model image (a), the algorithm computes a function mapping the model to an input image (b). To illustrate this mapping, the contours of the model (c) are extracted using a simple gradient operator and used as a validation texture which is overlaid on the input image using the recovered transformation (d). Additional results are obtained in different conditions (e)-(h). Note that in all cases, the white outlines project almost exactly at the right place, thus indicating a correct registration and shape estimation. The registration process, including image acquisition, takes about 80 ms and does not require any initialization or a priori pose information. (Reproduced from Pilet et al., 2005a, © 2005 IEEE, used with permission)

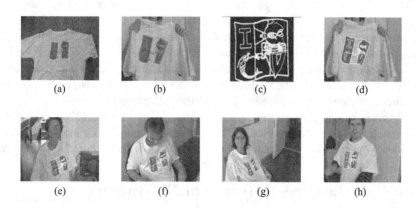

Figure 7. Augmenting a deformable object: (a) Reference image with overlaid mesh; (b) input image; (c) deformed mesh registered to the input image. (d) The original pattern has been erased and replaced by a blank but correctly shaded image. (e) A virtual pattern replaces the original one; it is correctly deformed but not yet relighted. (f) The virtual pattern is deformed and relighted (Reproduced from Pilet et al., 2005b, © 2005 IEEE, used with permission)

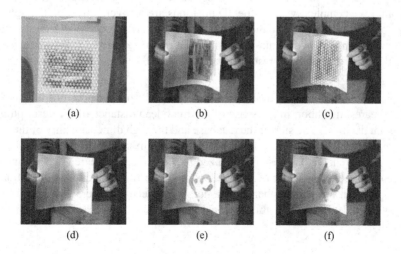

conditional distribution over the classes given that a patch reaches that leaf. A new image is classified by simply dropping it down the tree. Since only pixel intensities comparisons are involved, this procedure is very fast and robust to illumination changes. Thanks to the efficiency of randomized trees, it yields reliable classification results. As depicted by Figure 5, this method has been successfully used to detect and compute the 3D pose of both planar and non-planar objects.

As shown in Figure 6, this approach has been extended to deformable objects by replacing the rigid models by deformable meshes and introducing a well designed robust estimator. This estimator is the key to dealing with the large number of parameters involved in modeling deformable surfaces and rejecting erroneous matches for error rates of up to 95%, which is considerably more than what is required in practice (Pilet, Lepetit, & Fua, 2005a, 2005b). It can then be combined with a dynamic approach to estimating the amount of light that reaches individual image pixels by comparing their gray levels to those of the reference image. This lets us either erase patterns from the original images and replace them by blank but correctly shaded areas, which we think of as *Diminished Reality*, or to replace them by virtual ones that convincingly blend-in because they are properly lighted. As illustrated by Figure 7, this is important because adequate lighting is key to realism. Not only is this approach very fast and fully automated, but it also handles complex lighting effects, such as cast shadows, specularities, and multiple light sources of different hues and saturation.

From Wide Baseline Matching to 3D Tracking

As mentioned before, wide baseline matching techniques can be used to perform 3D tracking. To illustrate this, we briefly describe the SIFT-based implementation reported in Skrypnyk and Lowe (2004).

First, during a learning stage, a database of scene feature points is built by extracting SIFT keypoints in some reference images. Because the keypoints are detected in scale-space, the scene does not necessarily have to be well-textured. Their 3D positions are recovered using a structure-from-motion algorithm. Two-view correspondences are first established based on the SIFT descriptors, and chained to construct multi-view correspondences while avoiding prohibitive complexity. Then the 3D positions are recovered by a global optimization over all camera parameters and these point coordinates, which is initialized as suggested in Szeliski and Kang (1994). At run-time, SIFT features are extracted from the current frame, matched against the database, resulting in a set of 2D/3D correspondences that can be used to recover the pose.

The best candidate match for a SIFT feature extracted from the current frame is assumed to be its nearest neighbor, in the sense of the Euclidean distance of the descriptor vectors in the point database. The size of the database and the high dimensionality of these vectors would make the exhaustive search intractable, especially for real-time applications. To allow for fast search, the database is organized as a k-d tree. The search is performed so that bins are explored in the order of their closest distance from the query description vector, and stopped after a given number of data points has been considered as described in Beis and Lowe (1997). In practice, this approach returns the actual nearest neighbor with high probability.

As discussed in this chapter, recovering the camera positions in each frame independently and from noisy data typically results in jitter. To stabilize the pose, a regularization term that smoothes camera motion across consecutive frames is introduced. Its weight is iteratively estimated to eliminate as much jitter as possible without introducing drift when the motion is fast. The full method runs at four frames per second on a 1.8 GHz ThinkPad.

The End of Recursive Tracking?

Since real-time tracking-by-detection has become a practical possibility, one must wonder if the conventional recursive tracking methods that have been presented in the previous sections of this survey are obsolescent.

We do not believe this to be the case. As illustrated by the case of the SIFT-based tracking system (Skrypnyk & Lowe, 2004) previously discussed, treating each frame independently has its problems. Imposing temporal continuity constraints across frames can help increase the robustness and quality of the results. Furthermore, wide baseline matching tends to be both less accurate and more computationally intensive than the short baseline variety.

As shown, combining both kinds of approaches can yield the best of both worlds; Robustness from tracking-by-detection, and accuracy from recursive tracking. In our opinion, this is where the future of tracking lays. The challenge will be to become able, perhaps by taking advantage of recursive techniques that do not require prior training, to learn object descriptions online so that a tracker can operate in a complex environment with minimal *a priori* knowledge.

Conclusion

Even after more than 20 years of research, practical vision-based 3D tracking systems still rely on fiducials because this remains the only approach that is sufficiently fast, robust, and accurate. Therefore, if it is practical to introduce them in the environment the system inhabits, this solution surely must be retained. ARToolkit is a freely available alternative that uses planar fiducials that may be printed on pieces of paper. While less accurate, it remains robust and allows for fast development of low-cost applications. As a result, it has become popular in the augmented reality community.

However, this state of affairs may be about to change as computers have just now become fast enough to reliably handle natural features in real-time, thereby making it possible to completely do away with fiducials. This is especially true when dealing with objects that are polygonal, textured, or both (Drummond & Cipolla, 2002; Vacchetti et al., 2004b). However, the reader must be aware that the recursive nature of most of these algorithms makes them inherently fragile. They must be initialized manually and cannot recover if the process fails for any reason. In practice, even the best methods suffer such failures all too often, for example because the motion is too fast, a complete occlusion occurs, or simply because the target object moves momentarily out of the field of view.

This can be addressed by combining image data with data provided by inertial sensors, gyroscopes, or GPS (Foxlin & Naimark, 2003; Klein & Drummond, 2003; Jiang, Neumann, & You, 2004; Ribo & Lang, 2002). The sensors allow a prediction of the camera position or relative motion that can then be refined using vision techniques similar to the ones described in this chapter. When instrumenting the camera is an option, this combination is very effective for applications that require positioning the camera with respect to a static scene. However, it would be of no use to track moving objects with a static camera.

A more generic and desirable approach is therefore to develop purely image-based methods that can detect the target object and compute its 3D pose from a single image. If they are fast enough, they can then be used to initialize and re-initialize the system as often as needed, even if they cannot provide the same accuracy as traditional recursive approaches that use temporal continuity constraints to refine their estimates. Techniques able to do just this are just beginning to come online (Lepetit et al., 2005; Lepetit & Fua, 2006; Skrypnyk & Lowe, 2004). And, since they are the last missing part of the puzzle, we expect that we will not have to wait another twenty years for purely vision-based commercial systems to become a reality.

Camera Models

Most cameras currently used for tracking purposes can be modeled using the standard pinhole camera model that defines the imaging process as a projection from the world to the camera image plane. It is often represented by a projection matrix that operates on projective coordinates and can be written as the product of a camera calibration matrix that depends on the internal camera parameters and an rotation-translation matrix that encodes the rigid camera motion (Faugeras, 1993). Note, however, that new camera designs, such as the so-called omni-directional cameras that rely on hyperbolic or parabolic mirrors to achieve a very wide field of views, are becoming increasingly popular (Geyer & Daniilidis, 2003; Swaminathan & Nayar, 2003).

Camera Matrices

The 3D tracking algorithms described here seek to estimate the rotation-translation matrix. It is computed as the composition of a translation and a rotation that must be appropriately parameterized for estimation and numerical optimization purposes. While representing translations poses no problem, parameterizing rotation is more difficult to do well. Several representations have been proposed, such as Euler angles, quaternions, and exponential maps. All of them present singularities, but it is generally accepted that the exponential map representation is the one that behaves best for tracking purposes (Grassia, 1998).

Since distinguishing a change in focal length from a translation along the camera Z-axis is difficult, in most 3D tracking methods, the internal camera parameters are assumed to be fixed. In other words, the camera cannot zoom. These parameters can be estimated during an offline camera calibration stage, for example by imaging once a calibration grid of known dimensions (Faugeras, 1993; Tsai, 1987) or several times a simpler 2D grid seen from several positions (Sturm & Maybank, 1999; Zhang, 2000).

Handling Lens Distortion

The pinhole camera model is very realistic for lenses with fairly long focal lengths but does not represent all the aspects of the image formation. In particular, it does not take into account the possible distortion from the camera lens, which may be non-negligible especially for wide angle lenses.

Since they make it easier to keep target objects within the field of view, it is nevertheless desirable to have the option to use them for 3D tracking purposes. Fortunately, this is easily achieved because lens distortion mostly is a simple 2D radial deformation of the image. Given an estimate of the distortion parameters, it can be efficiently undone at run-time using a look-up table, which allows the use of the standard models previously discussed.

The software package of OpenCV allows the estimation of the distortion parameters using a method derived from Heikkila and Silven (1997). This is a convenient method for desktop systems. For larger workspaces, plumb line based methods (Brown, 1971; Fryer & Goodin, 1989) are common in photogrammetry. Without distortion, the image of a straight line will be a straight line, and conversely the distortion parameters can be estimated from images of straight lines by measuring their deviations from straightness. This is a very practical method in man-made environments where straight lines, such as those found at building corners, are common.

The Camera Calibration Matrix

In most 3D tracking methods, the internal parameters are assumed to be fixed and known, which means that the camera can not zoom because it is difficult to distinguish a change in focal length from a translation along the camera Z-axis. These parameters can be estimated during an offline camera calibration stage, from the images themselves. Classical calibration methods make use of a calibration pattern of known size inside the field of view. Sometimes it is a 3D calibration grid on which regular patterns are painted (Faugeras, 1993; Tsai, 1987). Zhang (2000) and Sturm and Maybank (1999) simultaneously introduced similar calibration methods that rely on a simple planar grid seen from several positions. They are more flexible since the pattern can be simply printed, attached to a planar object, and moved in front of the camera.

References

Amit, Y., & Geman, D. (1997). Shape quantization and recognition with randomized trees. *Neural Computation, 9*(7), 1545-1588.

Armstrong, M., & Zisserman, A. (1995). Robust object tracking. In *Proceedings of the Asian Conference on Computer Vision* (pp. 58-62).

Basu, S., Essa, I., & Pentland, A. (1996). Motion regularization for model-based head tracking. In *Proceedings of the International Conference on Pattern Recognition*, Vienna, Austria.

Baumberg, A. (2000). Reliable feature matching across widely separated views. In *Proceedings of the Conference on Computer Vision and Pattern Recognition* (pp. 774-781).

Beis, J., & Lowe, D. G. (1997). Shape indexing using approximate nearest-neighbour search in high-dimensional spaces. In *Proceedings of the Conference on Computer Vision and Pattern Recognition* (pp. 1000-1006). Puerto Rico.

Brown, D. C. (1971). Close range camera calibration. *Photogrammetric Engineering, 37*(8), 855-866.

Cascia, M., Sclaroff, S., & Athitsos, V. (2000, April). Fast, reliable head tracking under varying illumination: An approach based on registration of texture-mapped 3D models. *IEEE Transactions on Pattern Analysis and Machine Intelligence, 22*(4).

Chia, K. W., Cheok, A. D., & Prince, S. J. D. (2002). Online 6 DOF augmented reality registration from Natural Features. In *Proceedings of the International Symposium on Mixed and Augmented Reality*.

Cho, Y., Lee, W. J., & Neumann, U. (1998). A multi-ring color fiducial system and intensity-invariant detection method for scalable fiducial-tracking augmented reality.In *Proceedings of the International Workshop on Augmented Reality*.

Claus, D., & Fitzgibbon, A. (2004, May). Reliable fiducial detection in natural scenes. *European Conference on Computer Vision* (Vol. 3024, pp. 469-480). Springer-Verlag.

Comport, A. I., Marchand, E., & Chaumette, F. (2003, September). A real-time tracker for markerless augmented reality. In *Proceedings of the International Symposium on Mixed and Augmented Reality*, Tokyo, Japan.

DeCarlo, D., & Metaxas, D. (2000). Optical flow constraints on deformable models with applications to face tracking. *International Journal of Computer Vision, 38*, 99-127.

Deriche, R., & Giraudon, G. (1993). A computational approach for corner and vertex detection. *International Journal of Computer Vision, 10*(2), 101-124.

Drummond, T., & Cipolla, R. (2002, July). Real-time visual tracking of complex structures. *IEEE Transactions on Pattern Analysis and Machine Intelligence, 27*(7), 932-946.

Faugeras, O. D. (1993). *Three-dimensional computer vision: A geometric viewpoint*. MIT Press.

Fischler, M. A., & Bolles, R. C. (1981). Random sample consensus: a paradigm for model fitting with applications to image analysis and automated cartography. *Communications ACM, 24*(6), 381-395.

Förstner, W. (1986). A feature-based correspondence algorithm for image matching. *International Archives of Photogrammetry and Remote Sensing, 26*(3), 150-166.

Foxlin E., & Naimark L. (2003). Miniaturization, calibration and accuracy evaluation of a hybrid self-tracker. In *Proceedings of the International Symposium on Mixed and Augmented Reality*, Tokyo, Japan.

Fryer, J. G., & Goodin, D. J. (1989). In-Flight Aerial Camera Calibration from Photography of Linear Features. *Photogrammetric Engineering and Remote Sensing, 55*(12), 1751-1754.

Genc, Y., Riedel, S., Souvannavong, F., & Navab, N. (2002). Marker-less tracking for augmented reality: A learning-based approach. In *Proceedings of the International Symposium on Mixed and Augmented Reality.*

Geyer, C. M., & Daniilidis, K. (2003, October). Omnidirectional video. *The Visual Computer, 19*(6), 405-416.

Grassia, F. S. (1998). Practical parameterization of rotations using the exponential map. *Journal of Graphics Tools, 3*(3), 29-48.

Hager, G. D., & Belhumeur, P. N. (1998). Efficient region tracking with parametric models of geometry and illumination. *IEEE Transactions on Pattern Analysis and Machine Intelligence, 20*(10), 1025-1039.

Harris, C. (1992). *Tracking with rigid objects.* MIT Press.

Harris, C. G., & Stephens, M. J. (1988). A combined corner and edge detector. In *Proceedings of the 4th Alvey Vision Conference*, Manchester.

Heikkila, J., & Silven, O. (1997). A four-step camera calibration procedure with implicit image correction. In *Proceedings of the Conference on Computer Vision and Pattern Recognition* (pp. 1106-1112).

Hoff, W. A., Nguyen, K., & Lyon, T. (1996, November). Computer vision-based registration techniques for augmented reality. In *Proceedings of Intelligent Robots and Control Systems XV, Intelligent Control Systems and Advanced Manufacturing* (pp. 538-548).

Jiang, B., Neumann, U., & You, S. (2004). A robust tracking system for outdoor augmented reality. In *IEEE Virtual Reality Conference 2004.*

Jurie, F. (1998). Tracking objects with a recognition algorithm. *Pattern Recognition Letters, 3-4*(19), 331-340.

Jurie, F., & Dhome, M. (2001, July). A simple and efficient template matching algorithm. In *Proceedings of the International Conference on Computer Vision*, Vancouver, Canada.

Jurie, F., & Dhome, M. (2002, July). Hyperplane approximation for template matching. *IEEE Transactions on Pattern Analysis and Machine Intelligence, 24*(7), 996-100.

Kato, H., & Billinghurst, M. (1999, October). Marker tracking and HMD calibration for a video-based augmented reality conferencing system. In *Proceedings of the IEEE and ACM International Workshop on Augmented Reality.*

Kato, H., Billinghurst, M., Poupyrev, I., Imamoto, K., & Tachibana, K. (2000). Virtual object manipulation on a table-top AR environment. In *Proceedings of the International Symposium on Augmented Reality* (pp. 111-119).

Klein, G., & Drummond, T. (2003, October). Robust visual tracking for non-instrumented augmented reality. In *Proceedings of the International Symposium on Mixed and Augmented Reality* (pp. 36-45).

Koller, D., Klinker, G., Rose, E., Breen, D. E., Whitaker, R. T., & Tuceryan, M. (1997, September). Real-time Vision-based camera tracking for augmented reality applications.

In *Proceedings of the ACM Symposium on Virtual Reality Software and Technology* (pp. 87-94). Lausanne, Switzerland.

Lepetit, V., & Fua, P. (2006). Keypoint recognition using randomized trees. *IEEE Transactions on Pattern Analysis and Machine Intelligence.*

Lepetit, V., Lagger, P., & Fua, P. (2005, June). Randomized trees for real-time keypoint recognition. In *Proceedings of the Conference on Computer Vision and Pattern Recognition*, San Diego, CA.

Li, H., Roivainen, P., & Forchheimer, R. (1993, June). 3D motion estimation in model-based facial image coding. *IEEE Transactions on Pattern Analysis and Machine Intelligence, 15*(6), 545-555.

Lindeberg, T. (1994). Scale-space theory: A basic tool for analysing structures at different scales. *Journal of Applied Statistics, 21*(2), 224-270.

Lowe, D. G. (1991, June). Fitting parameterized three-dimensional models to images. *IEEE Transactions on Pattern Analysis and Machine Intelligence, 13*(5), 441-450.

Lowe, D. G. (1999). Object recognition from local scale-invariant features. In *Proceedings of the International Conference on Computer Vision* (pp. 1150-1157).

Lowe, D. G. (2004). Distinctive image features from scale-invariant keypoints. *International Journal of Computer Vision, 20*(2), 91-110.

Marchand, E., Bouthemy, P., & Chaumette F. (2001). A 2D-3D model-based approach to real-time visual tracking. *Journal of Image and Vision Computing, 19*(13), 941-955.

Matas, J., Chum, O., Martin, U., & Pajdla, T. (2002, September). Robust wide baseline stereo from maximally stable extremal regions. *British Machine Vision Conference*, London (pp. 384-393).

Mikolajczyk, K., & Schmid, C. (2002). An affine invariant interest point detector. In *Proceedings of the European Conference on Computer Vision* (pp. 128-142). Copenhagen: Springer.

Mikolajczyk K., & Schmid C. (2003, June). A performance evaluation of local descriptors. In In *Proceedings of the Conference on Computer Vision and Pattern Recognition* (pp. 257-263).

Mikolajczyk, K., Tuytelaars, T., Schmid, C., Zisserman, A., Matas, J., Schaffalitzky, F., Kadir, T., & VanGool, L. (2005). A comparison of affine region detectors. Accepted to *International Journal of Computer Vision.*

Mindru, F., Moons, T., & VanGool, L. (1999). Recognizing color patterns irrespective of viewpoint and illumination. In *Proceedings of the Conference on Computer Vision and Pattern Recognition* (pp. 368-373).

Moravec, H. (1981). *Robot rover visual navigation*. Ann Arbor, MI: UMI Research Press.

Moravec, H. P. (1977, August). Towards automatic visual obstacle avoidance. In *Proceedings of the International Joint Conference on Artificial Intelligence* (pp. 584). Cambridge, MA: MIT.

Nayar, S. K., Nene, S. A., & Murase, H. (1996). Real-time 100 object recognition system. *IEEE Transactions on Pattern Analysis and Machine Intelligence, 18*(12), 1186-1198.

Open Source Computer Vision Library. Intel. (n.d.). Retrieved from http://www.intel.com/research/mrl/research/opencv/

Pilet, J., Lepetit, V., & Fua, P. (2005a, October). Augmenting deformable objects in real-time. *International Symposium on Mixed and Augmented Reality*, Vienna.

Pilet, J., Lepetit, V., & Fua, P. (2005b, June). Real-Time non-rigid surface detection. In *Proceedings of the Conference on Computer Vision and Pattern Recognition*, San Diego, CA.

Ravela, S., Draper, B., Lim, J., & Weiss, R. (1995). Adaptive tracking and model registration across distinct aspects. In *Proceedings of the International Conference on Intelligent Robots and Systems* (pp. 174-180).

Rekimoto, J. (1998). Matrix: A realtime object identification and registration method for augmented reality. In In *Proceedings of the Asia Pacific Computer Human Interaction*.

Ribo, P., & Lang, P. (2002). Hybrid tracking for outdoor augmented reality applications. In *Computer graphics and applications* (pp. 54-63).

Schaffalitzky, F., & Zisserman, A. (2002). Multi-view matching for unordered image sets, or "How do I organize my holiday snaps?" In *Proceedings of European Conference on Computer Vision* (pp. 414-431).

Schmid, C., & Mohr, R. (1997, May). Local grayvalue invariants for image retrieval. *IEEE Transactions on Pattern Analysis and Machine Intelligence*, *19*(5), 530-534.

Se, S., Lowe, D. G., & Little, J. (2002). Mobile robot localization and mapping with uncertainty using scale-invariant visual landmarks. *International Journal of Robotics Research*, *22*(8), 735-758.

Shi, J., & Tomasi, C. (1994, June). Good features to track. In *Proceedings of the Conference on Computer Vision and Pattern Recognition*, Seattle.

Simon, G., & Berger, M. O. (1998, January). A two-stage robust statistical method for temporal registration from features of various type. In *Proceedings of the International Conference on Computer Vision*, Bombay, India (pp. 261-266).

Skrypnyk, I., & Lowe, D. G. (2004, November). Scene modelling, recognition, and tracking with invariant image features. In *Proceedings of the International Symposium on Mixed and Augmented Reality*, Arlington, VA (pp. 110-119).

Smith, S. M., & Brady, J. M. (1995). *SUSAN: A new approach to low level image processing*. Technical Report TR95SMS1c, Oxford University, Chertsey, Surrey, UK.

State, A., Hirota, G., David, T., Garett, W. F., & Livingston, M. A. (1996, August). Superior augmented-reality registration by integrating landmark tracking and magnetic tracking. *ACM SIGGRAPH*, New Orleans, LA (pp. 429-438).

Sturm, P., & Maybank, S. (1999, June). On plane-based camera calibration: A general algorithm, singularities, applications. In *Proceedings of the Conference on Computer Vision and Pattern Recognition* (pp. 432-437).

Swaminathan, R., & Nayar, S. K. (2003, June). A perspective on distortions. In *Proceedings of the Conference on Computer Vision and Pattern Recognition*.

Szeliski, R., & Kang, S. B. (1994). Recovering 3D shape and motion from image streams using non linear least squares. *Journal of Visual Communication and Image Representation, 5*(1), 10-28.

Tordoff, B., Mayol, W. W., de Campos, T. E., & Murray, D. W. (2002). Head pose estimation for wearable robot control. In *Proceedings of the British Machine Vision Conference* (pp. 807-816).

Tsai, R. Y. (1987). A versatile cameras calibration technique for high accuracy 3D machine vision mtrology using off-the-shelf TV cameras and lenses. *Journal of Robotics and Automation, 3*(4), 323-344.

Tuytelaars, T., & VanGool, L. (2000). Wide baseline stereo matching based on local, affinely invariant regions. In *Proceedings of the British Machine Vision Conference* (pp. 412-422).

Vacchetti, L., Lepetit, V., & Fua, P. (2004a, November). Combining edge and texture information for real-time accurate 3D camera tracking. In *Proceedings of the International Symposium on Mixed and Augmented Reality*, Arlington, VA.

Vacchetti, L., Lepetit, V., & Fua, P. (2004b, October). Stable real-time 3D tracking using online and offline information. *IEEE Transactions on Pattern Analysis and Machine Intelligence, 26*(10), 1385-1391.

Viola, P., & Jones, M. (2001). Rapid object detection using a boosted cascade of simple features. In *Proceedings of the Conference on Computer Vision and Pattern Recognition* (pp. 511-518).

Zhang, Z. (2000). A flexible new technique for camera calibration. *IEEE Transactions on Pattern Analysis and Machine Intelligence, 22*, 1330-1334.

Zhang, Z., Deriche, R., Faugeras, O., & Luong, Q. (1995). A robust technique for matching two uncalibrated images through the recovery of the unknown epipolar geometry. *Artificial Intelligence, 78*, 87-119.

Chapter II

Developing AR Systems in the Presence of Spatial Uncertainty

Cindy M. Robertson, Georgia Institute of Technology, USA

Enylton Machado Coelho, Georgia Institute of Technology, TSRB, USA

Blair MacIntyre, Georgia Institute of Technology, USA

Simon Julier, Naval Research Laboratory, USA

Abstract

This chapter introduces spatially adaptive augmented reality as an approach to dealing with the registration errors introduced by spatial uncertainty. It argues that if program-mers are given simple estimates of registration error, they can create systems that adapt to dynamically changing amounts of spatial uncertainty, and that it is this ability to adapt to spatial uncertainty that will be the key to creating augmented reality systems that work in real-world environments.

Introduction

Augmented reality (AR) systems merge computer-generated graphics with a view of the physical world. Ideally, the graphics should be perfectly aligned, or *registered*, with the physical world. Perfect registration requires the computer to have accurate knowledge of the structure of the physical world and the spatial relationships between the world, the display, and the viewer. Unfortunately, in many real-world situations, the available information is not accurate enough to support perfect registration. Uncertainty may exist in world knowledge (e.g., accurate, up-to-date models of the physical world may be impossible to obtain) or in the spatial relationships between the viewer and the world (e.g., the technology used to track the viewer may have limited accuracy).

In this chapter, we present an approach to creating usable AR systems in the presence of *spatial uncertainty*, implemented in a toolkit called OSGAR. In OSGAR, *registration errors* arising from spatial uncertainty are estimated in real-time and programmers are provided with the necessary scaffolding to create applications that adapt dynamically to changes in the estimated registration error. OSGAR helps programmers adapt both the output (e.g., creating augmentations that are understandable even though they are not perfectly registered) and input (e.g., interpreting user interaction) of AR systems in the presence of uncertain spatial information. While the effects of registration error are most obvious on the output side (i.e., misregistration between the graphics and the physical world), the impact of spatial uncertainty on the input side of an AR system is equally important. For example, a user might point at one object in the real world (using their finger, a 3D input device, or even a 2D cursor on a display) but, because of tracking errors, the computer could infer that they are pointing at an entirely different object.

This work has been motivated by two complementary observations. First, AR could be useful in many environments where it is impractical or impossible to obtain perfect spatial knowledge (e.g., many military, industrial, or emergency response scenarios). Second, many of the applications envisioned in these environments could be designed to work without perfect registration, if registration error estimates were available to the programmer. Consider, for example, an emergency-response scenario where personnel have AR systems to display situation awareness information (e.g., sensor information from unmanned air- and ground-vehicles, directions, or status updates from co-located or remote personnel). Much of this situational information would benefit from tight registration with the world (e.g., "life signs detected below here" with an arrow pointing to a specific pile of rubble) but would also be useful if only moderate registration was possible (e.g., "life signs detected within 10 feet"). Such a system will need to be robust enough to adapt to the variable accuracy of wide-area outdoor tracking technologies like GPS, and to withstand unpredictable changes in the physical environment (e.g., from fire, flooding, or explosions). The key observation behind OSGAR is that developers could implement these sorts of applications, which adapt to changing tracking conditions, if they have estimates of the uncertainty of that world knowledge and of the accuracy of the tracking systems being used.

In this chapter, we will first briefly define what we mean by "spatially adaptive AR," summarize the sources of registration error in AR systems, and highlight some prior work relevant to AR systems that adapt to spatial uncertainty. To motivate the design of OSGAR, we then present the idea of adaptive intent-based augmentations that automatically adapt to registration error estimates. Next, we summarize the mathematical framework we use to estimate registration errors in OSGAR. Then, we describe the major features of OSGAR that provide programmers with registration error estimates and support the creation of AR systems that adapt to spatial uncertainty. We conclude this chapter with some thoughts about designing meaningful AR systems in the face of spatial uncertainty.

Spatially Adaptive Augmented Reality Systems

We believe that perfect registration is not a strict requirement for many proposed applications of AR. Rather, the domain, the specific context, and the intent of the augmentation determine how accurate the registration between the graphics and the physical world must be. For instance, a medical AR application used during surgery will certainly require much better registration than an AR tour guide. In either case, if a programmer is given an estimate of the registration error that will be encountered during runtime, he or she can design the input and output of an AR system to deal with these errors in a manner appropriate for the domain.

We call an AR system that can dynamically adapt its interface to different amounts of spatial uncertainty a *spatially adaptive AR system*. OSGAR is designed to provide the programmer with runtime estimates of the registration error arising from spatial uncertainty, allowing applications to adapt continuously as the user works with them. By providing programmers with simple estimates of the impact of spatial uncertainty on registration error, programmers can focus on how to deal with these errors. For example, what is the best way to display an augmentation when there is a certain amount of error? Which kinds of augmentations should be used, and in which situations? How should transitions between different augmentations be handled when the amount of error changes? How does registration error limit the amount of information that can be conveyed? By freeing programmers from dealing with devices directly and worrying about the impact of each source of uncertainty, they can begin to focus on these important questions.

From the application developer's point of view, OSGAR provides a layer of abstraction that enables the application to be fine-tuned to the capabilities and limitations of the tracking technology available at runtime. Such an abstraction layer is analogous to that provided by the graphical interfaces on modern computers. The abstraction layers allow one to develop device independent applications, decoupling the application from the underlying hardware infrastructure. Beyond simply providing device independence, such libraries allow the programmer to query the capabilities of the hardware and adapt to them. Similar kinds of abstractions are needed before AR applications (indeed, any application based on sensing technologies) will ever leave the research laboratories and be put to use in real life situations.

From the user's point of view, spatially adaptive AR systems are much more likely to convey reliable information. As spatial uncertainty (and thus registration error) changes, the system adapts to help ensure the intent of the augmentation is clear, rather than having to gear output to the worst-case registration error to avoid misinformation.

Registration Error

There are many causes for registration error in AR systems, which (for this discussion) we classify as *tracking errors*, *alignment and calibration errors*, *modeling errors,* and *latency*. For an in-depth discussion of the causes of registration error, see Holloway (1997).

Tracking errors are perhaps the best-known and best-studied causes of uncertainty. Any tracking system measures the pose (position and orientation) of the camera using some kind of physical sensor. There are literally hundreds of papers which describe different methods based on a variety of sensing technologies (e.g., magnetic, ultrasonic, inertial, computer vision, etc.), as well as hybrid systems that combine more than one of these technologies. However, as noted by Welch and Foxlin (2002), there is no "Silver Bullet" that is likely to solve the tracking problem.

Related to, but distinct from tracking, are the issues of alignment and calibration. *Alignment errors* arise when multiple sensors and/or cameras are used, and are errors in the rigid body transformation between the sensor and camera coordinate frames. Alignment can be addressed using precision machining (so the dimension and location of sensors are known very accurately), but such solutions are very brittle (i.e., changing the physical configuration causes alignment information to be lost). As a result, there are many algorithms for calculating the needed rigid body transformations from a set of sensor measurements, especially for the so-called *wrist-hand calibration problem*. Although the errors introduced by these algorithms are often small (on the order of millimeters in position and less than a degree in orientation), they are still sufficient to produce visibly noticeable registration errors. *Calibration errors* arise when it is necessary to calculate other characteristics of the sensors (such as the scale factors) or when calculating the intrinsic parameters of the display (a camera or a head mounted display). The intrinsic parameters of a camera are its field of view, its center of projection, and the distortion in the image. These can be computed very precisely using automated camera calibration techniques. However, in optical see-through systems, users must be involved in the alignment and calibration process. Algorithms such as SPAAM (Tuceryan & Navab, 2000) have been proposed, but are highly intrusive and user fatigue can lead to errors in the calibration parameters.

Modeling errors occur because any model approximates the real object it represents. Whether a model is created by hand using a ruler, or using more advanced methods to automatically generate the models, the mere use of these processes introduces uncertainty into the final models. The development of automated, large-scale building models, for example, using LIDAR data, yields further errors, typically on the order of meters. Furthermore, in many real world contexts, the environment will often be modified subsequent to the modeling step.

A final source of registration error is the end-to-end *latency* through all components of the system. This includes the time that passes between an action happening in the physical world (e.g., the user moving), the action being sensed, the sensor communicating the updated information to the application and, finally, the application updating the display accordingly. Other temporal issues include time synchronization across multiple devices and the discrete update times of displays and the rendering subsystems, all of which have the effect of increasing registration error.

The common message of Holloway (1997) and Welch and Foxlin (2002) is that registration error is unlikely to be eliminated except under carefully controlled conditions. For example, in UNC's Ultrasound-guided breast biopsy system, great care was taken to minimize relative and end-to-end latency (Jacobs, Livingston, & State, 1997). Research aimed at developing better tracking systems or reducing end-to-end system latency is important, but it will not alone solve the problems preventing AR systems from gaining acceptance in many real-world environments. For example, while AR prototypes are usually "tuned" to compensate for registration errors induced by the available tracking technology, such approaches are brittle. If the tracker characteristics or environment changes for the worse, the tuned application will fail.

The brittleness of tuned applications manifests itself in ways besides complete failure. Tracking quality is rarely uniform, especially in wide-area scenarios (such as a factory or a whole city), and is likely to improve as technology changes. If the application is tuned for a given technology, it will not take advantage of situations where performance is substantially better. Worse, as technology improves, such applications may need to be entirely rewritten to leverage the possibilities afforded by tighter registration.

The approach presented here avoids these problems by discouraging application developers from tuning applications to a specific technology or expected registration error. By implementing a layer of abstraction between the sensors and the application developer that provides continuous estimates of the current registration errors, application developers are encouraged to create applications that adapt as registration errors change. In doing so, they must implement a range of interface options for different amounts of registration error, possibly including support for tighter registration than is currently possible. The reasons for run-time changes in the magnitude of registration error are hidden from the programmer, and may be the result of non-uniformity in tracking quality, updated hardware, or unusual environmental conditions (e.g., weather effects, power failures).

Background and Related Work

Since the early 1990s, many different augmented reality application prototypes have been developed, many of which are discussed elsewhere in this book. Most application prototypes have relied on the characteristics of a specific tracking system and been tuned to perform appropriately with that system, as previously discussed. We will not provide a complete overview of the range of applications that have been proposed or prototyped over the years, but instead focus on those applications that have dealt with registration error in some non-trivial way, or serve to highlight the need for flexible estimates of registration error.

The medical domain is one in which tight registration is necessary for AR to be useful. Prototypes supporting in-situ visualization of medical data (Bajura, Fuchs, & Ohbuchi, 1992; Navab, Bani-Hashemi, & Mitschke, 1999) require the data to be correctly aligned with the patient, especially when the visualization is used during a medical procedure such as ultrasound-guided needle biopsy (State et al., 1996) or robotically assisted minimally invasive cardiovascular surgery (Traub et al., 2004). Medical systems can achieve excellent registration because the environment can be carefully controlled, modeled, and instrumented.

Most system prototypes have ignored the impact of changing tracker quality on registration error. For example, outdoor applications that use GPS and sourceless orientation sensors cannot reasonably rely on accurate registration. As a result, applications tune their output to the expected accuracy. For example, the Touring Machine (Feiner, MacIntyre, Höllerer, & Webster, 1997) was a mobile AR system designed to provide information about the Columbia University campus. Building-level registration could be achieved but pixel-level registration could not. As a result, only building labels were displayed. Most prototypes, however, have simply ignored registration error and rendered the graphics assuming they would align with the physical world. As an example, the various GUI techniques implemented in the Tinmith system assume that the graphics are properly registered (Piekarski & Thomas, 2001). In fact, most prototypes do not even account for simple tracker errors, such as the loss of GPS accuracy (or even total GPS failure) when a person goes to a place surrounded by buildings or trees.

The bulk of the work on reducing registration error in AR systems has focused on reducing error by increasing tracking quality or reducing apparent system latency. For example, Azuma and Bishop (1994) offer improved registration in two areas. First, they demonstrate accurate static registration across a wide variety of viewing angles and positions through accurate tracking and careful calibration and modeling. Second, they reduce dynamic errors that occur from user head motion by using inertial sensors to predict future head locations.

While most AR applications would benefit from improved registration, a more important factor affecting deployment and acceptance is that the application must function properly under varying environmental conditions. AR applications need to be useful not only when all conditions are ideal and every component of the system is functioning properly; they need to be guaranteed to degrade gracefully when one or multiple subsystems present some deficiency.

The problem of dealing with registration error has received more attention on the output side of AR system design than on the input side. While claims that "improved trackers will fix graphical misalignment" can be used to dismiss the impact of misregistered graphics, the effect of spatial uncertainty on user interaction is often to make an AR prototype completely unusable. To ameliorate the impact of spatial errors on interaction with AR systems, various ad-hoc methods have been attempted. For example, Olwal, Benko, and Feiner approximate intrinsic errors through the use of geometric shapes (Olwal et al., 2003). Kaiser et al. employ multi-modal interaction techniques to help the user select objects, in the hope that one mode of interaction can compensate for the deficiencies in the other modes (Kaiser et al., 2003). However, neither approach is based on accurate estimates of the registration error.

Adaptive Intent-Based Augmentations

To show how estimates of registration error can be used, we have built some example augmentation widgets that modify their graphical representation based on the magnitude of the error estimate, such that the intent of the augmentation is preserved (Robertson & MacIntyre, 2003). We refer to such augmentations as *adaptive intent-based augmentations*, because the widgets encapsulate a semantically meaningful augmentation (e.g., "highlight object," "label object with text") and use those semantics to generate and continuously modify the graphical representation at runtime. We build on the concept of *intent-based illustrations* introduced by Seligmann and Feiner (1991). Their intent-based illustration system used a set of style strategies, or visual effects, to implement the communicative goals in a 3D virtual environment.

The design of our adaptive augmentations is informed by principles developed in cognitive psychology, particularly those that attempt to explain how we perceive the world around us. Two important sources for our designs are *Gestalt psychology* and Beiderman's concept of *geons*. Gestalt psychologists believe that humans see and recognize objects as a whole, not by identifying individual features (Koffka, 1935). They believe in five main principles of perceptual organization: *proximity* (why people group things that are close to each other in physical space), *similarity* (why people group similar objects together), *good continuation* (why we group together objects whose contours form a continuous straight or curved line), *closure* (why humans mentally fill in gaps in an object to see a complete figure), and *common fate* (why elements that move together get grouped together). More recently, Biederman argued that when people view objects they divide them into simple geometric components, such as cylinders, cones, and blocks, called geons (Biederman, 1987). He proposed 36 such primitives from which humans can quickly construct mental representations of a very large set of common objects. For instance, rather than seeing a flashlight as a complicated object, a person might break the flashlight up into one short, thick cylinder for the light portion, one longer, slender cylinder for the handle portion, and a flat rectangular block for the switch. He also showed that when people view incomplete drawings, they are still capable of identifying the objects if the intact portions of the picture include object vertices. Without the vertices, the person's ability to perceive the underlying geons is compromised.

Intent-Based Augmentation Examples

Our intent-based augmentations use *visual context* to help the user understand the intent of the augmentation. Adding additional graphical detail around the augmentation leverages the viewer's ability to perceive the overall structural similarities of the physical and virtual worlds, and quickly deduce their relationship even though they are not aligned with each other. We have identified several strategies for creating visual context that can help viewers understand the intent of an augmentation: *general visual context*, *detailed visual relationships*, and *inset windows*.

General visual context refers to additional details provided to give the user a frame of reference to situate the graphical augmentation relative to the physical target object. In our implementation, the amount of detail increases with the magnitude of the estimated registration error between the augmentation and its intended target.

Figure 1 shows an example of adding general visual context to an augmentation. The intent of Figure 1(a) is to show where a red block and a blue block are located on a Lego board. However, there are two red and two blue blocks located on the board and they are placed in exactly the same configuration. Registration error prevents a user from knowing which pair of blocks is the intent of the augmentation. Figure 1(b) shows the same scene with the edges of the base-plate added. By showing their location relative to the edges of the Lego board, the user can reason that the blocks closest to the edges are actually the intended tar-

Figure 1. In (a) no additional context is given; in (b) general visual context (the outline of the Lego board) is added to the augmentation, disambiguating which pair of pieces the augmentation belongs with

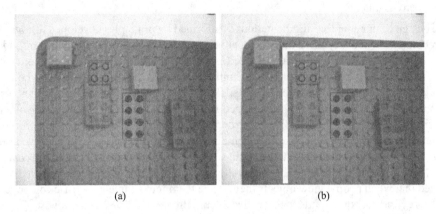

(a)   (b)

gets of the augmentation. (Note that in each of these examples and the examples to follow, the Lego board is shown as a perfect square, when in reality the Lego board has rounded edges. This was done to simplify the model, but does not reduce the disambiguating power of this cue.)

Detailed visual relationships are more detailed graphics intended to convey the precise relationship between the target of the augmentation and other objects close to it. These objects are used by the user when there are many similar objects close to each other and it is unclear which object is the actual target of the augmentation.

Figure 2 shows an example of adding detailed visual relationships to an augmentation. A user is supposed to place the yellow block onto the correct squares of the Lego board. Figure 2(a) shows the minimal output of an AR system. Because there are registration errors, the user cannot determine where the block needs to be placed. Figure 2(b) shows the same scene, but now the AR system provides some general visual context in the form of the loca-

Figure 2. In (a) no additional context is given; in (b) general visual context (the outline of the Lego board) is added to the augmentation; in (c) additional detailed visual relationships are shown (white Lego peg outlines), further clarifying the intent of the augmentation

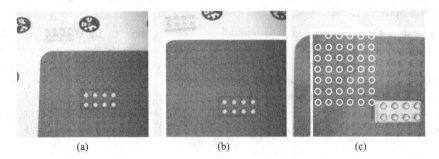

(a)   (b)   (c)

tion of the Lego board. Because the corner of the board in the display roughly aligns with that in the real world, the user can roughly determine where the block should be placed. However, the display does not provide enough information to specify exactly where the block should be located. Figure 2(c) extends the context by drawing the Lego pegs from the corner of the board to the corner of the yellow blocks. Therefore, the user can quickly and accurately confirm the accurate placement of the block by counting the number of pegs from the corner.

Finally, when a target is not visible in the user's view frame or if a registration error is particularly large, an *inset window* can be used to show what the user should be seeing.

Testing each of these strategies is the subject of ongoing research. Which style strategies convey the intent of different augmentations in the most appropriate manner? How much context is too much context? How much is too little? Do various rendering techniques convey intent better than others? Do the visualizations actually help the users or just distract them? However, to answer these questions different cues must be implemented and tested. We describe below an online framework to support the implementation and testing of these cues.

A Framework for Estimating Registration Errors

The foundation of our research is the ability to take estimates of the spatial uncertainty affecting an AR system and use them to estimate the resulting registration error impacting the user experience. We have implemented our ideas in OSGAR, an AR toolkit built on top of the open-source 3D scene-graph OpenSceneGraph (OSG). Before we discuss the mechanisms used by programmers to create adaptive displays and interaction techniques, we first describe how these estimates are obtained in our system. For a detailed discussion, see Coelho, MacIntyre, and Julier (2004).

In our implementation, we allow spatial uncertainty to be associated with any transformation in an AR system. A transformation matrix is therefore considered to be the mean of a probability distribution function (PDF) that approximates the actual value of that transformation. No restrictions are placed on the content of the transformation matrices; the system is assumed to be composed of a sequence of arbitrary 4x4 transformations. We encode the accuracy of the transformation as the covariance of an independent Gaussian distribution of each of the matrix elements, giving the programmer a relatively simple representation for the error estimate of a transformation, in a form that can be efficiently manipulated. While such a Gaussian model is an obvious simplification, it is unclear how better to measure and quantify the distribution of an arbitrary transformation matrix without sacrificing simplicity, consistency and efficiency.

The spatial location of any 3D point in the AR system is specified by a sequence of transformations. Uncertainty estimates are considered to be *view-independent*, and estimate the accuracy of a point's pose in the world as determined by the aggregated accuracy of this sequence of transformations. By combining the view-independent uncertainty of a point with the view-independent uncertainty of the viewer, *view-dependent* registration error estimates

Figure 3. OSGAR automatically computes registration error estimates for objects in the scene graph; the "*" ellipse is the error region around a 3D pointer

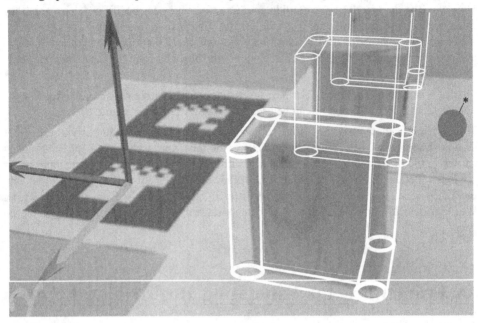

in screen-space can be computed as a 2D probability distribution of the projection of the point onto the view plane, shown as ellipses around the vertices of the cubes in Figure 3. The error ellipses of its vertices can be aggregated to approximate the registration error of an object. Two useful approximations are the "outer" region (shown in green in Figure 3) or an "inner" region (shown in white in Figure 3), indicating where some part of the object could or should occupy (respectively).

Figure 4. Creating graphics for a point in space: In (a) a point associated with a series of rigid transformations is displayed; in (b) there is uncertainty associated with the same point's position in space

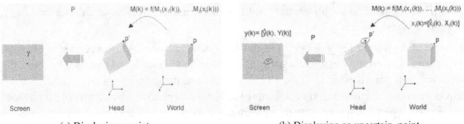

(a) Displaying a point   (b) Displaying an uncertain point

Estimating Registration Error

The effects of spatially uncertain transformations in the form of registration error can be estimated by observing the effect of the uncertainty on the projection equations. Because the analysis is fundamentally time varying, all the following quantities are referenced with respect to the discrete time index k. Each time step can, for example, refer to an individual frame. It is not necessary for each time step to be of equal length.

Consider the problem of determining the pixel coordinate $y(k)$ of a point $p(k)$ in world coordinates, as illustrated in Figure 4. Assume that the position of $p(k)$ is known perfectly. If there is some uncertainty, due to modeling errors or the fact that $p(k)$ might be a tracked object, the model can be easily extended to include these additional terms.

The projection can be broken into two steps: transforming from world coordinates to head coordinates (with coordinates $p'(k)$) and then applying the perspective transformation to project the point to the view plane. The transformation from $p(k)$ to $p'(k)$ is governed by the (homogeneous) model transformation matrix $M(k)$:

$$p'(k)=M(k)p(k)$$

$M(k)$ is a composite transformation that includes the inverses of the transformation matrices formed by the sensor readings. Therefore, tracking errors contribute to registration errors through an erroneous value of $M(k)$. These errors can be both spatial and temporal. Furthermore, the tracker value used is likely to be predicted from raw measurements using an implicit motion model and an assumed time step length. Both the model and the time step length can be inaccurate.

The problem of calculating the error bounds can therefore be stated as follows. For a 3D point $p(k)$ with tracker measurement $[x(k),X(k)]$, calculate the 2D mean and covariance of $y(k)$, $[y(k.)\ Y(k)]$, when $p'(k)$ is projected into screen space.

Originally, we used a parametric representation for the sequence of matrices that were composed to form the transformation matrix $M(k)$. Given this set of independent uncertain parameters, we used the unscented transform (Julier & Uhlmann, 2004) to estimate $y(k)$ regardless of the number of uncertain parameters influencing the transformation $M(k)$. However, the current implementation of OSGAR uses linearization. Although the limitations of linearization are widely known, we adopted this route for expediency when switching from a parametric representation to a matrix-based representation. This approach allows us to recursively propagate the error down a scene graph that applies arbitrary matrix transformations, which was not possible using the parametric representation and the unscented Transform.

Propagating Spatial Uncertainty

Each transformation is assumed to be associated with a graph node. Specifically, let M_i^j be the true relative transformation from node **I** to node **J**, M_r^n is the cumulative transformation matrix from the root node **R** to an arbitrary node **N**. Let $\hat{M}_i^j$ be the measured relative transformation from node i to node j.

The problem is to estimate the statistics of $\hat{M}_i''$ given that errors could be introduced at the transformation of any node in the tree. The error introduced at a node is assumed to be the additive matrix:

$$\hat{M}_r^i = M_r^i + \delta M_r^i$$

Assuming that the error introduced at a node is independent of the error introduced at preceding nodes, the equation to propagate the error recursively down the scene graph is as follows:

$$\hat{M}_r^i = \hat{M}_{i-1}^i \hat{M}_r^{i-1}$$

$$\delta M_r^i = M_{i-1}^i \delta M_r^{i-1} + \delta M_{i-1}^i M_r^{i-1}$$

Discussion

Choosing to represent the transformation as a generic transformation matrix of sixteen independent values and assuming uncertainty to be additive has three main difficulties:

1. It is more computationally expensive. If one assumed, for example, that the matrix only encoded translation rotation and scale then only nine parameters would be required. However, this is at the cost of introducing complicated nonlinear transformations at each node to recover the parameters (and their uncertainties) after a transformation is applied.

2. It does not capture the nonlinear constraints which exist between matrix elements. For example, large orientation errors are additive. These could be partially overcome by using more sophisticated models. For example, the error could be treated as being multiplicative and of the form $I + \delta M_{i-1}^i$ where I is the identity matrix. A recursive relationship exists in this case. The mean term is the same but the error propagation term becomes $\delta M_r^i = \delta M_r^{i-1} + (M_r^{i-1})^{-1} \delta M_{i-1}^i M_r^{i-1}$.

3. It only supports unimodal distributions. Some trackers may need more complex distributions to accurately represent their error characteristics. For example, tracking systems based on ultrawideband suffer from multipath signal interference and so there are several discrete potential solutions.

Despite these limitations, we believe the chosen representation is appropriate for our needs for the following reasons:

1. The transformation operations on each node are simple. The transformation consists of a single matrix multiplication which only involves basic arithmetic operations. More

elaborate models could be used, but at the risk of introducing lag and thus causing larger registration errors.

2.   The complexity of specifying nonlinearities (e.g., tracker errors) are only introduced at the nodes where these errors are generated.

3.   If nodes do not introduce their own sources of error, the first term in the error propagation is not needed, reducing complexity even further.

4.   Any type of matrix operation can be supported. Therefore, not just errors in the location of objects, but also their sizes, the position and projection properties of the viewer, etc., can be handled in a uniform way.

5.   Chains of static transformations can be exactly combined together into a single transformation step.

Error Estimation

The 2D elliptical region that estimates the registration error of an individual point in 3D space is computed statistically. The registration error represents the region on the screen that corresponds to where the 2D projection of the 3D point is likely to be. To compute the registration error for an object, not just a single point, we follow a simple two-step process:

1.   Compute the region on the screen for each vertex of the object, and

2.   Aggregate the regions computed in the previous step to generate two regions representing the object as a whole.

The *error ellipse* corresponds to applying step one of the computation of the error estimation, while both the *inner* and *outer* regions correspond to step two, when the vertex-related estimates are aggregated to generate on object estimate. These regions form the basis for designing both proper adaptive augmentations and suitable user interaction mechanisms.

The Architecture of OSGAR

OSGAR is based on the mathematical framework described above. Figure 5 shows the architecture of OSGAR, emphasizing how OSG and OSGAR are integrated. The first, fundamental, difference between OSGAR and other 3D scene graphs is the addition of the *OSGAR Transform*, a subclass of *OSG Transform* (the OSG 3D transformation node, analogous to that found in any scene-graph library) that supports uncertain transformations. In OSGAR, any transformation matrix is considered to be the mean of a probability distribution function (PDF) for that transformation, instead of just a single known transformation.

Using OSGAR Transform, internal nodes in the scene graph can have spatial uncertainty associated with them, and uncertain transformations can be mixed freely in the scene graph

Figure 5. OSGAR main components: OSGAR is built on top of OpenSceneGraph

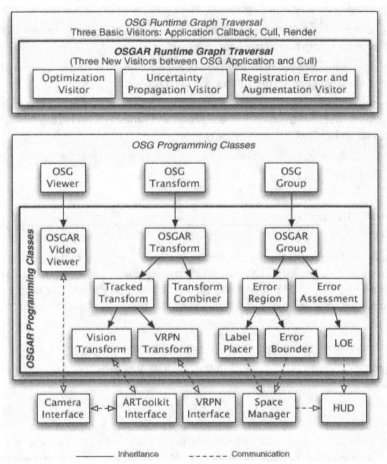

with exact (OSG Transform) ones. A covariance matrix inside the OSGAR Transform nodes represents the uncertainty associated with a transformation (if no uncertainty information is specified for a transformation, it is assumed to be exact and its covariance is zero). The mean of the PDF (i.e., the original transformation) is used for culling, rendering, and so on, as in regular scene graphs. Uncertainty is propagated down the scene graph by a pre-processing pass through the graph, as described next, and stored as matrix estimates at the internal group nodes.

The second difference between OSGAR and other scene graphs is the addition of new *OSGAR Group* nodes (the nodes internal to the graph, used to structure the hierarchical relationships in the world) that use the view-dependent error estimate to compute a 2D view-dependent convex hull of the points in the 3D hull of the geometry in the scene graph under the node.

The points in the 2D hull are used to compute the registration error estimates. The OSGAR Group subclasses, *Error Assessment* and *Error Region,* provide methods for programmers to retrieve two different representations of the registration error estimates of the objects in the subgraph under them.

The Region subclasses provide the programmer with a collection of closed regions (illustrated in Figure 3). An error ellipse for each vertex in the 2D hull, an outer region (the convex hull of all points in the error ellipses) representing the region that the object *might* intersect, and an inner region representing the region the object *should* intersect.

The Assessment subclasses provide the programmer with a single floating-point value representing an assessment of the magnitude of the registration error. The assessment is computed using two user-defined methods: *metric* is run on each of the vertices in the 2D hull, giving a floating-point value for each. An *aggregator* is run on the set of vertices and floating point values, and returns the single floating value for the object. There are many possible metrics that could be used by an Assessment object, such as the maximum of the main axis of the ellipses, the area of the ellipse, etc. As an aggregator function, one can consider the closest vertex, the average of all vertices, etc.

Implementation Details

Since scene graphs allow multiple paths to reach a node, a list of error estimates, tagged with the corresponding path, is stored on each of these group nodes. To handle these new nodes, three new specialized scene graph traversals (called *visitors* in OSG) were implemented. These three visitors are responsible for optimizing, computing the view independent uncertainty and the view dependent error estimate respectively.

Optimization Traversal

A number of pre-preprocessing steps are performed on the scene graph so that unnecessary computation is avoided during the next two traversals. For example, this visitor determines which nodes need to have their error estimates recomputed based on changes to the graph and transformations, limiting the nodes the subsequent visitors must visit. It also precomputes a simpler representation for complex objects, dramatically reducing the number of vertices processed.

View Independent Traversal

This visitor propagates the spatial uncertainty estimates down the graph, computing the *view independent spatial uncertainty* at each node in the graph. As an example, the uncertainty in the location of a tracked object is independent of the direction from which that object was viewed. These values are stored at the group nodes. Since there might be more than one path to a group node, a list of estimates is stored in these nodes. Each estimate is tagged with the path so that the proper one can be retrieved when needed.

View Dependent Traversal

This visitor uses the view independent spatial uncertainty to compute the final registration error estimate in 2D screen space for a point located at the origin of a node (for *Error Assessment OSGAR Group* nodes) or for the geometry contained in the subgraph rooted at a node (for *Error Region OSGAR Group* nodes). The error estimate is only computed where the programmer has requested it by using a subclass of one of these two nodes in their graph structure.

First, the view independent value computed for the camera node is combined with the view independent uncertainty at the node, giving the total uncertainty for a node relative to the viewer (the 3D camera). The spatial uncertainty from the viewer's perspective is then projected into 2D screen space in one of the two ways mentioned above. This computation also takes into account the uncertainty associated with the projection matrix, allowing uncertainty in the camera's intrinsic parameters to be accounted for.

Adapting Output with OSGAR

We have implemented one subclass of error assessment (LOE) and two subclasses of error region (bounding regions, label placer) as examples of how programmers can leverage the OSGAR Group classes to build applications that adapt their output to spatial uncertainty.

- **Level of error (LOE) switches:** The LOE automatically chooses between different children of the graph, allowing the application developer to specify different augmentations corresponding to the same real object. The most appropriate augmentation will be chosen accordingly, depending on the registration error estimate computed in real time.

- **Bounding regions:** This group displays a graphical representation of the 2D convex hulls computed by the Region node. This class can display the vertex ellipses, the inner region, the outer region, or any combination. Figure 3 shows three cubes with all regions displayed. It can be used for prototyping, debugging or as a crude highlight for the region an object is expected to occupy.

- **Label placer:** The label placer computes where to position the labels for a given object based on the computed inner and outer regions of the model. One has the option to keep the label always inside the object or guarantee that the label will never block the object. This class computes where to place the label to follow one of those constraints. The label placer uses a callback that specifies how to position the labels, for which we have implemented two very simple examples. The first callback positions the label where there is the most space available, computed from the sides of the object to the limits of the screen. The second callback always tries to position the label in this order: right, top, bottom, and then left.

Disambiguating Input Using OSGAR

Handling interaction in augmented reality (AR) systems is a challenging problem. Many compelling AR systems in military, industrial and entertainment domains envision users operating in mobile 3D environments where they interact with the world, such as by pointing at physical objects to obtain information about them. While AR interaction shares many traits with interaction in other 3D environments, such as virtual reality, it differs in one important way: much of what the user sees and interacts with are physical objects about which the system has imperfect information, especially regarding their geometry and pose (position and orientation) relative to the user.

Errors in tracking the pose and modeling the geometry of objects in the world most obviously manifest themselves to the user in the form of *registration error* between the object and any virtual augmentation being rendered in relation to that object (e.g., a label on a piece of equipment or a virtual lamp sitting on a physical table). These errors also introduce ambiguity into user interaction, especially in *selection* tasks. Furthermore, registration error is rarely constant, so it can be difficult for a user to adapt to.

This section shows how to leverage registration error estimates, such as those provided by OSGAR, to calculate selection probabilities for objects in AR systems (Coelho, MacIntyre, & Julier, 2005). This approach provides a simple yet robust foundation for creating interaction techniques in AR environments, and can feed directly into the multi-modal approaches described by other authors (Kaiser et al., 2003; Olwal, Benko, & Feiner, 2003).

Selection in OSGAR is achieved by detecting the collisions between the selection pointer and objects in the scene. The key difference is that by using the registration error estimates computed by OSGAR, it is possible to robustly tell what a user *might* be trying to select and provide feedback to help them make unambiguous selections.

Figure 6. Direct selection: When direct selection is possible, the system reports the likelihood of each object been selected

(a) Likelihoods   (b) Selections

Figure 7. Indirect selection: When the location of the selection targets can be controlled by the application, positioning the interaction elements in well spaced locations allows the user to interact with the system unambiguously

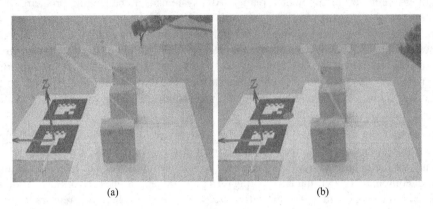

(a)   (b)

Given the registration error estimate regions in Figure 3, the basic selection algorithm is as follows:

1. **Intersect** the (solid magenta) region around the pointer with the regions around objects (green hulls) or points (blue ellipsoids) of interest, and

2. **Return** a list of all hits with additional useful information about each hit target, including the relative depth and likelihood of this being the target.

One metric for the likelihood is the area of intersection between the error estimation regions, but (as discussed next) the implementation gives programmers the flexibility to define their own evaluation callbacks.

Programmers can use the information in the hit list to implement domain-specific interaction techniques, analogous to how the OpenGL selection mechanism (which returns a list of all objects under a pixel, along with their depth ordering) is used to implement more complex techniques. In OpenGL, the simple selection technique is to select the closest object; similarly, a simple selection in OSGAR might be to select the closest object, or to select the object with the highest likelihood. In Figure 6(a), the highest likelihood is highlighted the darkest red. In Figure 6(b), two possible selection targets are shown in blue.

OSGAR error estimates can be further leveraged to implement indirect selection methods for when the user cannot unambiguously select a single object. An implementation of indirect selection is illustrated in Figure 7. A set of target labels is created, one for each possibly selected object. The labels are positioned automatically by the system (in this case, horizontally) depending on the magnitude of the error estimate of the pointer; the labels automatically spread themselves out further as the pointer error estimate increases. The user can select a single object unambiguously by selecting the corresponding label, since this indirect selection mechanism guarantees that the location on the screen of the targets will allow each target to be selected individually.

Conclusion

Registration errors caused by spatial uncertainty are an inherent problem in most AR applications. Rather than assume that spatial uncertainty can be eliminated, we have presented an approach to AR system design where the programmer is provided with estimates of registration error that they can use to create AR applications that function robustly in dynamically changing real world settings.

This chapter presented a framework that allows the application developer to reason about the constantly changing characteristics in the environment in a form that is straight-forward to use. That is, error is presented in terms of pixels on the screen, rather than absolute 3D distances in the environment. We introduced new concepts for adapting augmentations and disambiguating input based on these changing characteristics.

Acknowledgments

The authors would like to thank Brendan Hannigan for many of the low-level AR libraries used by OSGAR and Mike Ellison for the VidCapture wrappers for DirectShow (which are the basis for our video library). We also would like to thank UNC Chapel Hill for use of the VRPN library (which we used to communicate with sensors and trackers) and the UW HIT Lab for the ARToolkit (which we use for fiducial marker tracking). This work was supported by the Office of Naval Research under Contract N000140010361.

References

Azuma, R., & Bishop, G. (1994). Improving static and dynamic registration in an optical see-through HMD. *Computer Graphics (Proceedings of Siggraph)* (pp. 197-204).

Bajura, M., Fuchs, M., & Ohbuchi, R. (1992, July 26-31). *Merging virtual objects with the real world: Seeing ultrasound imagery within the patient.* Paper presented at the SIGGRAPH, Chicago.

Biederman, I. (1987). Recognition by components: A theory of human image understanding. *Psychological Review, 1994*, 115-147.

Coelho, E. M., MacIntyre, B., & Julier, S. (2004, November 2-5). *(osgAR): A scenegraph with uncertain transformations.* Paper presented at The International Symposium on Mixed and Augmented Reality, Arlington, VA.

Coelho, E. M., MacIntyre, B., & Julier, S. (2005, October 23-26). *Supporting interaction in augmented reality in the presence of uncertain spatial knowledge.* Paper presented at The ACM Symposium on User Interface Software and Technology, Seattle, WA.

Feiner, S., MacIntyre, B., Höllerer, T., & Webster, A. (1997). A touring machine: Prototyping 3D mobile augmented reality systems for exploring the urban environment. *Personal Technologies, 1*(4), 208-217.

Holloway, R. L. (1997). Registration error analysis for augmented reality. *Presence: Tele-operators and Virtual Environments, 6*(4), 413-432.

Jacobs, M., Livingston, M. A., & State, A. (1997, April 27-30). *Managing latency in complex augmented reality systems.* Paper presented at The Symposium on Interactive 3D Graphics, Providence, RI.

Julier, S. J., & Uhlmann, J. K. (2004). Unscented filtering and nonlinear estimation. *Proceedings of the IEEE, 92*(3), 401-422.

Kaiser, E., Olwal, A., McGee, D., Benko, H., Corradini, A., Li, X., et al. (2003, November 5-7). *Mutual disambiguation of 3D multimodal interaction in augmented and virtual reality.* Paper presented at The International Conference on Multimodal Interfaces Vancouver, BC. Canada.

Koffka, K. (1935). *Principles of Gestalt psychology.* New York: Harcourt Brace & Company.

Navab, N., Bani-Hashemi, A., & Mitschke, M. (1999). *Merging visible and invisible: Two camera-augmented mobile C-arm (CAMC) applications.* Paper presented at The 2nd International Workshop on Augmented Reality, San Francisco.

Olwal, A., Benko, H., & Feiner, S. (2003, October 7-10). *SenseShapes: Using statistical geometry for object selection in a multimodal augmented reality system.* Paper presented at the International Symposium on Mixed and Augmented Reality, Tokyo, Japan.

Open Scene Graph. (n.d.). Retrieved from http://www.openscenegraph.org

Piekarski, W., & Thomas, B. (2001, October 29-30). *Tinmith-evo5: An architecture for supporting mobile augmented reality environments.* Paper presented at the International Symposium on Augmented Reality, New York.

Robertson, C., & MacIntyre, B. (2003). Adapting to registration error in an intent-based augmentation system. In A. Y. C. Nee & S. K. Ong (Eds.), *Virtual and augmented reality applications in manufacturing* (pp. 143-163). London: Springer Verlag.

Seligmann, D., & Feiner, S. (1991). Automated generation of intent-based 3D illustrations. *Computer Graphics, 25*(4), 123-132.

State, A., Livingston, M. A., Hirota, G., Garrett, W. F., Whitton, M. C., Fuchs, H., et al. (1996, August 4-9). *Technologies for augmented-reality systems: Realizing ultrasound-guided needle biopsies.* Paper presented at the SIGGRAPH, New Orleans, LA.

Traub, J., Feuerstein, M., Bauer, M., Schirmbeck, E. U., Najafi, H., Bauernschmitt, R., et al. (2004, June 23-26). *Augmented reality for port placement and navigation in robotically assisted minimally invasive cardiovascular surgery.* Paper presented at the Computer Assisted Radiology and Surgery, Chicago.

Tuceryan, M., & Navab, N. (2000, October 5-6). *Single Point Active Alignment Method (SPAAM) for optical see-through HMD calibration for AR.* Paper presented at the The International Symposium on Augmented Reality, Munich, Germany.

Welch, G., & Foxlin, E. (2002). Motion tracking: No silver bullet, but a respectable arsenal. *IEEE Computer Graphics and Applications, 22*(6), 24-38.

Chapter III

An Introduction to Head Mounted Displays for Augmented Reality

Kiyoshi Kiyokawa, Osaka University, Japan

Abstract

This chapter introduces design and principles of head mounted displays (HMDs), as well as their state-of-the-art examples, for augmented reality (AR). Section 2 introduces a brief history of head mounted displays, human vision system, and application examples of see-through HMDs. Section 3 describes designs and principles of HMDs, such as typical configurations of optics, typical display elements, and major categories of HMDs. Section 4 gives typical characteristics of HMDs, such as resolution, field of view, and distortion. Section 5 describes human perceptual and health issues such as depth perception and safety. Finally, Section 6 gives conclusions with future challenges and prospects. For researchers, learners, and HMD developers, this chapter is a good starting point to learn basics, state of the art technologies, and future research directions of HMDs. For system developers and end-users, this chapter will give a good insight to HMDs to choose a suitable HMD for their purposes.

Introduction

Ever since Sutherland's first see-through HMD in the late 1960s, attempts have been made to develop a variety of HMDs by researchers and manufacturers in the communities of virtual reality (VR), AR, and wearable computers. Because of HMD's wide application domains and technological limitations, however, no single HMD is perfect. This is why it is extremely important to appropriately appreciate pros and cons of each HMD, its abilities, and limitations. As an introduction to the following discussion, this section introduces three issues related to HMDs; a brief history of HMDs, human vision system, and application examples of HMDs.

Brief History of Head Mounted Displays

The idea of a head mounted display was first patented by McCollum in 1945 (McCollum, 1945). Heilig also patented a stereoscopic television HMD in 1960 (Heilig, 1960), then he developed and patented a stationary VR simulator, the Sensorama Simulator in 1962, which was equipped with a variety of sensory devices including a binocular display to give the user virtual experiences. Comeau and Bryan at Philco Corporation built Headsight in 1961, the first actual HMD (Comeau & Bryan, 1961). This was more like a today's telepresence system. Using a magnetic tracking system and a single CRT mounted on a helmet, Headsight shows a remote video image according to the measured head direction. Bell Helicopter Company studied a servo-controlled camera-based HMD in the 1960's. This display provides the pilot with an augmented view captured by an infrared camera under the helicopter for landing at night. In a sense that the real world image is enhanced in real-time, this is the first video see-through AR system, though computer-generated imagery was not yet used.

The first HMD coupled with head tracking facility and real-time computer-generated image overlay was demonstrated by Sutherland in the late 1960's (Sutherland, 1965, 1968). This tethered display, called "Sword of Damocles," has a set of CRT-based optical see-through relay optics for each eye, allowing each eye to observe a synthetic imagery and its surrounding real environment simultaneously from a different vantage point.

Since the early 1970s, the U.S. Air Force has studied HMD systems as a way of providing the aircrew with a variety of flight information. As the first system in this regard, the AN/PVS-5 series Night Vision Goggle (NVG) was first tested in 1973. The Honeywell Integrated Helmet and Display Sighting System (IHADSS) is one of the most successful see-through systems in Army aviation, which was first fielded in 1985 (Rash & Martin, 1988). In 1982, Furness demonstrated the Visually Coupled Airborne Systems Simulator (VCASS), the US Air Force's "super-cockpit" VR system (Furness, 1986).

The large expanse, extra perspective (LEEP) optical system, developed in 1979 by Eric Howledtt, has been widely used in VR. The LEEP system, originally developed for 3D still photography, provides a wide field of view (~110°(H) x 55°(V)) stereoscopic viewing. Having a wide exit pupil of about 40 mm, the LEEP requires no adjustment mechanism for interpupillary distance. Employing the LEEP optical system, McGreevy and Fisher have developed the virtual interactive environment workstation (VIEW) system at the NASA Ames Research Center in 1985. Using the LEEP optics, VPL Research introduced the first

Figure 1. (a) Human eye structure; (b) density of cones and rods

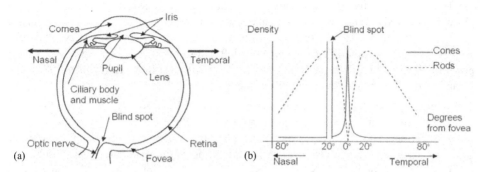

commercial HMD, EyePhone, in 1989. The EyePhone encouraged VR research at many institutes and laboratories. Since then, a variety of HMDs have been developed and commercialized.

Human Vision System

Vision is the most reliable and complicated sensory, providing more than 70% of the total sensory information. Figure 1(a) shows the structure of a human eye. When light travels through the cornea, it enters the pupil. The pupil is a round opening in the center of the iris, which adjusts the pupil's aperture size. After the light travels through the pupil, it will enter the crystalline lens, which refracts the light on the retina. There are two types of photoreceptor cells; rods and cones, on the retina. The retina contains about seven million cone cells and 120 million rod cells. As shown in Figure 1(b), most cones exist in the fovea, while rods widely exist on the retina except for the fovea. Three types of cone cells, corresponding to different peak wavelength sensitivities, cooperatively provide color perception within spectral region of 400 to 700 nm. The cones function under the daylight (normal) condition and provide very sharp visual acuity, the ability to resolve spatial detail. The rods function even under the dim light condition, though they provide lower visual acuity than cones do. Normal visual acuity can identify an object that subtends an angle of 1 to 0.5 minute of arc.

Field of view (FOV) of the human eye is an oval of about 150°(H) by 120°(V). As both eyes' FOVs overlap, the total binocular FOV measures about 200°(H) by 120°(V) (Barfield, Hendrix, Bjorneseth, Kaczmarek, & Lotens, 1995). The innermost region corresponding to the fovea is only 1.7° in diameter. Outside this region, the visual acuity drops drastically. To compensate, one needs to move the eyes and/or the head. An area in the view that fixation can be accomplished without head motion is called the field of fixation, which is roughly circular with a radius of about 40° to 50°. However, head motion will normally accompany to maintain the rotation angle of the eyes smaller than 15°. The horizontal FOV slowly declines with age. From nearly 180°(H) at age 20, to 135°(H) at age 80.

Depth perception occurs with monocular and/or binocular depth cues. These cues can be further categorized into physiological and psychological cues. Physiological monocular depth cues include accommodation, monocular convergence, and motion parallax. Psychological monocular depth cues include apparent size, linear perspective, aerial perspective, texture gradient, occlusion, shades, and shadows. Binocular convergence and stereopsis are typical physiological and psychological binocular depth cues, respectively. Binocular convergence is related to the angle between two lines from a focused object to the both eyes, while stereopsis is about the lateral disparity between left and right images. Stereopsis is the most powerful depth cue for distance up to 6 to 9 meters (Boff, Kaufman, & Thomas, 1986), and it can be effective up to a few hundreds of meters.

The human eye has the total dynamic sensitivity of at least 10^{10}, by changing the pupil diameter from about 2 mm to 8 mm. According to the intensity of the light, the dynamic range is divided into three types of vision; photopic, mesopic, and scotopic (Bohm & Schranner, 1990). Photopic vision, experienced during daylight, features sharp visual acuity and color perception. In this case, rods are saturated and not effective. Mesopic vision is experienced at dawn and twilight. In this case, cones function less actively and provide reduced color perception. At the same time, peripheral vision can be effective to find dim objects. Scotopic vision is experienced under starlight conditions. In this case, peripheral vision is more dominant than the foveal vision with poor visual acuity and degraded color perception because only the rods are active.

AR Applications of Head Mounted Displays

As readers may find elsewhere in this book, HMDs have a variety of applications in AR including military, medicine, scientific visualization, manufacturing, education, training, navigation, and entertainment. When considering the use of an HMD, it is important to identify crucial aspects in the target application.

A wide FOV HMD is preferred when the image overlay needs to surround the user. Army aviation is an example, in this regard, where the aviator often needs to see in every direction. Through the HMD, the aviator sees a variety of situational information, including pilotage imagery, tactical, and operational data (Buchroeder, 1987). In this case, a monocular display is often sufficient, as most targets are distant. Size and weight of the HMD are relatively less crucial, as the display-integrated helmet can be suspended from the cockpit ceiling.

A high resolution HMD is preferred for a dexterous manipulation task. For example, angular pixel resolution as well as registration accuracy is crucial in medical 3D visualization. Medical 3D visualization eliminates necessity for frequent gaze switching between the patient's body at hand and images of the small camera inside the body on a monitor during laparoscopic and endoscopic procedures (Rolland, Wright, & Kancherla, 1996). Stereoscopic view is also important for accurate operations. Wide FOV, on the other hand is not crucial, as the image overlay is needed in a small area.

A lightweight, less-tiring HMD is especially preferred for end-users and/or for tasks with a large workspace. Early examples in this regard include Boeing's AR system for wire harness assembly (Caudell & Mizell, 1992), KARMA system for end-user maintenance (Feiner, MacIntyre, & Seligmann, 1993), and an outdoor wearable tour guidance system (Feiner, Macintyre, Tobias, & Webster, 1997). In these systems, moderate pixel resolution and registration accuracy often suffice. Safety and user acceptance issues, such as periphery vision and a mechanism for easy attachment/detachment, are of importance.

Figure 2. Optical see-through display: (a) Configuration; (b) example HMD (Image courtesy of i-O Display Systems)

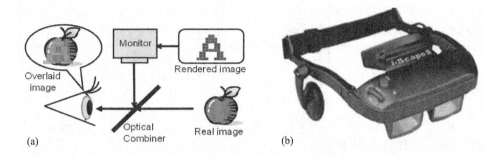

(a)   (b)

Hardware Issues

Optical and Video See-Through Approaches

There are mainly two types of see-through approaches in AR; optical and video. Figure 2 shows (a) a typical configuration and (b) a commercial product of an optical see-through display. With an optical see-through display, the real and synthetic imagery are combined with a partially transmissive and reflective optical device, typically half-silvered mirror. The real world is left almost intact through the optical combiner, while the synthetic imagery is optically overlaid on the real image. In most optical see-through HMDs, the optical combiner is normally placed at the end of the optical path just in front of the user's eyes. In the case of a half-silvered mirror, the real scene is simply seen through it, whereas the synthetic imagery is reflected on it. The imaging device cannot be placed in front of the eyes. Instead, it is normally located above the optical combiner, or to the side of the user's head with relay optics. Advantages of optical see-through HMDs include a natural, instantaneous

Figure 3. Video see-through display: (a) Configuration, and (b) example HMD (used with permission from Trivisio Prototyping GmbH)

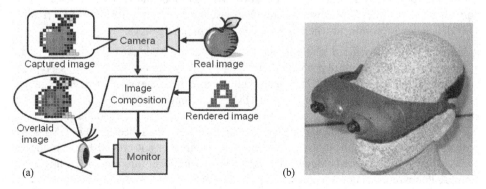

(a)   (b)

Table 1. Combinations of ocularity and see-through types

	Binocular (Stereo)	Biocular	Monocular
Optical see-through	Very good	Confusing	Good
Video see-through	Very good	Good	Confusing

view of the real scene, seamlessness between aided and periphery views, and (generally) simple and lightweight structures.

Figure 3 shows (a) a typical configuration and (b) a commercial product of a video see-through display. With a video see-through display, the real world imagery is first captured by a video camera, then the captured image and the synthetic imagery are combined electronically, and finally the combined imagery is presented to the user. Electronic merging can be accomplished by frame grabbers or chroma-keying devices. As there are very few commercial video see-through HMDs, most of them are manually built, using a closed-view (non see-through) HMD and one or two video cameras. Advantages of video see-through HMDs over optical see-through HMDs include pictorial consistency between the real and the synthetic views and the availability of a variety of image processing techniques. With appropriate vision-based tracking and synchronous processing of the captured and the rendered images, geometric and temporal consistencies can be accomplished.

Ocularity

Ocularity is another criterion for categorizing HMDs. There are three types of ocularity; monocular, biocular, and binocular. These categories are independent of the type of see-through. Table 1 shows applicability of each combination of ocularity and see-through types.

A monocular HMD has a single viewing device, either see-through or closed. It can be relatively small and provides unaided real view to the other eye. A monocular HMD is preferable, for example, for some outdoor settings, where less obtrusive real view is crucial and stereoscopic synthetic imagery is not necessary. The Army aviation and wearable computing are good examples of the application. With a monocular HMD, the two eyes see quite different images. This causes an annoying visual experience called binocular rivalry. This deficiency is prominent when using video see-through displays.

A biocular HMD provides a single image to both eyes. As both eyes always observe an exact same synthetic image, a problem of binocular rivalry does not occur. This is a typical configuration for consumer HMDs, where 2D images such as televisions and video games are primary target contents. Some biocular HMDs have optical see-through capability for safety reasons. However, an optical see-through view with a biocular HMD is annoying in AR systems because of binocular rivalry. For AR, biocular video see-through HMDs are preferable for casual applications, where stereo capability is not crucial but convincing overlaid imagery is needed. MagicBook is a good example in this regard (Billinghurst, Kato, & Poupyrev, 2001).

A binocular HMD has two separate displays with two input channels, one for each eye. Because of the stereo capability, binocular HMDs are preferred in many AR systems. There is often confusion between binocular and stereo. A binocular HMD can function as a stereoscopic HMD only when two different image sources are properly provided.

Eye-Relief

A HMD needs to magnify a small image on the imaging device to produce a large virtual screen at a certain distance to cover the user's view (Figure 4(a)). For small total size and rotational moment of inertia, the eye-relief (the separation between the eyepiece and the eye) is desirable to be short. However, too small eye-relief causes the FOV to be partially shaded off, and it is inconvenient for users' with eyeglasses. As a compromise, eye-relief of a HMD is normally set between 20 to 40 mm.

Eye-relief and the actual distance between the eye and the imaging device (or the last image plane) are interlinked to each other, because a magnifying lens (the eyepiece functions as a magnifying lens) has normally equivalent front and back focal lengths. For example, when the eye-relief is 30 mm, the distance between the eye and the image will be roughly 60 mm. Similarly, the larger the eye-relief becomes, the larger the eyepiece diameter needs to be, which introduces heavier optics but a larger exit pupil size. The exit pupil should be as large as possible, at least around 10 mm in diameter. The eyepiece diameter cannot exceed the interpupillary distance (IPD) that varies among individuals from 53mm to 73 mm (Robinett & Rolland, 1992).

Relay Optics Design

Once the eye-relief is determined, the size of the imaging device can be calculated based on the required FOV. For example, if the required horizontal FOV is 30° and the eye-relief is 30 mm, an imaging device of 0.8 inch in diagonal is needed (30[mm] × $tan(30[deg]/2)$

Figure 4. (a) Eye-relief and viewing distance; (b) an off-axis relay optics design (Image taken from U.S. Patent 4,854,688, Hayford & Koch, 1989)

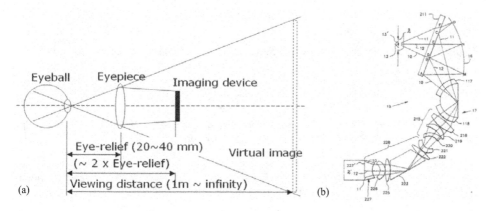

× 2 × (5/4) / 25.4 = 0.79). In this sense, if the eyepiece is solely used for the entire optics, flexibility in the selection of the imaging device is severely limited. Relay optics solve this problem and allow larger FOV in exchange for larger total size and weight. Relay optics are normally folded and placed around the head to minimize rotational moment of inertia. Relay optics form virtual images and an exit pupil that are collimated by the eyepiece. In such pupil-forming systems, the pupil needs to be positioned within a specific area to avoid eclipse.

Most of the relay optics designs are on-axis, that is, each optical element is aligned on the center of the optical axis. Off-axis design is more attractive as it can provide a larger FOV in a smaller layout. Figure 4(b) is an example of off-axis design that achieves a FOV of 50° (Hayford & Koch, 1989). However, in off-axis design, trapezoidal distortion and astigmatism occur as well as aberrations, which are difficult to eliminate.

Eyepiece Design

Mainly due to recent progress of high-resolution, small imaging devices, HMDs with a modest FOV that are lightweight and small have become possible by using the simple eyepiece design. Figure 5 shows three typical eyepiece designs. In early HMDs, refractive optics have been used (Figure 5(a)). In this case, at least three lenses are normally required for aberration correction and the size in depth and weight of the optics are difficult to reduce. Optical see-through capability is achieved by placing an optical combiner between the eyepiece and the eye.

Catadioptric designs (Figure 5(b)) contain a concave mirror and a half-silvered mirror. Light emitted from the imaging device is first reflected on the half-silvered mirror toward the concave mirror. The light is then reflected on the concave mirror, travels through the half-silvered mirror, and focuses on the eye. This configuration reduces the size and weight significantly. Besides, chromatic aberration is not introduced, which is the inability of a lens to focus different colors to the same point. Optical see-through is achieved by simply making the concave mirror semi-transparent. However, the eye receives only 1/4 of the original light of the imaging device at most, because of the half-silvered mirror. A beam-splitting prism is often used in place of the half-silvered mirror to increase the FOV at the expense of weight.

Figure 5. Typical eyepiece designs: (a) Refractive; (b) catadioptric; (c) free-form prism

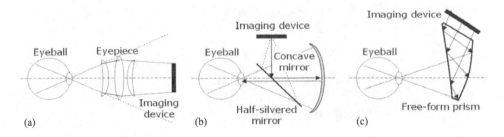

More advanced eyepiece designs use a free-form prism, developed by Canon in 1995 (Figure 5(c)). This configuration reduces the thickness and weight without loss of light efficiency. For example, 34° horizontal FOV is achieved with the prism's thickness of 15 mm. The inner side of the front surface functions as a concave mirror. The inner side of the back surface is carefully angled. At first, the light from the imaging device bounces off this surface with total reflection. Second, the reflected light travels through this surface to the eye, because of small incident angles. To provide optical see-through capability, a compensating prism can be attached at the front side (on the right side of Figure 5(c)).

Other Types of HMD Design

A Holographic Optical Element (HOE), a kind of diffractive grating, has been used for lightweight optics in HMDs. Due to its diffractive power, a variety of curved mirror shapes can be formed on a flat substrate. A HOE can also function as a highly transparent optical combiner due to its wavelength selectivity. Based on these unique characteristics, very thin (a few millimeters), lightweight, and bright optical see-through HMDs have been proposed (e.g., Kasai, Tanijiri, Endo, & Ueda, 2000). Small exit pupils and color alternation in see-through vision are typical drawbacks of HOE-based HMDs.

Light-guide Optical Element (LOE) developed by Lumus Vision Ltd. offers fairly large field of view (>40°) with extremely thin (4 mm) optics and a large exit pupil (~15mm) (Allen, 2002). As shown in Figure 6, image components from an image source are first coupled into the LOE with total internal reflection. Those image components are then coupled out of the LOE using carefully designed reflecting surfaces. Advantages of the LOE include thin and lightweight structure, bright see-through capability, clear periphery view, and potentially inexpensive manufacturing.

While normal HMDs present a virtual screen at a certain distance in front of the user's eye, some HMDs form no virtual screen (Figure 7). The virtual retinal display (VRD), developed at the University of Washington, scans modulated light directly onto the retina of the eye based on the principle of Maxwellian-view. The VRD eliminates the need for screens and imaging optics, theoretically allowing for very high resolution and wide FOV. A VRD

Figure 6. Light-guide optical element (LOE)

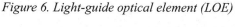

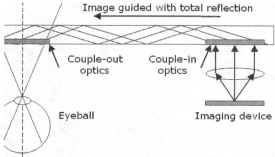

Figure 7. Locations of the image with regard to the type of HMD

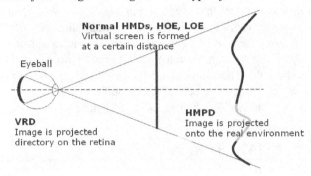

assures focused images all the time regardless of accommodation of the eye, in exchange for a small exit pupil.

Head mounted projection displays (HMPD) present a stereo image onto the real environment from a pair of miniature projectors (Fisher, 1996). A typical configuration and an example of HMPD are shown in Figure 8. From the regions in the real environment that are covered with retroreflective materials, the projected stereo image is bounced back to the corresponding eyes separately. Without the need for eyepiece, this design is less obtrusive, and it gives smaller aberrations and larger binocular FOV up to 120° horizontally. The HMPD in Figure 8(b), developed by Rolland et al. is an extra lightweight one with external fabric using OLED as a microdisplay and having 2 arcmin resolution, 42° diagonal FOV.

Display Elements

Miniature cathode ray tubes (CRTs) have been used in early and high-end HMDs, primarily due to their availability, high contrast, and high resolution (~1600x1200). CRTs generate

Figure 8. Head mounted projection display: (a) Configuration; (b) example HMPD (Image courtesy of Professor Jannick Rolland, ODALab and Nvis)

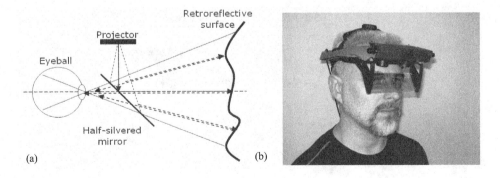

images by scanning an electron beam to strike a phosphor-coated surface. Main drawbacks of CRTs include weight, size (especially in depth), power consumption, high voltage, and heat. Field-sequential (time-multiplexed) full-color capability is normally provided by using liquid crystal shutters or a spinning color-wheel, because a shadow mask for miniature CRTs (~1 inch) is difficult to fabricate. CRTs, however, have been replaced by flat panel (FP) devices in most HMDs, except for some applications that require very high luminance.

FP devices offer miniature imaging devices with reduced thickness, weight, and power consumption. Liquid crystal displays (LCDs), the most common FP devices, consist of matrix cells, each of which functions as a separate light valve by applying an electric field. Among a variety types of LCD, active matrix LCDs (AMLCDs) driven by thin film transistors (TFTs) in the twisted nematic (TN) mode are most commonly used. They are normally coupled with a light source, such as the cold-cathode fluorescent tube (CCFT). To achieve color LCDs, a subpixel approach with RGB color filters is commonly employed. A resolution of XGA (1024×768) is achieved in today's commercial LCD-based HMDs.

Liquid Crystal on Silicon (LCOS) is a liquid crystal matrix array formed on a reflective silicon-based mirror substrate. Because switching devices are hidden under the mirror surface, the aperture ratio can be very high. For this reason, LCOS technology offers very high resolution ($>\sim 1280 \times 1024$). As a variation, ferroelectricity liquid crystal on silicon (FLCOS) uses ferroelectricity liquid crystal, which has very short response time ($1\sim100$ μs) enough to achieve full-color by a field-sequential technique.

An organic light emitting diode (OLED) is a variation of electroluminescence (EL) which has a matrix array of phosphor material between glass substrates. By applying an electric field, each cell emits light. Without the need for a dedicated light source, an OLED-based HMD offers reduced thickness and weight, low power consumption, and a wide viewing angle. Drawbacks of an OLED include short life span and low color purity, which have recently been improved.

Characteristics of Head Mounted Displays

Resolution

Resolution of the display system defines the fidelity of the image. Resolution of the total system is limited by those of optics and the imaging device. In the case of video see-through, resolution of the camera must be taken into consideration as well. A modulation transfer function (MTF) is often used to quantify the way modulation is transferred through the system. If the system is linear, convolution of the individual components' MTFs give the MTF of the entire system. However, angular resolution and the number of total pixels are conveniently used to assess each component. Regarding resolution of the synthetic image, an ideal HMD will need to have as many as 12000×7200 pixels to compete with the human vision. This is, unfortunately, unobtainable from the current technology.

To compromise, one needs to choose either of three options; (1) higher angular resolution with a narrower FOV, (2) lower angular resolution with a wider FOV, and (3) array multiple screens (called tiling). Medical visualization and Army aviation are suitable for first and second options, respectively. The border between first and second options is not clear, but 50° horizontally is a reasonable threshold. Third option is promising, but it also introduces increased weight, size, and rendering complexity. The Kaiser Electro-Optics "full immersion head mounted display" is the extreme in this regard (non see-through), which has 12 LCD in 3×2 arrangements for each eye, providing $176° \times 47°$ (However, resolution of each screen is only about 254×227). Another way of using multiple screens is a combination of first and second options (Longridge, Thomas, Fernie, Williams, & Wetzel, 1989). The idea is to provide a high-resolution screen and a wide FOV screen in a concentric layout. Mimicking the human vision system, this configuration gives highest resolution to where needed.

In AR systems, resolution of the real scene is a different story. Optical see-through displays provide close to the best scene resolution that is obtained with the unaided eye. Aberrations and distortions introduced by the optical combiner are negligible. Video see-through displays, on the other hand, provide digitized real images. The resolution in this case is limited by that of both the camera and the display. Captured images by a standard NTSC video camera typically have a resolution of 640 (or 720) × 480, but recent IEEE 1394 digital video cameras have higher resolution up to 1600×1200 at 15 fps, or 1024×768 at 30 fps.

Field of View

For an HMD for AR, a field of view can be classified into a number of regions. An aided (or overlay) FOV is the most important visual field in AR where the synthetic imagery is overlaid onto the real scene. An aided FOV of a stereo HMD typically consists of a stereo FOV and monocular FOVs. Narrow FOV HMDs ($<\sim60°$(H)) commonly have 100% overlap, whereas wide FOV HMDs ($>\sim80°$(H)) often have a small overlap ratio, e.g., 50%. Outside of the aided FOV consists of the peripheral FOV and occluded regions blocked by the HMD structure. The real scene is directly seen through the peripheral FOV, whereas none of the real or synthetic imagery is viewed in the occluded regions. The real view's transition between the aided and peripheral views is designed to be as seamless as possible. The occluded regions must be as small as possible.

A necessary aided FOV is task-dependent. In medical 3D visualization, such as breast needle biopsy, only a limited region in the visual field needs to be aided. Some studies claim that performance gain is saturated at the FOV of around 60°. However, aided peripheral vision is important for situation awareness and navigation tasks (Arthur, 2000). Larger peripheral FOVs reduce required head motion and searching time.

In optical see-through HMDs, overlay FOVs larger than around 60° are difficult to achieve due to aberrations and distortions. However, optical see-through HMDs tend to have a simple and compact structure, leaving wide peripheral FOV for direct view of the real scene. In the video see-through approach, the FOV of the display needs to match that of the camera to maximize both undistorted overlay FOV and unaided real world FOV in periphery. A camera with a viewing angle narrower than that of the display will only result in expanded blocked regions. Nagahra, Yagi, and Yachida (2005) proposed a very wide FOV HMD (180°(H) with 60°(H) overlap) using a pair of ellipsoidal and hyperboloidal curved mirrors (see Figure 9). Coupled with a pair of omni-directional cameras, this display can be a very wide FOV video see-through HMD.

Figure 9. A 180-degree FOV HMD: (a) Optics of the HMD unit; (b) prototype HMD (Images taken from Nagahara, Yagi, and Yachida, 2005, © 2005 The Institute of Electronics, Information and Communication Engineers, used with permission)

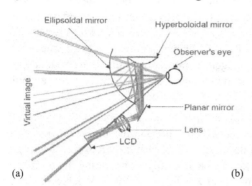
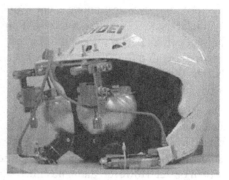

(a)   (b)

Distortions and Aberrations

Image distortions and aberrations cause incorrect registration and rendered depths, eyestrain and disorientation in AR. In a stereo HMD, differences in distortion between left and right images must be minimized to achieve correct stereopsis. CRT-based HMDs are prone to image distortion. First, producing a square image by scanning electron beams is not trivial. Second, as it takes several milliseconds to scan an image, image distortion on the retina will occur with rapid head motion. Rapid head motion also induces annoying color separation with field-sequential color systems.

Lenses and curved mirrors introduce a variety of optical aberrations. Typical distortions include pincushion, barrel and trapezoidal. Without introducing additional optical elements, optical distortions can be corrected electronically by pre-distorting the source image. In optical see-through HMDs, distortion must be corrected optically, which may increase weight and size of the optics. The HMPDs are generally free from distortion, as they do not have eyepiece-related problems.

Chromatic aberrations occur due to refractive power (a prism effect) of the lenses. To compensate, achromatic lenses are normally used, which consist of convex and concave lenses. Reflective optical elements such as concave mirrors do not induce chromatic aberrations. Considering that "full-color" displays actually have only RGB components, chromatic aberrations can be compensated by separately pre-distorting R, G, and B planes at the expense of increased rendering costs. Although not widely used to date, this technique is worth considering when designing wide FOV systems.

Spherical aberrations are induced by the spherical shape of the lens surface. With lateral shift of the eye, the image gets distorted and blurred. Similarly, field curvatures cause blurred imagery in the periphery. Pre-distorting techniques are not effective to correct these aberrations. Instead, aspheric and/or achromatic lenses can be used.

Occlusion

Occlusion is a strong depth cue. In the real world, orders of objects in depth can be recognized by observing overlaps among them. Correct mutual occlusion between the real and the synthetic scenes is often essential in AR applications, such as architectural previewing. To present correct occlusion, depth information of both the real and the synthetic scenes are needed. Depth information of the synthetic imagery is normally available from the depth buffer. While depth information of the real scene can be acquired in advance for a static scene, or by real-time range sensors such as a high-speed stereovision system.

Once the depth information is acquired, occlusion is represented differently with optical and video see-through approaches. In both cases, a partially occluded virtual object can be represented by simply omitting rendering the occluded regions. Similarly, a partially occluded real object can be presented in a video see-through approach simply by rendering the occluded virtual object. However, the same effect in an optical way is quite difficult to achieve, as the real scene is always seen through the partially transmissive optical combiner.

Some approaches to tackle this problem include (1) using a luminous synthetic imagery to make the real scene virtually invisible, (2) using a pattern light source in a dark environment to make part of real objects invisible, (3) using a HMPD with retroreflective screens. First approach is common in flight simulators but it also restricts available colors (to only bright ones). Second and third approaches need a special setup in the real environment. Another approach is a pixel-based light-modulating mechanism embedded in the see-through optics. The most advanced prototypical HMD to date in this regard is ELMO-4 (Kiyokawa, Billinghurst, Campbell, & Woods, 2003), which employs a relay design to introduce a transparent LCD panel positioned at an intermediate focus point. Figure 10 shows design and image examples of ELMO-4.

Latency

Latency in AR systems is a temporal lag from the measurement of the head position to the moment the rendered imagery is presented to the user. This leads to inconsistency between visual and vestibular sensations. In an optical see-through HMD, latency is observed as a severe registration error with the head motion, which further introduces motion sickness, confusion, and disorientation. In such a situation, the synthetic imagery swings around the real scene. In a video see-through HMD, this problem can be minimized by delaying the real image to synchronize it with the synthetic imagery. This approach eliminates apparent latency between the real and the synthetic scenes, at the expense of artificial delay introduced in the real scene.

To compensate latency, prediction filters such as an extended kalman filter (EKF) have been successfully used. Frameless rendering techniques can minimize the rendering delay by continuously updating part of the image frame. Taking advantage of nonuniformity of visual acuity and/or saccadic suppression, limiting regions and/or resolution of the synthetic imagery using an eye-tracking device helps reduce the rendering delay (Luebke & Hallen, 2001). Viewport extraction and image shifting techniques take a different approach. With these techniques, a synthetic imagery larger than the screen resolution is first rendered, and

Figure 10. (a) ELMO-4 optics design; (b) its appearance, and overlay images seen through ELMO-4; (c) without occlusion; (d) with occlusion and real-time range sensing (Images taken from Kiyokawa et al., 2003, © 2003 IEEE, used with permission)

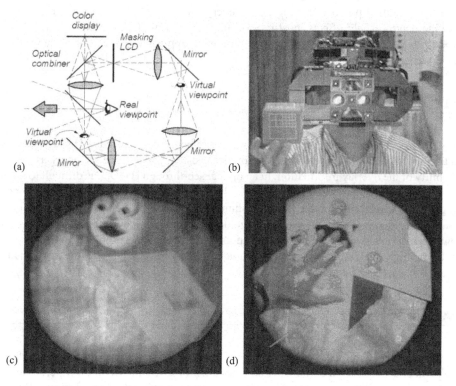

then a portion of it is extracted and presented to the user according to the latest measurement (Kijima & Ojika, 2002).

Depth of Field

Depth of field refers to the range of distances from the eye (or a camera) in which an object appears in focus. In the real life, the eye's accommodation is automatically adjusted to focus on an object according to the distance, and objects outside the depth of field appear blurred. On the other hand, the synthetic imagery is normally seen at a fixed distance. Therefore, it is impossible to focus on both the real and the synthetic imagery at the same time with an optical see-through HMD, unless the focused object is at or near the HMD's viewing distance.

This problem does not occur with a video see-through display, though captured real objects can be defocused due to the camera. To avoid blurred video images, the camera is preferable to be auto-focus, or to have a small aperture size. However, fixed focus of the synthetic imagery is problematic because accommodation and convergence are closely interlinked in the human vision system. Adjusting one of these while keeping the other causes eyestrain.

To support natural accommodation-convergence coupling, 3DDAC developed at ATR uses movable relay lenses and eye-tracking mechanisms embedded in the headset (Omura, Shiwa, & Kishino, 1996).

Due to a standard pinhole camera model, every rendered object is always in focus. To provide depth-of-field effects, post-process filtering and multi-pass rendering have been proposed. Varicose mirror displays are a promising approach to solve all of these issues (Schowengerdt & Seibel, 2004).

Brightness and Contrast

Brightness and contrast of the synthetic imagery should be adjusted to those of the real image. These factors severely affect pictorial consistency and sense of reality as well as visibility of the overlay information. In an optical see-through HMD, it is difficult to match them for a very wide range of luminance values of the real scene. No imaging device is bright enough to be comparable to the sunshine. Instead, some products allow transparency control. In video see-through systems, brightness matching is achieved inherently. Instead, low contrast (low dynamic range) of the captured image is often a problem. To compensate, real-time high dynamic range (HDR) techniques could be used, though the author is not aware of a successful example.

Eyepoint Offset

Unlike optical see-through systems, video see-through HMDs are difficult to eliminate the eyepoint offset between the user's eye and the camera viewpoint. Mounting a stereo camera above the HMD introduces a vertical offset, causing a false sense of height. Horizontal offsets introduce errors in depth perception. Canon's COASTAR display eliminates eyepoint offset with a fairly wide FOV (51°(H) × 37°(V)) by using a free-form prism (Takagi, Yamazaki, Saito, & Taniguchi, 2000). As another problem, the viewpoint for rendering must match that of the eye (for optical see-through) or the camera (for video see-through). As a rendering viewpoint, the center of eye rotation is better for position accuracy, whereas the center of the entrance pupil is better for angular accuracy (Vaissie & Rolland, 2000). Although human IPD alters dynamically because of eye rotation, this dynamic IPD has not yet been compensated in real-time to the author's knowledge.

Human Perceptual Issues

Depth Perception

Even when geometrical consistency is achieved, it is often difficult to determine depths of virtual objects correctly in augmented reality. This is due primarily to (1) HMDs' inability to support depth cues, (2) lack of standard rendering approaches, and (3) visual congestion.

First, as we have seen in this chapter, standard HMDs do not support every depth cue of the human vision system. Depth perception can be improved by rendering other types of monocular depth cues (e.g., shades, shadows, aerial perspective, texture gradient and so on) when appropriate.

Second, some of those rendering techniques may not be preferable in some situations. Virtual objects in an AR application are often rendered in a simple way (e.g., wire-framed) purposely so as not to obstruct visibility of the real scene. Such objects are less informative in terms of depth perception. The typical X-ray vision effect also causes confusion in depth perception. To support correct depth perception in such situations, Livingston et al. (2003) proposed a variety of combinations of visualization techniques, varying for example edge drawing styles and surface opacity.

Third, in some AR applications, virtual annotations and labels may overlap or congest. Visual congestion degrades the visibility of the object of interest, making it difficult to perceive its distance. To alleviate label overlaps, relocation techniques in the screen space have been proposed (Bell, Feiner, & Hollerer, 2001).

User Acceptance

Inappropriately worn HMDs will induce undesirable symptoms including headaches, shoulder stiffness, motion sickness, or even severe injuries. From an ergonomic point of view, HMDs must be as small, lightweight, and comfortable to wear as possible, as long as the visual performance satisfies the application requirements. Center of mass of a HMD must be positioned as close to that of the user's head as possible. A well-balanced heavy HMD feels much lighter than a poorly balanced lightweight HMD.

Safety issues are of equally importance. By its nature, AR applications distract user's voluntary attention to the real environment by overlaying synthetic information. Paying too much attention to the synthetic imagery could be highly dangerous to the real world activity. To prevent catastrophic results, AR applications may need to display minimal information as long as the target task is assisted satisfactory. Furthermore, HMDs restrict peripheral vision, which obstructs situation awareness of the surroundings. In video see-through, central vision will be lost under a system failure. To accommodate these problems, a flip-up display design is helpful (Rolland & Fuchs, 2001). When safety issues are of top priority, optical see-through HMDs are recommended.

From a social point of view, HMDs should have a low profile or "cool" design to be widely accepted. Video cameras used in the video see-through HMDs may face severe privacy and/or security issues. Bass, Mann, Siewiorek, and Thompson (1997) describe the ultimate test of obtrusiveness of a HMD as "whether or not a wearer is able to gamble in a Las Vegas casino without challenge." When skilled experts are main target users, social issues are not crucial.

Adaptation

The human vision system is quite dynamic. It takes some time to adapt to and recover from a new visual experience. For example, wearing a HMD will cause the pupil's dilation slightly. However, complete dilation may take over 20 minutes whereas complete constriction may take less than one minute (Alpern & Campbell, 1963). Even though the visual experience is inconsistent with the real world, the human vision system adapts to the new environment very flexibly. For example, a great ability of adaptation to the inverted image on the retina has been proven for more than 100 years (Stratton, 1896). Similar adaptation occurs with AR systems with an eyepoint offset. Biocca and Rolland (1998) found that performance in a depth-pointing task was improved significantly over time using a video see-through system with an eyepoint offset of 62 mm in vertical and 165 mm in horizontal. Also found was a negative aftereffect, which can be harmful in some situations.

Long-term use of a HMD will increase the likelihood of user's encounter to a variety of deficiencies, such as red eyes, fatigue, double vision, and motion sickness. Therefore, a recovery period should be given to the user whenever needed. The National Institute for Occupational Safety recommends a 15 minute of rest each after two hours of continuous use of a video display unit (VDU) (Rosner & Belkin, 1989). Extensive user studies must be conducted to develop similar recommendations for see-through HMDs.

Conclusion

Although decades have past since the first appearance of the HMD, there is no single "right" HMD due to technical limitations and wide variety of applications. Therefore, appropriate compromise must be made depending on the target application. Issues discussed in this chapter give some insights into the selection of a HMD. One must first consider whether optical or video see-through approach is more suitable for the target task. This is, in short, a trade-off between the real world visibility and pictorial consistency. Next consideration would be a trade-off between the field of view and angular resolution. The wider the FOV is, the heavier, the larger, and the more expensive the optics is likely to become. When the user needs to observe both near and far overlay information, an accommodation-capable (e.g., 3DDAC) or accommodation-free (e.g., virtual retinal displays) HMD may be the first choice. If true occlusion within nearly intact real views is necessary, the bulky ELMO-4 is the best candidate to date.

Technologies adaptable to HMDs have slowly but steadily progressed. In the near future, high-resolution (> ~1600 × 1200) and high-speed (> ~60Hz) digital video cameras, high-resolution (> ~2560 × 2048) miniature FP displays will become common. As size and weight of a display unit decrease, the technique of tiling multiple displays may be revisited. High-end products and research prototypes will enjoy those technical advancements. It is a different story, however, if these technologies are adapted to consumer HMDs. Unfortunately, some manufacturers have given up the consumer HMD business due to the small market in past ten years. Researchers and system designers have an important role not only to expand the cutting-edge AR technology, but also to enlighten the public to the AR technology and foster its potential market.

References

Allen, K. (2002, July). A new fold in microdisplay optics. In *Emerging displays review, emerging display technologies* (pp. 7-12). Stanford Resources.

Alpern, M., & Campbell, F. W. (1963). The behavior of the pupil during dark adaptation. *Journal Physiology, 65*, 5-7.

Arthur, K. W. (2000). *Effects of field of view on performance with head-mounted displays.* University of North Carolina at Chapel Hill Doctoral Thesis.

Barfield, W, Hendrix, C., Bjorneseth, O., Kaczmarek, K. A., & Lotens, W. (1995). Comparison of human sensory capabilities with technical specifications of virtual environment equipment. *Presence, 4*(4), 329-356.

Bass, L., Mann, S., Siewiorek, D., & Thompson, C. (1997). Issues in wearable computing: A CHI 97 Workshop. *ACM SIGCHI Bulletin, 29*(4), 34-39.

Bell, B., Feiner, S., & Hollerer, T. (2001). View management for virtual and augmented reality. In *Proceedings of the ACM UIST 2001* (pp. 101-110).

Billinghurst, M., Kato, H., & Poupyrev, I. (2001). The MagicBook: Moving seamlessly between reality and virtuality. *IEEE Computer Graphics and Applications, 21*(3), 6-8.

Biocca, F. A., & Rolland, J. P. (1998). Virtual eyes can rearrange your body: Adaptation to virtual-eye location in see-thru head-mounted displays. *Presence: Teleoperators and Virtual Environments (MIT Press), 7*(3), 262-277.

Boff, K. R., Kaufman, L., & Thomas, J. P. (1986). Handbook of perception and human performance. John Wiley and Sons.

Bohm, H. D. V., & Schranner, R. (1990). Requirements of an HMS/D for a night-flying helicopter. Helmet-mounted displays II. In *Proceedings of SPIE* (Vol. 1290, pp. 93-107).

Buchroeder, R. A. (1987). Helmet-mounted displays, Tutorial Short Course Notes T2. In *Proceedings of the SPIE Technical Symposium Southeast on Optics, Electro-optics, and Sensors.*

Caudell, T. P., & Mizell, D. W. (1992). Augmented reality: An application of heads-up display technology to manual manufacturing processes. In *Proceedings of the 1992 IEEE Hawaii International Conference on Systems Sciences* (pp. 659-669).

Comeau, C. P., & Bryan, J. S. (1961, November). Headsight television system provides remote surveillance. *Electronics, 10*(34), 86-90.

Feiner, S., Macintyre, B., & Seligmann, D. (1993). Knowledge-based augmented reality. *Communications of the ACM, 36*(7), 53-62.

Feiner, S. B., Macintyre, B., Tobias, H., & Webster, A. (1997). A touring machine: Prototyping 3D mobile augmented reality systems for exploring the urban environment. In *Proceedings of ISWC '97* (pp. 74-81).

Furness, T. A. (1986). The super cockpit and its human factors challenges. In *Proceedings of the Human Factors Society* (Vol. 30, pp. 48-52).

Hayford, M. J., & Koch, D. G. (1989). *Optical arrangement.* U.S. Patent No. 4854688, issued August 8, 1989.

Heilig, M. (1960). *Stereoscopic television apparatus for individual use.* U.S. Patent No. 2955156, issued October 4, 1960.

Kasai, I., Tanijiri, Y., Endo, T., & Ueda, H. (2000). A forgettable near eye display. In *Proceedings of 4th International Symposium on Wearable Computers (ISWC) 2000* (pp. 115-118).

Kijima, R., & Ojika, T. (2002). Reflex HMD to compensate lagand correction of derivative deformation. In *Proceedings of International Conference on Virtual Reality (VR) 2002* (pp. 172-179).

Kiyokawa, K., Billinghurst, M., Campbell, B., & Woods, E. (2003). An occlusion-capable optical see-through headmount display for supporting co-located collaboration. In *Proceedings of International Symposium on Mixed and Augmented Reality (ISMAR) 2003* (pp. 133-141).

Livingston, M. A., Swan, J. E., Gabbard, J. L., Hollerer, T. H., Hix, D., Julier, S. J., Yohan, B., Brown, D. (2003). Resolving multiple occluded layers in augmented reality. In *Proceedings of International Symposium on Mixed and Augmented Reality (ISMAR) 2003* (pp. 56-65).

Longridge, T., Thomas, M., Fernie, A., Williams, T., & Wetzel, P. (1989). Design of an eye slaved area of interest system for the simulator complexity testbed. In T. Longridge (Ed.), *Area of interest/field-of-view research using ASPT* (pp. 275-283). National Security Industrial Association, Air Force Human Resources Laboratory, Air Force Systems Command.

Luebke, D., & Hallen, B. (2001). Perceptually-driven simplification for interactive rendering. In *Proceedings of the ACM 12th Eurographics Workshop on Rendering Techniques* (pp. 223-234).

McCollum, H. (1945). *Stereoscopic television apparatus.* U.S. Patent No. 2,388,170.

Nagahara, H., Yagi, Y., & Yachida, M. (2005). "Wide Field of View Catadioptrical Head Mounted Display." *Transaction of the IEICE, J88-D-II*(1), 95-104 (in Japanese).

Omura, K., Shiwa, S., & Kishino, F. (1996). 3D Display with accommodative compensation (3DDAC) employing real-time gaze detection. *SID 1996 Digest*, 889-892.

Rash, C. E., & Martin, J. S. (1988). *The impact of the U.S. Army's AH-64 helmet mounted display on future aviation helmet design* (USAARL Rep. No. 88-13). Fort Rucker, AL: U.S. Army Aeromedical Research Laboratory.

Rolland, J. P., & Fuchs, H. (2001). Optical versus Video see-through head-mounted displays. In W. Barfield & T. Caudell (Eds.), *Fundamentals of wearable computers and augmented reality*. Mahwah, NJ: Lawrence Erlbaum Associates.

Rolland, J. P., Wright, D. L., & Kancherla, A. R. (1996). Towards a novel augmented-reality tool to visualize dynamic 3D anatomy. In *Proceedings of Medicine Meets Virtual Reality*, San Diego, CA, 1997 (Vol. 5, Tech. Rep. No. TR96-02). University of Central Florida.

Rosner M., & Belkin, M. (1989). Video display units and visual function. *Survey of Ophthalmology, 33*(6), 515-522.

Schowengerdt, B. T., & Seibel, E. J. (2004). True 3D displays that allow viewers to dynamically shift accommodation, bringing objects displayed at different viewing distances into and out of focus. *CyberPsychology & Behavior, 7*(6), 610-620.

Stratton, G. M. (1896). Some preliminary experiments on vision without inversion of the retinal image. *Psychological Review, 3*, 611-617.

Sutherland, I. (1965). The ultimate display. In *Information Processing 1965: Proceedings of IFIP Congress* (Vol. 2, pp. 506-508).

Sutherland, I. (1968). A head-mounted three-dimensional display. In *Fall Joint Computer Conference, AFIPS Conference Proceedings* (Vol. 33, pp. 757-764).

Takagi, A., Yamazaki, S., Saito, Y., & Taniguchi, N. (2000). Development of a stereo video see-through HMD for AR systems. In *Proceedings of International Symposium on Augmented Reality (ISAR) 2000* (pp. 68-80).

Vaissie, L., & Rolland, J. (2000). Accuracy of rendered depth in head-mounted displays: Choice of eyepoint locations. In *Proceedings of SPIE AeroSense 2000* (Vol. 4021, pp. 343-353).

Chapter IV

Projector-Based Augmentation

Oliver Bimber, Bauhaus University, Germany

Abstract

Projector-based augmentation approaches hold the potential of combining the advantages of well-established spatial virtual reality and spatial augmented reality. Immersive, semi-immersive, and augmented visualizations can be realized in everyday environments—without the need for special projection screens and dedicated display configurations. Limitations of mobile devices, such as low resolution and small field of view, focus constrains, and ergonomic issues can be overcome in many cases by the utilization of projection technology. Thus, applications that do not require mobility can benefit from efficient spatial augmentations. Examples range from edutainment in museums (such as storytelling projections onto natural stone walls in historical buildings) to architectural visualizations (such as augmentations of complex illumination simulations or modified surface materials in real building structures). This chapter describes projector camera methods and multi-projector techniques that aim at correcting geometric aberrations, compensating local and global radiometric effects, and improving focus properties of images projected onto everyday surfaces.

Introduction

Their increasing capabilities and declining cost make video projectors widespread and established presentation tools. Being able to generate images that are larger than the actual display device virtually anywhere is an interesting feature for many applications that cannot be provided by desktop screens. Several research groups discover this potential by applying projectors in unconventional ways to develop new and innovative information displays that go beyond simple screen presentations.

Projector-based displays have clearly replaced head-attached displays for most virtual reality (VR) applications. Immersive surround screen displays and semi-immersive wall-like or table-like configurations are being used for visualizing two-dimensional or three-dimensional graphical content.

Today, the majority of augmented reality applications focus on mobility. Thus, wearable or portable devices have become dominant in this area. However, an increasing trend toward projector-based displays for AR can be noticed. Projector-based augmentation approaches hold the potential of combining the advantages of well-established spatial virtual reality and spatial augmented reality (Bimber & Raskar, 2005d). Immersive, semi-immersive, and augmented visualizations can be realized in everyday environments–without the need for special projection screens and dedicated display configurations. Limitations of mobile devices, such as low resolution and small field of view, focus constrains, and ergonomic issues can be overcome by the application of projection technology. For many applications, this requires the abdication of mobility, but not necessarily of portability. Several applications, however, do not require mobility and rather benefit from efficient spatial augmentations. Examples range from edutainment in museums (such as storytelling projections onto natural stone walls in historical buildings) to architectural applications (such as augmentations of complex illumination or surface material simulations in real building structures). The problems, limitations, potentials, and details of a variety of existing techniques toward projector based augmentations are described in this chapter.

A variety of stationary, movable, and hand-held projectors have been proposed for displaying graphical information directly on real objects or surfaces instead of performing optical overlays or video compositions.

The Luminous Room (Underkoffler, Ullmer, & Ishii, 1999) for instance, describes an early concept for providing graphical display and interaction on each surface of an interior architecture space. Co-located two-way optical transducers, called I/O bulbs, that consist of projector camera pairs capture the user interactions and display the corresponding output. With the Everywhere Displays projector (Pinhanez, 2001), this concept has been extended technically by allowing a steerable projection using a pan/tilt mirror. A similar approach is followed by Ehnes, Hirota, and Hirose (2004). Recently, it was demonstrated how context-aware hand-held projectors, so-called iLamps, can be used as mobile information displays and interaction devices (Raskar et al., 2003).

Another concept called Shader Lamps (Raskar, Welch, Low, & Bandyopadhyay, 2001) attempts to lift the visual properties of neutral diffuse objects that serve as projection screen. The computed radiance at a point of a non-trivial physical surface is mimicked by changing the bidirectional reflectance distribution function and illuminating the point appropriately with projector pixels. Animating the projected images allows creating the perception of motion without physical displacement of the real object (Raskar, Ziegler, & Willwacher, 2002). This type of spatial augmentation is also possible for large, human-sized environments, as demonstrated in Low, Welch, Lastra, and Fuchs (2001).

Projector-based illumination has become an effective technique in augmented reality to achieve consistent occlusion (Bimber, 2002; Noda, Ban, Sato, & Chihara, 1999) and illumination (Bimber, Grundhöfer, Wetzstein, & Knödel, 2003) effects between real artifacts and optically overlaid graphics. Video projectors instead of simple analog light bulbs are used to illuminate physical objects with arbitrary diffuse reflectance. The per-pixel illumination is controllable and can be synchronized with the rendering of the graphical overlays. This also makes the combination of high-quality optical holograms with interactive graphical elements possible (Bimber, 2004). Using a video projector to produce a controlled reference wave allows reconstructing the hologram's object wave partially—not at those portions that are overlaid by integrated graphical elements.

New optical combiners, together with real-time radiometric compensation methods, allow superimposing arbitrarily textured, flat surfaces, such as paintings efficiently (Bimber, Emmerling, & Klemmer, 2005a).

Other methods allow augmenting arbitrary—flat (Fujii, Grossberg, & Nayar, 2005; Nayar, Peri, Grossberg, & Belhumeur, 2003; Wang, Sato, Okabe, & Sato, 2005; Yoshida, Horii, & Sato, 2003) or geometrically non-trivial (Bimber, Wetzstein, Emmerling, & Nitschke, 2005b; Grossberg, Peri, Nayar, & Bulhumeur, 2004)—textured surfaces without the application of special optical combiners, such as transparent projection screens. They scan the surfaces' geometric and reflectance properties and carry out a per-pixel displacement and radiometric compensation before the images are projected.

Besides these examples, a variety of other techniques and applications have been described that utilize projectors and a structured illumination to achieve special effects and augmentations. To describe them all is out of the scope of this chapter. More details can be found in the book *Spatial Augmented Reality: Merging Real and Virtual Worlds* (Bimber et al., 2005d).

Fundamental Problems and Overview of Solutions

For conventional projection systems, the screen material is optimized for a projection, and its reflectance is uniform across the surface. If images are projected onto everyday surfaces, however, the following fundamental problems arise (cf. Figure 1, left):

1. If the surface is not planar, the projected images are geometrically warped and appear distorted to an observer.

2. If the surface is not white but has a colored texture, the projected light is blended with the reflecting surfaces' pigments.

3. Diffused light is scattered from one surface portion to others and is blended together with the direct illumination.

4. Conventional projectors can focus on planar surfaces only. Projections onto geometrically complex surfaces cause a regional defocus in the projected images.

5. Even if problems 1-4 can be avoided by pre-correcting the images before displaying them, slight misregistrations of projected pixels and the corresponding surface pigments can lead to extreme visual artifacts.

6. Multiple projectors can have varying chrominance and luminance parameters, which leads to inconsistent image contributions.

7. If the surface is not Lambertian (i.e., not perfectly diffuse), a projector-based augmentation might not be possible.

These points represent particular problems if the projected images contain stereo pairs to enable a stereoscopic 3D visualization on screen surfaces that are not optimized for projection. The reason for this is that the human visual system strongly relies on the extraction of salient structure features (such as edges, corners, etc.) for estimating disparities. Several of the image distortions previously described simply wash out these features (4), blend these features with physical features on the surface (2 and 5) or with scattered light from other surface portions (3), or misalign them (1). In the following, it is assumed that the projection surface is Lambertian to enable a projector-based augmentation. It is out of the scope of this chapter to describe photometric calibration techniques (such as chrominance mapping and luminance matching) and other multi-projector methods, such as cross-fading or shadow removal. The interested reader is referred to Brown, Majumder, and Yang (2005) for an overview of this area. This chapter also does not describe other important issues related to projector-based augmentation, such as projector hardware (electronic and optics), tracking and registration, networked rendering frameworks, projector-based interaction techniques and devices, etc.

Instead, this chapter presents a self-contained framework of basic rendering techniques that strive for a projector-based augmentation of everyday environments and surfaces (cf. Figure 1, right). The corpus of this chapter describes projector-camera methods and multi-projector techniques that aim at correcting geometry, local and global radiometric effects, and focus

Figure 1. Four exemplary problems resulting from a conventional projection onto a complex surface, and corrected projection (left); main components for enabling consistent stereoscopic projections on everyday (Lambertian) surfaces (right) (Right image reprinted from Bimber, 2005b, © IEEE)

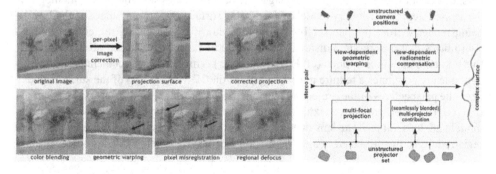

properties of projected images to minimize the distortions previously described. Based on these fundamental techniques, further methods are explained that enable the view-dependent correction of projected images. The rendering techniques described in this chapter can all be implemented as hardware-accelerated pixel shaders, and consequently support a pixel-precise correction at interactive frame-rates. Thus, the four modules shown in Figure 1—right are projector individual pixel shaders. Finally, a brief overview over current limitations and an outlook of future developments is discussed.

Projecting onto Optimized Surfaces

For surfaces whose reflectance is optimized for projection (i.e., surfaces with a homogenous white reflectance), a geometric correction of the projected images is sufficient to provide an undistorted augmentation for an observer. Slight misregistrations of the images on the surfaces in the order of 2-3 pixels lead to geometric artifacts that, in most cases, can be tolerated. This section gives a brief overview over general geometry correction techniques for single and multiple projectors.

If multiple projectors (P) have to be registered to a planar surface via camera feedback (cf. Figure 2, left), collineations with the plane surface can be expressed as camera-to-projector homographies (H). A homography matrix can be automatically determined by correlating a projection pattern to its corresponding camera image. The homographies are usually extended to homogenous 4×4 matrices to make them compatible with conventional transformation pipelines and consequently benefit from single pass rendering. Multiplied after the projection transformation, they map normalized camera coordinates into normalized projector coordinates. An observer located at the position of the calibration camera (C) perceives a correct image in this case. In cases where a head-tracked observer has to be supported the calibration camera can be placed orthogonal to the surface. The virtual scene is rendered from the perspective of the observer with an off-axis projection over the rectangular portion of the plane surface that is visible to the camera. The resulting image is then warped to the perspectives of the individual projectors via their camera-to-projector homographies.[1] This can all be done within a single rendering pass.

If the geometry of the projection surface is non-planar but known, a two-pass rendering technique can be applied for projecting the image in an undistorted way[2] (Raskar et al., 1999b). In the first pass, the image that has to be displayed is off-screen rendered from the perspective of the observer (C). This image O is then read back into the texture memory. In the second step, the geometry model of the display surface is texture-mapped with O while being rendered from the perspective of the projector. For computing the correct texture coordinates that ensure an undistorted view from the perspective of the observer projective texture mapping is applied (cf. Figure 2, center). This hardware accelerated technique dynamically computes a texture matrix that maps the 3D vertices (p_i) of the surface model from the perspectives of the projectors (P_i) into the texture space of the observer's perspective (C). However, projective texture mapping assumes a simple pinhole camera/projector model and does not take the lens distortion of projectors into account. This can cause misregistrations of the projected images in the range of several pixels—even if other intrinsic

Figure 2. Geometric correction via homographies (left) and projective texture mapping (center), example for using projective texture mapping (right) (Right image reprinted from Raskar et al., 2001, © Springer-Verlag)

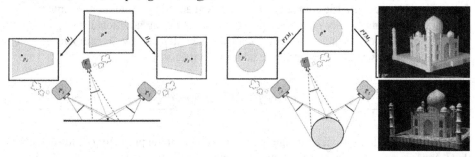

and extrinsic parameters have been determined precisely. Projecting corrected images onto textured surfaces with misregistrations in this order causes immediate visual intensity artifacts that can make the fusion of projected stereo-pairs difficult. In Section 4, two pixel-precise registration techniques are described. The first method is also being applied by related approaches (Grossberg et al., 2004; Nayar et al., 2003). In Section 6, this method is extended toward view-dependent rendering. Note that some of the techniques described next (e.g., compensating secondary scattering and multi-focal projection) are also relevant for projection optimized surfaces.

Projecting onto Complex Surfaces

For projections onto colored or textured surfaces, the images have to be color corrected in addition to a geometry correction. Recent work on radiometric compensation uses cameras in combination with projectors for measuring the surface reflectance as well as the contribution of the environment light. These parameters are then used for correcting the projected images in such a way that blending artifacts with the underlying surface are minimized.

Nayar et al. (2003), for instance, express the color transform between each camera and projector pixel as pixel-individual 3×3 color mixing matrices. These matrices are estimated from measured camera responses of multiple projected sample images. They can be continuously refined over a closed feedback loop and are used to correct each pixel during runtime. Later, a refined version of this technique was used for controlling the appearance of two- and three-dimensional objects, such as posters, boxes, and spheres (Grossberg et al., 2004). Wang et al. (2005) adapt this method to the properties of the human vision system by compressing the contrast of the input images. Fujii et al. (2005) applies a variation of the closed feedback loop method to handle dynamic environments by applying a co-axial projector-camera alignment.

This section begins with a simple implementation of geometric and radiometric image correction (Bimber et al., 2005a). In contrast to Fujii et al. (2005), Grossberg et al. (2004), Nayar et al. (2003), and Wang et al. (2005), it uses single disjoint camera measurements of surface reflectance, environment light contribution, and projector form-factor components for a per-pixel radiometric compensation using hardware accelerated pixel shaders. However, it does not take the color mixing of the individual RGB channels into account. Furthermore, it is described how radiometric compensation can be enhanced by using multiple interplaying projectors for geometrically complex surfaces, or by applying additional transparent film materials overlaid over planar surfaces. Finally, it is explained how to compensate global illumination effects, such as scattering in addition to local ones.

Radiometric Compensation with a Single-Projector

In its simplest configuration, an image is displayed by a single projector (P) in such a way that it appears correct (color and geometry) for a single camera view (C). Thereby, the display surfaces must be Lambertian, but can have an arbitrary color, texture, and shape.

The first step is to determine the geometric relations of camera pixels and projector pixels over the display surface. Well known structured light techniques (e.g., gray code scanning with phase shift) can be used for measuring the 1-to-n mapping of camera pixels to projector pixels (cf. Figure 3, left). This mapping is stored in a 2D look-up-texture having a resolution of the camera, which in the following is referred to as $C2P$ map. A corresponding texture that maps every projector pixel to one or many camera pixels can be computed by reversing the $C2P$ map. This texture is called $P2C$ map. It has the resolution of the projector. The 1-to-n relations (note that n can also become 0 during the reversion process) are finally removed from both maps through averaging and interpolation.

Once the geometric relations are known, the radiometric parameters are measured. It can be assumed that a light ray with intensity I is projected onto a surface pigment with reflectance M. The fraction of light that arrives at the pigment depends on the geometric relation between the light source and the surface. A simple representation of what is known as form factor can be used for approximating this fraction: $F=f*cos(\alpha)/r^2$, where α is the angular correlation between the light ray and the surface normal and r the distance (square distance attenuation) between the light source and the surface. The factor f allows scaling the intensity to avoid clipping (i.e., intensity values that exceed the luminance capabilities of the projector) and to consider the simultaneous contributions of multiple projectors.

Together with the environment light E, the projected light fraction I is blended with the pigment's reflectance M (cf. Figure 3, center):

$$R= EM+IFM \qquad (1)$$

Thereby R is the diffuse radiance that can be captured by the camera. If R, F, M, and E are known, I can be computed with:

$$I=(R-EM)/FM \qquad (2)$$

Figure 3. Pixel-precise geometric correction (left) and radiometric compensation (center); example of a projection onto a scruffy room corner (right): (a) two projectors uncorrected, (b) registered projectors, (c) geometry corrected projections, (d) radiometric compensated projections (Right image reprinted from Bimber et al., 2005c, © IEEE)

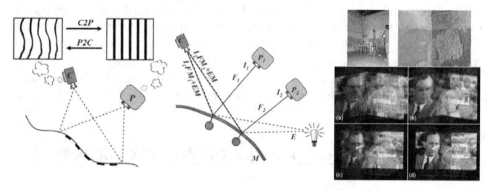

In the single-projector approach, E, F, and M cannot be determined independently. Instead, FM is measured by projecting a white image ($I=1$) and turning off the entire environment light ($E=0$), and EM is measured by projecting a black image ($I=0$) under environment light. Note that EM also contains the black-level of the projector.

Since this holds for every discrete camera pixel, R, E, FM, and EM are entire textures and equation 2 can be computed[3] in real-time by a pixel shader.

During runtime pixel, displacement mapping is realized by rendering a full-screen quad into the frame buffer of the projector. This triggers fragment processing of every projector pixel. A fragment shader maps all pixels from the projector perspective into the camera perspective (via texture look-ups in the $P2C$ map) to ensure a geometric consistency for the camera view. All computations are then performed in camera space. The projection of the resulting image I onto the surface leads to a geometry and color corrected image that approximates the desired image R for the target perspective of the camera.

Radiometric Compensation with Multi-Projectors

The simultaneous contribution of multiple projectors increases the total light intensity that arrives at the surface. This can overcome the limitations of equation 2 for extreme situations (e.g., small FM values or large EM values) and can consequently avoid an early clipping of I.

If N projectors are applied, equation 1 extends to (cf. Figure 3, center):

$$R=EM+\sum_i^N I_i FM_i \qquad (3)$$

One strategy is to balance the projected intensities equally among all projectors i which leads to:

$$I_i = \frac{(R-EM)}{\sum_j^N FM_j} \qquad (4)$$

This equation can also be solved in real-time by projector-individual pixel shaders (based on individual parameter textures FM_i, $C2P_i$, and $P2C_i$—but striving for the same final result R). Note that EM also contains the accumulated black-level of all projectors.

If all projectors provide linear transfer functions (e.g., after a linearization) and identical brightness, a scaling of $f_i = 1/N$ used in the form factor balances the load among them equally. However, f_i might be decreased further to avoid clipping and to adapt for differently aged bulbs.

Amplification Through Transparent Projection Screens

A clipping of I can also be minimized if the projection surface is coated with a transparent projection screen (e.g., a flexible transparent film material that diffuses a portion d and transmits a fraction t of the light projected onto it). This is a practical option for augmenting pictorial artwork, such as paintings or sketches (Bimber et al., 2005c).

If a light beam with incident radiance L is projected onto the transparent film material that is located on top of the surface (e.g., the canvas of a painting), a portion d of L is directly diffused from the film while the remaining portion t of L is transmitted through the film. The transmitted light tL interacts with the underlying pigment's diffuse reflectance M on the canvas, and a color blended light fraction tLM is diffused. The portion $tLMt$ is then transmitted through the film, while the remaining part $tLMd$ is reflected back toward the canvas where it is color blended and diffused from the same pigment again. This ping-pong effect between film material and canvas is repeated infinitely while for every pass a continuously

Figure 4. Interaction of projected light and environment light with the screen canvas and the transparent projection film—sequence diagram (right); examples of interactive projections onto real painting (right) (Images reprinted from Bimber et al., 2005a, © IEEE)

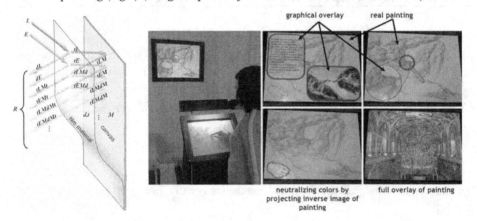

decreasing amount of light is transmitted through the film that contributes to the resulting radiance R. Mathematically, this can be expressed as an infinite geometric series that converges toward a finite value. The same is true for the environment light with incident radiance E that is emitted from uncontrollable light sources. Since these light sources also illuminate the canvas and the film material, the environment light's contribution to R has to be considered as well.

Figure 4 describes this process in form of a sequence diagram. Note that in contrast to this conceptual illustration, there should be no physical gap between film material and canvas, and that the light interaction occurs at the same spot.

If all parameters (L, E, M, t, and d) are known the resulting radiance R that is visible to an observer in front of the canvas can be computed:

$$R = (L+E)d + (L+E)t^2 M \sum_{i=0}^{\infty}(Md)^i =$$

$$(L+E)\left(d + \frac{t^2 M}{1-Md}\right) \tag{5}$$

Since R (image that is expected to be seen) is known, the previous equation needs to be solved for L:

$$L = \frac{R}{\left(d + \dfrac{t^2 M}{1-Md}\right)} - E \tag{6}$$

This allows computing the incident radiance L that needs to be projected onto the film and the canvas to create the known result R. The radiant intensity I of the projector that is required to create L is related to a discretized pixel value and is given by:

$$I = L\frac{1}{F}f \tag{7}$$

where $F = f * cos\alpha / r^2$ is the form factor of the projector (see section 4.1).

As described earlier, the contribution of multiple (N) projectors allows minimizing the clipping problem with:

$$L = \sum_{i=1}^{N} L_i \quad , \quad I_i = L_i \frac{1}{F_i} \tag{8}$$

Compensating Secondary Scattering Through Reverse Radiosity

The techniques described above can compensate only radiometric effects that result from a direct illumination of the surface. However, diffuse surface portions scatter a fraction of light to other surface portions. This amount of indirect illumination adds to the direct illumination and has to be compensated as well (Bimber, Grundhöfer, Zeidler, Danch, & Kapakos, 2006b) (cf. Figure 5). Problematic is the fact that the amount of scattering depends on the projected compensated image (I) and vice versa. In computer graphics, the reverse situation (i.e., the global radiosity of each surface element) is determined based on a known illumination (I) and is computed by numerically solving a linear equation system. Some modern approaches implement this finite element model—which is commonly known as radiosity rendering—with pixel shaders and achieve interactive frame rates.

Assume that the surface is subdivided into A discrete patches (e.g., in camera space or in parametric space). The form factor F_{ji} describes the amount of radiance that is scattered from patch j to patch i. This can either be measured or be computed (if the surface geometry is known). The amount of radiance (S_i) that is reflected by patch i which is a result of indirect scattering of light from all other patches can be described as:

$$S_i = \sum_{j,j \neq i}^{A} (I_j F_j M_j + E_j M_j) F_{ji} M_i + \sum_{j,j \neq i}^{A} \sum_{k,k \neq j}^{A} [(I_k F_k M_k + E_k M_k) F_{kj} M_j] F_{ji} M_i + ... \qquad (9)$$

Note, that equation 9 presents only the first two scattering levels to a patch i (i.e., the radiance that is scattered directly from the patches j to patch i, and the radiance that is scattered from all patches k over all patches j to patch i). This can be rewritten into a recursive from:

Figure 5. Scattering of light between two surface patches (left): Example of compensated scattering (right): (a) uncorrected projection onto two-sided projection screen (c), (b) corrected projection, (d) corrected amount of scattering (subtraction of images a and b) (Images reprinted from Bimber et al., 2006b, © IEEE)

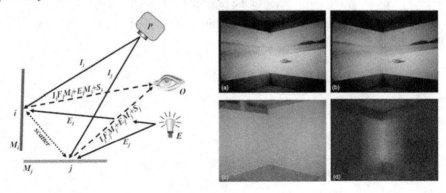

$$S_i^1 = \sum_{j, j\neq i}^{A} (I_j F_j M_j + E_j M_j) F_{ji} M_i \quad , \quad S_i^h = \sum_{j, j\neq i}^{A} S_j^{h-1} F_{ji} M_i \tag{10}$$

Note, that S_i^h indicates the h-th scattering level at patch i (i.e., the reflected radiance at patch i that can be contributed to scattering which arrives over h-1 intermediate patches). To compensate the direct illumination and the scattering, the following computation has to be performed:

$$I_i = \frac{1}{F_i M_i} \left(R_i - E_i M_i - \sum_{h=1}^{H} S_i^h \right) \tag{11}$$

As previously mentioned, the difficulty in this case is that I_i depends on S_i^h and vice versa. This linear equation system can be solved numerically by approximating I_i through several iterations:

Initially, I_i is computed for the direct case (equation 2). The result is used in the second iteration to compute a first estimate of scattering, and to compensate the direct and the approximated indirect illumination (equation 11). The result of this iteration is then used in a third iteration, and so on. This process is repeated until I_i converges (i.e., the results of two consecutive iterations do not reveal significant differences).

While equations 10 and 11 can be implemented as pixel shaders, the iterations can be realized as individual rendering passes. While frame-buffer objects offer an efficient way of exchanging the resulting textures I_i between different rendering passes, occlusion queries support the hardware accelerated comparison of two consecutive results I_i. Both techniques avoid the time consuming read-back of textures from the graphics card. The patches' form factors F_{ji} are efficiently compressed into a single parameter texture to keep the memory requirements on the graphics card at a minimum. This can be done offline. Note that only patches with form factors larger than a predefined threshold are selected. This leads to additional resources and performance optimizations and does not affect the outcome's quality significantly. Thus, the form-factor matrix F is a sparse matrix.

A more efficient analytical solution to equations 10 and 11 exists. It was recently shown by Seitz, Matsushita, and Kutulakos (2005) that global interreflections can be removed from photographs of unknown scenes under unknown illuminations by applying an interreflection cancellation operator. It can also be shown that equation 10 equals a geometric series that converges when the number of scatter levels h approaches infinity. Thus the analytical complement to equation 11 is:

$$I_i = \frac{1}{F_i M_i} \left(R_i - E_i M_i - \sum_{j, j\neq i}^{A} R_j F_{ji} M_j \right) \tag{12}$$

This is similar to Seitz's approach—but with a main difference. The interreflection cancellation operator is not applied to an image that contains interreflections to remove them, but to an image that does not contain interreflections to compensate them when projecting the compensated image. This also proofs that the amount of indirect scattering which is produced by the compensated image throughout all scatter levels equals the amount of indirect scattering that is produced by the original image in the first level.

It is clear that equations 10-12 cannot be computed in real-time if A equals the resolution of the projector (or a camera with similar resolution). Consequently, all parameter textures have to be down-sampled to an acceptable patch resolution (e.g., $A=128 \times 128$). The final compensated image can then be computed as follows:

$$I'_B = I_B - \uparrow (\downarrow I_B - I'_A) \tag{13}$$

Thereby, I_B is the compensated image for direct illumination (computed as described in equations 2 or 4) in the projector resolution (B), I'_A is the compensated image in patch resolution A (solved as previously described), and $\uparrow$ and $\downarrow$ indicate up and down sampling image operators (from B to A and vice versa). The result I'_B contains the compensation of the direct illumination and the scattering, and is finally being displayed.

The extensions of equations 10-12 to support multi-projector configurations based on the balancing strategy described in section 4.2 are simply derived by replacing the single projector form factors by the sum of form factors of all projectors (see equations 3 and 4). As previously described, the projected intensities are then balanced equally among all projectors. Thus I_i is the same for each projector, and can easily be computed.

Multi-Focal Projection

Today's consumer projectors are designed and engineered to focus images on planar display surfaces. The Schleimpflug principle describes how to offset the focal plane by an off-axis configuration of the optical system. However, plane-focused images are partially blurred if projected onto surfaces with substantial depth differences. Special lenses, such as f-theta lenses, allow generating focused images on spherical surfaces. Planetariums and some cylindrical projection displays (Biehling et al., 2004) apply laser projectors to overcome this problem. Direct-writing-scanning-laser-beam projectors scan almost parallel beams of laser light onto the projection screen. Thereby, the laser beams remain constant in diameter over a substantial depth range. This results in a large focal depth and in the possibility to display sharp images in large dome-like or cylindrical theatres. The cost of a single laser projector, however, can quickly exceed the cost of several hundred conventional projectors. But the development of low-cost laser-diodes is promising and can overcome these drawbacks in future.

If the projection surface is multi-planar, multiple projectors can be arranged in such a way that they focus on individual planar sections (e.g., Low et al., 2001). This, however, becomes inefficient and sometimes impossible the more complex the surface becomes.

Figure 6. Multi-focal projection concept (left): Unstructured projector set, multiple projection units integrated in one projector, and two projectors projecting on plane. Example of multi-focal projection onto a curved screen (right). (Images reprinted from Bimber et al., 2005b, © IEEE)

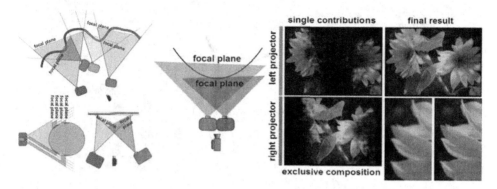

In this section a multi-focal projection technique (Bimber et al., 2006a) is described that projects images with minimal defocus onto geometrically and radiometric complex surfaces. This is essential to enable, for instance, stereoscopic projections supporting disparity-based depth perception on arbitrary surfaces (Bimber et al., 2005b).

The multi-projector technique works as follows: Multiple conventional projectors with differently adjusted focal planes, but overlapping image areas are used (cf. Figure 6). They can be either arbitrarily positioned in the environment, or can be integrated into a single projection unit. The defocus created on the surface is estimated automatically for each projector pixel via camera feedback and structured light projection. If this is known, a final image with minimal defocus can be composed in real-time from individual pixel contributions of all projectors.

The technique is independent of the surfaces' geometry, color and texture, the environment light as well as of the projectors' position, orientation, luminance and chrominance. In the following subsections it is explained how intensity spreads are measured, how relative focus values are estimated from the measured intensity spreads, and how the final images are composed from the simultaneous contributions of multiple projectors.

Measuring Intensity Spreads

The goal of a multi-focal projection is to estimate relative focus values caused by each projector pixel on all portions of an arbitrary display surface. Having this information, a final image with minimal defocus can be composed from multiple projector contributions.

This sub-section describes the approach of measuring the intensity spreads of projected sample points. They are proportional to the defocus of the sampling projector on the corresponding surface portion.

Figure 7. Measuring intensity spreads on geometric and radiometric complex surfaces (left).Example of color coded focus estimations for the example shown in Figure 6, right (right): blue to green = best to worst focus. (Images reprinted from Bimber et al., 2006a, © IEEE)

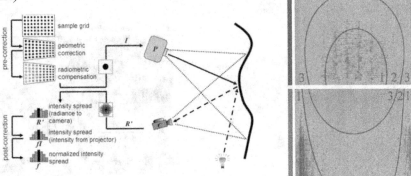

Like for the geometric and radiometric image correction (Section 4), a structured light projection is applied in combination with camera feedback to estimate the focus values (cf. Figure 7, left). However, instead of displaying horizontal and vertical scan lines, a uniform grid pattern of circular sample points is used. Applying points instead of strips also allows determining the defocus parameters in multiple directions simultaneously.

Displaying a sample point from the projector's view leads to a color and geometry distorted image of it in the camera's view. This situation makes it impossible to estimate focus values for the corresponding surface area. The reason for this is that it is not detectable in this case whether the recorded intensity spreads of the sample point can be contributed to defocus or to external factors (e.g., geometric or radiometric distortion, or blending with the environment light on the surface, the projector's position or orientation).

To overcome this problem, the surface is sampled from the perspective of the camera instead of from the perspective of the projector. Measuring relative focus values within the same space and under the same conditions, enables a qualitative comparison between individual projector contributions. Thus, a sample point is initially defined in the camera perspective and is then geometrically warped into the perspective of the projector with the beforehand determined *C2P* map (Section 3.2). In addition, the sample point is color corrected with equation 2 to compensate the surface reflectance, the environment light, and the projector's form factor contribution. Thereby, $R>0$ for pixels that belong to the sample point and $R=0$ for all other pixels.

If a perfectly sharp image is assumed (perfectly focused by the projector and by the camera) the image recorded by the camera contains the initially defined and undistorted sample point. In this case, it has retained its original circular shape in the defined size and appears in a uniform intensity that approximates the defined intensity and color R.

However, due to blur effects (caused either by the projector or by the camera) the shape and the intensity of the sample point are no longer uniform. The resulting intensity spread and intensity loss can be measured in the camera image. They are proportional to the relative defocus of the projector at this point. Measuring the defocus caused by different projectors at the same sample point enables a qualitative and relative comparison and finally an optimal image composition. The camera's parameters must not be changed during the measurements for multiple projectors that need to be compared.

Relative Focus-Estimation

As previously explained, a defocused sample point creates an intensity spread on the surface that is captured in the camera image. The intensities in the blurred area are not projected in a controlled way. They are also blended with the underlying surface reflectance. To estimate the focus values of a sample point consistently, the intensity spread has to be normalized in such a way that it becomes independent of the surface reflectance, the environment light and the projectors' form factor contributions at the spread areas. Note that this normalization cannot be carried out during the pre-correction step because the intensity spread has to be measured first.

The pre-correction applies equation 2 to compute and project the corrected sample point in such a way that it appears at coordinate x,y in the camera image:

$$I_{x,y} = (R_{x,y} - EM_{x,y})/FM_{x,y} \tag{14}$$

As previously outlined, $R_{x,y} > 0$ for pixels that belong to the sample point, and $R_{x,y} = 0$ for all other pixels.

The intensity spread $R'_{x',y'}$ in the blurred area x', y' is measured by the camera as well. It results from defocus and is a fraction f of the sample original point's intensity that is blended with the surface reflectance in the blur area:

$$R'_{x',y'} = fI_{x,y}FM_{x',y'} + EM_{x',y'} \tag{15}$$

To normalize the intensity spread, f has to be determined. For this, the intensity the projector would have to produce in terms of creating the same radiance $R'_{x',y'}$ by a direct illumination has to be estimated:

$$fI_{x,y} = \frac{(R'_{x',y'} - EM_{x',y'})}{FM_{x',y'}} \tag{16}$$

Finally, f can be computed by comparing the results of equations 14 and 16:

$$f = \frac{fI_{x,y}}{I_{x,y}} \tag{17}$$

If the pixels in the captured camera image are normalized, a normalized intensity distribution of the sample point is received. This is independent of the surface reflectance of the projector's form factor. Due to limitations of the projectors (brightness and dynamic range) and the camera (response and noise) their maxima of the intensity spreads might not equal one. A second normalization that lifts their maxima intensities to one (and the other intensities accordingly) enhances the quality of focus estimation that does not analyze the intensity loss of the spread.

Each sample point in the camera view corresponds to a distinct area on the display surface. The focus of every projector is estimated within the same surface area (i.e., the same sample point in the camera view). To do this for the entire surface, multiple sample points are shifted within two-dimensional scan windows in the entire camera view. A pixel-by-pixel shift results in exact focus estimations for every single camera pixel. Thereby the projector-individual focus values computed for a sample point that is larger than a camera pixel are mapped to its center pixel. Alternatively, the same focus values can be mapped to all pixels of the sample point. This allows shifts in the size of the sample points' radii and leads to shorter scanning times with lower precision. A third alternative is to map the focus values to the center pixel while performing larger shifts. The resulting voids can then be interpolated. This leads to even shorter scanning times but also to a further reduction of the precision. A planar surface, for example, requires capturing only one image with a coarse grid of sample points.

Thus, the normalized intensities f are used to estimate relative focus values. Common focus operators, such as intensity-based and frequency-based techniques, or point-spread methods can be applied for this. Frequency-based focus operators, such as Laplacian, discrete cosine transformation, or fast Fourier transformation, are often referred to in related literature. However, an even better result can be received by using the focus operator described in Tsai and Chou (2003), which is originally used to measure the blur on CRT screens. Applying the momentum preserving principle, this operator segments any discrete geometry of the intensity spread inside the corresponding search window into its foreground and background. The proportion of foreground relative to the background is used as focus value.

The focal plane of the camera causes additional blur and influences the absolute focus values. However, since it remains constant for all projectors, the same amount of defocus is added in each measurement. This applies also to secondary scattering effects. Note that if the defocus of the camera is too high, small focus variations between the projectors might not be detectable with resolution, intensity response, and dynamic range provided by the camera. Consequently, the camera's focus should be adjusted adequately to avoid extreme blur effects in the camera image. This allows computing relative focus values Φ that enable a quantitative comparison of corresponding projector pixels.

The focus values are first determined for each color channel separately and the results are averaged. The momentum preserving operator in Tsai et al. (2003) proved also to be stable among the RGB channels. The operator is fast and robust against camera noise.

Image Compositions

The relative focus values $\Phi_{i,x,y}$ of each projector i that reaches a surface area which is visible in the camera pixel x,y are now known. An image from multiple projector contributions with minimal defocus can then be composed in real-time. Two general techniques are imaginable: An exclusive composition or a weighted composition.

Exclusive Composition

An exclusive image composition allows only one projector (the one with the largest focus value) to cover a surface area which appears at pixel x,y in camera space:

$$I_i = w_i(R\text{-}EM)/FM_i, \quad w_i = \begin{cases} 1 & \Phi_{i,x,y} \geq \Phi_{j,x,y} \\ 0 & else \end{cases} \tag{18}$$

The binary weights w_i are determined from the focus values Φ offline, coded into a single texture map, and are passed to the projector-individual pixel shaders. Alternatively, a stencil mask can be computed for each projector. The mapping from camera space to projector space is given by the *C2P* maps.

Neighboring pixels of different projectors might not be correctly aligned on the surface. This is due to their potentially unequal sizes and orientations, as well as due to imprecision of the geometric calibration. The resulting overlaps and gaps can lead to visible artifacts. To reduce these artifacts, the weight texture must be smoothened using a low-pass filter. This results in soft edges and in non-binary weight values. Since neighboring pixel-contributions from different projectors can now overlap partially, a different composition method has to be applied to ensure a correct radiometric compensation. The weighted composition described in equation 19 can be used for this. But instead of computing normalized weights directly from the focus values, the softened weights of the exclusive weight texture are normalized.

Weighted Composition

Another disadvantage of the exclusive composition method is that the total light intensity that arrives at the surface cannot be larger than that produced by a single projector. This causes visual artifacts at surface pigments with extremely low reflectance or bright environment light.

As explained in Section 4, the simultaneous contribution of multiple projectors can overcome this problem. A weighted image composition represents a tradeoff between intensity enhancement and focus refinement:

$$I_i = \frac{w_i(R-EM)}{\sum_j^N w_j FM_j}, w_{i,x,y} = \frac{\Phi_{i,x,y}}{\sum_j^N \Phi_{j,x,y}} \tag{19}$$

The intensity contribution and the form factor component of each projector i that covers the same surface area x,y in camera space is weighted. The weights w_i are derived from the focus values and are normalized. They are not binary in this case. Projector contributions with high focus values are up-weighted, and contributions of projectors with low focus values are down-weighted. Together, however, all contributions will always produce the correct result R when being reflected by the surface.

The weighted composition allows also to scale the focus values Φ_i up or down during runtime. This makes it possible to amplify or attenuate the contribution (and consequently the focus properties) of an individual projector i under retention of a correct radiometric compensation.

Similarly as for the exclusive composition, a static alpha mask can be used alternatively for blending each projector's output instead of weighing the result inside the pixel shaders.

View-Dependent Pixel-Precise Augmentations

For view-dependent applications (e.g., head-tracked stereoscopic visualizations), however, a single sweet spot (i.e., a single camera view) as assumed in Sections 4.1 and 4.2 is not sufficient. The extension toward a view-dependent correction of geometry and radiometric measurements is described in two variations: as an image-based and as a geometry-based approach.

Image-Based Approach

To create a radiometrically compensated and geometrically corrected projection for a single camera perspective, the geometric mapping between camera and projector(s), as well as the

Figure 8. Image-based rendering approach (left): Five source cameras (1-5), one destination camera (d). Example of stereoscopic and head-tracked projection onto complex surface (right): With and without radiometric compensation, and occlusion effects. (Images reprinted from Bimber, 2005b, © IEEE)

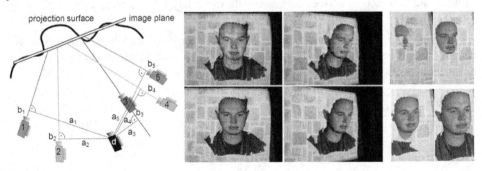

radiometric parameters have to be measured during calibration. This results in the parameter textures *C2P*, *P2C*, *EM*, and *FM* that are used by projector-individual pixel-shaders to perform a pixel-precise geometric and radiometric correction for the actual perspective in real-time. This process was described in Section 4.

Figure 8 (left) illustrates how this approach can be extended toward view-dependent image-based rendering (Bimber et al., 2005b) that was inspired by unstructured Lumigraphs (Buehler, Bosse, McMillan, Gortler, & Cohen, 2001).

The set of parameters for multiple, unstructured source camera positions are measured: P_i2C_j, FM_{ij}, and EM_{ij}, where i is the projector index and j is the camera index. The camera can be tracked and its position and orientation can be stored together with each corresponding parameter set. Figure 8—left illustrates this for five unstructured source camera positions. For rendering the image correctly, it has to be defined where the image plane will appear in space. This can be done once before calibration by interactively aligning a 3D model of the image plane at the desired position in the real environment.[4] If the camera is moved, the registered image plane has to be rendered according to the new camera perspective. Two different image plane types can be supported: An on-axis image plane remains at a fixed position in space but its orientation is updated in such a way that it is perpendicular to the vector that is spanned by the camera's position and the central position of the image plane. The orientation and position of an off-axis image plane remains constant in space—no matter where the camera is located.

If it is assumed to render a correct image only for one of the calibrated source cameras j, the following step is performed: The projection of the image plane into the camera's perspective has to be computed first. This is done by off-screen rendering the registered image plane model from the perspective of this camera. The image plane is shaded with texture coordinates that allow a correct perspective mapping of the original image O onto it. These texture coordinates range from $u=0..1$ and $v=0..1$ for addressing and displaying the entire image O. In the following, this image plane texture is referred to as IP. Projector-individual pixel shaders can then carry out the following tasks: For each pixel of projector i find the corresponding radiometric parameters in FM_{ij} and EM_{ij} using P_i2C_j. Then find the corresponding pixel of the original image O by referencing P_i2C_j first to look-up the texture coordinate of O in IP. Using this texture coordinate, perform a look-up in O. Having all parameters, the color correction is performed (see Section 4) and the pixel is displayed.

For a novel destination camera position that does not match any of the source camera positions, however, all parameters have to be computed rather than being measured: The geometric and radiometric parameter textures, as well as the direction vector for this novel camera perspective are interpolated from the measured parameters of the source cameras. A new image plane texture IP is then rendered from this interpolated perspective. For a correct interpolation, the position of the destination camera is projected onto the direction vectors of the source cameras. Two distances can now be computed for each source camera j (cf. Figure 8, left): The distance from the destination camera to its projection points on each source cameras' direction vector (a_j). And the distance from the destination camera's projection points to each source cameras' position (b_j). These distances are used for computing penalty weights for each source camera with:

$$p_j = \alpha a_j + (1-\alpha)b_j \qquad (20)$$

Note that all distances a_j and b_j have to be normalized over all source cameras before computing the penalties. The factor α allows weighting the contribution of each distance. Since a shift of the destination camera along a source direction vector causes less distortion than a shift away from it, a_j must be weighted higher than b_j. One possibility is to choose $\alpha=0.75$. Note that neither the orientation of the destination camera, nor the intrinsic parameters of source or destination cameras have to be taken into account for computing the penalty weights.

From all source cameras, a subset of k cameras with the smallest penalties is selected. This has to be done due to memory restrictions of current graphics cards. Only these k source cameras are considered for sampling the destination camera's new parameter textures. For each of the k source cameras, a weight factor can be computed with:

$$w_j = \left(1 - \frac{P_j}{\max_{pk}} \right) \frac{1}{P_j} \qquad (21)$$

where $\max_{pk}$ is the maximum penalty among the k selected source cameras. Note that all weights have to be normalized after being computed. This implies that the source camera with the largest penalty ($\max_{pk}$) among the k selected ones is weighted with 0. A source camera with close-to-zero penalty is first weighted with a value approaching infinity, but is then mapped to 1 after normalization.

The parameter textures and interpolated direction vector for the destination camera can now be computed, rather than being measured. This is performed with the pixel shaders by interpolating each parameter entry t_j of P_i2C_j, FM_{ij}, EM_{ij}, and the original direction vectors among the k selected source cameras as follows:

$$t_d = \sum_j^k w_j t_j \qquad (22)$$

Note that look-ups in FM_{ij} and EM_{ij} have to be carried out with the original (non-interpolated) P_i2C_j map while look-ups in IP have to be done with the interpolated projector-to-camera map. This allows the computation of the geometric warping, the image plane projection, and the radiometric parameters (surface reflectance, environment contribution, and black-level) for a novel destination camera. For completely diffuse surfaces, the radiometric parameters do not change. Weak specular effects, however, are taken into account with this method as well. To handle a flexible number of source cameras, the pixel shaders are not hard-coded, but dynamically generated and loaded onto the graphics card during runtime. This happens only if k is modified.

The view-independent parameter textures, such as the scattering described in section 4.4 or the focus values described in Section 5 do not have to be interpolated.

Geometry-Based Approach

As explained earlier, projective texture mapping and two-pass rendering can be applied for image warping if the surface geometry is known. It is easy to see that the precision of this method strongly depends on the quality of the surface model and on an adequate registration between surface model and projectors. Misregistrations of 2-3 pixels that lead to geometric image distortions can be tolerated in case of simple non-textured surfaces. Performing the radiometric compensation with wrong parameters, however, leads to immediately visible color and intensity artifacts. They make the fusion of stereo pairs difficult. Next a variation of this geometric rendering method that is applicable for view-dependent radiometric compensation is described.

Knowing the pixel correspondence between two or more camera positions allows computing each surface point's 3D position in space which is stored in projector individual geometry maps (GM_j). A definite mapping of 3D surface points to projector pixels is provided implicitly through indexing GM_i. The radiometric parameters (EM_{ij} and FM_{ij}) are measured for each camera-projector combination. The parameter textures that belong to the same projector are then averaged and C_j2P_i-mapped to projector individual look-up textures (EM_i and FM_i) that correspond to the indexing of GM_i.

A texture matrix (TM) that transforms the 3D surface points into the perspective of the observer camera can then be computed. This matrix is a composition ($TM = N*I*E$) of extrinsic (E: position and orientation transformations) and intrinsic (I: perspective projection) parameters of the observer camera followed by a transformation from normalized device coordinates into normalized texture space (N=translate[0.5,0.5,0.0]*scale[0.5,0.5,1.0] for OpenGL). Note that the same matrix is also applied for texturing by conventional projective texture mapping methods. The rendering of the geometry from the perspective of the projector(s), however, is different in the described approach.

For every projector pixel, the corresponding surface point SP_i is looked up in GM_i and is mapped into the perspective of the observer camera with $TM*SP_i$. Consistent occlusion effects can be achieved by performing a depth test with the transformed scene points and the depth map of the virtual scene. Being in the camera space, the pixel of the original image O can be referenced in the corresponding look-up textures, as described in Section 6.1. Remember that for performing a look-up in O, the texture coordinates of the defined image plane have to be referenced. Thus the image plane texture IP has to be computed for the perspective of the observer camera and passed to the pixel shader exactly as described in section 6.1. The radiometric parameters can be looked-up in EM_i and FM_i. Note that EM_i, FM_i, and GM_i have projector resolution.

In contrast to conventional projective texture mapping approaches, this variation ensures that the look-up of the radiometric parameters for each projector pixel always matches with its corresponding surface pigment. Only the mapping into the observer's camera perspective depends on the quality of the estimated geometry map and the precision of the tracking device. This, however, can only cause a geometric misalignment of the image–but no color or intensity artifacts. Intrinsic and extrinsic parameters of the projectors do not have to be acquired. Non-linear projector distortions are corrected by this method as well.

Potentials and Limitations

Projector-based augmentation has a great potential in many areas. However, there are also several technical limitations that have to be reported on current projector-camera approaches that are used for augmented reality. The fixed resolution of both—cameras and projectors—prevent from measuring and correcting small geometric details and colored pigments that fall below their resolutions. The solution to this problem is to ensure a higher spatial resolution (projector and camera) on a smaller surface area. This can be achieved by a larger number of stationary projectors and cameras[5] or by an interactively tracked projector/camera device. Furthermore, off-the-shelf projectors and cameras suffer from a low dynamic range, which makes the capturing and compensation of a large color space impossible. Potential solutions are multi-channel projectors that provide a high-dynamic range in combination with multi-spectral imaging technology (Hill, 2002). High-dynamic range or dynamic range increase techniques represent further software solutions that can enhance the camera measurements.

The high black-level of conventional projectors also makes it difficult to produce absolutely dark areas. For multi-projector configurations, the black-level of each projector is being added. This prevents current projector-based AR configurations from using a large number of overlapping projectors for creating very bright images with a high contrast that can compensate all possible pigment colors. Optical filters can reduce the black-level–but they will also reduce the brightness. In some situations, local contrast effects (dark areas surrounded by bright areas are perceived darker than they actually are) reduce this problem on a perceptual level.

Diffuse materials that perfectly absorb light in one or more bands of the spectrum are not well suited for a radiometric compensation approach. Fortunately, such materials are not very common in the real world. Most diffuse surfaces scatter at least a small portion of the light being projected onto them. Thus, this challenge reduces to the question of how much light can be projected for achieving the desired result. Strongly specular surfaces, however, will make a projector-based augmentation fail in general. To find a solution to this problem remains a challenge in the future of projector-based augmentation. Alternative concepts, such as mobile and spatial optical or video see-through technologies might be preferable in these situations.

Future projectors will become compact in size and require little power and cooling. Conventional lamps will be replaced by powerful LEDs. This makes them suitable for mobile augmented reality applications or spatial augmented reality configurations (Bimber et al., 2005d) that apply large number projectors which are seamlessly integrated into everyday environments. Reflective technology (such as DLP or LCOS) will more and more replace transmissive technology (e.g., LCD). This leads to an increased brightness and extremely high update rates that will easily support multi-user stereoscopic visualizations with a single projection unit. Such enabling technologies make the implementation of novel imaging and display techniques possible, such as a simultaneous acquisition and display (Cotting, Naef, Gross, & Fuchs, 2004), or a programmable imaging directly over the digital micromirror array of the projector (Nayar & Boult, 2004).

Another advantage of projection technology over traditional display technology applied by the AR community is that its technological development is strongly driven by a large consumer electronics market. This will also lead in future to a fast technical progress and to continuously falling prices.

Acknowledgments

I would like to thank and acknowledge all students and colleagues who contributed to the work summarized in this chapter. Namely Andreas Emmerling, Gordon Wetzstein, Anselm Grundhöfer, Christian Nitschke, Daniel Danch, Petro Kapakos, Thomas Klemmer, Franz Coriand, Alexander Kleppe, Stefanie Zollmann, Tobias Langlotz, Erich Bruns, and Thomas Zeidler.

References

Bell, I. E. (2003). Neutralizing paintings with a projector. In *Proceedings of SPIE/IS&T* (Vol. 5008, pp. 560-568).

Biehling, W., Deter, C., Dube, S., Hill, B., Helling, S., Isakovic, K., Klose, S., & Schiewe, K. (2004). LaserCave: Some building blocks for immersive screens. In *Proceedings of International Status Conference on Virtual and Augmented Reality*.

Bimber, O. (2004) Combining Optical holograms with interactive computer graphics. *IEEE Computer, 37*(1), 85-91.

Bimber, O., & Emmerling, A. (2006a). Multi-focal projection: A multi-projector technique for increasing focal depth. *IEEE Transactions on Visualization and Computer Graphics (TVCG)*.

Bimber, O., & Fröhlich, B. (2002). Occlusion shadows: Using projected light to generate realistic occlusion effects for view-dependent optical see-through displays. In *Proceedings of International Symposium on Mixed and Augmented Reality (ISMAR'02)* (pp. 186-195).

Bimber, O., & Raskar, R. (2005d). *Spatial augmented reality: Merging real and virtual worlds*. A K Peters LTD.

Bimber, O., Coriand, F., Kleppe, A., Bruns, E., Zollmann, S., & Langlotz, T. (2005c). Superimposing pictorial artwork with projected imagery. *IEEE MultiMedia, 12*(1), 16-26.

Bimber, O., Emmerling, A., & Klemmer, T. (2005a). Embedded entertainment with smart projectors. *IEEE Computer, 38*(1), 56-63.

Bimber, O., Grundhöfer, A., Wetzstein, G., & Knödel, S. (2003). Consistent illumination within optical see-through augmented environments. In *Proceedings of IEEE/ACM International Symposium on Mixed and Augmented Reality (ISMAR'03)* (pp. 198-207).

Bimber, O., Grundhöfer, A., Zeidler, T., Danch, D., & Kapakos, P. (2006b). Compensating indirect scattering for immersive and semi-immersive projection displays. In *Proceedings of IEEE Virtual Reality (IEEE VR'06)*.

Bimber, O., Wetzstein, G., Emmerling, A., & Nitschke, C. (2005b). Enabling view-dependent stereoscopic projection in real environments. In *Proceedings of IEEE/ACM International Symposium on Mixed and Augmented Reality (ISMAR'05)* (pp. 14-23).

Brown, M., Majumder, A., & Yang, R. (2005). Camera-based calibration techniques for seamless multi-projector displays. *IEEE Transactions on Visualization and Computer Graphics, 11*(2), 193-206.

Buehler, C., Bosse, M., McMillan, L., Gortler, S.J., & Cohen, M. F. (2001). Unstructured Lumigraph rendering. In *Proceedings of ACM Siggraph'01* (pp. 425-432).

Cotting, D., Naef, M., Gross, M., & Fuchs, H. (2004). Embedding imperceptible patterns into projected images for simultaneous acquisition and display. In *Proceedings of IEEE/ACM International Symposium on Mixed and Augmented Reality (ISMAR'04)* (pp. 100-109).

Ehnes, J., Hirota, K., & Hirose, M. (2004). Projected augmentation–Augmented reality using rotatable video projectors. In *Proceedings of IEEE/ACM International Symposium on Mixed and Augmented Reality (ISMAR'04)* (pp. 26-35).

Fujii, K., Grossberg, M. D., & Nayar, S. K. (2005). A projector-camera system with real-time photometric adaptation for dynamic environments. In *Proceedings of Computer Vision and Pattern Recognition (CVPR'05)* (Vol. 2, pp. 20-25).

Grossberg, M. D., Peri, H., Nayar, S. K., & Bulhumeur, P. (2004). Making one object look like another: Controlling appearance using a projector-camera system. In *Proceedings of IEEE Conference on Computer Vision and Pattern Recognition (CVPR'04)* (Vol. 1, pp. 452-459).

Hill, B. (2002). (R)evolution of color imagining systems. In *Proceedings of the 1st European Conference on Color in Graphics, Imagining and Vision (CGIV'02)* (pp. 473-479).

Low, K. L., Welch, G., Lastra, A., & Fuchs, H. (2001). Life-sized projector-based dioramas. In *Proceedings Symposium Virtual Reality Software and Technology (VRST'01)* (pp. 93-101).

Nayar, S. K., & Boult, T. E. (2004). Programmable imaging using a digital micromirror array. In *Proceedings of Computer Vision and Pattern Recognition (CVPR'04)* (pp. 436-443).

Nayar, S. K., Peri, H., Grossberg, M. D., & Belhumeur, P. N. (2003). A projection system with radiometric compensation for screen imperfections. In *Proceedings of International Workshop on Projector-Camera Systems (ProCams'03)*.

Noda, S., Ban, Y., Sato, K., & Chihara, K. (1999). An optical see-through mixed reality display with real-time rangefinder and an active pattern light source. *Transactions of the Virtual Reality Society of Japan, 4*(4), 665-670.

Pinhanez, C. (2001). The everywhere displays projector: A device to create ubiquitous graphical interfaces. In *Proceedings of Ubiquitous Computing (UbiComp'01)* (pp. 315-331).

Raskar, R. (1999a). Oblique projector rendering on planar surfaces for a tracked user. In *Proceedings of ACM Siggraph '99*, sketch.

Raskar, R., Brown, M. S., Yang, R., Chen, W., Welch, G., Towles, H., Seales, B., & Fuchs, H. (1999b). Multi-projector displays using camera-based registration. In *Proceedings of IEEE Visualization (IEEE Viz '99)* (pp. 161-168).

Raskar, R., van Baar, J., Beardsly, P., Willwacher, T., Rao, S., & Forlines, C. (2003). iLamps: Geometrically aware and self-configuring projectors. In *Proceedings of ACM Siggraph '03* (pp. 809-818).

Raskar, R., Welch, G., Low, K. L., & Bandyopadhyay, D. (2001). Shader lamps: Animating real objects with image-based illumination. In *Proceedings of Eurographics Rendering Workshop* (pp. 89-102).

Raskar, R., Ziegler, R., & Willwacher, T. (2002). Cartoon dioramas in motion. In *Proceedings of International Symposium on Non-photorealistic Animation and Rendering* (pp. 7-ff).

Seitz, S. M., Matsushita, Y., & Kutulakos, K. N. (2005). A theory of inverse light transport. In *Proceedings of IEEE International Conference on Computer Vision (IEEE ICCV '05)* (pp. 1440-1447).

Tsai, D. M., & Chou, C. C. (2003). A fast focus measure for video display inspection. *Machine Vision and Applications, 14*(3), 192-196.

Underkoffler, J., Ullmer, B., & Ishii, H. (1999). Emancipated pixels: Real-world graphics in the luminous room. In *Proceedings of ACM Siggraph* (pp. 385-392).

Wang, D., Sato, I., Okabe, T., & Sato, Y. (2005). Radiometric compensation in a projector-camera system based on the properties of human vision system. In *Proceedings of IEEE International Workshop on Projector-Camera Systems (ProCams '05)*.

Yoshida, T., Horii, C., & Sato, K. (2003). A virtual color reconstruction system for real heritage with light projection. In *Proceedings of Virtual Systems and Multimedia* (pp. 158-164).

Endnotes

[1]   Consistent depth values have to be ensured (Raskar, 1999a).

[2]   The intrinsic and extrinsic parameters of the projectors have to be determined first.

[3]   For each color channel separately.

[4]   Visual feedback for this process can be provided by rendering the image plane perspectively correct into the video stream of one source camera.

[5]   Or a single mobile camera covering a larger number of sample positions sequentially.

Chapter V

Mobile Phone Based Augmented Reality

Anders Henrysson, Norrköping Visualisation and Interaction Studio, Sweden

Mark Ollila, Norrköping Visualisation and Interaction Studio, Sweden

Mark Billinghurst, Human Interface Technology Laboratory, New Zealand

Abstract

Mobile phones are evolving into the ideal platform for augmented reality (AR). In this chapter, we describe how augmented reality applications can be developed for mobile phones and the interaction metaphors that are ideally suited for this platform. Several sample applications are described which explore different interaction techniques. User study results show that moving the phone to interact with virtual content is an intuitive way to select and position virtual objects. A collaborative AR game is also presented with an evaluation study. Users preferred playing with the collaborative AR interface than with a non-AR interface and also found physical phone motion to be a very natural input method. This results discussed in this chapter should assist researchers in developing their own mobile phone based AR applications.

Introduction

In recent years, mobile phones have developed into an ideal platform for augmented reality (AR). The current generation of phones has full color displays, integrated cameras, fast processors, and even dedicated 3D graphics chips. It is important to conduct research on the types of AR applications that are ideally suited to mobile phones and user interface guidelines for developing these applications. This is because the widespread adoption of mobile phones means that they could be one of the dominant platforms for AR applications in the near future.

Traditionally AR content is viewed through a head mounted display (HMD). Wearing an HMD leaves the users hands free to interact with the virtual content, either directly or by using an input device such as a mouse or digital glove. However, for handheld and mobile phone based AR, the user looks through the screen and needs at least one hand to hold the device. The user interface for these applications is very different than those for HMD based AR applications. Thus, there is a need to conduct research on interaction techniques for handheld AR displays, and to produce formal user studies to evaluate these techniques.

In this chapter, we give an overview of the development path from mobile AR to mobile phone AR. We explain in detail how we developed an AR platform suited for mobile phones and discuss the uniqueness of mobile phone interaction for AR. We present sample applications and user studies performed to evaluate interaction techniques and metaphors.

Related Work

The first mobile AR systems, such as Feiner's Touring Machine (Feiner, MacIntyre, & Webster, 1997), relied on bulky backpack worn computers and custom-built hardware. However, it was obvious that what was carried in a backpack would one day be held in the palm of the hand. Feiner showed the potential of mobile AR systems for outdoor context sensitive information overlay, while ARQuake (Thomas et al., 2002) showed how these same systems could be used for outdoor gaming.

At the same time these early mobile systems were being developed, Schmalstieg et al. (2002), Billinghurst, Weghorst, and Furness (1996), and Rekimoto (1996) were exploring early face-to-face collaborative AR interfaces. Billinghurst's Shared Space work showed how AR can be used to seamlessly enhance face-to-face collaboration (Billinghurst, Poupyrev, Kato, & May, 2000) and his AR Conferencing work (Billinghurst & Kato, 1999) showed how AR can be used to create the illusion that a remote collaborator is actually present in the local workspace. Schmalstieg's Studierstube (Schmalstieg et al., 2002) software architecture is ideally suited for building distributed AR applications, and his team has developed a number of interesting collaborative AR systems.

Using Studierstube, Reitmayr, and Schmalstieg (2001) brought the mobile and collaborative research directions together in a mobile collaborative augmented reality interface based on a backpack configuration. Prior to this, Höllerer, Feiner, Terauchi, and Rashid (1999) had added remote collaboration capabilities to the University of Columbia's touring machine, allowing

Figure 1. The pioneering system, Transvision, which consisted of a small LCD display and camera and allowed collaborative hand-held augmented reality interaction (Rekimoto, 1996) (Image courtesy of Jun Rekimoto, Sony CSL)

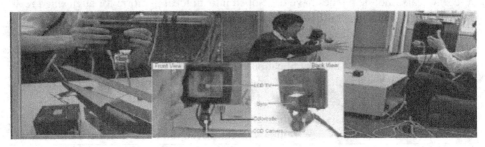

a wearable AR user to collaborate with a remote user at a desktop computer. Piekarski and Thomas (2002) also added similar remote collaboration capabilities to their Tinmith system, once again between a wearable AR user and a colleague at a desktop computer. However Reitmayr's work was the first that allowed multiple users with wearable AR systems to collaborate in spontaneous ways, either face-to-face or in remote settings.

These projects showed that the same benefits that tethered AR interfaces provided for collaboration could also extend to the mobile platform, and new application areas could be explored, such as location based gaming.

Rekimoto's Transvision system explored how a tethered handheld display could provide shared object viewing in an AR setting (Rekimoto, 1996) (see Figure 1). Transvision consists of a small LCD display with a camera mounted on the back. Two users sit across the table and see shared AR content shown on the phone displays. The ARPAD interface (Mogilev, Kiyokawa, Billinghurst, & Pair, 2002) is similar, but it adds a handheld controller to the LCD panel. ARPAD decouples translation and rotation. A selected object is fixed in space relative to the LCD panel and can be moved by moving the panel. Rotation is performed using a trackball input device.

As significant computing and graphics power became available on the handheld platform, researchers have naturally begun to explore the use of personal digital assistants (PDAs) for AR applications as well. First, there was work such as the AR-PDA project (Geiger, Kleinnjohan, Reiman, & Stichling, 2001) and BatPortal (Ingram & Newman, 2001) in which the PDA was used as a thin client for showing AR content generated on a remote server. Then in 2003, Wagner and Schmalstieg (2003b) ported the ARToolKit (2005) tracking library to the PocketPC and developed the first self-contained PDA AR application. Unlike the backpack systems, handheld collaborative AR interfaces are unencumbering and ideal for lightweight social interactions.

Mobile phone-based AR has followed a similar development path. Early phones did not have enough processing power so researchers explored thin client approaches. For example, the AR-Phone project (Cutting, Assad, Carmichael, & Hudson, 2003) used Bluetooth to send phone camera images to a remote sever for processing and graphics overlay. However, Henrysson recently ported ARToolKit over to the Symbian phone platform (Henrysson & Ollila, 2003), while Moehring developed an alternative custom computer vision and tracking library (Moehring, Lessig, & Bimber, 2004). This work enables simple AR applications to be developed which run at 7-14 frames per second.

An additional thread that our work draws on is AR interaction techniques. As mobile AR applications have moved from a wearable backpack into the palm of the hand, the interface has changed. The first mobile AR systems used head mounted displays to show virtual graphics and developed a number of very innovative techniques for interacting with the virtual data. For example, in the Tinmith system (Piekarski et al., 2002), touch sensitive gloves were used to select menu options and move virtual objects in the real world. Kurata's handmouse system (Kurata, Okuma, Kourogi, & Sakaue, 2001) allowed people to use natural gesture input in a wearable AR interface, while Reitmayr et al. (2001) implemented a stylus based interaction method.

PDA-based AR applications do not typically use head mounted displays, but are based instead around the LCD display on the PDA or handheld device. At least one of the user's hands is needed to hold the PDA so some of the earlier mobile interaction techniques are not suitable. It is natural in this setting to use stylus input but there are other possibilities as well. In the AR-PAD project (Mogilev et al., 2002), buttons and a trackball on the display are used as input in a face-to-face collaborative AR game. Träskbäck and Haller (2004) use a tablet-PC and pen input for an AR-based refinery education tool. In Wagner's indoor navigation tool (Wagner & Schmalstieg, 2003c), user input is also a combination of stylus interaction and knowledge of display position from visual tracking of markers in the environment.

Handheld AR applications, such as the Invisible Train (Wagner, Pintaric, Ledermann, & Schmalstieg, 2005), also show an interesting combination of interacting with the AR content by interacting in the world and with the device itself. In this case, the user moves around in the real world to select the view of the virtual train set and then touches the screen with a stylus to change the position of tracks on the train set (see Figure 2). Similarly in Wagner's AR-Kanji collaborative game (Wagner & Barakonyi, 2003a), the user looks through the PDA screen to view real cards that have Kanji symbols printed on them. When the cards

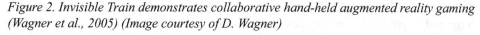

Figure 2. Invisible Train demonstrates collaborative hand-held augmented reality gaming (Wagner et al., 2005) (Image courtesy of D. Wagner)

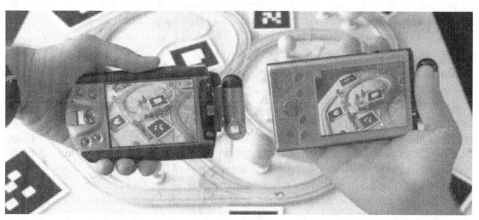

are seen through the screen, virtual models are seen corresponding to the translation of the Kanji characters. These can be manipulated by hand and the PDA shows the model from different viewpoints. There is very little stylus input required. These projects show that if the AR display is handheld, the orientation and position of the display can be used as an important interaction tool.

Bringing Augmented Reality to the Mobile Phone

To bring AR to the mobile phone we had to develop a robust, lightweight tracking solution. Given the widespread adoption of built-in cameras in mobile phones, optical tracking was an obvious choice. There are various optical tracking techniques including fitting a projection of a 3D model onto detected features in the video image and matching a video frame with photos from known positions and orientations. However, we wanted to have a general tracking method suitable for interaction studies with minimal preparation. We choose to work with the ARToolKit software library, which provided a well-tested solution for optical tracking. ARToolKit can be used to calculate the 3D pose of a camera relative to a single square tracking marker.

In order to develop self-contained AR applications for Symbian based mobile phones we needed to port the ARToolKit tracking library to the Symbian operating system. The original implementation of ARToolKit uses double precision floating-points. However, both the mobile phones we are targeting and the PDA used by Wagner lack a floating-point unit, making floating-point arithmetic orders of magnitude slower than integer arithmetic. To overcome this, Wagner identified the most computational heavy functions and rewrote them to fixed-point using Intel's GPP library.

Fixed-point representations use the integer datatype to provide both range and precision. If great precision is required (e.g., for trigonometric functions), 28 of the 32 integer bits are used for precision. Since there was no equivalent fixed-point library featuring variable precision available for Symbian, we wrote our own. We did extensive performance tests to select the algorithms that ran the fastest on the mobile phone. The average speed-up compared to corresponding floating-point functions was about 20 times. We started out by porting the functions rewritten by Wagner and continued backwards to cover most of functions needed for camera pose estimation. The resulting port runs several times faster than the non fixed-point version of ARToolKit. This speed-up was essential for developing interactive applications.

To provide 3D graphics capabilities, we decided on OpenGL ES (OpenGL ES, 2002), which is a subset of OpenGL 1.3 suitable for low-power, embedded devices. To make it run on these limited devices some members of the Khronos group removed redundant APIs and functions. Memory and processor demanding functions such as 3D texturing and double precision floating-point values have been removed along with GLU. A 16:16 fixed-point data type has been added to increase performance while retain some of the floating-point precision. The most noticeable difference is the removal of the immediate mode in favor of vertex arrays. Since Symbian does not permit any global variables the vertex and normal arrays must be declared constant, which limits the dynamic properties of objects. While

Figure 3. These two images demonstrate visualizations of complex objects using mobile phone augmented reality

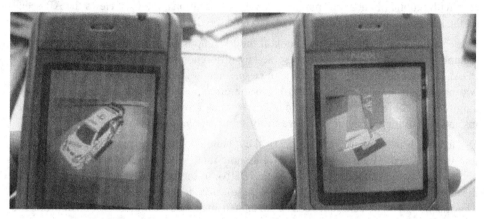

OpenGL ES takes care of the low level rendering there is still need for a higher-level game engine with ability to import models and organize the content into a scene graph. To import textured models from a 3D animation package we used the Deep Exploration tool from Right Hemisphere. This converts the exported model to C++ code with OpenGL floating-point vertex arrays, which are converted into OpenGL ES compatible fixed-point vertex arrays using a simple program we wrote. This conversion is not perfect since the exported OpenGL array indexing differs slightly from the OpenGL ES one.

Having this platform we were able to import complex 3D models and visualize them in an Augmented Reality application (see Figure 3). In this case, when the application recognizes the ARToolKit tracking marker a simple 3D model is overlaid on the live camera view. On a Nokia 6630 phone, this typically runs at 6-7 frames per second.

Interaction Design for
Mobile Phone Augmented Reality

In order to explore methods for virtual object manipulation in AR applications on a mobile phone, we need to consider the appropriate interaction metaphor. There are several key differences between using a mobile phone AR interface and a traditional head mounted display-based AR system. Obviously, the display is handheld rather than head worn meaning that the phone affords a much greater peripheral view of the real world. On the phone the display and input device are connected while they are separate for the HMD configuration. This means that with a mobile phone there is no need for a second device for interaction, configuration, or 2D menu browsing, which is the case for most HMD configurations.

These differences mean that interface metaphors developed for HMD-based systems may not be appropriate for handheld systems. For example, applications developed with a Tangible

AR metaphor (Kato, Billinghurst, Poupyrev, Tetsutani, & Tachibana, 2001) often assume that the user has both hands free to manipulate physical input devices; this will not be the case with mobile phones. For phone-based AR applications, the user views the AR scene on the screen and needs at least one hand to hold the device.

These differences suggest that we look at the PDA applications for appropriate interface metaphors. However, there are also some key differences between a mobile phone and a PDA. The mobile phone is operated using a one-handed button interface in contrast to the two-hand stylus interaction of the PDA. It is therefore possible to use the mobile phone as a tangible input object itself. In order to interact we can move the device relative to the world instead of moving the stylus relative a fairly static screen.

Our approach is to assume the phone is like a handheld AR lens providing a small view into the AR scene. With this in mind, we assume that the user will more likely move the phone-display than change their viewpoint relative to the phone. The small form factor of the mobile phone lets us go beyond the looking-glass metaphor to an object-based approach. This means that input techniques can be developed largely based around motion of the phone itself, rather than keypad or button input on the phone.

For complex applications, we need 6 degree of freedom (DOF) manipulation. There have been many 6 DOF interface techniques developed for desktop applications, however there are a number of important differences between using a phone AR interface and a traditional desktop interface. Phone input options are limited since there is no mouse and keyboards are limited to a handful of high-end models. Limited screen resolution severely restricts the use of menus and multiple view-ports. We need input techniques that can be used one handed and only rely on a phone joypad and keypad input. Since the phone is handheld we can also use the motion of the phone itself to interact with the virtual object.

New opportunities in mobile phone interaction have emerged with the integration of cameras into the phones. Using simple image processing on the phone, it is possible to estimate the movement of the device, and implement 6 DOF manipulation. For example, we can fix the virtual object relative to the phone and then position and rotate objects by moving the phone relative to the real world. Bimanual interaction techniques can also be used; the dominant hand holding the phone and the non-dominant manipulating a real object on which AR graphics are overlaid.

Sample Application: Object Manipulation

To explore different object manipulation techniques, we have implemented tangible (iso-morphic) interaction as well as keypad (isometric) interaction methods. In the tangible case, objects are selected by positioning virtual cross hairs over them, clicking, and holding down the joypad controller. Once selected, the object is fixed relative to the phone and moves when the user moves the phone. When the joypad is released, the object orientation and position is set to the final phone orientation and position. These two transformations can also be handled separately where the orientation or position is reset upon release. The keypad interface allows the user to isolate one axis at the time.

To explore object rotation we implemented an ArcBall rotation technique (Chen, Mountford, & Sellen, 1988). The relative motion of the phone is used to rotate the currently selected object. The ArcBall allows the user to perform large 3DOF rotations using small movements. In a desktop implementation, the mouse pointer is used to manipulate an invisible ball that contains the object to be rotated. The resulting rotation depends on where on the ball the user clicked and in which direction the pointer was dragged. In our phone interface, the center of the object is projected into screen coordinates and a virtual crosshair acts as a mouse pointer rotating the object.

In the keypad/joypad method, the objects continuously rotate or translate a fixed amount for each fraction of a second while the buttons are pressed. In contrast, when the virtual object is fixed relative to the phone (tangible input), the user can move the object as fast as they can move the phone. Therefore, the user should be able to translate or rotate the objects faster using tangible input techniques than with keypad input.

To test the interaction methods and explore how they could be combined, we implemented a scene assembly application. The application consists of a minimal scene with two boxes and a ground plane (see Figure 4). The boxes can be moved freely above the ground plane. When selected, the object is locked to the phone and highlighted in white. The virtual model

Figure 4. Example of object manipulation using a mobile phone; in this case, the user is performing scene assembly

Figure 5. The semi-transparent menu for selecting transformation mode

is fixed in space relative to the phone and so can be rotated and translated at the same time by moving the phone. When the keypad button is released the new transformation in the global (marker) space is calculated.

The keypad interface is used to modify all six degrees of freedom of the virtual objects. We chose to use the same buttons for both translation and rotation. To switch between the translation and rotation mode we implemented a semi-transparent menu activated by pressing the standard menu button on the joypad (see Figure 5). The menu layout consists of a 3 by 3 grid of icons that are mapped to the keypad buttons 1 to 9. Once the translation or rotation mode is entered the menu disappears.

In both modes, we are handling transformation in three dimensions corresponding to the x, y, and z-axes of the local object coordinate system. Since the joypad is 5-way and pressing it always means selection, it can only handle two of the dimensions. Therefore, to translate the object in the x-y plane we use the four directions of the joypad and complement it with the 2 and 5 keys for translation along the y-axis. For rotation, we use the joypad to rotate around the x and z-axis, while the 2 and 5 buttons rotate the object around the y-axis.

User Study: Object Manipulation

We performed a user study in order to test the usability of the manipulation techniques previously described. In the study, the users tried to position and orient blocks. The subject sat at a table, which had a piece of paper with a number of tracking makers printed on it. When the user looked through the phone display at the tracking marker, they saw a virtual ground plane with a virtual block on it and a wireframe image of a target block. The study was done in two parts, evaluating positioning and translating techniques separately. In the first, we tested the following three positioning conditions:

1.   Object fixed to the phone (one handed).
2.   Button and keypad input.
3.   Object fixed to the phone (bimanual).

In each case, the goal was to select and move the block until it was inside the target wireframe block. In the second part of the experiment we tested the following rotation techniques:

1.   ArcBall.
2.   Keypad input for rotation about the object axis.
3.   Object fixed to the phone (one handed).
4.   Object fixed to the phone (bimanual).

For each condition, the virtual block was shown inside a wireframe copy and the goal was to rotate the block until it matched the orientation of the wireframe copy.

In the bimanual cases, the user was able to manipulate the tracking paper with one hand while moving or rotating the phone with the other, while in the other conditions the user wasn't allowed to move the tracking marker. When the block was positioned or rotated correctly inside the target wire-frame it changed color to yellow showing the subject that the trial was over. For each trial, we measured the amount of time it took the user to complete the trial and also continuously logged the position or rotation of the block relative to the target.

After three trials in one condition we asked the subject to subjectively rate his or her performance and how easy was it for him or her to use the manipulation technique. Finally, after all the positioning or orientation conditions were completed we asked the users to rank them all in order of ease of use.

Results

We recruited a total of nine subjects for the user studies, seven male and two female, aged between 22 and 32 years. None of the subjects had experience with 3D object manipulation on mobile phones but all of them had used mobile phones before and some of them had played games on their mobile phone.

Positioning

There was a significant difference in the time it took users to position objects depending on the positioning technique they used. Conditions **A** and **C** took less time than the keypad condition (condition **B**). Using a one factor ANOVA ($F(2,24) = 3.65$, $P < 0.05$) we found a significant difference in task completion times (see Table 1).

For each of the conditions, subjects were asked to answer the following questions:

Q1: How easy was it for you to position the object?
Q2: How accurately did you think you placed the block?
Q3: How quickly did you think you placed the block?
Q4: How enjoyable was the experience?

Using a scale of 1 to 7 where 1 = very easy, 7 = not very easy. Table 2 shows the average results.

Table 1. Average task completion times for positioning objects

Condition	A: Fixed to Phone	B: Keypad	C: Bimanual
Average Time (s)	8.51	21.15	14.01

Table 2. Average responses for the subjective survey

Condition	A: Fixed to Phone	B: Keypad	C: Bimanual
Q1:Ease of use	5.8	5.0	5.8
Q2: Accuracy	5.4	6.0	5.1
Q3: Speed	5.9	4.4	5.1
Q4: Enjoyable	5.7	4.6	5.3

Table 3. Average ranked choice between conditions (1 = highest)

Condition	A: Fixed to Phone	B: Keypad	C: Bimanual
Average Rank	1.44	2.56	2.00

The users thought that when the object was fixed to the phone (conditions **A** and **C**) it was easier to position the object correctly (**Q1**) but they could position the model more accurately (**Q2**) with the keypad input. A one factor ANOVA finds a near significant difference in the results for Q1 ($F(2,24) = 2.88$, $P = 0.076$) and Q2 ($F(2,24) = 3.32$, $P = 0.053$).

There was a significant difference in the other conditions. The users thought they could place the objects more quickly when they were attached to the phone (**Q3**) and the tangible interfaces were more enjoyable (**Q4**). A one factor ANOVA finds a significant difference in the results for Q3 ($F(2,24) = 5.13$, $P < 0.05$) and Q4 ($F(2,24) = 3.47$, $P < 0.05$).

The users were asked to rank the conditions in order of ease of use (1 = easiest, 3 = most difficult). Table 3 shows the average ranking. Condition **A** and **C** were the best ranked conditions. A one factor ANOVA gives a significant difference ($F(2,24) = 5.36$, $P < 0.05$).

Orientation

There was also a significant difference in the time it took users to orient objects depending on the technique they used. Table 4 shows the average time it took the users to rotate the

Table 4. Average task completion times for positioning objects

Condition	A: ArcBall	B: Keypad	C: Fixed	C: Bimanual
Avg Time (s)	21.8	20.1	42.3	37.4

virtual block to match the wireframe target. Conditions **A** (ArcBall) and **B** (keypad input) are on average twice as fast as the Tangible Input rotation conditions (**C** and **D**). A one-factor ANOVA finds a significant difference between these times $(F(3,32) = 4.60, P < 0.01)$.

Subjects were also asked to answer the same survey questions as in the translation task, except **Q1** was changed "How easy was it for you to rotate the virtual object?" There were no significant differences between these survey responses. The subjects thought that the conditions were equally easy to use and enjoyable. The users were asked to rank the conditions in order of ease of use. There was also no significant difference between these results.

User Feedback

In addition to survey responses, many users gave additional comments about the experience. Several commented that when the virtual object was attached to the phone they felt like they were holding it. In contrast, when the keypad was used they felt that they were looking at a screen. They felt like they were more in control and they could use their spatial abilities when manipulating the virtual object with tangible input. In contrast, those that preferred the keypad liked how it could be used for precise movements and also how you didn't need to physically move yourself to rotate the object. Some users also commented on a lack of visual feedback about the rotation axis.

The block changed color when it was released inside the target but subjects thought it would have been good to change before it was released. They also felt visual cues showing the axis of rotation would be helpful, especially in the case of the ArcBall implementation. Those subjects that used two-handed input said that they felt they had more control because they could make gross movements with the camera and then fine tune the block position with small marker movements.

Sample Application-Face-to-Face Collaborative AR

To explore face-to-face collaborative AR we developed a simple two player game; AR Tennis. Tennis was chosen because it could be played in either a competitive or cooperative fashion, awareness of the other player is helpful, it requires only simple graphics and it is a game that most people are familiar with. For a multiplayer game, we needed a way to

Figure 6. Tennis court superimposed on a marker visible from the mobile camera phone. The marker is placed between the players and the mobile phone is used like a racquet. (Image courtesy of Games Lab, Australian Centre for the Moving Image)

transfer data between phones. Since our game is a face-to-face collaborative application we chose Bluetooth and wrote a simple peer-to-peer communications layer that enables data to be shared between the phones.

Our tennis application uses a set of three ARToolKit markers arranged in a line. When the player points the camera phone at the markers they see a virtual tennis court model superimposed over the real world (see Figure 6). As long as one or more of these markers are in the field of view then the virtual tennis court will appear. This marker set is used to establish a global coordinate frame and both of the phones are tracked in this coordinate frame.

There is a single ball that initially starts on one of the phones. To serve the ball the player points their phone at the court and hits the "2" key on the keypad. Once the ball is in play, there is no need to use the keypad any more. A simple physics engine is used to bounce the ball off the court and respond to when the player hits the ball with their camera phones. The racket is defined as a circle centered on the z-axis in the xy-plane of the camera space. This means that holding the phone corresponds to holding a virtual racket. If there is an intersection between the racket plane and the ball, the direction of ball is reversed. The direction and position vectors of the ball are sent over to the other phone using Bluetooth. By sending the position the simulations will be synchronized each round. When receiving data the device switches state from outgoing to incoming and starts to check for collision with the racket. Both devices check for collision with the net and if the ball is bounced outside the court. If an incoming ball is missed the user gets to serve. Each time the ball is hit there is a small sound played and the phone of the person that hits the ball vibrates, providing haptic and audio multi-sensory cues.

In order to evaluate the usability of mobile phones for collaborative AR we conducted a small pilot user study. We were particularly interested in two questions:

1.   Does having an AR interface enhance the face-to-face gaming experience?

2.   Is multi-sensory feedback useful for the game playing experience?

To explore these questions we conducted two experiments, both using the AR tennis game we have developed.

Experiment One: The Value of AR

In this first study, we were interested in exploring how useful the AR view of the game was, especially in providing information about the other player's actions. Pairs of subjects played the game in each of the following three conditions:

A.   Face-to-face AR: Where they have virtual graphics superimposed over a live video view.

B.   Face-to-face non-AR: Where they could see the graphics only, not the live video input.

C.   Non face-to-face gaming: Where the players could not see each other and also could see the graphics only. There was no live video background used.

In the face-to-face conditions (**A** and **B**) players sat across a table facing each other sharing a single set of tracking markers. In condition **C**, the players sat with a black cloth dividing them and each used their own tracking marker.

Players were allowed to practice with the application until they felt proficient with the game. Then they were told to play for 3 minutes in each of the conditions. The goal was to work together to achieve the highest number of consecutive ball bounces over the net. This was to encourage the players to cooperate together. After each condition the number of ball bounces was recorded and also a simple survey was given asking the subjects how well they thought they could collaborate together. Six pairs of subjects completed the pilot study, all of them male university staff and students aged between 21 and 40 years.

Experiment One Results

In general, there was a large variability in the number of ball bounces counted for each condition and there was no statistically significant difference across conditions. This is not surprising because pairs used many different strategies for playing the game. However, we did get some significantly different results from the subjective user surveys. At the end of each condition, subjects were asked the following four questions:

Q1:   How easy was it to work with your partner?

Q2:   How easily did your partner work with you?

Table 5. Average subjective survey scores for AR Tennis

	A: FtF AR	B: FtF non-AR	C: Non FtF
Q1	4.83	4.13	3.75
Q2	4.50	4.25	3.83
Q3	5.92	3.17	2.50
Q4	5.17	5.25	5.33

Q3:   How easy was it to be aware of what your partner was doing?

Q4:   How enjoyable was the game?

Each questions was answered on a scale from 1 to 7 where 1 = Not Very Easy and 7 = Very Easy. Table 5 shows the average scores for each question across all conditions.

The users found each condition equally enjoyable (**Q4**). Interestingly enough, despite simple graphics and limited interactivity the enjoyment score was relatively high. However, there was a significant difference in response to the first three questions. The user felt that there was a difference between the conditions in terms of how easy it was to work with their partner (**Q1**) and how easily their partner worked with them (**Q2**). For question 1 (ANOVA $F(2,33) = 8.17$, $p < 0.05$) and for question 2 (ANOVA $F(2,33) = 3.97$, $p < 0.05$). The face-to-face AR condition was favored in both cases. Users felt that it was much easier to be aware of what their partner was doing (**Q3**) in the face-to-face AR condition with the live video background than in the other two conditions which had no video background (ANOVA $F(2,15) = 33.4$, $p < 0.0001$).

Subjects were also asked to rank the three conditions in order of how easy it was to work together. All but one of the users (11 out of 12) ranked the face-to-face AR condition first, confirming the results from the survey questions.

Experiment Two: Multi-Sensory Feedback

A second study was conducted to explore the value of having multi-sensory feedback in the collaborative AR application. In the game it was possible to play with audio and vibration feedback when the ball was hit. Players played the game in the following conditions:

A: Face-to-face AR with audio and haptic feedback.

B: Face-to-face AR with no audio feedback but with haptic.

C: Face-to-face AR with audio but no haptic feedback.

D: Face-to-face AR with no audio and no haptic feedback.

These four conditions were used to explore which of the audio and tactile options the players found most valuable. Each pair of players played in each condition for one minute, once again counting the highest number of consecutive ball bounces over the net and also completing a survey after each condition. The same six pairs who completed experiment one also completed experiment two. After finishing the conditions for experiment one they would continue to complete the conditions for experiment two, so that they were trained on the system.

Experiment Two Results

As with the first experiment, there was a wide variability in the average number of ball bounces counted and no statistical difference across conditions. However, we did get some significantly different results from the subjective user surveys. At the end of each condition subjects were asked the following three questions:

Q1: How easy was it to be aware of when you had hit the ball?

Q2: How easy what it to be aware of when your partner had hit the ball?

Q3: How enjoyable was the game?

Table 6. Subjective survey results from multi-sensory game play

	A: Audio + Haptic	B: No Audio + Haptic	C: Audio + No Haptic	D: No Audio + No Haptic
Q1	5.75	5.00	5.33	3.17
Q2	5.42	4.17	5.17	3.33
Q3	5.83	4.83	4.83	4.17

Once again each questions was answered on a scale from 1 to 7 where 1 = Not Very Easy and 7 = Very Easy. Table 6 shows the average scores for each question across all conditions.

For awareness (**Q1** and **Q2**) the conditions using audio (**A** and **C**) were ranked the best. For question 1 (ANOVA $F(3,44) = 11.1$, $p < 0.0001$) and for question 2 (ANOVA $F(3,44) = 6.59$, $p < 0.001$). They almost unanimously rated the condition that provided the most sensory output (audio, visual, haptic) as the most enjoyable (**Q3**) (ANOVA $F(3,44) = 6.53$, $p < 0.001$).

Subjects were also asked to rank the four conditions in order of how easy it was to work together. Almost all of the subjects ranked condition **A** best (10 out of 12 responses), followed by condition **C** (audio but no haptic feedback), then condition **B** (haptic but no audio feedback) and finally condition **D** (no audio or haptic feedback). Thus, they almost unanimously rated the condition which provided the most sensory output (audio, visual, haptic) as easiest to work in and also as the most enjoyable. There also appears to be a clear preference for audio only output over haptic output. This could be in part due to great awareness cue that audio provides for both the user and their partner when they hit the ball. With haptic only feedback, for the player that is not hitting the ball it is equivalent to having no feedback at all.

Design Recommendations

Users found that the tangible interface metaphor provides a fast way to position AR objects in a mobile phone interface because they just have to move the real phone where the block is to go. The subjects also felt that it was more enjoyable.

However, there seems to be little advantage in using our implementation of a tangible interface metaphor for virtual object rotation. When the virtual object is fixed to the phone then the user often has to move themselves and the phone at the same time to rotate the object to the orientation they want, which takes time. Even when the person can use a second hand to rotate the tracking marker, this is still more time consuming than using the ArcBall or keypad input.

One of the main advantages of the keypad is that it just rotates the object around one axis at a time and so makes it easy for the user to understand what the rotation axis is and how to undo any mistakes. There is also a compromise between speed and accuracy that may affect performance. Tangible input techniques may be fast, but because they provide full six degree of freedom input, they may not be the best methods for precise input.

The collaborative AR game showed that face-to-face mobile games could benefit from combining computer graphics with views of the real world. The use of multi-sensory feedback, especially audio and visual is important for increasing game enjoyment. There are certain types of games that appear suitable for collaborative AR on mobile phones. If visual tracking is used then the ideal games have a focus on a single shared game space. This enables the players to easily see each other at the same time as the virtual content.

The screens on mobile phones are very small so collaborative AR games need only to use a limited amount of graphics and should mainly focus on enhancing the face-to-face interaction. For example in our tennis game a very simple ball, court, and net model was used, but this was enough to keep users happily engaged.

The use of an appropriate tangible object metaphor is also important for the usability of mobile phone AR applications. In our case we wanted the player to feel like the phone was a tennis racket hitting balls over a virtual net. This is why the phone vibrated when a ball was hit and a racquet sound was made. Once they understood this metaphor, it was easy for users to move the phone around the court space to hit the ball. Physical manipulation of a phone is very natural so it provides an intuitive interaction approach for collaborative AR games.

Conclusion and Future Work

Mobile phones provide an interesting opportunity for augmented reality technology to move into the mainstream, used by millions of people. However before this happens more research has to be conducted on the best AR interaction metaphors and techniques for mobile devices.

In this chapter we present our experiences with mobile phone based AR. We have developed an optimized version of ARToolKit for the mobile phone, and then using that explored a tangible input metaphor where we use the real phone motion to interact with AR content. We developed a basic interaction application for 6DOF object manipulation, and the first collaborative AR game for mobile phones.

One of the main limitations of our platform is the tracking. To be able to track the phone position using ARToolKit, the complete marker pattern must be visible. We have begun to experiment with feature tracking to allow one corner of the marker square to be outside the viewfinder. Another problem is that the current ARToolKit tracking only works in a limited range. If the user is too close to the marker, one or more corners will fall outside of the viewfinder. Too far away and the resolution is too low for marker identification.

Though the focus will remain on optical tracking due to the widespread availability of camera phones, other tracking techniques might be commonly available and make the transition to wide-area mobile phone AR possible. Many 3G phones have built-in GPS, which enables outdoor positioning. Some phones have also electronic compasses and tilt sensors built-in. These sensors combined will make it possible to obtain the orientation and position of the device.

We will continue to explore mobile phone based augmented reality. In the future we would like to employ the 6DOF manipulation techniques in a collaborative set-up and conduct more in-depth user studies. Other applications will also be developed to explore other aspects of mobile phone AR such as content creation and interfacing with intelligent environments.

References

ARToolKit (2005). ARToolKit Web site. Retrieved from www.hitl.washington.edu/artool-kit/

Billinghurst, M., & Kato, H. (1999). Real world teleconferencing. *Proceedings of CHI '99: CHI '99 Extended Abstracts on Human Factors in Computing Systems* (pp. 194-195). New York: ACM Press.

Billinghurst, M., Poupyrev, I., Kato, H., & May, R. (2000). Mixing realities in shared space: An augmented reality interface for collaborative computing. In *Proceedings of the Multimedia and Expo. IEEE International Conference* (Vol. 3, pp. 1641-1644). New York: IEEE Computer Society.

Billinghurst, M., Weghorst, S., & Furness, T. (1996). Shared space: Collaborative augmented reality. In *Proceedings of the Workshop on Collaborative Virtual Environments (CVE 96)*, Nottingham, UK.

Chen, M., Mountford, S. J., & Sellen, A. (1988). A study in interactive 3D rotation using 2-D control devices. In *SIGGRAPH '88: Proceedings of the 15th Annual Conference on Computer Graphics and Interactive Techniques* (pp. 121-129). New York: ACM Press.

Cutting, D., Assad, M., Carmichael, D. J., & Hudson, A. (2003, November 26-28). AR phone: Accessible augmented reality in the intelligent environment. In *Proceedings of OZCHI 2003*. Brisbane, Australia: University of Queensland.

Feiner, T. S., MacIntyre, B., & Webster, T. (1997, October 13-14). A touring machine: Pro-toyping 3D mobile augmented reality systems for exploring the urban environment. In *Proceedings of the 1st IEEE International Symposium on Wearable Computers (ISWC 97)* (pp. 74-81). Cambridge, MA: IEEE Computer Society.

Geiger, C., Kleinnjohan, B., Reiman, C., & Stichling, D. (2001). Mobile AR4ALL. In *Proceedings of the 2nd IEEE and ACM International Symposium on Augmented Reality (ISAR 2001)*. New York: IEEE Computer Society.

Henrysson, A., & Ollila, M. (2003). Augmented reality on smartphones. In *Proceedings of the 2nd IEEE International Augmented Reality Toolkit Workshop*. Tokyo, Japan: Waseda University.

Höllerer, T., Feiner, S., Terauchi, T., & Rashid, G. (1999). Exploring MARS: Developing indoor and outdoor user interfaces to a mobile reality system. *Computers Graphics, 23*(6), 779.

Ingram, D., & Newman, J. (2001). Augmented reality in a WideArea sentient environment. In *Proceedings of the IEEE and ACM International Symposium on Augmented Reality (ISAR'01)* (pp. 77-85). Washington, DC: IEEE Computer Society.

Kato, H., Billinghurst, M., Poupyrev, I., Tetsutani, N., & Tachibana, K. (2001). Tangible aug-mented reality for human computer interaction. In *Proceedings of Nicograph 2001*.

Kurata, T., Okuma, T., Kourogi, T., & Sakaue, K. (2001). The hand-mouse: A human in-terface suitable for augmented reality environments enabled by VisualWearables. In *Proceedings of International Symposium on Mixed Reality (ISMR 2001)*, Yokohama, Japan (pp. 188-189).

Moehring, M., Lessig, C., & Bimber, O. (2004). Video see-through AR on consumer cell phones. *Proceedings of the International Symposium on Augmented and Mixed Reality (ISMAR '04)* (pp. 252-253).

Mogilev, D., Kiyokawa, K., Billinghurst, M., & Pair, J. (2002). AR Pad: An interface for face-to-face AR collaboration. *Proceedings of CHI '02: CHI '02 Extended Abstracts on Human Factors in Computing Systems* (pp. 654-655). New York: ACM Press.

OpenGL ES (2002). *OpenGL ES Web site.* Retrieved from www.khronos.org/opengles

Piekarski, W., & Thomas, B. (2002). ARQuake: The outdoor augmented reality gaming system. *Communications of the ACM, 45*(1), 36-38.

Reitmayr, G., & Schmalstieg, D. (2001, October). Mobile collaborative augmented reality. In *Proceedings of the International Symposium on Augmented Reality 2001 (ISAR 2001)* (pp. 114-123). New York.

Rekimoto, J. (1996, September). Transvision: A hand-held augmented reality system for collaborative design. In *Proceedings of Virtual Systems and Multi-Media 1996 (VSMM '96)*, Gifu, Japan (pp. 18-20).

Schmalstieg, D., Fuhrmann, A., Hesina, G., Szalavari, Z., Encarnacao, L., Gervautz, M., & Purgathofer, W. (2002). The Studierstube augmented reality project. *Presence: Teleoperators and Virtual Environments, 11*, 33-54.

Thomas, B., Close, B., Donoghue, J., Squires, J., Bondi, P. D., & Piekarski, W. (2002). First person indoor/outdoor augmented reality application: ARQuake. *Personal and Ubiquitous Computing, 6*(1), 75-86.

Träskbäck, M., & Haller, M. (2004). Mixed reality training application for an oil refinery: User requirements. In *Proceedings of the 2004 ACM SIGGRAPH International Conference on the Virtual Reality Continuum and its Applications in Industry (VRCAI '04)* (pp. 324-327). New York: ACM Press.

Wagner, D., & Barakonyi, I. (2003a). Augmented reality Kanji learning. In *Proceedings of the 2nd IEEE and ACM International Symposium on Mixed and Augmented Reality (ISMAR 2003)* (pp. 335-343). Washington, DC: IEEE Computer Society.

Wagner, D., Pintaric, T., Ledermann, F., & Schmalstieg, D. (2005). Towards massively multi-user augmented reality on handheld devices. In *Proceedings of the 3rd International Conference on Pervasive Computing (Pervasive 2005)*, Munich, Germany.

Wagner, D., & Schmalstieg, D. (2003b). ARToolKit on the PocketPC platform. In *Proceedings of the 2nd IEEE International Augmented Reality Toolkit Workshop.* Tokyo, Japan: Waseda University.

Wagner, D., & Schmalstieg, D. (2003c, October 21-23). First steps towards handheld augmented reality. In *Proceedings of the 7th IEEE International Symposium on Wearable Computers (ISWC 2003)* (pp. 127-135). White Plains, NY: IEEE Press.

Chapter VI

Representing and Processing Screen Space in Augmented Reality

Blaine Bell, Columbia University, USA

Steven Feiner, Columbia University, USA

Abstract

View management involves computing what a user sees within a 3D environment when it is projected onto a display screen. Doing this interactively to create effectively laid out user interfaces for augmented reality, virtual reality, or any other kind of 3D user interface requires representing and processing screen space. In this chapter, we describe how to compute a 2D screen-space representation that corresponds to the visible portions of the projections of 3D objects on the screen. We describe in detail two visible-surface determination algorithms that are used to generate these representations: one based on a binary space partitioning tree, and one based on a hardware accelerated z-buffer and object buffer. We compare the performance and accuracy tradeoffs of these algorithms, and present examples of how to use our representation to satisfy visibility constraints that avoid unwanted occlusions, making it possible to label and annotate objects in 3D environments.

Introduction

Augmented reality (AR) makes it possible to concurrently visualize both the real world and overlaid virtual information. While designing a conventional user interface requires deciding what information should be presented, and how and where it should be shown, designing an AR user interface thus requires addressing another crucial problem: the superimposed virtual information can occlude things that we would otherwise see in the real world. Therefore, to avoid obscuring important objects, it is necessary to determine the position and size of virtual objects within the user interface relative to what is seen in the real world.

View management (Bell, Feiner, & Höllerer, 2001) refers to the layout decisions that determine spatial relationships among objects in a 3D user interface. For an application to perform view management, it must compute the visibility of objects of interest in a 3D environment, as seen from a selected 3D viewpoint, taking into account visibility constraints. It also must represent and process the visibility information once it has been projected onto the 2D screen space representing the user's view.

Figure 1 shows the order in which computations are done in our view management pipeline (Bell, Feiner, & Höllerer, 2005). To precisely maintain the specified visual constraints, this pipeline should get executed for each frame rendered. However, since some of these computations can take a considerable amount of time to compute, asynchronous execution of the pipeline, as in the decoupled simulation model (Shaw, Green, Liang, & Sun, 1993), can preserve interactive rendering frame rates at the expense of view management accuracy. (These tradeoffs might be preferable depending on the user's preference or task.)

In this chapter, we focus on how to compute the visibility information on which view management is based, as performed in step 3 of Figure 1. This occurs after the viewing specification has been determined (step 2), and the 3D projection has been defined. The resulting visibility information will be used further down the pipeline to satisfy view management constraints, such as avoiding occlusion or determining placements for annotations that are close to the visible portions of associated objects.

Figure 2 demonstrates how we apply view management to a collaborative augmented reality environment. It is photographed through an optical see-through head-worn display, in which

Figure 1. View management computational pipeline: Screen space processing occurs in step 3

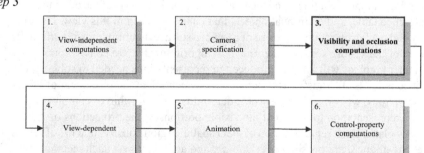

Figure 2. View management in an augmented reality meeting scenario (Imaged through a tracked, optical see-through, head-worn display)

the user directly views the real world through optics that also reflect graphics rendered on miniature LCDs. One user is sitting across from another, discussing a virtual model of the Columbia campus located between them. In response to a request from the user whose view is displayed, all virtual buildings have been annotated with their names. Each label is scaled within a user-selectable range and positioned automatically. A label is preferentially placed within a visible portion of its building's projection. If there is no space to accommodate a label legibly within that projection, it is instead placed near the projection, but not overlapping other buildings or annotations, and is connected to its building by an arrow. Additional annotations in the scene include a meeting agenda (shown at the left), a virtual copy of a building that one of the users has created, and popup information related to that building (both shown at the right). The projections of these annotations avoid other objects, including the visible user's head, to maintain a clear line of sight between users.

In this example, the system needs to compute visibility for the virtual 3D environment, which consists of the campus buildings, and the real world, which consists of the other user's body, the conference table, and additional objects that cannot be seen in this view. Determining visibility and occlusion requires the use of a visible-surface determination algorithm. However, none of the visible-surface determination algorithms that are conventionally used in 3D computer graphics will directly produce the representations needed to solve view management constraints. To satisfy these constraints, which affect the placement of labels and other annotations, we use a visible-surface determination algorithm in combination with a 2D spatial representation to represent the visible portions of the projections of 3D objects on the view plane. Each representation of a 2D spatial region consists of a list of rectangles that are axis-aligned, are possibly overlapping, and are the largest such rectangles that lie wholly inside that region.

We have used two different visible-surface determination algorithms: one based on a binary space partitioning (BSP) tree (Fuchs, Kedem, & Naylor, 1980), and one based on a hardware-accelerated z-buffer (Catmull, 1974) and object buffer (Atherton, 1981). In the rest of this chapter, we discuss the 2D spatial representation, we describe how to generate the desired 2D spatial representations using the BSP tree and the z-buffer, and we compare their performance and accuracy tradeoffs for different kinds of 3D applications. We then present examples of how to use these visibility representations to label and annotate objects in 3D environments.

Related Work

Visible-surface determination algorithms have long been a research topic in computer graphics (Sutherland, Sproull, & Schumacker, 1974). However, standard visible-surface determination algorithms do not create a 2D screen-space representation that is suitable for view management. For example, the most common algorithm used for visible-surface determination is the z-buffer or depth-buffer algorithm (Catmull, 1974), in which the frame buffer is paired with a z-buffer of the same width and height as the frame buffer. Each frame buffer pixel thus has an associated z-value (depth value) in the z-buffer that represents the depth of the closest object rendered for that pixel. This makes it possible to account for scene visibility by iterating through the scene polygons and rendering each pixel only if its z-value is closer than the z-value already associated with that pixel. If a unique value is rendered into the frame buffer for each object, then the frame buffer becomes an *object buffer* (Atherton, 1981) that can be used to determine the object visible at each pixel. However, since the results produce a discrete representation on the image plane with pixel granularity, we describe how additional processing can generate a representation that better supports view management.

List-priority visible-surface determination algorithms rely on explicit sorting of polygons in a view-dependent (back-to-front or front-to-back) order, splitting polygons to eliminate visibility conflicts. For example, the binary space partitioning (BSP) tree algorithm (Fuchs et al., 1980; Paterson & Yao, 1990; Schumaker, Brand, Gilliland, & Sharp, 1969; Thibault & Naylor, 1987) splits polygons during a preprocessing step in which a tree data structure is constructed. The visibility order for an arbitrary projection of a scene is determined by a view-dependent traversal of the tree, which needs to be modified only when the scene geometry changes. These algorithms assume that some additional representation is provided to accumulate the image-plane representation that results from rendering the polygons in the proper order. In this chapter, we also describe how a sorted list of polygons in visibility order can be used to generate an appropriate 2D image-plane representation. (Similarly, the visibility skeleton (Durand, Drettakis, & Puech, 1997)—graph data structure that encodes all possible visibility relationships in a polygonal scene—could also be used to derive an image-plane representation for view management.)

There are also other ways of representing what is visible on the image plane. Area-subdivision algorithms partition the 2D image plane into regions of common visibility. For example, Warnock's algorithm (Warnock, 1969) recursively subdivides the image plane into quadrants, creating a representation that would later be known as a quad tree (Samet, 1990). Unfortunately, this representation partitions the image plane into non-overlapping pieces. Consequently, it makes it relatively expensive to determine placements that are larger than any of the individual non-overlapping pieces, which is necessary for effective view management.

View management has also been accomplished using other types of representations and techniques. In one approach (Ali, Hartmann, & Strothotte, 2005), a scene object buffer is directly evaluated and annotations are laid out using a force-directed approach (Fruchterman & Reingold, 1991). Azuma and Furmanski (Azuma, 2003) perform interactive label placement by executing a radial search around a point to be labeled to find a free position, in the spirit of earlier work on static map label placement (Christensen, Marks, & Shieber, 1995). While these approaches perform view management without using our separate 2D image-plane representation, it is more difficult for them to avoid overlap completely.

2D Representation

The 2D visibility representation that we use to solve view management constraints consists of a list of axis-aligned rectangles for each visible region. Each of these rectangles within the lists is as large as it can be without extending past the boundaries of the region. Furthermore, there are no redundant rectangles (i.e., no rectangle is enclosed by another in the list), and the rectangles exhaustively cover the entire region. Once this representation is calculated, many view-management constraints can be solved by searching the 2D visible space of the objects on the view plane. For example, if any axis-aligned rectangle were to be drawn within the region, then at least one of these largest space rectangles will completely enclose the drawn rectangle. This makes it very easy for programmers to determine whether a desired rectangle can be drawn within the region by sequentially comparing it with each rectangle in the region's representation.

Figure 3. 2D empty-space representation consists of axis-aligned largest rectangles (horizontal stripes): (a) No scene objects; (b) one scene object (solid) is added; (c) second scene object (dotted) is added

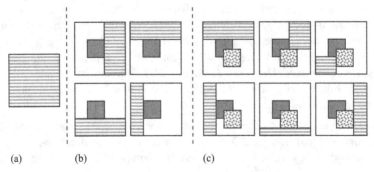

(a)   (b)   (c)

Figure 3 shows the rectangles that represent the empty space (i.e., the area where objects do not exist) within a rectangular area when there are no objects (part a), one object (part b), and two objects (part c). We have developed algorithms for adding, deleting, and moving objects within an arbitrary 2D space, which maintain the representation so that applications can query the empty space at any time (Bell & Feiner, 2000). Since these lists of rectangles represent an arbitrary space, they can also be used to represent the visible space of an object on the 2D view plane.

Computing Visibility Using a Binary Space Partitioning (BSP) Tree

We can perform visible-surface determination by using the BSP tree algorithm (Fuchs et al., 1980) to efficiently sort the upright extents of the objects' projections to produce the visibility order for an arbitrary projection of a scene. A BSP tree is a binary tree whose nodes typically represent actual polygons (or polygon fragments) in the scene. Because we need to determine the visibility order for objects, we use BSP tree planes to separate objects rather than individual polygons (Paterson & Yao, 1990; Schumaker et al., 1969). We choose these planes using the heuristics of Thibault and Naylor (1987). Although BSP trees are often used for purely static scenes, dynamic objects can be handled efficiently by adding these objects to the tree last and removing and adding them each time they move (Chrysanthou & Slater, 1992).

Figure 4. (a) 3D view of our campus; (b) bird's eye view of the campus scene, which includes semi-transparent splitting planes for the BSP tree; eye icon and lines indicate the user's view frustum in (a) with respect to the model

(a)

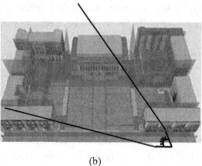

(b)

Determining the Visible Portions of Each Object

When visibility computations are needed, we determine the visible portions of the scene objects by using our 2D space representation. As objects are processed in a front-to-back order using the BSP tree, the space representation is populated with *full-space* rectangles that represent the 2D projections of the 3D scene objects. A complementary empty-space representation encodes the 2D screen space of the view plane that is not populated by any previously processed object. By evaluating the empty-space representation before an object is processed, the visible (i.e., unoccluded) space for that object is determined to be the empty space within the object's 2D projection (i.e., the space that has no projections of previously processed objects). We obtain the largest visible-space representation for each object by clipping the largest empty-space rectangles that overlap the object's projected area and eliminating redundant rectangles that are wholly contained in any others. This visible-space representation provides an efficient way to find suitable locations for annotations that must be placed relative to the visible area of an object's projection.

Figure 4(a) shows an example of a 3D view of our campus, along with a bird's eye view of the scene (Figure 4b) that includes semi-transparent splitting planes for the BSP tree and an eye icon (▲) with lines that indicate the user's view frustum. For each node obtained from the BSP tree in front-to-back order, the 2D upright extent of its projection is computed by projecting each vertex and adding the encompassing axis-aligned bounding rectangle to the space representation. Each row from top to bottom in Figure 5 shows how each node's projection is processed in order to compute each node's visible space, from front-to-back relative to the user's viewpoint. Initially, the 2D spatial representation of the view plane has no full-space rectangles and consists of one largest space rectangle that represents the entire rectangular-shaped view plane (Figure 5a, upper right).

When processing each node, the upright extent of its 2D projection is intersected with the members of the current list of largest empty-space rectangles, as shown in Figure 6. This can be performed efficiently because we maintain the largest empty-space rectangles in a 2D interval tree (Samet, 1990), allowing an efficient window query to determine the members that intersect the extent. (The intersection operation itself is simple because all rectangles are axis-aligned.) The intersection yields a set of rectangles (not necessarily contiguous), some of which may be wholly contained within others; these subset rectangles are eliminated. The result is a set of largest rectangles whose union is the visible portion of the node (Figure 6c). In our example, the visible space of the first two nodes is computed as their entire projections (Figure 5a-b). This is because there are no previously processed projections that overlap each node's projected area (i.e., the dashed outline in the middle column), which both lie completely within the 2D empty space (Figure 5, right column).

Each subsequent object processed (Figure 5c-g), has a projection that overlaps the previously processed projections, and thus, its visible space includes only a portion of the projected area. Consider the third node processed (Figure 5c): the detail presented in Figure 7(a) shows the upright extent of its 2D projection as a dashed outline overlaid onto the 3D projection (left) and overlaid onto the 2D space representation (right). The empty space is evaluated within the dashed outline, as shown in Figure 7(a), and results in the one dark grey rectangle (right)

Figure 5.   Computing screen space of each object from front-to-back relative to the user's viewpoint. Each row, from top to bottom, shows the processing of an additional object. The current BSP tree object being processed is shaded in the bird's eye view (left column), its projection is shown in the same shade on the 2D view plane (middle column), and its projection is outlined with dashes in the 2D spatial representation (right column). The spatial representation is used to determine visible space for the object by computing the empty space within the BSP tree node's projection. After a projection has been processed, it is added as full-space to the 2D spatial representation. (h) Screen-space representation after the last object is processed.

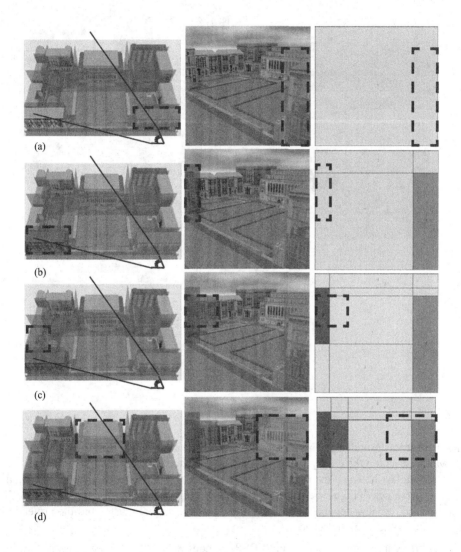

Figure 5. continued

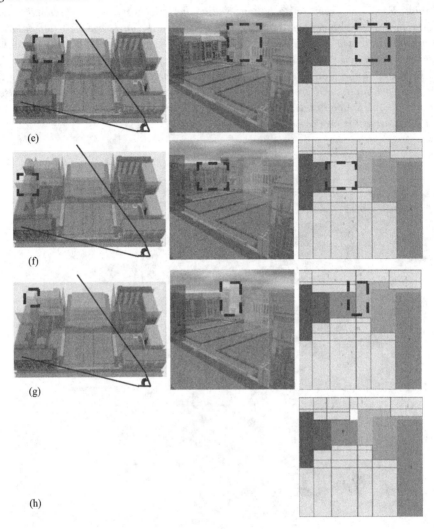

(e)

(f)

(g)

(h)

that represents the node's visible space. The fourth node's projection (light grey in Figure 5d) is evaluated within the empty space and the visible space is determined to be the two dark grey rectangles shown on the right in Figure 7(b). The rest of the nodes are processed in the same way (shown in Figure 5e-g), and the resulting empty-space representation (Figure 5h) can be used, in view-dependent computations, for objects that must avoid the projections of all of the objects in the scene.

Some objects are represented by a single BSP tree node, while others are split across multiple nodes. Consider Figure 8, where objects are placed so that it is not possible to create a plane

Figure 6. Adding a new object to the view-plane representation: (a) Original object (solid), shown separately with each of the four original largest empty spaces (striped); (b) new object extent (dotted) is added; (c) resulting visible largest spaces of new object extent (dotted)

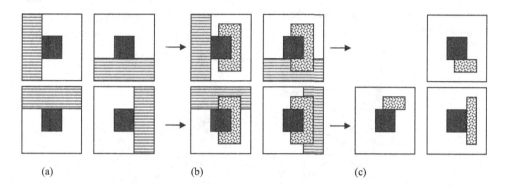

(a)   (b)   (c)

that will partition the scene without splitting one or more objects. In this case, we continue to use the heuristics of Thibault and Naylor (1987) to minimize the amount of splitting in the BSP tree. However, there are certain objects, specifically concave objects, which often do not get split well using these heuristics. This can result in large screen space approximations for concave objects, including empty space, which can inappropriately increase the area allocated to them on the view plane. To address this, we create splitting planes manually to assure that the BSP tree has multiple parts for some of the objects. This makes it possible to support concave objects, which could alternatively be supported automatically by using convex decomposition algorithms (Lien & Amato, 2004; Mangan & Whitaker, 1999).

Figure 9 shows an example of an object split into multiple parts by a BSP tree plane, along with the approximation of each part's projection transparently overlaid. For each part of an object, the largest visible rectangles are computed, as described previously in this section, and are shown for these specific parts in Figure 7(c-d). Once the visible rectangles have been computed for each part of an object, they must now be combined to obtain the visible space rectangles for the entire object. To do this, each part of the same object is coalesced into an accumulated list of visible rectangles, which represents the screen space for the entire object. In the next section, we describe how the visible space rectangles of two parts of an object are coalesced. This algorithm can be used sequentially on multiple parts to obtain one unified visible-space representation for an entire object.

Coalescing Lists of Largest Visible Rectangles

To coalesce two lists of largest visible rectangles, we merge each visible rectangle from one list with the visible rectangles of the other list. This operation is similar to the space management deletion algorithm (Bell & Feiner, 2000), in which the largest empty-space rectangles that are revealed when a covering rectangle is deleted are combined with all adjacent largest

Figure 7. Processing of projections (dashed outline) of visible BSP tree nodes (Figure 5c-d); projections are overlaid onto the 3D projection on the left of each subfigure, the empty space is evaluated within the area of these projections to result in the largest visible space rectangles (striped), shown on the right, that represent the visible spaces for the nodes: (a) Object added in Figure 5(c), (b) object added in Figure 5(d), (c) object added in Figure 5(e), (d) object added in Figure 5(g)

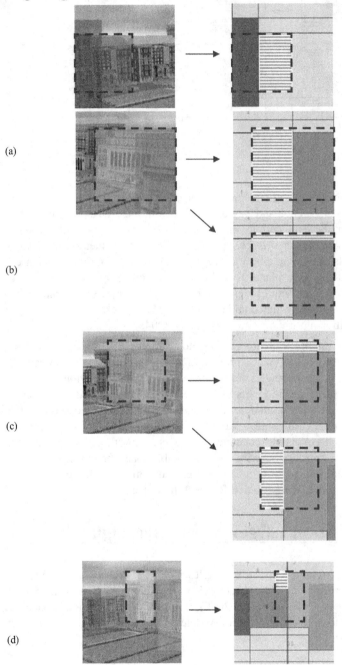

Figure 8. Example of an object layout (in 2D or in 3D as a plan view of a scene) that requires a BSP plane to split at least one of the objects; there is no plane that will partition the group of objects without cutting an object in parts; this requires us to split an object in the object BSP

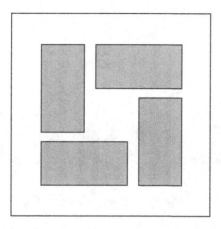

empty-space rectangles. Unlike the deletion algorithm, we combine lists of largest visible rectangles incrementally, which means that some pairs of rectangles being processed may overlap. To handle these cases, the function that combines two largest visible rectangles must support overlap, creating up to two new largest visible rectangles, as shown in Figure 10. Thus, for each rectangle in one list, we find all ways in which it can combine with the rectangles in the other list, and remove those that are enclosed by any other, to determine the largest visible rectangles in the union of the two lists. Figure 11 shows an example of coalescing the two projected BSP tree object parts from Figure 9. Each part consists of the visible space rectangles that result from processing the projections shown in Figure 7(c-d). The horizontal striped rectangle from the left part is combined with the two vertically striped rectangles from the right part, which results in the three circled rectangles that represent the largest visible spaces for this entire object.

The ability to coalesce two sets of rectangles offers the opportunity to combine the visibility results of multiple objects. When laying out a new object, a rectangle can then be selected that lies within one object. Alternatively, the coalescing algorithm can be used to merge the largest rectangles of multiple objects to create a meta-object that corresponds to the union of those objects. This enables the system to lay out a new object whose projection spans the space of multiple objects. Objects can either be coalesced as they are added to the representation or after the representation is built. If both the original objects and the coalesced objects are desired, the coalesced objects can be created in a second space manager representation.

Since full space objects are represented the same way as empty space, both can be coalesced; for example, to treat certain objects as empty space (e.g., the grass, pavement, and sky shown

Figure 9. The last building added to the representation in Figure 5(f-g) has two BSP tree object parts: (a) Building in the top part of the image is split by a plane, (b) projections of both parts are used to determine the visible space for this object. The lighter rectangle represents the projection of the left building part, and the overlapping darker rectangle represents the projection of the right building part.

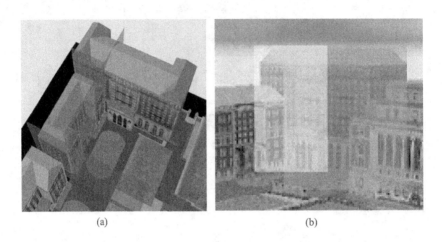

(a)   (b)

Figure 10. Two overlapping largest rectangles (white boxes) create an additional largest rectangle (grey boxes) in each dimension in which their combined extent is greater than that of either original rectangle

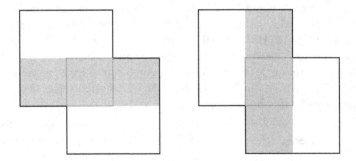

in the campus view of Figure 4). Note that coalescing full space with empty space is not the equivalent of simply not processing the objects when constructing the representation: some objects might obscure parts of others. For example, in our model, the grass and pavement obscure underground infrastructure that would be treated as visible if the grass and pavement were not added.

Figure 11.   Coalescing lists of visible space rectangles of the two BSP tree parts (from Figure 9) of the center building, which is partially occluded by the buildings highlighted on the left and right. (a) Initial visible spaces of both parts include the horizontal striped rectangle from one BSP tree part and two vertically striped rectangles from the other BSP tree part (resulting from computations in Figure 7c-d). (b) The rectangle (horizontal striped) from one part's visible representation is combined with the two adjacent rectangles (vertically striped) of the other part. (c) Results of the two combine operations. The three circled rectangles represent the largest visible spaces of the building. The two original rectangles in (a) that are not circled are not included in the largest visible spaces because they are wholly contained within at least one resulting circled rectangle.

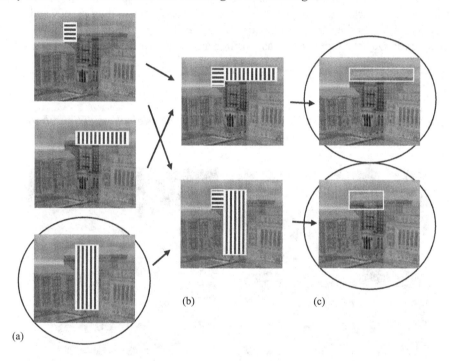

(a)   (b)   (c)

Computing Visibility Using a Z-Buffer

Alternatively, we can compute the 2D spatial representation of the visible regions of objects in a 3D scene using a z-buffer algorithm (Catmull, 1974). By rendering each object in a distinct color with the current viewing specification, we can use the frame buffer as an object buffer (Atherton, 1981), in which each pixel's color encodes the identity of the object visible at that pixel. Figure 12 shows an example of a rendered image (a, upper left) with three object buffers (b-d), each with a different resolution. While higher resolutions provide more accuracy, we need to process these object buffers to convert them into our 2D representation; therefore, performance decreases as the number of pixels to be processed increases.

Note that we must be careful to avoid the problems that can occur when two adjacent polygons in the same object fail to share a vertex on a shared edge, potentially causing missed pixels

(Foley, van Dam, Feiner, & Hughes, 1996). If there are unshared vertices of the polygons on each side of an edge of an object, the pixels close to the edge's projection might not all render as the same object. This can result in a few misrendered pixels, which, when converted into our representation, will cause a large area to be improperly split into a set of smaller ones. To prevent this, we add the necessary extra vertices to polygons in our models.

We use a scan line-order sweep algorithm to convert the resulting pixel representation to the spatial representation that is needed to satisfy our constraints (illustrated in Figure 13, with pseudo-code shown in Figures 14-15). Since it is likely that adjacent pixels will have the same value, we evaluate each pixel, starting at the top left corner of the buffer, moving across the width of the image (in Figure 14, the for loops in lines 7-29), with the variables x and y to keep track of positions in the object buffer, and the variables pixelX and pixelY to keep track of positions in the rendered image). We also must maintain the current object value (currentObjectValue) and the last position at which the pixel value has changed (pre-

Figure 12. Object buffer rendering: (a) Frame buffer at original resolution, (b-d) object buffers at different lower resolutions

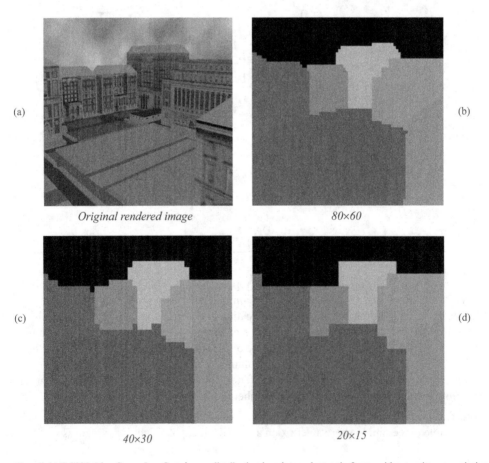

(a)   *Original rendered image*   *80×60*   (b)

(c)   *40×30*   *20×15*   (d)

Figure 13. Z-buffer visibility sweep algorithm. At this stage of processing, a new rectangle (outlined in dotted black and grey) is being added to the visible space for the given object labeled "2" in the object-buffer representation shown in each subfigure. (a) Visible space for object "2" highlighted in grey. Marker shows the end of the span of pixels for object "2" which initiates the processing of the new rectangle. (b-e) Four highlighted grey rectangles on the left are processed and, if adjacent, are combined with the new rectangle. (f–h) The results of these combinations consist of the three highlighted grey-filled rectangles on the right. Rectangle in (g) is a subset of the rectangle in (f) and is therefore discarded (indicated by an "X"); after the entire z-buffer is processed, the accumulated final visible space representation for each visible object consists of a list of largest space rectangles.

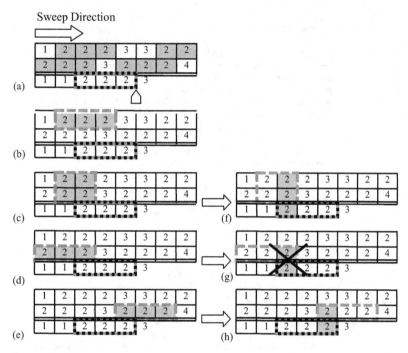

viousObjectValue). Once a change is detected (e.g., Figure 13a, and shown in pseudo-code in Figure 14, lines 17-19) or the end of the scan line is reached (Figure 14, lines 22-28), a rectangle is created from the last to the current position (with unit height) and is combined with the current object's visible-space representation. The current object and last position are then reset, and the algorithm continues. The function processRectangle, which is used Figure 14 and shown in Figure 15, does the necessary processing, once a new rectangle has been detected.

Since rectangles on the current scan line are combined with rectangles from the previous scan line, a one-dimensional interval tree of all rectangles from the previous scan line for each object is kept for fast lookup (objectXIT is an array of 1D interval trees, initialized in Figure 14, line 2). Any rectangle from the last scan line that is not a result of a combine

Figure 14. Pseudocode for the sweep algorithm to convert the discrete object-buffer repre-sentation to our 2D space representation. Iterating through each row to detect rectangles to process.

```
0    computeVPRectanglesForEachObjectFromZBuffer
                                  (double offscreenToScreenRatio){
1      IntervalTree2D objectVPRep [ ] = new IntervalTree2D[N];
2      IntervalTree1D objectXIT[ ] = new IntervalTree1D[N];
3      ImageBuffer buffer = createandRenderObjectBuffer();
4      int width = buffer.getWidth(), height = buffer.getHeight();
5      int startX, lastX, previousObjectValue, currentObjectValue;
6      double pixelX = 0, pixelY = 0;
7      for (y = 0, pixelX = 0; y < height; y++, pixelY += offscreenToScreenRatio){
8        previousObjectValue = -1;
9        for (x=0; x < (width-1); x++, pixelX += offscreenToScreenRatio){
10         currentObjectValue = buffer.getPixel(x,y);
11         if (previousObjectValue==-1){   /* No object in previous pixel */
12           startX = lastX = Math.round(pixelX);
13           previousObjectValue = currentObjectValue;
14         } else if (previousObjectValue==currentObjectValue){
               /* pixel is same as previous, increment last and continue */
15           lastX = Math.round(pixelX + offscreenToScreenRatio);
16         } else {
               /* change detected, combine region to all adjacent spaces for object */
17           processRectangle( objectVPRep[currentObjectValue],
                     objectXIT[currentObjectValue], currentObjectValue,
                     startX, placeX, placeY, offscreenToScreenRatio);
18           startX = lastX = Math.round(pixelX);
19           previousObjectValue = currentObjectValue;
20         }
21       }
           /* for the last pixel in each row */
22       currentObjectValue = buffer.getPixel(x,y);
23       if (previousObjectValue != currentObjectValue){
24         processRectangle( objectVPRep[previousObjectValue],
                 objectXIT[previousObjectValue], previousObjectValue, startX,
                 Math.round(pixelX), pixelY, offscreenToScreenRatio);
25         processRectangle( objectVPRep[currentObjectValue],
                 objectXIT[currentObjectValue], currentObjectValue,
                 Math.round(pixelX),  Math.round(pixelX + offscreenToScreenRatio),
                 pixelY, offscreenToScreenRatio);
26       } else {
27         processRectangle(objectVPRep[previousObjectValue],
                 objectXIT[previousObjectValue], previousObjectValue, startX,
                 Math.round(pixelX + offscreenToScreenRatio), pixelY,
                 offscreenToScreenRatio);
28       }
29     }
30     for each object O from 0 to N             /* all resulting spaces in interval
31       objectVPRep[O].addAll(objectXIT[O])        tree are spaces for objects */
32   }
```

operation is considered part of the final result and does not need further processing. The set of largest visible space rectangles for each visible region consists of all resulting rectangles, including the rectangles that have been combined on the last scan line. These resulting rectangles are kept in variable objectVPRep, which is an array of 2D interval trees, initialized in Figure 14, line 1.

Figure 13 shows the z-buffer visibility sweep algorithm at the stage of processing a new rectangle (outlined in dotted black and grey) within a small portion of the object buffer, where the numbers associate each square pixel to a related object in the scene. Each pixel is evaluated in the sweep direction (left to right on rows from top to bottom) to find new rectangles for objects, which are found when the next pixel's associated object is different from the previous pixel's associated object or the end of the row is reached. In this example, the new rectangle in Figure 13(a) is processed because the next pixel to the right of the pointer is labeled "3." To process the new rectangle, it is added to the visible space associated with the same object labeled "2," which is highlighted in grey in Figure 13(a). The visible space for each object in the scene is accumulated as a list of largest empty space rectangles throughout the sweep process.

To add the new rectangle, it must be compared with each rectangle in the same object's visible-space representation that overlaps it in the sweep direction. In this example, the comparisons are executed on the four solid grey rectangles shown on the left in Figure 13(b-e). The grey highlighted rectangle in Figure 13(b) is not adjacent to the current row (solid double line) and is therefore added to the visible space of the object, since it is no longer needed for processing. (Note that this rectangle could have been detected as no longer needed for processing at the end of the previous line, at the expense of extra processing at the end of each row.) The grey highlighted rectangles in Figure 13(c-e) are adjacent to the new rectangle, and thus are combined with the new rectangle in the vertical direction to create the three new grey-filled rectangles highlighted in Figure 13(f-h), respectively. The new combined rectangle in Figure 13(g) is a subset of the rectangle highlighted in Figure 13(f) and is therefore discarded (indicated by an "X," and removed in Figure 15, line 11). After the rectangles in Figure 13(c-d) are processed to produce the proposed rectangles in Figure 13(f-g), they can no longer be adjacent to any more processed space and therefore are added to the visible space of the object (shown in the pseudo-code in Figure 15, lines 13-16). All other computed rectangles in Figure 13(e, f, h) and the new rectangle (outlined in dotted black and grey) are kept for this object in the 1D interval tree for further processing (Figure 15, line 22).

Visibility Computation Performance

The two methods we have described, using a BSP tree and using a z-buffer, have considerably different performance behaviors and results. Depending on the type of 3D application, different methods and algorithms should be used to query the resulting 2D spatial representations. In this section, we compare these two methods by discussing some measurements of their performance and accuracy. Next, we discuss the benefits and drawbacks of each method to

Figure 15. Pseudo-code for the sweep algorithm to convert the discrete object-buffer representation to our 2D space representation

```
0     processRectangle(IntervalTree2D objectVP,IntervalTree1D objectXIT, int objectValue,
                      int startX, int placeX, double placeY, double offscreenToScreenRatio){
1       Rectangle newRect = new Rectangle(startX,
                                      Math.round(placeY- offscreenToScreenRatio),
                                      placeY, Math.round(placeY));
2       List allNewPotentialRects = new List();
3       allNewPotentialRects.add(newRect);
4       List allOverlappingInXRects =objectXIT.getOverlappingWithoutEdges(newRect);
5       for each rectangle R in allOverlappingInXRects {
6           if (isAdjacentinY(newRect, R)){
7               Rectangle combinedRect = consensusInY(newRect, R);
8               if (R isEnclosedBy combinedRect){
9                   objectXIT.remove(R);
10              }
11              remove any Rectangle in allNewPotentialRects
                      enclosed by combinedRect;
12              add combinedRect to allNewPotentialRects if it is
                      not enclosed by any Rectangle in allNewPotentialRects;
13              if (R.maxX < placeX){
14                  objectVP.add(R);
15                  objectXIT.remove(R);
16              }
17          } else {
18              objectVP.add(R);
19              objectXIT.remove(R);
20          }
21      }
22      add all Rectangles in allNewPotentialRects to objectXIT;
23  }
```

help clarify the applications for which they are most appropriate, and then provide some tips we have found useful for querying the resulting spatial representations.

Figures 16-18 show an evaluation of the performance, results, and accuracy of the two visibility algorithms on a Pentium 4 Mobile 2GHz CPU with 1GB of RAM and an NVidia Quadro 4GoGL. In these examples, the camera is moving around our 3D campus model, which consists of 32 buildings. The camera automatically follows a predetermined path around the campus so that approximately 14.5 buildings on average are visible in every frame rendered. While these results were generated from only one example, representing a single way of controlling the view, they provide us with useful data for discussing the important differences between the algorithms.

Figure 16 shows the performance when computing the visibility for every frame rendered in the evaluation. In this case, the BSP tree performed better than even an extremely low resolution z-buffer (10×7 pixels, shown in the far right column). Since the z-buffer algorithm processes each individual pixel, the resolution has a direct impact on the performance, while the resolution has no effect on the performance of the BSP tree algorithm itself.

Performance is correlated with the number of 2D rectangles that are produced in the resulting representation, as shown in Figure 17. As the buffer resolution decreases, so does the number of rectangles in the resulting representation. Although the BSP tree algorithm results in more rectangles than the low-resolution z-buffer, it still performs better. This is because the BSP tree algorithm uses the empty space result, which represents the 2D space that does not contain the visible projections of any objects and requires no further processing. If this region, which we use for outside labels and annotations, is calculated using the z-buffer algorithm, each unrendered pixel needs to be processed, just like every other region in the frame buffer.

Figure 16. Performance comparison computing visibility using the two methods; the z-buffer is rendered with different resolutions

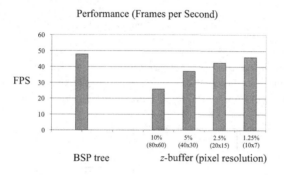

Figure 17. The number of 2D upright rectangles in the resulting 2D representation for the two methods; the z-buffer algorithm is rendered with different resolutions, fraction of full resolution is shown for each z-buffer resolution

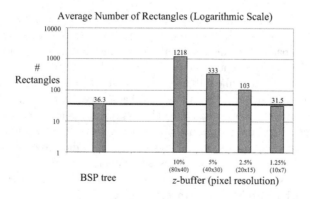

Figure 18. Difference measured between the visibility of objects determined by the algo-rithms and the actual visibility of objects at final rendered resolution, computed as percent-age of pixels with correct visibility, percentage of full resolution is shown for each z-buffer resolution

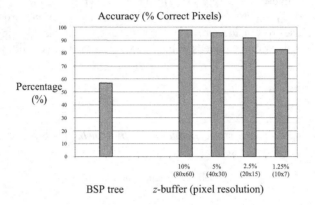

Figure 19. 2D upright rectangular approximations: (a,c) Rectangular projections that do not need better approximations; (b, d) multiple rectangles (black outlines) can be used to create a better approximation of an object's projection to increase accuracy

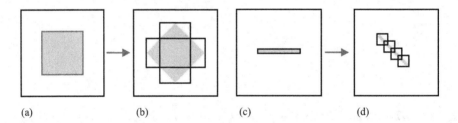

The results of these visibility algorithms are approximations. To measure their accuracy, we compare the visibility in the full-size rendered image (by computing an object buffer of the same size) and compare it with the results of each of the algorithms. Figure 18 shows these comparison results as the percentage of pixels computed by the algorithms that matched the actual visibility determined in the full-size object buffer. The z-buffer accuracy far exceeds the BSP tree projection accuracy, even when used at a very low resolution. In the BSP tree algorithm, the objects are approximated by a low polygonal count to minimize the number of vertices projected and the projections are also approximated as upright 2D rectangles. Incorrect approximation regions typically arise whenever the projections do not project as upright 2D rectangles, and can be addressed by approximating these projections using more rectangles, as shown in Figure 19. Using more rectangles increases the accuracy of the representation, but also increases processing time.

Using Representations for
Labeling and Annotating

The resulting 2D representation supports a variety of layout strategies. Each object is represented by the largest rectangles contained within the visible parts of the object's projection. Thus, an appropriate position and size can be selected for a new object within the visible portion of the projection of any object or group of objects. This makes it possible to perform the equivalent of area feature labeling (Roessel, 1989) in a 3D environment in which objects can partially occlude each other; in this situation, we determine which parts of an object are visible, and select that one that would be best to contain a label. For example, Figure 20 shows an indoor augmented reality application that automatically places labels within the projections of their associated objects. If there is not room within the spatial representation, then an object's label is placed outside but close to the projection of its object.

For computing visibility interactively, the benefits of the BSP tree algorithm for static scene geometry far exceed the benefits of using the z-buffer. The frame rate (Figure 16) is most important, since, for typical 3D environments, the BSP tree algorithm produces a small number of rectangles. Alternatively, using the z-buffer with a low resolution has some negative effects, as well. Although the accuracy (Figure 18) remains fairly high, when the resolution is extremely low (e.g., 10×7 pixels), each z-buffer pixel represents a large number of frame-buffer pixels (e.g., in an 800×600 image, each pixel in a 10×7 z-buffer represents an 80×86 pixel area in the full-resolution frame-buffer). At this coarse z-buffer resolution, it is difficult to detect smaller changes and object movement; for example, if an object moves 50 pixels, it is possible that the visibility representation will not change at all. This produces problems; for example, an arrow that points out an object may not move when it is supposed to move, because its placement is determined by the visibility representation. Furthermore, objects may experience large discontinuities in size and motion between frames in an animation. In contrast, since the BSP tree algorithm computes the projections in floating point coordinates, even slight object motion changes the visibility representation, so that the layouts change accordingly.

Nevertheless, there are interactive applications in which using a z-buffer can be worthwhile. For example, in the outdoor mobile augmented reality application shown in Figure 21, the user is walking around, looking at buildings and restaurants. Here, the head-worn display has a small field of view, the objects are quite large, and the users are sufficiently close to the objects that many project onto large areas of the screen. In these cases, a high-resolution visibility solution is not needed, and a relatively low-resolution z-buffer can be used.

The z-buffer is also useful for highly dynamic scenes in which many objects are moving relative to each other. Assuming that the entire scene is rendered for each frame, there is no rendering overhead. In contrast, the BSP tree data structure needs to be updated whenever an object is moved to properly determine the front-to-back order for the objects in the scene (Chrysanthou & Slater, 1992).

A high-resolution z-buffer is well suited for labeling and annotating a static image. If computational performance is not an issue, the z-buffer produces a representation with high accuracy (Figure 18). At the expense of increased processing time, view management is performed more accurately and the labels and other annotations are laid out more precisely.

Figure 20. Indoor augmented reality environment with labels

Conclusion and Future Work

We have described two methods for computing visibility and how we use them to compute screen space. Converting the output of these visibility algorithms into our 2D screen-space representation requires a considerable amount of processing, especially since there is no hardware acceleration. For interactive graphics, the amount of processing is extremely important, since it has a direct relationship to the rendering frame rate. If the frame rate is too low, then the application may not be usable. Therefore, it is important for the programmer to choose the appropriate algorithm based on the needs of the application.

We are extending our view management research to address new ways of placing labels and other annotations, while also affecting how visibility is computed. Instead of placing labels and other annotations relative to the visible projections of entire objects, we wish to place them relative to specific faces of objects, possibly oriented so that each is parallel to its specified face. This requires that visibility information be computed for each of the involved faces.

Performance and scalability are the most challenging issues for computing visibility in a 3D environment. As the number of objects increase, more processing is needed. We plan to examine in more detail how our algorithms scale as a function of the number of objects. We also intend to apply standard computer graphics techniques based on bounding-volume hierarchies (Kay & Kajiya, 1986; Rubin & Whitted, 1980) to help support view management in large scale environments.

Figure 21. Outdoor augmented reality environment: (a) Backpack system, (b) information about the restaurant is seen in the user's view through a head-worn display

Figure 22. Augmented reality user interface that incorporates a world-in-miniature to give the user a better understanding of their environment

There are situations in which two or more 3D environments must be processed. For example, Figure 22 (Bell et al., 2002) shows a virtual "world-in-miniature" (Stoakley, Conway, & Pausch, 1995) rendered in front of the real world. In this case, none of the objects in the virtual world-in-miniature requires visibility computations (other than those used for rendering) since there are no associated annotations to lay out. However, the virtual objects in the world-in-miniature block objects in the real world, and thus must be taken into account when computing labels and annotations for the real world. Instead of traversing the BSP tree for the virtual world-in-miniature and projecting each virtual object, we can use an approximation of all their projections. This would improve the performance of our algorithms, since the 2D spatial representation would have fewer rectangles than if all world-in-miniature objects had been processed.

These optimizations can potentially be applied in many parts of a 3D application, depending on the situation. Therefore, we have begun to develop a rule-based system that a view management component could use to determine when and how to use these techniques to minimize performance cost.

Acknowledgments

This work was supported in part by ONR Contract N00014-04-1-0005, DAFAFRL Contract FA8650-05-2-6647, NSF Grant 0121239, NLM Contract R01 LM06593-01, and gifts from Intel, Microsoft, and Mitsubishi Electric Research Labs. Blaine Bell was supported during part of this work by an IBM Graduate Research Fellowship. Ryuji Yamamoto created the campus model shown in the figures.

References

Ali, K., Hartmann, K., & Strothotte, T. (2005). Label layout for interactive 3D illustrations. *Journal of WSCG, 13*, 1-8.

Atherton, P. R. (1981). A method of interactive visualization of CAD surface models on a color video display. In *Proceedings of SIGGRAPH '81* (pp. 279-287).

Azuma, R. T. (2003). Evaluating label placement for augmented reality view management. In *Proceedings of the 2nd IEEE and ACM International Symposium on Mixed and Augmented Reality* (pp. 66-75).

Bell, B., & Feiner, S. (2000). Dynamic space management for user interfaces. In *Proceedings of ACM Symposium on User Interface Software and Technology 2000* (pp. 239-248). San Diego, CA.

Bell, B., Feiner, S., & Höllerer, T. (2001). View management for virtual and augmented reality. In *Proceedings of ACM Symposium on User Interface Software and Technology 2001*, Orlando, FL (pp. 101-110).

Bell, B., Feiner, S., & Höllerer, T. (2005). Maintaining visibility constraints for view management in 3D user interfaces. In O. Stock & M. Zancanaro (Eds.), *Multimodal intelligent information presentation* (pp. 255-277). Kluwers.

Bell, B., Höllerer, T., & Feiner, S. (2002). An annotated situation-awareness aid for augmented reality. In *Proceedings of the ACM Symposium on User Interface Software and Technology 2002* (pp. 213-216). Paris.

Catmull, E. (1974). *A subdivision algorithm for computer display of curved surfaces.* PhD Thesis, University of Utah, Salt Lake City.

Christensen, J., Marks, J., & Shieber, S. (1995). An empirical study of algorithms for point-feature label placement. *ACM Transactions on Graphics, 14*(3), 203-232.

Chrysanthou, Y., & Slater, M. (1992). Computing dynamic changes to BSP trees. In *Computer Graphics Forum, Proceedings of Eurographics '92* (Vol. 11, pp. 321-332).

Durand, F., Drettakis, G., & Puech, C. (1997). The visibility skeleton: A powerful and efficient multi-purpose global visibility tool. In *Proceedings of the 24th Annual Conference on Computer Graphics and Interactive Techniques.* ACM Press/Addison-Wesley Publishing.

Foley, J., van Dam, A., Feiner, S., & Hughes, J. (1996). *Computer graphics: Principles and practice* (2nd ed.). Reading, MA: Addison-Wesley.

Fruchterman, T. M. J., & Reingold, E. M. (1991). Graph drawing by force-directed placement. *Softw. Pract. Exper., 21*(11), 1129-1164.

Fuchs, H., Kedem, Z., & Naylor, B. (1980). On visible surface generation by a priori tree structures. In *Proceedings of SIGGRAPH*, Seattle, WA (pp. 124-133).

Kay, T. L., & Kajiya, J. T. (1986). Raytracing complex scenes. *Computer Graphics (SIGGRAPH '86 Proceedings), 20*(4), 269-278.

Lien, J. M., & Amato, N. M. (2004). Approximate convex decomposition. In *Proceedings of the 20th Annual Symposium on Computational Geometry* (pp. 457-458). Brooklyn, New York: ACM Press.

Mangan, A. P., & Whitaker, R. T. (1999). Partitioning 3D surface meshes using watershed segmentation. *IEEE Transactions on Visualization and Computer Graphics, 5*(4), 308-321.

Paterson, M. S., & Yao, F. F. (1990). Optimal binary space partitions for orthogonal objects. In *Proceedings of the 1st Annual ACM-SIAM Symposium on Discrete Algorithms* (pp. 100-106). San Francisco: Society for Industrial and Applied Mathematics.

Roessel, J. (1989). An algorithm for locating candidate labeling boxes within a polygon. *The American Cartographer, 16*(3), 201-209.

Rubin, S. M., & Whitted, T. (1980). A 3-dimensional representation for fast rendering of complex scenes. In *Proceedings of the 7th Annual Conference on Computer Graphics and Interactive Techniques.* Seattle, WA: ACM Press.

Samet, H. (1990). *The design and analysis of spatial data structures.* Reading, MA: Addison-Wesley.

Schumaker, R. A., Brand, P., Gilliland, M., & Sharp, W. (1969). *Study for applying com-puter-generated images to visual simulation* (Rep. No. AFHRL-TR-69-14). U.S. Air Force Human Resources Laboratory.

Shaw, C., Green, M., Liang, J., & Sun, Y. (1993). Decoupled simulation in virtual reality with the MR toolkit. *ACM Transactions on Information Systems (TOIS), 11*(3), 287-317.

Stoakley, R., Conway, M., & Pausch, R. (1995). Virtual reality on a WIM: Interactive worlds in miniature. In *Proceedings of CHI '95*, Denver, CO (pp. 265-272).

Sutherland, I. E., Sproull, R. F., & Schumacker, R. A. (1974). A characterization of ten hid-den-surface algorithms. *ACM Computer Survey, 6*(1), 1-55.

Thibault, W., C., & Naylor, B., F. (1987). Set operations on polyhedra using binary space partitioning trees. In *Proceedings of SIGGRAPH '87* (pp. 153-162).

Warnock, J. E. (1969). *A hidden surface algorithm for computer generated halftone pictures*. PhD Thesis, University of Utah.

Section II:

Augmented Reality
Development Environments

Chapter VII

Abstraction and Implementation Strategies for Augmented Reality Authoring

Florian Ledermann, Vienna University of Technology, Austria

István Barakonyi, Graz University of Technology, Austria

Dieter Schmalstieg, Vienna University of Technology, Austria

Abstract

Augmented reality (AR) application development is still lacking advanced authoring tools—
—even the simple presentation of information, which should not require any programming,
is not systematically addressed by development tools. Moreover, there is also a severe lack
of agreed techniques or best practices for the structuring of AR content. In this chapter, we
present APRIL, the augmented presentation and interaction language, an authoring platform
for AR applications which provides concepts and techniques that are independent of specific
applications or target hardware platforms, and should be suitable for raising the level of
abstraction at which AR content creators can operate.

Introduction

While augmented reality (AR) technology is steadily maturing, application and content development for those systems still mostly takes place at source code level. Besides limiting developer productivity, this also prevents professionals from other domains such as writers, designers, or artists from taking an active role in the development of AR applications and presentations. Previous attempts to adapt authoring concepts from other domains such as virtual reality or multimedia have met with only partial success.

In order to develop authoring tools that genuinely support AR content creation, we have to look into some of the unique properties of the AR paradigm. We argue that a successful AR authoring solution must provide more than an attractive graphical user interface for an existing AR application framework. It must provide conceptual models and corresponding workflow tools, which are appropriate to the specific domain of AR.

In this chapter, we explore such models and tools and describe a working solution, the augmented presentation and interaction language (APRIL). In particular, we discuss aspects relating to real-world interfaces, hardware abstraction, and authoring workflow.

Requirements

The requirements for an appropriate AR authoring solution have been derived from our own experience in realizing AR applications, both by expert programmers and by our students, and from published work in this field that points out the need for authoring solutions (Navab, 2004; Regenbrecht, Baratoff, & Wilke, 2005). To illustrate these requirements and the proposed solutions in the context of this article, we will use a widely known example of an AR application scenario: construction assistance (Figure 1). This scenario is well suited to our analysis for a number of reasons. It is a widely known example with existing case stud-

Figure 1. The interactive furniture construction guide is an example for an application created with APRIL by undergraduate students; the construction process is modeled with a state engine, and possible parts for the next step are shown to the user

ies and implementations (Webster, Feiner, MacIntyre, Massie, & Krueger, 1996, Zauner, Haller, & Brandl, 2003).

It is a moderately complex, non-linear task involving untrained end-users—exactly fitting the type of application that we want to support with our solution. It is related to a wide range of industrial and engineering applications. The realization of this application can be decomposed into separate tasks and delegated to individuals in a team of collaborating experts.

Roles in the Authoring Process

One of the main reasons to move away from graphics programming to a more flexible authoring solution is the support of labor division among different collaborators fulfilling different roles in the development process. These roles may be embodied by distinct professionals (or teams of professionals), or by fewer, even a single person, authoring a simple presentation on her own, yet profiting from a clearly structured design process. We identified the following roles of people contributing to an AR presentation:

- **Domain expert:** The domain expert is the individual or group with the necessary knowledge of the subject dealt with in the presentation. In the furniture example, this would be an engineer or designer who is familiar with every detail of the assembly process.

- **Story author:** The story author translates the knowledge of the domain expert(s) into ideas and a specification of how the subject should be presented in an interactive way.

- **Content creator:** Content creators design and deliver multimedia content for the presentation, following a storyboard. Content creators deliver images, graphics, video, sound, and 3D-models to be used in the presentation, and often work with domain experts to transform original content into representations understandable by end-users.

- **Component implementer:** For sophisticated presentations, static media content has to be turned into components that can expose behavior and react to user input, using a programming or scripting language.

- **Presentation integrator:** The presentation integrator puts together the components and media elements according to the storyboard, and specifies interaction techniques offered to the user depending on the availability of devices. While the story author acts a priori to the content creation to specify the details of the presentation, the story integrator takes the results of the content creation phase and assembles them together.

- **End user:** A person using the running application. In our example, this will be a customer who wants to assemble his new piece of furniture.

Conceptual Model and Structured Design Process

To allow teams of different professionals to work together on an application, we have to provide a conceptual model and terminology that leads to a shared understanding of the project. Since augmented reality is a relatively new paradigm, there is only a small set of terms that apply to AR authoring which are consistently and widely used. One of our goals was to identify existing and introduce new key concepts that can be used by all contributors to the project, to avoid misunderstandings and support collaboration and shared documentation.

On the basis of the identified roles and this conceptual model, a structured design process can be established which defines tasks and deliverables for each role and allows tools supporting these tasks to be developed.

Real-World Interfaces

One aspect that makes AR setups fundamentally different from other media is the presence of the real world in the user's perception of the application space—a feature that we have to take into account when structuring application space and interaction. Furthermore, in applications like our furniture construction example, the world is not only a passive container for the application's content, but parts of the real world (e.g., pieces of furniture to assemble, real-world tools) are part of the applications user interface. In our conceptual model, we have to address the different possibilities of relating application content to the real world. For example, the parts of furniture to be assembled must be explicitly modeled as application objects despite the fact that they will not be rendered graphically.

Hardware Abstraction

Another fundamental aspect of AR is the heterogeneity of hardware setups, devices, and interaction techniques that usually prohibit a "write once, run anywhere" approach or the development of standardized interaction toolkits. We will present strategies for hardware abstraction and an interaction concept that can be transparently applied to a wide range of input devices. By applying these abstractions, application portability can be improved, enabling applications to be developed on desktop workstations or in other test environments instead of directly on the target AR system, which may be scarce or expensive to use. Note that this virtualization of resources is equally useful for classic virtual reality (VR) development.

An important requirement is that the framework should support the manifold combination possibilities of input and output peripherals found in the hybrid, distributed AR systems we are developing in our research. In some cases, such as when working with mobile systems or handheld devices, it is also much more convenient to develop the application on a desktop PC and then run it on the target system exclusively for fine-tuning and final deployment. Applications and their components should be reusable in different setups, and applications developed for one system should run on another setup, with little or no modification. The furniture construction application can be configured to run on a Web cam-based home setup, as well as on the tracked see-through augmented reality head-mounted displays in our lab.

Modularization

To support a distributed workflow and allow future reuse of parts of applications, it is desirable to be able to modularize applications. This applies to individual parts of an application's content, but also for abstract parts of the application like the storyboard, the interaction specifications, or the hardware description.

Runtime Engine Support

Obviously, an authoring system cannot exist in isolation, but requires a runtime engine to execute the application and present the content created in the authoring system. In particular, the runtime engine must provide structuring of space and time to support the conceptual model of our authoring system.

Authoring Workflow and Tool Support

As far as possible, the authoring workflow should build on existing tools and standards, providing interfaces for integrating these tools into a consistent workflow. The professional tools used by content creators and domain experts should be supported in the AR authoring process, removing the need to re-implement successful solutions in these areas.

In our approach, we have chosen to use a declarative scripting language as the integrating component for authoring. It abstracts the low-level technical aspects of the system, and exposes high-level concepts to the author in an open format, which can be created using any combination of manual text entry, graphical user interfaces, or automatic generators. Rather than relying on a monolithic graphical user interface, we support third-party standard tools for multimedia content (graphics, sound, 3D modeling, video, etc.) and process description (UML state charts) as a front-end to the authoring process. Users will typically spend only a small amount of time directly with the scripting language.

Contribution

The aforementioned requirements have been implemented in an authoring system called APRIL. We will present this system as a proof of concept implementation of the presented ideas, and discuss results and experiences. The contributions presented in this chapter are: (1) identification of key concepts and properties of AR systems that are relevant for content creation, (2) description of the state-of-the-art in AR authoring, (3) a consistent conceptual model for content creators covering hardware abstraction, interaction, spatial and temporal structuring, (4) presenting a reference implementation of an authoring system using the aforementioned model.

Related Work

There is an extensive body of work on authoring tools for interactive 3D graphics, ranging from scripting languages to fully integrated graphical tools. For example, many of today's commercial computer games ship with an editor for the creation of new levels, artifacts, or characters. However, authoring desktop 3D content meets only a subset of the requirements of authoring for AR. Moreover, we have to distinguish authoring solutions targeted at a specific purpose, such as a particular game or application, from general purpose authoring solutions.

3D Modeling and Scripting

The first attempts to support rapid prototyping for 3D graphics were based on text file formats and scripting languages such as Open Inventor (Strauss & Carey, 1992), VRML (VRML Consortium, 1997), or X3D (Web3D Consortium, 2005). New types of objects and behaviors can only be added by implementing them in C++ and compiling them to native code. While scriptable frameworks represent an improvement in the workflow of programmers, who can create application prototypes without the need to compile code, they do not offer the necessary concepts and abstractions for controlling an application's temporal structure and interactive behavior, and provide no built-in support for AR/VR devices. Platforms like Avango (Tramberend, 1999) or *Studierstube* (Schmalstieg et al., 2002) add the necessary classes to such frameworks to support the creation of AR/VR applications. However, from the perspective of an author the power of these frameworks further complicates matters rather than providing the required level of abstraction.

Among the tools targeted towards beginners, the Alice system (Conway, Pausch, Gossweiler, & Burnette, 1994) is particularly noteworthy. It was designed as a tool to introduce novice programmers to 3D graphics programming. Alice comes with its own scene editor and an extensive set of scripting commands, but is clearly targeted at an educational setting. For creating "real world" applications, the reusability and modularity of Alice is insufficient. Also, Alice focuses on animation and behavior control of individual objects and does not offer any high-level concepts for application control.

Application Specific Authoring

Another set of authoring solutions provides high-level support for AR/VR, but concentrates on providing optimal support for a particular domain, or within the bounds of a specific host application. One example is the Virtual Reality Slide Show system (VRSS) (Fuhrmann, Prikryl, Tobler, & Purgathofer, 2001), which provides a set of high-level concepts for authoring through a collection of Python macros. VRSS draws inspiration from conventional slide shows, and provides the concepts necessary to the user when creating similar slide shows within a VR environment.

Powerspace (Haringer & Regenbrecht, 2002) allows users to use Microsoft Powerpoint to create conventional 2D slides, which are then converted to 3D presentations by a converter script. These slide shows can be further refined in an editor that allows the adjustment of the spatial arrangement of the objects of the application, as well as the import of 3D models into the slides. Clearly, the Powerspace system is limited by the capabilities of the Powerpoint software and the slideshow concept, but it offers an interesting perspective on integrating pre-existing content into the Augmented Reality domain.

The Geist project (Kretschmer et al., 2001) aims at the presentation of historical and cultural information for mobile AR users roaming a city. The Geist engine builds on a detailed analysis of drama theory and interactive storytelling and provides several runtime modules to support applications based on these concepts. Using Prolog, authors can create semiotic functions that drive the story. Virtual characters that are controlled by an expert system demonstrate compelling conversational and emotional behavior. While this approach is very general and powerful, it can only reveal its full potential in fairly complex applications, incorporating dynamic behavior of multiple real and virtual actors, and hence requires a correspondingly high effort in content creation.

The situated documentaries application developed at Columbia University has similar goals for mobile AR users, but uses a more straightforward hypermedia approach towards content authoring. The hypermedia narratives are bound to locations in an outdoor environment, and can be browsed by the user by roaming the environment. The researchers have developed a custom visual editor for situated documentaries (Güven & Feiner, 2003), allowing them to implement an authoring paradigm tailored to the needs of their system. While the visual editor looks very promising, the underlying hypermedia system limits the scope of possible applications.

The need for an additional abstraction layer to support hybrid setups and AR specific features has been recognized by some researchers. For example, AMIRE provides a component model for authoring and playback of AR applications. On top of the AMIRE system, a graphical authoring tool for AR assembly instructions has been created (Zauner et al., 2003). However, this tool is limited to the domain of step-by-step instructions for assembly tasks. A similar approach is taken by researchers at Fraunhofer IGD (Knöpfle, Weidenhausen, Chauvigne, & Stock, 2005), who present a graphical editor for describing AR support for car maintenance procedures.

General Purpose AR/VR Authoring

There are few systems that support authoring (as opposed to programming) for general purpose AR/VR. An initial inspiration for the work presented in this paper is alVRed (Beckhaus, Lechner, Mostafawy, Trogemann, & Wages, 2002) developed Fraunhofer IMK. The alVRed project is an authoring solution which uses a hierarchical state machine to model the temporal structure of VR applications. In their model, a state represents a scene of the application, while the transitions between states represent changes in the application triggered by user interaction. alVRed provides a runtime engine built on top of the Avango environment (Tramberend, 1999) for executing the state machines, as well as a number of editors for supporting various stages of content creation. Particularly interesting is an editor for fine-tuning graphics and animation parameters from within an immersive projection environment. The one area not adequately addressed by alVRed encompasses key AR requirements such as interaction abstraction and multi-user operation.

The designers augmented reality toolkit (DART) (MacIntyre, Gandy, Dow, & Bolter, 2004) developed at GeorgiaTech is built on commercial software: DART extends Macromedia Director, the premier authoring tool for creating classical screen based multimedia applications. DART allows design students who are already familiar with Director to quickly create compelling AR applications, often using sketches and video based content rather than 3D models as a starting point. Director is an extremely versatile platform used by an extensive community of multimedia developers for a large variety of applications, and these properties are inherited by the DART plug-in. However, DART is ultimately limited by the technical constraints of Director, such as inadequate support for 3D models, stereoscopic rendering, optical see-through displays or multi-user applications.

Finally, the distributed wearable augmented reality framework (DWARF) (MacWilliams et al., 2003) deserves mentioning, although it is not strictly an authoring solution. DWARF is a strongly component-oriented middleware, composed of communicating objects. A graphical monitor program allows convenient inspection and remote control of the components. DWARF's dynamic reconfiguration capabilities allow the developers to replace software components and restart parts of an application on the fly without re-starting the whole system. This is exceptional insofar as it pertains to a distributed multi-user system with full hardware abstraction capabilities rather than a single computer authoring workplace.

The APRIL Language

APRIL, the augmented reality presentation and interaction language, covers all aspects of AR authoring defined in the requirements analysis. APRIL provides elements to describe the hardware setup, including displays and tracking devices, as well as the content of the application and its temporal organization and interactive capabilities. Rather then developing APRIL from scratch, we built the authoring and playback facilities on top of our existing *Studierstube* runtime system. However, it should be possible to use other runtime platforms for playing back applications created using our framework.

We decided to create an XML-based language for expressing all aspects needed to create compelling interactive AR content. This language acts as the "glue-code" between those parts where we could use existing content formats. XML was chosen for three reasons: It is a widely used standard for describing structural data, allows the incorporation of other text or XML based file formats into documents, and offers a wide range of tools that operate on XML data, such as parsers, validators, or XSLT transformations.

Enumerating all elements and features that APRIL provides is beyond the scope of this chapter. Interested readers are referred to Ledermann (2004), where detailed information and the APRIL schema specification can be found. In this chapter, we focus on the illustration of the main concepts of the APRIL language and an analysis of the implications of our approach. Whenever references to concrete APRIL element names are made, these will be set in typewriter letters.

Overview

The main aspects that contribute to an application are encapsulated in four top-level elements —setup, cast, story, behaviors, and interactions—that can be easily exchanged, allowing customization of the application for different purposes (Figure 2).

Figure 2. Main components of APRIL

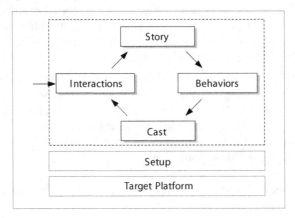

The *story* is an explicit representation of the temporal structure of the application, composed of individual *scenes*. In each scene, a predefined sequence of *behaviors* is executed by *actors*, which are instances of reusable components which expose certain fields for input and output. The transitions that advance the story from one scene to the next are triggered by user interaction, potentially provided by interaction components.

The decision to have a central storyboard controlling the application was made in full knowledge of other agent-centric approaches, where the overall behavior of an application is the result of emergent behaviors of one or more autonomous agents. In contrast to other applications, for our AR applications we want the results to be predictable and easily controllable by a human author. Hence, a single central instance of a storyboard seemed best suited to model such an application. In addition, a central storyboard is a valuable document for discussing ideas and monitoring the progress of a larger project involving multiple collaborating authors.

The hardware setup provides a layer of abstraction that hides details of the underlying hardware setup from the user. Using different hardware description files, applications can be run on different hardware setups without changing their content.

Stages, Scenes, and Actors

The two fundamental dimensions, along which an application is organized, have already been mentioned: temporal organization, determining the visibility and behavior of the objects of the application over time, and spatial organization, determining the location and size of these objects in relation to the viewer.

We call all objects that are subject to this organization, and therefore make up an application's content, actors. An actor may have a geometric representation, like a virtual object or a character that interacts with the user, but it could also be a sound or video clip or even some abstract entity that controls the behavior of other actors. APRIL allows nesting of actors, such that a single actor can represent a group of other actors that can be moved or otherwise controlled simultaneously. Each actor is an instance of a component that has a collection of input and output fields allowing reading and writing of typed values. Details of the APRIL component model will be explained.

When we refer to the behavior of an actor, we mean the change of the fields of the actor over time. Aspects of the behavior can be defined in advance by the author by arranging field changes on a timeline, parts of which will be dynamic, determined by user interaction at runtime.

We decided to use UML state charts to model applications, a formalism that has been used successfully by other projects like alVRed and for which professional graphical modeling tools exist. UML state charts can be hierarchical and concurrent, meaning that a state can contain sub-states, and there might be several states active at the same time (Figure 3). Each state represents a scene in the APRIL model, and has three timelines associated with it: The enter timeline is guaranteed to execute when the scene is entered, the do timeline is executed as long as the scene remains active (this means that behaviors on that timeline are not guaranteed to be executed and can be interrupted whenever the scene is left), and the exit timeline, which is executed as soon as a transition to the next scene is triggered. On each of the timelines, field changes of actors can be arranged by setting or animating the field to a new value.

The temporal organization of applications can borrow from pre-existing concepts already used for developing virtual reality content. However, the spatial organization of content in an AR application differs from existing approaches. In VR applications, typically a single scene is rendered for all users, while one of the specific strengths of Augmented Reality systems is to provide multiple users with different views on the world. Even for a single-

Figure 3. The storyboard of a simple APRIL application, modeled as a UML state diagram; for the "introduction" scene, the three timelines enter, do, and exit are emphasized

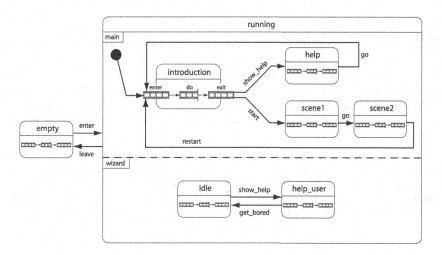

user AR system, there may be several "realities" that are simultaneously viewed: the real world and corresponding registered computer generated overlays, user interface elements like head up displays (HUDs) or interaction panels, world in miniature (Stoakley, Conway, & Pausch, 1995) for navigation or scenes rendered-to-texture for use as a 2D information display, and so on.

In APRIL, the top-level spatial containers for the content of an application are called stages. For each stage, authors can not only define spatial relationships with respect to the world and to other stages, but also the rendering technique used (e.g., three-dimensional or as a texture on a flat surface) and the association of stages with certain displays (to provide "private" content for particular users). By default, actors appear on the main stage, the area that is aligned with the real world. Interaction objects can be placed on interaction stages, where they will be rendered depending on the setup, for example as a HUD or as an interaction panel.

Stages require a coupling between the individual hardware setup and the application—the available stages are different for each setup, and therefore have to be defined in the hardware description. If these stages were simply referenced in the application (e.g., by name), the portability of the application would be reduced, because the application could then only be run on similar setups with the same number of stages. To overcome this problem, the concept of roles has been introduced. Each stage is assigned one (or more) roles from a predefined set that describe the function of a particular stage. These roles are tokens, for example, MAIN would identify the world stage that is visible to all users, UI_ALL the user interface stage for all users, UI1 the user interface of the primary user and so on. Actors can then be assigned to a list of stages, and the runtime system would look for the first stage on the list that is available on the target platform. If none of the substitution possibilities is available, a warning message is generated and the corresponding content is not displayed.

Another type of content specific to AR applications is the real world. Usually, for more advanced applications, some sort of world model is required, for calculating occlusions between real objects and virtual ones, or to be able to render content that is projected onto real world objects correctly. APRIL provides the `world` element as a container for geometry of the real world. The geometry can be obtained by careful modeling or by scanning the objects with a 3D scanner.

Hardware Abstraction

Flexibility in AR authoring requires separation of the content of the application from all aspects that depend on the actual system that the application will run on. However, the mapping from the hardware-dependent layer to the application must be sufficiently expressive to allow the application to make full use of the hardware features like tracking devices or displays.

APRIL allows all hardware aspects to be placed into a separate setup description file and supports the running of an application on different setups each with their respective setup description files. Each of these files contain XML code that describes the arrangement of computers, displays, pointing and other interaction devices that the system is composed of, and the definition of stages and input devices that will be available in the application.

Each computer that is part of the setup is represented by a corresponding host element, that defines the name and IP-address of that host, and the operating system and AR platform that runs on that machine. For each display, a display element carries information about its size and the geometry of the virtual camera generating the image. For configuring tracking devices, we use the existing OpenTracker configuration language (Reitmayr & Schmalstieg, 2001), that is simply included in the APRIL file by using a namespace for OpenTracker elements. OpenTracker allows the definition of tracking sources and a filter graph for transforming and filtering tracking data. Rather than reinventing a similar technology, we decided to directly include the OpenTracker elements into the APRIL setup description files.

OpenTracker only defines tracking devices and their relations, but not the meaning of the tracking data for the application. In APRIL, OpenTracker elements are used inside appropriate APRIL elements to add semantics to the tracking data: headtracking or displaytracking elements inside a display element contain OpenTracker elements that define the tracking of the user's head or the display surface for the given display, pointer elements define pointing devices that are driven by the tracking data, and station elements define general-purpose tracking input that can be used by the application.

Pointing at objects and regions in space plays a central role in Augmented Reality applications, and several techniques have been developed to allow users to perform pointing tasks under various constraints. APRIL provides the pointer element to define a pointing device, allowing the author to choose from several pointing techniques. The simplest case would be a pointing device that operates in world space. Other applications have used a ray-picking technique, using a "virtual laser pointer" to select objects at a distance. Some techniques work only in combination with a display, such as performing ray-picking that originates from the eye point of the user, effectively allowing her to use 2D input to select objects in space. These pointers can only be used in conjunction with a specific display and are placed inside the corresponding display element.

Stages, the top-level spatial containers for the application's content, are also defined in the setup description file. A stage can be defined inside a display element, in which case the content of the stage will only be visible on that specific display. Content placed in stages that are defined at the top level of the configuration file is publicly visible for all users. For each stage, it is possible to choose whether the content should be rendered in 3D or as a 2D texture, and whether it should be positioned relative to the global world coordinate system or located at a fixed offset from the display surface.

Figure 4 lists an example hardware configuration file for a single-host setup using a pointer and four stages.

Component Model

As stated in the requirements, the content of APRIL applications should be assembled from reusable components. Components should be defined outside the application, in individual files, to allow for re-use across applications and setups.

As these components constitute the content of our applications, sophisticated means to express geometry and multimedia content will be needed. Instead of creating a new XML-based syntax for defining these objects, another approach has been chosen, which is loosely

Figure 4. Example hardware description file

```
<april XMLns="http://www.Studierstube.org/april"
       XMLns:ot="http://www.Studierstube.org/opentracker">
  <setup>
    <host name="mobile" ip="10.0.0.77" hwPlatform="Linux">
      <screen resolution="1280 1024"/>
      <screen resolution="1024 768"/>
      <display screen="1" screenSize="fullscreen" stereo="true"
        worldSize="-0.4 0.3" worldPosition="0.098 0.162 0"
        worldOrientation="-0.1856 0.9649 0.1857 1.6057" mode="AR">
        <headtracking>
          <ot:EventVirtualTransform translation="0.00 0.20 0.01">
          <ot:NetworkSource number="1" multicast-addr="10.0.0.7" port="12345"/>
          </ot:EventVirtualTransform>
        </headtracking>
        <stage role="WIM1" type="3D" location="DISPLAY" scaleToFit="true"
               translation="0 -0.5 0" scale="0.5 0.5 0.5"/>
        <stage role="UI1" type="2D" location="DISPLAY" scaleToFit="true"/>
        <pointer mode="2D-RAY"/>
      </display>
      <station id="tool">
        <ot:NetworkSource number="2" multicast-addr="10.0.0.7" port="12345"/>
      </station>
    </host>
    <stage role="WIM_COMMON" type="3D" location="WORLD" scaleToFit="true"
           translation="1.3 2.9 0.75" size="0.5 0.5 0.5"/>
    <stage role="MAIN" type="3D" location="WORLD"/>
  </setup>
</april>
```

inspired by the VRML97 EXTERNPROTO concept (VRML Consortium, 1997). An APRIL component is basically a template, using any existing, text based "host language" to express the intended content, plus additional XML markup to define the interface of the component, a collection of inputs and outputs that will be accessible from the APRIL application. The chosen content format must be supported by the target runtime platform. Therefore, it is necessary to provide multiple implementations, sharing the same interface, in different formats to support different runtime platforms. The APRIL component mechanism itself is platform independent and can make use of any host language.

Using a platform specific language for content definition reduces portability of components, but makes all features and optimizations of a given platform available to developers. We considered creating a platform-neutral content definition language that could only use a set of features supported by all platforms, which would however preclude the creation of sophisticated content that uses state-of-the-art real time rendering features.

An APRIL component definition file consists of two main parts: the components interface definition, and one or multiple implementations. A component's interface is composed of the available input and output fields, and the specification of possible sub-components (called parts) that can be added to the component. This interface definition is shared across all implementations, and defines the features of the component that are available for scripting in APRIL.

A component can have multiple implementations in different host languages—the software used for playing the APRIL application will choose the most suitable implementation. Therefore, authors can provide different implementations for different runtime systems, for example to provide a simpler implementation to be run on handheld computers. Each implementation contains the code for implementing the component's behavior in the chosen

Figure 5. Definition of the "model" component, used to load geometry from an external file (Simplified for demonstrational purposes)

```
<component id="model" XMLns="http://www.Studierstube.org/april">
  <interface>
    <field id="position" type="SFVec3f" default="0.0 0.0 0.0"/>
    <field id="visible" type="SFBool" default="TRUE"/>
    <input id="src" type="SFString" const="true"/>
    <part id="children"/>
  </interface>
  <implementation swPlatform="OpenInventor">
DEF <id/> Separator {
    DEF <id/>_Switch Switch {
        whichChild = DEF <id/>_Bool BoolOperation { # convert from Bool to Int32
            a <in id="visible"/>
            operation A
        }.output
        Group {} # Dummy Child for switching off
        Group { # actual content
            DEF <id/>_Transform Transform {
                translation <in id="position"/>
            }
            Separator {
                SoFileSubgraph { fileName <in id="src"/>}
            }
            <sub id="children"/>
        }
    }
}
    <out id="position"><id/>_Transform.translation</out>
    <out id="visible"><id/>_Bool.a</out>
  </implementation>
</component>
```

host language, where the inputs and outputs used in the interface definition are marked with special XML marker elements, to indicate the language-specific entry points for setting and retrieving values from the component's fields. Figure 5 shows a simple example component, containing the interface definition and a single implementation section for Open Inventor based frameworks (such as *Studierstube*).

Application Control and Interaction

As explained previously, each scene of the storyboard contains three timelines that are executed upon entering, execution and leaving the scene respectively. On these timelines, commands can be arranged to change the inputs of the application's actors. The two basic commands to change a field value are set and animate, that allow the author to set a field to a predefined value or to interpolate the value of the field over a given time span.

For more dynamic behavior of the application, the input of an actor can be connected to the output of another actor, or the control over a field value can be given to the user. In this case, either a pointing device can be referenced to provide the input, or a suitable user interface element is generated to control the value of the field. The connection or control possibility lasts as long as the state in which these behaviors are specified is active, so no elements for disconnecting and releasing control are needed.

The transitions between scenes are mapped to user interactions. APRIL provides built-in high-level user interactions, such as displaying a button on user interaction stages that triggers a transition when clicked (defined by the buttonaction element), or detecting the intersection of a pointer with the geometry of an actor (by using the touch element). APRIL also provides the pseudo-interactions timeout, always, and disabled, to automatically trigger or disable certain transitions.

Customized user interaction can be realized by defining a condition that must be met to trigger the transition with the evaluator element. For these conditions, an output field of an actor can be compared to a constant value, or to another output. With this element, it is possible to realize complex user interactions by providing a component that encapsulates the user interface and the necessary calculations to trigger a transition.

Since all interactions are defined within the interactions top-level element, they can be easily exchanged. This process, called interaction mapping, can be used to derive different versions of the same application, suiting different needs. For example, a non-interactive version of an application, using only timeout transitions to linearly step through the application, can be provided for demo purposes, while a fully interactive version of the same application is run in user sessions.

Implementation

Rather than implementing a runtime platform that reads and executes APRIL files directly, we adopted a translation approach which transforms the APRIL source files into the necessary configuration files for our *Studierstube* framework, which runs on PCs and PDAs.

Because of the powerful capabilities of *Studierstube*, we can support high-level concepts with very little implementation effort for the APRIL specific runtime system. An implementation of a generic state-engine that controls the application at runtime according to the storyboard was implemented as an extension node, and a few utility classes were added to the *Studierstube* API. Most of the high-level concepts were however implemented by introducing a pre-processing step of the APRIL files, implemented in XSLT.

XSLT is a template-based language for transforming XML documents into other, text-based document types. One or multiple input files can be processed in a non-linear fashion, generating arbitrary numbers of output files. XSLT is most often used to generate HTML pages from XML specification documents, or to transform and aggregate a collection of XML documents into other XML documents.

A typical *Studierstube* application consists of a number of input files—the application's content, tracking configuration, display configuration and user information are all stored in separate files, even for single user setups. One of the motivations that led to the development of APRIL is that, even in moderately complex setups, these files get quite large, and it is increasingly hard for the application developer to keep the information in the files consistent. In the APRIL preprocessing step, these files are generated by XSLT, using the information that is stored in the APRIL file in a concise way.

Figure 6. Schematic view of the APRIL transformation process

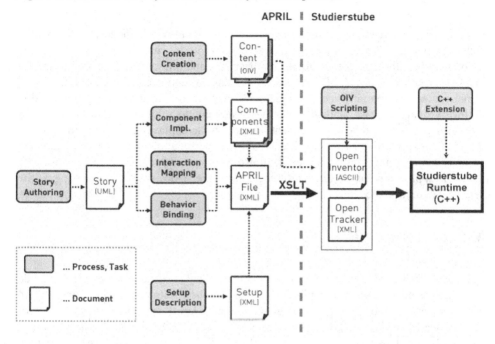

A schematic overview of this transformation process is shown in Figure 6. The story specification together with the corresponding interaction and behavior definitions constitutes the core of the APRIL application. Third party professional tools for content creation (for example, Maya for 3D modeling, Photoshop for image editing, and Poseidon UML for state chart editing) are employed to create the input files.

Components, defined in separate files for reusability, are included in the application and content like geometry or sound samples are included in their native file formats. At the time of the XSLT processing, the setup description file of the target platform is loaded, and the set of associated files is transformed into the necessary Open Inventor and OpenTracker files that serve as input for the *Studierstube* runtime.

Figure 6 also shows where human intervention in the APRIL authoring process is supported. APRIL transforms the approach to AR application authoring from a technology-oriented workflow that can only be performed by programmers—implementing extensions in C++ and scripting the application logic on a low level of abstraction–to an authoring-centric view, allowing a smooth workflow and the distribution of tasks between different domain experts contributing to the application. This workflow is also much more scalable from single individuals who create an entire application to entire teams of collaborating professionals, using the storyboard as a central artifact for communication to contribute at different levels to the final result.

Results

Over the past two years, we have created several applications with the help of the APRIL authoring platform. We already used the example of furniture construction described in the introduction to illustrate the requirements of an AR authoring solution. Other examples that have been realized with APRIL, both by our students and in collaboration with professional content creators, include a "Magic book" application, an archaeology presentation for the "Virtual showcase" and an interactive sightseeing tour through our institute, guided by a virtual companion. We will present the tour guide application in detail to illustrate the practical application of APRIL. It exemplifies encapsulation of independent, complex systems and communication between them using components and fields, and shows how the same application can be run on different hardware setups simply by exchanging the setup configuration file.

Virtual Tour Guide

The Virtual Tour Guide application embeds a virtual animated character acting as a tour guide into a mobile indoor navigation application called Signpost (Reitmayr & Schmalstieg, 2003). The user wears a mobile AR setup integrated into a backpack and a helmet, and perceives the augmented world through a head-mounted display (HMD). A camera mounted above the HMD tracks fiducials placed onto walls of the building area covered by the application. The markers help locate the user within this area since the system knows their exact position in a precisely measured virtual model of the building that has been registered with its real counterpart.

The virtual tour guide character is placed into the reference frame of the real building. While walking around, the character provides assistance to find selected destinations and provides location-specific explanation about the content of various rooms and people working in them using body gestures (e.g., gaze direction, pointing, asking the user to follow, etc.), 2D and 3D visual elements and sound. Since the tour guide is aware of the building geometry, it appears to walk up real stairs and go through real doors and walkways, thus further enhancing integrity with the user's physical environment.

The tour guide character is controlled by the AR Puppet framework (Barakonyi, Psik, Schmalstieg, 2004) that is a hierarchical character animation system enabling the use of embodied animated agents in AR applications. Both AR Puppet and the Signpost navigation application are large systems with a complex network of internal modules responsible for various subtasks, therefore it is difficult and undesirable to modify their internal structure in order to establish communication between them. Relying on the APRIL framework's component model and turning AR Puppet and Signpost into custom APRIL components enables the encapsulation of these frameworks' functionality. These components can be used as black boxes by content authors that expose relevant input and output fields for communication with other, external components while hiding internal implementation details. Figure 7 illustrates the fields exposed by Signpost and monitored by AR Puppet to provide the tour guide character with relevant navigation information.

Figure 7. Communication between the AR Puppet and Signpost systems within the APRIL framework

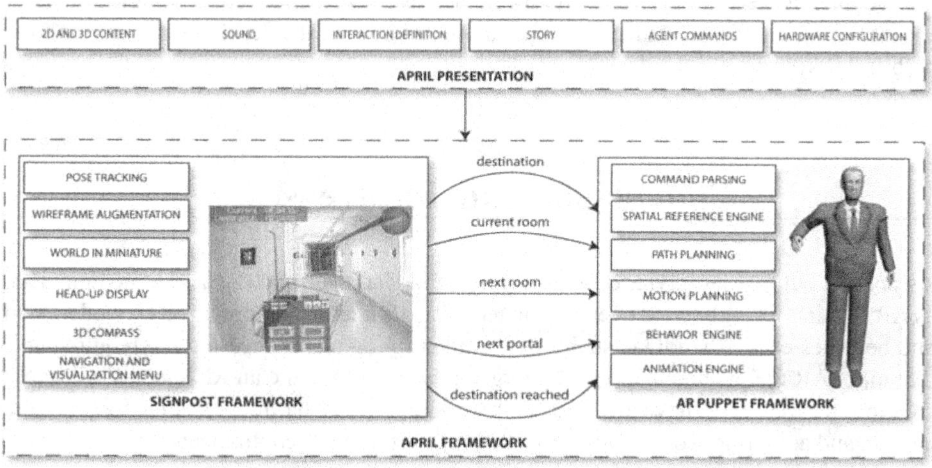

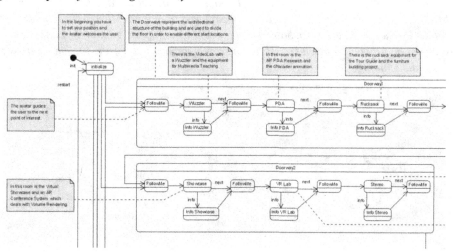

The tour itself is modeled by the APRIL storyboard as a UML state engine. A small part of the complete state engine is shown in Figure 10. Individual stations of the guided tour are modeled as states, triggering linear presentations when the user arrives. The structure of the building and the different modes for the guided tour (linear or free mode) are modeled by transitions and superstates.

The expensive and bulky mobile AR system required by the Signpost application in its original form makes content and application authoring, debugging and testing a difficult task, therefore we needed to develop a desktop simulator system that is able to run the same navigation application with simple keyboard input and screen based output. The hardware

Figure 8. A part of the tour guide storyboard

abstraction feature of APRIL conveniently hides details such as the type of display or exact tracking setup from authors and components. Only symbolic names are used, thus allowing the internal details of different hardware setups to be exchanged. See Figure 9 for an illustration of the virtual tour guide application running on the desktop simulator and the mobile AR system.

Conclusion and Future Work

As pointed out by MacIntyre, Bolter, Moreno, and Hannigan (2001), a new medium such as AR requires effort beyond overcoming technical difficulties before it is truly understood and becomes established. One such effort is identifying and addressing the requirements that make AR unique and that must be targeted in order to make an AR specific authoring solution successful. We have identified real-world interfaces, hardware abstraction, runtime engine, and authoring workflow tools as the most prominent requirements.

Previous work has only partially addressed these requirements, or has been limited to a specific application domain or software platform. APRIL is also limited in some respects, in particular it completely relies on third party graphical editors for compiling the content, and its current XSLT-based implementation only provides limited support for runtime reconfigurability. However, when applied to a number of application design problems, we have found that it combines the high level authoring concepts also found in DART and alVRed in a very comprehensive way with the technical virtues of flexible component systems such as DWARF and AMIRE. It can therefore cater to a wide audience ranging from artists to engineers, and provides good support for multi-disciplinary teams.

The XSLT-based reference implementation, using the *Studierstube* framework, provides templates for the implementation of the APRIL features. We found that these templates not

Figure 9. (a) The indoor tour guide application running on the desktop developer setup (b) The indoor tour guide application view captured from the HMD of a user wearing the mobile AR backpack system; in both setups a world-in-miniature view of the building model is shown and location-dependent HUD overlay graphics is presented to the user as she roams the building

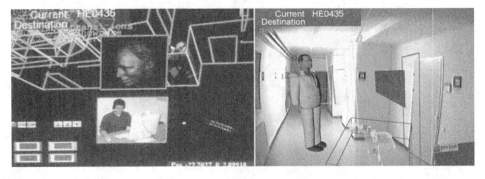

only provide a working implementation of APRIL, but implicitly document best practices for implementing common AR design patterns on top of the framework.

Having developed a description language and runtime engine, the next step is to concentrate on front-end tools for the interactive visual creation of AR applications. It will be challenging to examine whether such a tool proves more productive than using a conventional 2D user interfaces or direct manipulation in AR in a style similar to Lee, Nelles, Billinghurst, and Kim (2004).

Another interesting perspective is the automatic generation of APRIL presentations. While previously this required detailed knowledge of the target application framework to be able to create the complex, interdependent files necessary for a non-trivial application, APRIL provides the high level of abstraction that allows the content for an application to be auto-generated by software. This opens up possibilities of using large amounts of existing content (e.g., in museums) in an Augmented Reality context with little manual effort.

Acknowledgments

The authors would like to thank Gerhard Reitmayr for valuable suggestions throughout the development of APRIL and Joe Newman for proofreading this chapter. Licenses of the Maya software were donated by Alias Systems. This research was funded in part by EU contract #IST-2000-28610, FWF contract #Y193 and bm:bwk contract #TUWP16/2001.

References

Barakonyi, I., Psik, T., & Schmalstieg, D. (2004). Agents that talk and hit back: Animated agents in augmented reality. In *Proceedings of the IEEE and ACM International Symposium on Mixed and Augmented Reality 2004*, Arlington, VA (pp. 141-150).

Beckhaus, S., Lechner, A., Mostafawy, S., Trogemann, G., & Wages, R (2002). alVRed: Tools for storytelling in virtual environments. *Internationale Statustagung Virtuelle und Erweiterete Realität*. Leipzig, Germany.

Billinghurst, M., Kato, H., & Poupyrev, I. (2001). The Magic-Book—moving seamlessly between reality and virtuality. *IEEE Computer Graphics and Applications, 21*(3), 6-8.

Bimber, O., Fröhlich, B., Schmalstieg, & D., Encarnacao, L. M. (2001). The virtual showcase. *IEEE Computer Graphics and Applications, 21*(6), 48-55.

Conway, M., Pausch, R., Gossweiler, R., & Burnette, T. (1994). Alice: A rapid prototyping system for building virtual environments. In *Proceedings of ACM CHI '94 Conference on Human Factors in Computing Systems* (Vol. 2, pp. 295-296).

Fuhrmann A., Prikryl, J., Tobler, R., & Purgathofer, W. (2001). Interactive content for presentations in virtual reality. In *Proceedings of the ACM Symposium on Virtual Reality Software & Technology*, Baniff, Alberta, Canada (pp. 183-189).

Güven, S., & Feiner, S. (2003). Authoring 3D hypermedia for wearable augmented and virtual reality. In *Proceedings of the 7th International Symposium on Wearable Computers*, White Plains, NY (pp. 118-126).

Haringer, M., & Regenbrecht, H. (2002). A pragmatic approach to Augmented Reality authoring. In *Proceedings of ISMAR 2002*, Darmstadt, Germany (pp. 237-245).

Knöpfle, C., Weidenhausen, J., Chauvigne, L., & Stock, I. (2005). Template based authoring for AR based service scenarios. In *Proceedings of IEEE Virtual Reality 2005*, Bonn, Germany (pp. 237-240).

Kretschmer, U., Coors, V., Spierling, U., Grasbon, D., Schneider, K., Rojas, I., & Malaka, R. (2001). Meeting the spirit of history. In *Proceedings of the 2001 Conference on Virtual Reality, Archeology, and Cultural Heritage*, Athens, Greece (pp. 141-152).

Ledermann, F. (2004). *An authoring framework for augmented reality presentations*. Master's thesis, Vienna University of Technology.

Lee, G., Nelles, C., Billinghurst, M., & Kim, G. (2004). Immersive authoring of tangible augmented reality applications. In *Proceedings of the IEEE and ACM International Symposium on Mixed and Augmented Reality 2004*, Arlington, VA (pp. 172-181).

MacIntyre, B., Bolter, J., Moreno, E., & Hannigan, B. (2001). Augmented Reality as a new media experience. In *Proceedings International Symposium on Augmented Reality 2001*, New York (pp. 197-206).

MacIntyre, B., Gandy, M., Dow, S., & Bolter, J. (2004). DART: A toolkit for rapid design exploration of Augmented Reality experiences. In *Proceedings of User Interface Software and Technology (UIST'04)*, Sante Fe, NM (pp. 197-206).

MacWilliams, A., Sandor, C., Wagner, M., Bauer, M., Klinker, G., & Bruegge, B. (2003). Herding sheep: Live system development for distributed Augmented Reality. In *Proceedings International Symposium on Mixed and Augmented Reality 2003*, Tokyo, Japan (p. 123).

Navab, N. (2004). Developing killer apps for industrial Augmented Reality. *IEEE Computer Graphics and Applications, 24*, 16-20.

Regenbrecht, H., Baratoff, G., & Wilke, W. (2005). Augmented reality projects in the automotive and aerospace industries. *IEEE Computer Graphics and Applications, 25*, 48-56.

Reitmayr, G., & Schmalstieg, D. (2001). OpenTracker: An open software architecture for reconfigurable tracking based on XML. In *Proceedings of IEEE Virtual Reality 2001*, Yokohama, Japan (pp. 285-286).

Reitmayr, G., & Schmalstieg, D. (2003). Location based applications for mobile augmented reality. In *Proceedings of the 4th Australasian User Interface Conference*, Adelaide, Australia (pp. 65-73).

Schmalstieg D., Fuhrmann, A., Hesina, G., Szalavari, Z., Encarnacao, L. M., Gervautz, M., & Purgathofer, W. (2002). The Studierstube augmented reality project. *PRESENCE: Teleoperators and Virtual Environments, 11*(1).

Stoakley, R., Conway, M., & Pausch, R. (1995). Virtual reality on a WIM: Interactive worlds in miniature. In *Proceedings on Human Factors in Computing Systems*, Denver, CO (pp. 265-272).

Strauss, P., & Carey, R. (1992). An object oriented 3D graphics toolkit. In *Proceedings of the 19th Annual Conference on Computer Graphics and Interactive Techniques* (pp. 341-349).

Tramberend, H. (1999). Avocado: A distributed virtual reality framework. In *Proceedings of IEEE Virtual Reality 1999* (p. 14).

VRML Consortium. (1997). *VRML97 specification.* Specification 147721:1997, ISO/IEC.

Web3D Consortium. (2005). *X3D specification Web site.* Retrieved from http://www.web3d.org/x3d/specifications/

Webster, A., Feiner, S., MacIntyre, B., Massie, B., & Krueger, T. (1996). Augmented reality in architectural construction, inspection, and renovation. In *Proceedings of the 3rd ASCE Congress for Computing in Civil Engineering,* Anaheim, CA.

Zauner, J., Haller, M., & Brandl, A.. (2003). Authoring of a mixed reality assembly instructor for hierarchical structures. In *Proceedings of ISMAR 2003*, Tokyo, Japan (pp. 237-246).

Chapter VIII

Supporting Early Design Activities for AR Experiences

Maribeth Gandy, Georgia Institute of Technology, USA

Blair MacIntyre, Georgia Institute of Technology, USA

Steven Dow, Georgia Institute of Technology, USA

Jay David Bolter, Georgia Institute of Technology, USA

Abstract

In this chapter, we describe DART: the designer's augmented reality toolkit, an authoring environment for rapidly prototyping augmented reality experiences. We summarize the most significant problems faced by designers working with AR in the real world, and use DART as the example to guide a discussion of the AR design process which we have broken down into four stages (idea exploration, population of the virtual world, application development, and evaluation). The focus of our work with DART has been on supporting early design activities, especially a rapid transition from storyboards to working experience, so that the experiential part of a design can be tested early and often.

Introduction

Over the past few decades, augmented reality (AR) researchers (including ourselves) have explored a wide variety of task focused domains, ranging from equipment maintenance and repair to medicine to battlefield awareness. Over the past five years, we have also been collaborating with new media designers, shifting our thinking from "AR as technology" to "AR as medium," and turning our attention toward more experiential AR domains such as in-situ educational historic dramas, reflections on biased points of view in "Four Angry Men" (MacIntyre et al., 2003), and entertainment in "Alice's Adventures" (Moreno, MacIntyre, & Bolter, 2001). In this chapter, we use the term AR to refer to a broad class of user interface techniques that seek to augment a person's perception of the world around them with computer generated information, often using see-through head-worn displays to overlay graphics on the user's view of the world.

While there are significant technical challenges to creating working AR systems, these challenges can be overcome in specific situations through careful engineering and design. When working on a well-defined AR task, such as a printer maintenance system, it is feasible for a team of technology experts to work closely with design and human/computer interaction (HCI) experts to understand the particular problem and engineer a solution. Unfortunately, relying on collaboration between designers and technologists is problematic in less well-specified projects, where skilled designers are exploring a problem using AR as their medium. Designers are most effective when working directly with a medium, and working through an intermediary seriously hinders (or even destroys) the creative process. Consider the difference between a painter directing an assistant where to apply oil to a canvas, rather than holding the brush, or a 3D animator explaining to a programmer how a character should move, rather than manipulating the model directly. DART (the Designer's AR Toolkit) is the result of our collaborations with designers over the past four years, and is aimed at enabling them to work directly and effectively with AR (MacIntyre, Gandy, Dow, & Bolter, 2004). The design of DART addresses a collection of problems that, together, make AR a difficult medium to work with. DART is implemented on top of Macromedia Director, the de facto standard for multimedia content creation. Director was chosen because it is a powerful, widely used tool that is open and extensible, has a full-featured debugging and design environment, and is robust enough for final content delivery.

There are three major design goals for DART:

- **Support the entire design process:** Creating AR experiences can be difficult. The developer must handle the standard software development issues (e.g., performance, modularity, debugging) with the additional challenges of creating 3D content, working with technology such as cameras and trackers, and creating a compelling virtual experience that blends well with the physical world both literally and figuratively. In the past, the AR design process has been immature. The lack of tools and techniques has resulted in AR developers spending considerable time creating a single version of an experience that could not be evaluated (by users or even the developers themselves) until the content was created, the technology was in place, and the application was almost complete. As a result, the design of AR experiences has suffered since it was not possible to employ the kinds of rapid prototyping and iterative development techniques that are crucial to successful software design in other domains. Ironically, AR is a domain that is even more in need of early evaluation approaches due to the aforementioned complexities that are inherent in AR experiences. An AR design environment must have facilities that allow designers to brainstorm, test their ideas early and often, and evolve initial versions of the experience into the deployable system.

- **Provide a powerful, easy to use design environment:** Modern development environments (like Director) allow applications to be constructed using direct manipulation interfaces, support flexible content organization, and support the visual layout of applications to facilitate easy reconfiguration of the experience and the content. An AR design environment should use similar facilities to allow designers to rapidly replace content, and to flexibly switch between cameras, sensors, and other AR specific components.

- **Ameliorate the problems of working in the physical world:** Since AR experiences are situated in a particular space, designers are forced to develop and test their applications with the live hardware in the actual location. This is very limiting on the amount of testing and experimentation that a designer can do during development. Designers need to be able work away from the site of the AR experience, and to design experiences without having to first deploy the entire sensing infrastructure.

In the next section, we give a brief summary of related work in this domain followed by an overview of DART. Then in the following sections, we will use two DART applications to guide a discussion of the AR design process, how DART supports this process, and what our research has revealed about the requirements of AR authoring environments in general.

Related Work

Most work in the AR community has focused on improving tracking and display technology. There have been a number of AR toolkits developed over the years, such as Studierstube (Schmalstieg et al., 2002) the ARToolkit (Billinghurst, Bowskill, Jessop, & Morphett, 1998), Tinmith (Piekarski & Thomas, 2003), and DWARF (MacWilliams, Reicher, Klinker, & Bruegge, 2004). All of these tools require the application developer to work at a fairly low level, with languages like C or C++. None of these systems attempt to provide a designer focused prototyping environment, but instead are targeted at AR technologists. Of these, the most widely used is the ARToolkit, both because the technology requirements for using it are modest, allowing designers to explore AR using markers and VRML.

More recent projects have begun to tackle the other end of the design spectrum, exploring environments to simplify the creation of AR systems with minimal programming. APRIL[1] (a scripting environment built on Studierstube) is an XML-based language for authoring AR, but is still preliminary and does not yet provide the breadth or power of Director and Lingo. AMIRE is focused on creating graphical authoring tools for specific AR domains, rather than a general purpose environment. While certain applications can be more quickly developed in this tool, the designers are constrained to problems that the tool was designed to solve (Abawi, Dörner, Haller, & Zauner, 2004). CATOMIRE[2] is a graphical authoring environment that uses a dataflow approach, where their system components are hooked together with "wires." As with AMIRE, their system is currently very limited in scope, and would restrict designers to working on problems they have built components for.

Other relevant work can be found outside the AR community. The Phidget toolkit (Greenberg & Fitchett, 2001) aimed at making tangible devices available to designers, and solved some fundamental problems with prototyping beyond just "making it easy to get at the hardware." There have been numerous research systems created over the years to support the exploration of new electronic media by novice programmers with an eye toward developing better interface and programming technologies. The closest to our work is Alice (Pierce et al., 1997), although they are focused on lowering the threshold of entry into the world of 3D graphics and VR programming, rather than explicitly supporting early design activities. Most such systems took the approach of creating a custom programming environment, rather than enhancing an existing environment. The motivation for our sketch-based content comes from the work of Landay and his collaborators at CMU and Berkeley (e.g., Landay & Myers 2001). We hope to support designers in a similar manner, although their work focuses on doing so for more traditional applications.

Director and the DART Architecture

DART consists of a set of Lingo scripts and an Xtra plug-in that extends Macromedia Director to support the development of augmented, virtual, and mixed reality applications. We chose to develop on top of Director as it provides a very full featured development environment with an active developer community and cross platform support (Win and Mac/OSX). By leveraging the features that already existed in Director, including powerful 3D and physics engines, we have focused our efforts on integrating the necessary AR components with Director's programming model. The Director environment provides programmers with pre-built scripting components (in the Lingo scripting language) that can be used as they are, modified, or extended by the developer. All the scripts are open and editable, allowing a developer to easily create new components as needed.

The Xtra is a plug-in for Director written in C++. This plug-in adds low level AR related functionality into Director including video capture (from a variety of cameras), connection to virtual-reality peripheral network (VRPN)[3] sources (trackers, buttons, analogs and distributed shared memory objects), fast video-mixed AR via OpenGL, and marker tracking (ARToolkit and ARTag[4]).

The behavior scripts (written in Lingo) are part of the Director authoring environment and can be manipulated just like Director's built-in components. The DART scripts themselves are contained in a series of casts (the Director structure for organizing content for use in an application). These casts divide up the scripts into logical groups. The DART behaviors encapsulate the high level components that make up an AR application, and provide structured access to the various AR technologies. There are "actors" which represent the content of an application (3D models, sounds, text, lights, etc.) and a "3D camera" that represents the virtual camera in the 3D world. There are behaviors that connect into the functionality of the Xtra such as "live video" which configures the camera to be captured (for use in video-mixed AR applications), and "live trackers" which represent trackers (VRPN or marker) in the application. "Transforms" are placed on actors and 3D cameras to control their position, orientation, scale, and to define the parent/child relationships of the scene graph. Transforms can subscribe to trackers which form the connection between them and the objects in the application.

Interactivity in DART applications is achieved via a cue/action model. "Cues" are events that are fired when things happen in the application (e.g., the 3D camera reaches a certain position, an audio clip finishes playing, a timer reaches a defined value, a marker appears or disappears, etc.) "Actions" subscribe to cues and wait for them to occur. When the specified cue fires, the action will execute (e.g., start an animation on an object, move an Actor in the 3D world, change the volume on an audio clip, etc.)

The development of a DART application progresses, just as any Director application, by placing components on the Director score. To develop a DART application, you place scripts either on the 3D world sprite (provided with Director) or you place them in container sprites. When you place a script on the score it brings up a property page where you can configure the behavior. In this manner you can build up the parts of an AR application, placing container sprites on the score and filling them with the desired behavior scripts. For more advanced applications, the developer can simply edit code in the behavior scripts, add new scripts of her own, or copy an existing script to serve as a starting point for a new component. DART scripts and custom Lingo can be freely mixed together. DART applications can utilize all the standard Director components and Xtras.

DART and the AR Design Process

DART provides support for the entire AR design process from initial storyboarding and brain storming to evaluation, testing, and deployment of a finished experience. Throughout the process of developing DART and extending its features our focus has been on filling in the holes of the development process that are not currently supported. We have drawn on rapid prototyping concepts from ubiquitous computing such as wizard-of-oz testing and from the film domain for methods such as storyboard animatics.

The AR design process follows a similar progression as other media (e.g., the Web [Newman, Lin, Hong, & Landay, 2003], film [Katz, 1991], voice applications [Klemmer et al., 2001]), in that ideas move from informal, often sketch-based representations, to more concrete content and interactivity until a working application is complete. The iterative nature of any design process is not clear-cut and often returns back to early stages as constraints and user opinions are revealed. To guide our discussion of the features of DART and how they support the design process, we identify four general stages for AR design (Exploring Ideas, Populating the Virtual World, Developing the Application, and Evaluation and Deployment of the Application). We will illustrate DART's support for these stages with details from two DART applications: *Four Angry Men* and *The Voices of Oakland*.

Four Angry Men (FAM), shown in Figure 1, is the second version of our single-narrative, multiple point-of-view augmented reality experience, in which the viewer/user becomes a

Figure 1. A view of two of the virtual jurors of "Four Angry Men"

participant in an abridged version of the screenplay "Twelve Angry Men" (Rose, 1983). As with the first version (Three Angry Men [MacIntyre et al., 2003]), the user witnesses the drama from the viewpoint of one of four jurors, and her perception of the scene reflects the expectations, beliefs, and prejudices of that juror. The user sits in one chair in a physical space representing the jury room. Through the head-worn display, he or she can see three other virtual jurors (as texture-mapped video) occupying other chairs in the room. The user herself hears the words of the fourth juror (including his "inner thoughts"), whose seat he or she is occupying. At any time the user can get up, move to another chair, and assume the point of view (POV) of another juror

The Voices of Oakland (VOO), shown in Figure 2, uses AR technology to introduce visitors to the history and architecture of Oakland Cemetery, Atlanta's oldest cemetery (Dow et al., 2005). Wearing headphones and carrying a portable computer with tracking devices, the

Figure 2. A user experiencing "The Voices of Oakland"

visitors walk among the graves and listen to the voices of various historical figures. The visitors can tailor the experience to suit their interests through a hand-held interface.

In the following sections we use these examples from our own work to illustrate the evolution of an AR experience from initial idea to finished application, and the approaches we used in DART to address each step of the process.

Stage 1: Exploring Ideas

Being that AR applications are by definition *in situ*, it is important to begin the design process in the location where the experience will be situated. Focusing on ideas, concepts for the virtual content and user experience without incorporating the context of the space will result in more iterations and wasted work later in the process. Therefore, the first step is to gather information, both functional and aesthetic, to serve as a framework for the brain storming process.

The concept of video prototyping for early design exploration has been suggested for use in ubiquitous computing applications (Mackay, 1998). The designer takes video of a space with a video camera and then uses standard video editing tools to create a video mockup to illustrate what the finished application might look like to other members of the team or to users for early evaluation. A drawback of video prototypes is that they are tedious to create and once created it is not easy to swap out content or to visualize different scenarios. However, in the design of our AR experiences, we use this technique as it allows the designer to be completely technology agnostic and provides a mechanism for visualizing ideas relatively quickly.

Unfortunately, the effort and resources put into a video prototype does not reduce the amount of work needed to create a finished application, since the content is discarded once the initial design stage ends. To address this issue we have created a suite of services in DART that allow for the creation of early video prototypes that can be transformed into the final application as the design progresses.

Capture and Replay

Before the designer can begin experimenting with ideas, he or she must first gather data about the location where the experience will be situated. DART allows the designer to easily capture video as well as sensor and tracker data in a space. Any DART application can capture data by including "capture video" and "capture tracker" behaviors on the score. The capture function can be a fully functional AR experience, or it could be a bare bones application that simply records data. Captured data can be replayed in any DART application via the "playback tracker" and "playback video" behaviors. Since the designer can control the clock that drives a DART application the entire experience including captured data can be paused, rewound, and fast forwarded at run-time.

All of the captured data is stored into cast libraries, where it can be viewed and modified if necessary. During playback, a designer can choose to replay a certain portion of a captured data set, or they might mix/match data from several independent captures. When sensor data is played back, it is essentially fed back into the system as if it were a live sensor, allowing for swift replacement of live data with prerecorded data (and vice versa).

In the case of VOO (and in several other AR Design student projects situated in Oakland Cemetery), we began the design process by capturing video, GPS, and inertial sensor data in the cemetery. The designers simply walked through the space interacting in ways we thought would be relevant for the final experience (e.g., walking up to a certain head stone, looking a famous sculpture, etc.) Once the data was captured it could be used in a variety of ways in different stages of the design process.

Sketch Annotations and Video Prototyping

Sketched content is commonly used in pre-visualization to create animatics (animated story-boards, used during film and television pre-visualization [Katz, 1991]). Not only has sketched content been shown to be useful for rapid content creation, the use of sketches can enhance the design process by tacitly freeing people to suggest radical changes (Landay & Myers, 2001) and can convey more of the designer's intent than quickly created 3D content.

As a complement to the capture/playback infrastructure, we have created a DART component that allows for the creation and playback of sketch annotations overlaid on the scene (Presti, Gandy, MacIntyre, & Dow, 2005). Inspired by Pixar's Review Sketch (Wolff, 2004), this interface not only allows the AR designer to "draw" on top of the "real world" video, but also to generate virtual 3D objects from the 2D sketches.

This feature allows the designer to quickly get initial ideas into a concrete form. When the designer wishes to add a sketch on top of the scene, he or she pauses the playback in the application and draws whatever he or she wishes on the screen. When he or she is done, he or she simply starts up the replay again. Throughout the process, the images are saved along with

Figure 3. Sketch annotations drawn on top of captured video from Oakland Cemetery

their time codes synching their display to the captured video. The next time the application is run the sketches are replayed on top of the captured video automatically. Figure 3 shows one of these sketches drawn on top of a frame of captured data from Oakland Cemetery. The 2D sketch annotations can also be transformed into 3D content ("sketch actors" discussed below) in the scene for use in the next stage of design that incorporates tracking data.

Video prototypes can also be created using regular DART actors and time-based cues. The designer can simply place 3D object actors, sketch actors, audio actors etc., on the score and place the transform scripts to define their 3D positions and orientations. Once the designer has placed the actors, he or she can utilize time cues to bypass the need for application logic. The time cues simply fire an event at a specified time; actions placed on the actors will receive them and respond accordingly. In this way the designer can define the types of actions that might occur in the final experience without having to create the (possibly complex) logic to generate them from sensor input. For example, the designer might create a captured data set where at 5 seconds the user walks through the door and at 6.3 seconds he or she makes a gesture with his or her hand. The designer can then define time cues called "door_enter" and "wave_hand" that fire at those respective times. The actors can then respond to those cues in the desired way (e.g., an action "shows" an object while another action triggers a "start animation" on the same actor). Although these time cues will not be useful in the live application, the actions will be, and in the meantime the designer can explore various approaches rapidly even if complex algorithms or technology will be required to make it "real." Once the user experience has been fleshed out the designer can focus on how to add the necessary intelligence to the system. The result is a video prototype that does not require wasted effort, can be rapidly modified, and that can evolve into a deployable version at the end of the cycle.

This prototyping technique emerged naturally from students in our AR Design class. We intended for the students to use the captured data to create applications that would work in a live experience, but noticed that instead of programming complex behaviors early in the design process, the students were utilizing the time cues to make a prototype that looked correct with the captured data set. We realized this was a useful technique that allowed them to realize their ideas quickly and to iterate through several approaches. The creation of the application logic is more appropriately left for the next step in the design process.

Stage 2: Populating the Virtual World

As previously discussed, one challenge to creating AR experiences is the time and expertise needed to create compelling content (3D models, animations, video, sound, etc.). We have learned from our own experiences with FAM that it can be a mistake to put a large amount of resources into creating content before you have done proper testing. For both technical and artistic reasons we have re-shot the video of the jurors in FAM three times. The post-production on the video to create the virtual jurors is extensive, resulting literally in months of wasted effort. It was these struggles with the early versions of FAM that motivated and informed the creation of DART. In particular, we wanted the designer to be able to evaluate the whole user experience before too much effort is put into final content development (Pausch, Snoddy, Taylor, Watson, & Haseltine, 1996).

Sketch Actors

When exploring the ways that DART could support the use of rough "proxy" content we were influenced by the use of animatics and storyboards in the film industry. Using this approach in pre-production, directors are able to visualize their shots in a cheap and easy manner. Therefore, DART supports the concept of "sketch actors," or flipbook style animations created from a set of still images. The designer creates a set of sketches illustrating what an object in the scene will look like (e.g., these could be drawings done by the design team, or still images such as photographs) and edits a text file inside of DART to define at what time each image will be displayed. The sketch actor is placed in 3D space in the world just as any other actor and supports the common set of actor functionality (start, stop, hide, show, etc.)

Figure 4. (a) Initial prototype of FAM using sketch actors, (b) view of FAM using finished video content

(a)

(b)

In the most recent version of FAM, before we shot the video with our juror actors, we sketched a set of very rough storyboards (consisting of stick men) illustrating the types of movements and jurors' reactions we wanted, and created sketch actors from them (see Figure 4). These actors were placed in the 3D world so that they would appear to be sitting at the physical table, just as the final content would. We quickly recorded audio of the script with our own voices. This allowed us to debug content oriented issues before too much effort was put into creating the real videos and audio. Once post-production was complete on the final FAM video content we simply replaced the sketch actors in the application with video actors.

Proxy Content

DART supports the concept of virtual and physical objects, so that actors can represent either virtual content to be registered visually with the physical world or they can represent elements of the physical world that will be used for occlusion (see Figure 5). This feature, coupled with the direct manipulation method of application development on the Director score, results in a suite of techniques that allow a DART designer to quickly modify or swap content for debugging and evaluation. For example, when we begin placing 3D virtual objects in the physical world for a new AR experience, we often use proxy content (such as simple primitive objects or sketch actors), eliminating the problems that may arise with more complex models and allowing us to begin evaluation and testing before time is spent on final content. This proxy content is easily replaced later in the process.

Meanwhile, in this stage of the design, the designer often starts mapping the extent of the space, determining where virtual content should be placed, and verifying that the tracking is working. Proxy content that may not appear in the final experience has proven useful to support these activities, and serves as spatial markers to the designer (e.g., indicating the location of the origin of the world coordinate system or showing where a physical object will be placed in the world). For example, in "Four Angry Men" there are position cues

Figure 5. The physical object (the cup) occludes the virtual object (the dog)

defined that will fire when the user enters a zone around each juror. In the design stage we used semi-transparent spheres to visualize these zones to help us determine their optimum size and to debug the behavior of the position cue (i.e., we could see when the user entered the zone and could verify the cue fired appropriately). It is very easy to later swap out these stand-in actors for others, or (in the case of objects used for debugging) move them to an inactive portion of the score or make them temporarily invisible, keeping them available for later use.

Stage 3: Developing the Application

Once the designer has iterated through early designs and content, the next step is to begin developing the real experience using the sensing hardware, and implementing the necessary application logic that reacts to the sensors. At this stage, DART provides an infrastructure that supports rapid development and modification of applications as well as application specific extensions to the basic framework. During these tasks, the Director environment itself provides the interface and functionality to support application development in an efficient and robust manner with features that might not typically appear in academic software toolkits.

The Tracking Infrastructure

An important element of any AR application is tracking. One obstacle that prevents designers from creating AR applications is the expertise and domain knowledge required to understand the tracking and sensing technologies and the complexities intrinsic to working with the hardware. These technologies are often difficult to work with for a variety of reasons. They can be expensive and difficult to configure. Interfacing between the sensors and the computer application can be complicated and require low level programming expertise. The reliance on real-time sensors means that it is difficult to develop the application off-line without the hardware being available, and it can be difficult to change which type of tracking technology the application uses. In DART, we have implemented an approach to tracker management and leveraged existing technology such as VRPN to alleviate many of these problems (Gandy, MacIntyre, & Dow, 2004). The result is a flexible approach to tracking (see Figure 6) that allows for experimentation, off-line development, wizard-of-oz testing, and easy migration from one tracking technology to another (e.g., switching from a 6DOF tracker to marker-based tracking).

The DART tracking infrastructure also makes it easy to create various kinds of synthetic trackers because the tracking data is routed through a central location, all consumers of the tracking data use a common subscription model, and all tracking reports use uniform timestamps/formats. For example, a designer can choose to fuse the data from two different trackers to create a new "tracker," such as combining GPS position and inertial orientation data as the student projects situated in Oakland Cemetery did.

Figure 6. Diagram showing the tracking infrastructure in DART

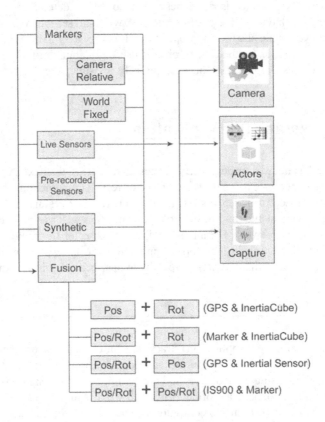

Working with the Score

The designer can reduce the complexity of the resulting application by leveraging aspects of the Director score. Most Director developers (DART or otherwise) do not use the score in a linear time-based manner. Rather, they typically use the score to lay out logical sections of the experience, in essence defining a state machine for the application with the vertical groups of sprites functioning as nodes and the cues and actions triggering transitions between states. This makes it easier to understand and modify the finished application; the overall structure of the application can be simplified if the designer uses the score intelligently.

Figure 7 shows the layout of the FAM experience on the Director score. The vertical groupings under each text marker represent a different state in the experience. In the FAM experience, these states are the user entering the room (the text marker "Begin"), the four states where the user is standing by any of the four juror locations (e.g. "POVA_stand"), and the four states where the user is sitting at one of the four locations (e.g. "POVA"). The sprites that are unique for each state are only present on those frames; these are the video actors

Figure 7. The layout of the FAM experience on the Director score

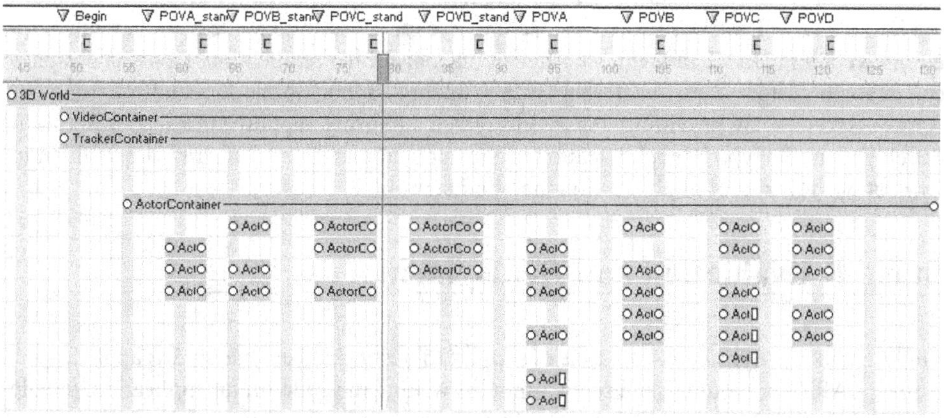

that represent each juror from that point-of-view. There are some sprites which are always present in the experience that span the entire length of the score, such as the 3D world, the live video, the live tracker, and the object actor representing the physical table.

The interaction in FAM involves the user standing up and moving to other seats at the table to switch between points-of-view. Cues are used to detect when the user stands up or sits down, and position cues detect which juror the user is closest to. These cues cause the execution to jump between the different states (indicated by text markers above the score).

The visual layout of the score and the direct manipulation interaction means that it is trivial to swap out one version of a sprite for another. The designer can always modify the property pages, but in our experiences, we often have different sprites stored in an inactive portion of the score. In FAM we have two versions of an experience in one application; a version for debugging purposes that uses captured video and tracking and the full version that uses live sources. We have different versions of the relevant sprites for the two cases and one version of the common components (e.g., the 30+ actors that made up the experience). To switch back and forth, we drag one set of sprites out of the way and replace them with the other set (Shown under the "Testing Version" marker in Figure 7).

Extending DART

It is not possible to provide all the functionality any designer would ever need for any AR experience with a development tool such as DART. Design tools that do not have facilities for creating custom code, where the applications must be designed entirely through ma-nipulation of the provided components, will result in the development of a narrow niche of applications. We have found that for any application of sufficient size or complexity, it is necessary for the designer to develop custom additions to DART. Fortunately, it is precisely this type of development that Director supports very well. When developing real applications, the benefit of DART lies in this ability to develop at many levels. At the highest level, the designer can simply use the components provided with DART and design the application visually. At the next level, the designer can take a standard component, copy it, and modify it to work differently for her app. The designer can also write custom Lingo code, hooking into the DART infrastructure (e.g., actors, tracker subscription, cue/action architecture etc.); leveraging DART in the most efficient manner for her application. Lastly, a designer can develop custom Xtras written in C/C++, adding support to the Director environment for new services. By providing this multi-layered authoring support DART does not limit developers in the type or sophistication of the applications they create and allows them to work at whatever level of abstraction they find comfortable.

Stage 4: Evaluation and Deployment

Traditionally there has been little time or support for testing and evaluating AR applications. Before DART, we would spend several months writing the code for an application, unable to truly evaluate the experience or fully test the application until it was almost complete, at which point it was often too late to make major changes. In the previous sections, we have shown how DART supports the crucial early design exercises. However, DART also provides facilities for user evaluation and debugging later in the process.

Wizard of Oz Prototyping Tools

The Wizard of Oz (WOz) simulation method is a prototyping approach widely used among researchers and professionals in HCI. A "wizard" operator generally plays some role in a work-in-progress computer system, manually simulating sensor data, contextual information, or system intelligence. In DART, we use the word "puppet" to refer to the mocked-up user interface controlled by the wizard.

The Wizard of Oz tools in DART leverage the cue broadcast/subscription architecture (Dow et al., 2005). To enable WOz communication, one must place the "Puppet of Oz" behavior on the machine running the experience and the "Wizard of Oz" behavior on a remote machine. The two scripts establish the networking connection and enable the wizard interface to trigger any actions available in the user application. By using common naming conventions, cues can be triggered locally or by a remote wizard.

Leveraging continuous notification of available actions from the puppet, DART can automatically generate a WOz interface consisting of GUI buttons that correspond to the list of possible actions on the puppet. The wizard generates a generic button interface (using a simple layout algorithm) and labels each button with the unique event name. As the puppet application runs, the wizard automatically refreshes the corresponding set of buttons. Automatic wizard generation lowers the barrier for using WOz prototyping as an evaluation strategy.

The wizard interface can also be customized to control the puppet using a mix of built-in Director widgets and DART behaviors. For example, in VOO the designer placed an overhead map image in the WOz application and attached a "map tracking" behavior that generated synthetic GPS tracker reports that appeared to the puppet application to be real GPS reports. Since both interfaces were developed in DART, we were able to integrate

Figure 8. Visualization of VOO created with a handful of DART behaviors (DataGraphs, Observers, TimeSlider) inside Director: (a) GPS data for 5 participants with dynamic circles showing the user's position at a particular time, (b) textual representations of GPS location and head rotation data, (c) Graph of button interaction over time, (d) slider for control of DART's abstract time, Dow, 2005 (© 2005 IEEE, used with permission)

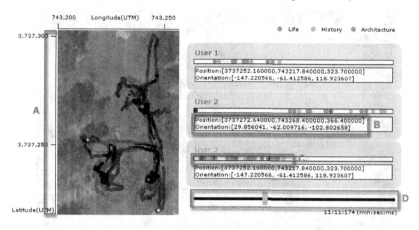

part of the user interface of the puppet into the wizard interface so that the wizard operator would experience the same application state as the user. In VOO, we used this strategy to allow the wizard to listen to the same audio segments, follow along with the user, and decide what content to display.

Visualization Tools

To help designers evaluate an experience, DART also includes tools for visualizing captured data textually and graphically. By having the tools integrated with DART, designers have the ability to visualize live data in parallel with previously collected data, enabling real-time analysis of user performance. Visualization tools in DART can show both static, cumulative data as well as a single data value at any particular time on the abstract clock. For example, in VOO we visualized the GPS data for each participant on the same image to get an overview of user movement (see Figure 8).

Debugging Support

Although we have not yet created a full suite of debugging related tools, there are some DART components that can be helpful in overcoming the challenges of debugging an AR application.

For example, one of the most common problems we have encountered when testing applications is the case where the virtual content is not appearing where expected. The most confusing case is when none of the virtual content is visible. In this situation, the designer

Figure 9. Simple DART application using the overhead map; the overhead map (in the upper left corner) shows the position and orientations of all the objects in the scene as well as the camera, the light gray icon represents the camera with the line pointing out from the circle showing the direction the camera is pointed, the black icons represent object actors in the scene, which are currently seen in the 3D camera's view

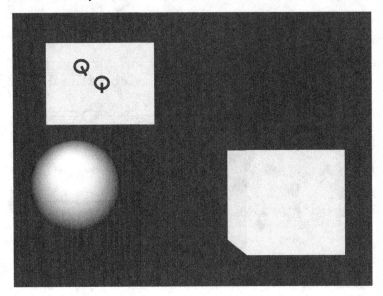

does not know if the objects are in the wrong 3D location, if the 3D camera is in the wrong location (possibly due to a problem with the tracker), or if the objects are there but are invisible/too small to be seen. To help with this problem we created an overhead map component (Gandy et al., 2005) (see Figure 9). The designer simply adds this map to the score and defines its size and placement as an overlay on top of the scene. The map will then automatically generate an overhead view of the 3D scene, using color and shape to indicate the continuous locations and orientations of the virtual camera as well as all the actors in the scene. This component allows the designer to see what actors are where and their relation to the virtual camera. This makes it easy to debug tricky problems such as the virtual camera having an incorrect 180-degree rotation, which results in it pointing away from where the user is looking.

How DART can Inform Other Authoring Environments

In the previous sections, we discussed a set of useful features for any AR authoring environment, and illustrated them in the context of DART. In this section, we provide a summary of these general concepts for each stage of the design process.

- Exploring Ideas
  - Rapid creation of early prototypes (e.g., video prototyping, story boards) focused on brainstorming and experience testing. Ideally, these prototypes can be used as the basis for future iterations of the application.
  - Capture and replay of sensor data (e.g., video, trackers). Enables designers to work effectively offline, away from the application space and technology.
- Populating the Virtual World
  - Proxy content. A tool should allow the designer to work with stand-in content for debugging and evaluation. The content can be easily replaced with final content as it is completed.
  - Virtual and physical objects as first-class entities. Allows the physical space to be modeled and to interact with all subsystems, such as graphics and physics.
  - Support for the user mapping out and exploring the physical space.
- Developing the Application
  - Multilayered development architecture. Allows for a continuum of programming ease and complexity.
    - Authoring tools do not need to anticipate all designer needs, but must provide the basic building blocks that can be modified and extended.
  - Reduce challenges of working with technology
    - Abstractions for hardware such as sensors, cameras, trackers.
    - Make it easy to switch between different technologies.
  - Provide visualizations or direct manipulation tools to aid in the design of application structure (e.g., GUI programming via the Director score).
- Evaluation and Deployment
  - Support for standard HCI evaluation tools such as Wizard-of-Oz.
  - Methods of storing and analyzing data gathered from evaluations.
  - Debugging support for common problems encountered by designers in AR.
    - Spatial errors and coordinate system confusion (e.g. incorrect transforms, objects in the wrong place, incorrectly sized, or inadvertently hidden).
    - Technology errors (e.g. hardware not working correctly or not as the designer expects).
  - Standard debugging tools from traditional programming environments (e.g., breakpoints, variable inspection, and error information).

Conclusion and Future Work

Version 2.0 of DART is in public release. In future versions, we have a number of directions we hope to move. Technically, we plan to enhance the camera infrastructure to support multiple simultaneous cameras, camera calibration from inside Director, a plug-in architecture for image processing operations, better multi-sensor integration, and automated multi-sensor calibration. Another direction is to tackle the problems of authoring and debugging. While we rely on the skills of designers, working in 3D is conceptually hard. The kinds of authoring and debugging facilities from environments such as Alice (Pierce et al., 1997) has would be quite useful in DART.

While DART is not a panacea for all of the problems encountered when working with AR (or any media that mixes physical and virtual worlds), it takes a significant step toward enabling designers to work with this exciting new medium. By focusing on rapid prototyping and early experience testing, and creating an environment which allows designers to work effectively at (and away from) a physical site, we help designers get over the initial hurdle of creating a first working prototype to explore the embodied experiences AR is appropriate for. We have demonstrated the importance of integrating a research toolkit with existing, powerful tools such as Director, and of addressing both technical (e.g., tracker integration) and practical problems (e.g., dealing with the annoyances of working in the physical world). DART places a heavy emphasis on rapidly moving informal content from storyboards into a functioning AR prototype, because we believe that it is not the final content creation that has limited AR experience prototyping, but rather the difficulty of exploring the design problems in the first place. It is this hole that DART has been designed to fill.

Acknowledgments

We would like to acknowledge the many students who have worked on and with DART over the years, especially Emmanuel Moreno, Jaemin Lee, Christopher Oezbek, and the students in all our AR Design and independent research classes. This work was supported by seed grants from the GVU Center at Georgia Tech and by NSF CAREER Grant 0347712. We also thank UNC Chapel Hill for use of the VRPN library, and the UW HIT Lab for the ARToolkit.

References

Abawi, D., Dörner, R., Haller, M., & Zauner, J. (2004). Efficient mixed reality application development. In *Proceedings of the 1ˢᵗ European Conference on Visual Media Production (CVMP)*, London.

Billinghurst, M., Bowskill, J., Jessop, M., & Morphett, J. (1998). A wearable spatial conferencing space. In *Proceedings of the 2nd International Symposium on Wearable Computers (ISWC)*, Pittsburgh, PA.

Dow, S., Lee, J., Oezbek, C., MacIntyre, B., Bolter, J. D., & Gandy, M. (2005). Exploring spatial narratives and mixed reality experiences in Oakland Cemetery. In *Proceedings of the ACM SIGCHI Conference on Advances in Computer Entertainment (ACE'05)*, Valencia, Spain.

Dow, S., Lee, J., Oezbek, C., MacIntyre, B., Bolter, J. D., & Gandy, M. (2005). Wizard of Oz interfaces for mixed reality applications. In *Proceedings of the CHI '05 Extended Abstracts on Human Factors in Computing Systems*, Portland, OR.

Dow, S., MacIntyre, B., Lee, J., Oezbek, C., Bolter, J. D., & Gandy, M. (2005, November). Wizard of Oz support throughout an iterative design process. *IEEE Pervasive Computing (Special Issue on Rapid Prototyping)*.

Gandy, M., MacIntyre, B., & Dow, S. (2004). Making tracking technology accessible in a rapid prototyping environment. In *Proceedings of the 3rd IEEE and ACM International Symposium on Mixed and Augmented Reality (ISMAR)*, Arlington, VA.

Gandy, M., MacIntyre, Presti, P., Dow, S., Bolter, J., Yarbrough, B., & O'Rear, N. (2005). AR karaoke: Acting in your favorite scenes. In *Proceedings of the International Symposium on Mixed and Augmented Reality (ISMAR)*, Vienna, Austria.

Greenberg, S., & Fitchett, C. (2001). Phidgets: Easy development of physical interfaces through physical widgets. In *Proceedings of the 14th Annual ACM Symposium on User Interface Software and Technology (UIST)*, Orlando, FL.

Katz, S. (1991). *Film directing shot by shot: Visualizing from concept to screen*. Studio City, CA: Michael Wiese Productions.

Klemmer, S. R., Sinha, A., Chen, J., Landay, J., Aboobaker, N., & Wang, A. (2001). SUEDE: A Wizard of Oz prototyping tool for speech user interfaces. *CHI Letters: ACM Symposium User Interface Software and Technology, 2*(2), 1-10.

Landay, J. A., & Myers, B. A. (2001). Sketching interfaces: Toward more human interface design. *IEEE Computer, 34*(3), 56-64.

MacIntyre, B., Bolter, J., Vaughn, J., Hannigan, B., Gandy, M., Moreno, E., Haas, M., Kang, S., Krum, D., & Voida, S. (2003). Three Angry Men: An augmented reality experiment in point-of-view drama. In *Proceedings of the 1st International Conference on Technologies for Interactive Digital Storytelling and Entertainment (TIDSE '03)*, Darmstadt, Germany.

MacIntyre, B., Gandy, M., Dow, S., & Bolter, J., (2004). DART: A toolkit for rapid design exploration of augmented reality experiences. In *Proceedings of the 17th Annual ACM Symposium on User Interface Software and Technology (UIST)*, Sante Fe, NM.

Mackay, W. E. (1988). Video prototyping: A technique for developing hypermedia systems. In *Proceedings of the Conference Companion of ACM CHI '88 Human Factors in Computing Systems,* Washington, DC.

MacWilliams, A., Reicher, T., Klinker, G., & Bruegge, B. (2004). Design patterns for augmented reality systems. In *Proceedings of the International Workshop Exploring the Design and Engineering of Mixed Reality Systems: MIXER 2004*, Funchal, Madeira.

Moreno, E., MacIntyre, B., & Bolter, J. D. (2001). Alice's adventure's in new media: An exploration of interactive narratives in augmented reality. In *Proceedings of the Conference on Communication of Art, Science, and Technology (CAST 01)*, Bonn, Germany.

Newman, M. W., Lin, J., Hong, J. I., & Landay, J. A. (2003). DENIM: An informal Web site design tool inspired by observations of practice. *Human-Computer Interaction, 18*(3), 259-324.

Pausch, R., Snoddy, J., Taylor, R., Watson, S., & Haseltine, E. (1996). Disney's Aladdin: First steps toward storytelling in virtual reality. In *Proceedings of the 23rd Annual Conference on Computer Graphics and Interactive Techniques*.

Piekarski, W., & Thomas, B. H. (2003). An object-oriented software architecture for 3D mixed reality applications. In *Proceedings of the 2nd International Symposium on Mixed and Augmented Reality (ISMAR)*, Tokyo, Japan.

Pierce, J., Audia, S., Burnette, T., Christiansen, K., Cosgrove, D., Conway, M., et al. (1997). "Alice: Easy to use interactive 3D graphics. In *Proceedings of the ACM Symposium on User Interface Software and Technology* (pp. 77-78).

Presti, P., Gandy, M., MacIntyre, B., & Dow, S. (2005). A sketch interface to support storyboarding of augmented reality experiences. In *Proceedings of the Conference on Computer Graphics and Interactive Techniques (SIGGRAPH)*, Los Angeles, CA.

Rose, R. (1983). *Twelve Angry Men: A play in three acts*. Dramatic Publications Company.

Schmalstieg, D., Fuhrmann, A., Hesina, G., Szalavári, Z., Encarnação, L. M., Gervautz, M., & Purgathofer, W. (2002). The Studierstube augmented reality project. *PRESENCE: Teleoperators and Virtual Environments, 11*(1), 32-54.

Wolff, E. (2004). *Tool time at Pixar*. Millimeter, The Professional Resource for Production and Post. Nov 1, 2004.

Endnotes

[1]   http://www.studierstube.org/april/

[2]   http://webster.fhs-hagenberg.ac.at/staff/jzauner/CATOMIR.html

[3]   http://www.cs.unc.edu/Research/vrpn/index.html

[4]   http://www.cv.iit.nrc.ca/research/ar/artag/

Chapter IX

Real-Time 3D Design Modelling of Outdoor Structures Using Mobile Augmented Reality Systems

Wayne Piekarski, University of South Australia, Australia

Abstract

This chapter presents a series of new augmented reality user interaction techniques to support the capture and creation of 3D geometry of large outdoor structures. Named construction at a distance, these techniques are based on the action at a distance concepts employed by other virtual environments researchers. These techniques address the problem of AR systems traditionally being consumers of information, rather than being used to create new content. By using information about the user's physical presence along with hand and head gestures, AR systems can be used to capture and create the geometry of objects that are orders of magnitude larger than the user, with no prior information or assistance. While existing scanning techniques can only be used to capture existing physical objects, construction at a distance also allows the creation of new models that exist only in the mind of the user. Using a single AR interface, users can enter geometry and verify its accuracy in real-time.

Construction at a distance is a collection of 3D modelling techniques based on the concept of AR working planes, landmark alignment, constructive solid geometry operations, and iterative refinement to form complex shapes. This chapter presents a number of different construction at a distance techniques, and are demonstrated with examples of real objects that have been modelled in the physical world.

Introduction

Current research in AR applications has focused mainly on obtaining adequate tracking and registration and then developing simple interfaces to present display information to the user (Azuma et al., 2001). One important problem that has not been fully addressed is the authoring of the content that is displayed to the user. Since most AR systems are being used simply as a visualisation tool, the data is prepared offline with standard editing tools and then transferred to the AR system. While ourselves (Piekarski & Thomas, 2003) and others (Baillot, Brown, & Julier, 2001) have started to investigate outdoor AR modelling, this work is very preliminary and incomplete. Brooks states that one of the still unsolved problems in VR is the creation and capture of 3D geometry (Brooks, 1999), which is also relevant for AR models. To develop content for AR systems, we have developed a number of techniques collectively termed *construction at a distance* (CAAD). These techniques use the AR system itself to capture the 3D geometry of existing structures in the physical world, and create new 3D models of virtual objects that do not yet exist. CAAD makes use of the AR working planes and landmark alignment techniques presented in a previous paper (Piekarski & Thomas, 2004), and builds higher-level operations to perform the capture and creation of 3D models. While some of these CAAD techniques have been presented previously (Piekarski et al., Thomas, 2003), in this chapter, I describe new body-relative plane techniques and expand on previous work with a discussion of how AR working planes are used in the implementation.

The introduction section in this chapter describes the advantages of these modelling techniques over other existing methods. Next, the techniques are described over three sections and how they are implemented on a mobile outdoor AR system. An overview of the user interface that supports these techniques is discussed, followed by a discussion on the use of different viewpoints to support situational awareness. The chapter is then concluded with a discussion of possibilities for collaboration, and how the accuracy of the techniques are affected by various environmental factors.

Supplement Physical Capture Limitations

The purpose of these techniques is not to replace existing object capture methods, such as image-based reconstruction (Debevec, Taylor, & Malik, 1996) or laser scanning. These techniques are highly accurate and can produce excellent results given the proper conditions. However, there are a number of limitations and CAAD provides an alternative to existing techniques in the following ways:

- A human operator is capable of accurately estimating the geometry of planar shapes, even when partially occluded by other objects in the environment. When trees occlude the edges of a building, a human can estimate the layout based on incomplete visual information and a knowledge of the volumetric properties of buildings.

- The eye is a highly accurate input device capable of aligning along the walls of buildings (Cutting & Vishton, 1995; Piekarski et al., 2004). Accurate modelling is still possible when working from a distance and direct access to the object is not available.

- Existing capture techniques (Debevec et al., 1996) have a fixed operation time no matter what the complexity of the scene is, whereas in my methods the human can judge the most appropriate level of detail. In many cases, the user wants to create only simple shapes such as boxes to represent buildings, and so these techniques are ideal for quick operations.

- Existing techniques require the object to already exist so it can be captured, whereas my methods allow the human to specify any geometry desired. My techniques allow the creation of new shapes that do not physically exist and may be used to plan future construction work.

It is important to realise that there are limitations introduced by the resolution and accuracy of the tracking devices used to record the inputs. For example, when using a GPS accurate to 50 centimetres the object size that can be modelled is in the order of metres (such as a car), while using a 1 millimetre magnetic tracker allows much smaller objects (such as a drink can). This research does not attempt to address problems with registration or accuracy of tracking devices, but instead works within the limitations of current technology to provide the best solutions that can be achieved.

Working at a Fixed Scale

A number of VR techniques have been developed for use in modelling applications. These applications traditionally provide tools to create and manipulate objects in a virtual world, and to fly around and perform scaling operations to handle a variety of object sizes. While techniques for action at a distance such as spot lights, selection apertures, and image plane techniques (Pierce et al., 1997) have been developed, these only perform simple selections on existing objects and cannot be used to create new ones due to the lack of generating distance values. Techniques such as flying, worlds in miniature (Stoakley, Conway, & Pausch, 1995), and scaled world grab (Mine, Brooks, & Sequin 1997), can perform the creation of points by bringing the world within arm's reach, but accuracy is affected by the scale. Due to their non-exact freehand input methods, all of these systems are also limited to conceptual modelling tasks and not precision modelling. CAD systems use snapping functions or exact numerical entry to ensure accurate inputs, but require an existing reference to snap to or non-intuitive command-based entry.

Although AR environments share some similar functionality with VR, AR is unique in that it requires registration of the physical and virtual worlds. Flying and scaling operations require the breaking of AR registration and so cannot be used. Scaled world representations force the user to divert their attention from the physical world to perform miniature operations within the hands. Existing VR techniques cannot create models of objects the size of skyscraper buildings without breaking the 1:1 relationship between the user and the virtual world. With CAAD techniques, the scale of the world is fixed and only the user's head position controls the view. The virtual geometry is created using absolute world coordinates and is always registered and verifiable against the physical world in real-time. By using the physical presence of the user as an input device, the body can be directly used to quickly and intuitively control the view rather than relying on a separate input device.

Humans are much more capable of accurately estimating and specifying horizontal and vertical displacements compared to distances (Cutting et al., 1995). By using the AR working planes and landmark alignment techniques described previously (Piekarski et al., 2004), simple 2D input devices can be used to draw points in 3D. An AR working plane can be defined at any time from the body along the direction of view (maximising accuracy with landmark alignment) or relative to an existing object (maintaining the same accuracy as the source object), and the user can then move around to a different angle to draw against this surface. With AR working planes, the user is able to draw points that are at large distances and at locations that are not normally reachable, maintaining a 1:1 relationship between the virtual and physical worlds. The techniques in this chapter require any simple 2D input device with a cursor to draw against the AR working plane, with this particular implementation using a glove with fiducial-marker based tracking.

Iterative Model Refinement

CAAD relies on a set of fundamental operations that by themselves cannot generally model a physical world object. Combining a series of these fundamental operations by making iterative improvements can produce complex shapes however. As the modelling operation is taking place the user can see how well the virtual and physical objects compare, repeatedly making changes until the desired quality is gained. Constructive solid geometry (CSG) techniques used by CAD systems also rely on this principle to produce highly complicated shapes that would otherwise be difficult to specify. The ability to instantly verify the quality of models against the physical world helps to reduce errors and decrease the total modelling time. The process of iterative refinement for VR modelling is discussed by Brooks (1999), and he recommends that a breadth-first iterative refinement strategy is the most efficient. I use these VR guidelines for the proposed CAAD techniques, and take the refinement process one step further by using the unique ability of AR to compare virtual and physical worlds simultaneously.

Simplified Techniques

Some techniques have been developed previously for the interactive creation of data in virtual environments with no prior information. The CDS system by Bowman can create vertices by projecting a virtual laser beam against the ground plane (Bowman, 1996). By connecting these points together and extruding the 2D outline upwards, full 3D solid objects can be created although they are limited in complexity by being constant across the height axis. Baillot et al. performed the creation of vertices located at the intersection of two virtual laser beams drawn from different locations (Baillot et al., 2001). After defining vertices, these can then be connected together to form other shapes of arbitrary complexity, limited only by the time available to the user. Since these techniques both operate using vertex primitives that are then connected into edges, polygons, and objects, the complexity of this task increases as the number of facets on the object increases. Rather than treating objects as collections of vertices like the previously mentioned work, CAAD mainly operates using surfaces and solid objects, so an object with 10 facets can be modelled in 10 steps rather than as 20 vertices and 30 edges.

Direct Object Placement Techniques

This section describes techniques involving the direct placement of objects within arm's reach. While not being truly CAAD, these techniques may be used as inputs for other operations. The simplest way to perform modelling is to use prefabricated objects and place them at the feet of the user as they stand in the environment, when commanded by the user. I have termed this technique street furniture, as it can be used to place down objects that commonly occur on the street (Piekarski et al., 2003). Furthermore, using the AR working planes techniques (Piekarski et al., 2003; Thomas 2004) the user is able to translate, scale, and rotate these objects in the AR environment. The street furniture method works well when objects to create are known in advance, and the user can avoid having to model the object each time. While this technique is not at a distance according to our requirements, it is the most basic and simplest operation that can be performed using a mobile outdoor AR computer. It is possible to use direct placement of markers at the feet to specify vertices and extrude the object upwards, but this is not always practical in the physical world because the user cannot stand on top of a building to mark its outline. Later techniques described in this chapter use direct placement for the creation of infinitely sized plane surfaces in the environment.

Body-Relative Plane Techniques

This section describes a series of CAAD techniques based on the user's physical presence in the environment. Using simple head-based pointing, the geometry of planes originating from the body can be specified, taking advantage of the user's sense of proprioception (Mine et al., 1997). Using CSG techniques, these planes can be used to easily define solid building shapes out of arm's reach. Since many buildings in the physical world can be modelled using planes, the process of modelling can be accelerated compared to the simplistic approach of creating each vertex and edge manually.

Orientation Infinite Planes

Buildings in the physical world tend to approximate collections of angled walls in many cases. A solid convex cube can be formed with the specification of six planes arranged perpendicular to each other and a CSG intersection operator. Instead of specifying these planes

Figure 1. Infinite carving planes used to iteratively create a convex shape from an infinite solid

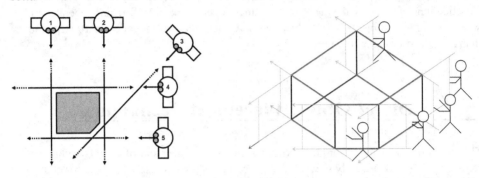

numerically, the user can create these same planes in an AR environment by projecting them along the line of sight. By looking along the plane of a wall of a building and aligning the two ends, the user can project an infinite plane along this wall in a similar way to AR working planes. Each plane defines a half space that when combined with a CSG intersect operation will form a finite solid shape.

Figure 1 depicts a five-sided building and the location of the mobile AR user as they are sighting down each of the walls, showing the infinite volume being iteratively bound by the infinite planes. At the beginning of the operation, the AR system creates an (approximately) infinite solid volume that will be used for carving. When the user is aligned with a wall, they project an infinitely long vertical plane along the view direction into the world. This plane divides the previous infinite solid into two parts and the left or right portion (decided by the user) is carved away from the solid and removed. As the user sights along each wall, the solid will be reduced down to an object that is no longer infinite in the X and Y axes. At completion, a floor is automatically created at ground level, and the roof is left unbounded for carving using other techniques, since it is impractical to sight along the roof of a very tall building. The final 3D shape is stored using absolute world coordinates and reflects the geometry of the physical building.

With this technique, the object can be carved away iteratively and the user receives real-time feedback of the infinite volume being bounded, allowing immediate undo in case of a mistake. Compared to the direct methods described previously, this plane-based technique allows the capture of buildings from a distance without having to actually stand next to or on top of the building. Since the user is in direct control of the modelling process, the positions of occluded surfaces can be estimated using their knowledge of the environment. These features are useful because many existing physical capture methods require a full view of the object, GPS trackers do not work well near large buildings, and standing on top of a building may not be possible or too dangerous. This technique is also much more efficient than vertex and edge specification since each wall is handled with a single primitive that is easy to create accurately. A limitation of this technique is that using only planes and a CSG intersection to define objects restricts usage to convex buildings with no indentations, and this will be addressed further at the end of this section.

Position Infinite Planes

Another limitation of the orientation infinite planes technique is the dependence on an orientation sensing device for the head. While RTK GPS units may have reliable accuracies in the order of 2 cm, orientation sensors vary in accuracy due to problems with interference and limitations of the technology. These variations affect the placement of planes in the environment and as the distance from the user increases, angular errors cause increasing positional errors, but using techniques that can avoid the use of orientation sensing should be able to produce much more accurate results.

In order to take advantage of the stability of position tracking, the orientation infinite planes technique described earlier can be modified to use two or more position points to specify orientation, making it invariant to errors in orientation tracking devices. Using the same landmark alignment concept discussed previously, the user can accurately sight along a wall and mark a position. To indicate direction, the user walks closer while maintaining their alignment and marks a second point. These two points can then be used to project an infinite carving plane. By increasing the spacing of the marker points or using a line of best fit amongst multiple points, the accuracy of this technique can be further improved.

The accuracy of this technique can be calculated based on the positional error of the GPS and the distance between the two marker points. To make this technique useful, it must have an accuracy that is better than is available using traditional orientation sensors. As an example, when a maximum allowable error of 1 degree is assumed, an RTK GPS unit with 2 cm accuracy will require a distance of 1.1 metres between the points. If 10 or more metres is used then the orientation accuracy will be orders of magnitude better than previously possible.

Fixed Infinite Planes

This technique is similar to the position infinite planes technique in that it is invariant to orientation sensing errors. The previous technique required the user to specify the orientation for each plane by using two points, but if the angles at each corner are known to be equal then only one orientation is needed and the others can be calculated automatically. The user creates the first plane using the same method described previously, but for each additional plane, only one position marker is recorded. Based on the number of positions marked, the system knows the number of walls to create and calculates the orientation for each position point based on the first plane. This technique uses nearly half the number of points and yet produces the same accuracy if the first plane is properly placed and the building meets the required properties.

CSG Operations

Many objects in the physical world are not the same shape as simple boxes, cylinders, spheres, and cones. While it may seem that many objects are too complicated to model, they may usually be described in terms of combinations of other objects. For example, the process of defining a cube with a hole using vertices is time consuming, but can be easily specified with a CSG operation. CSG is a technique commonly used by CAD systems, supporting Boolean set operations such as inversion, union, intersection, and subtraction. The manufacture of objects in the physical world is also performed in a similar manner—a drill can be used to bore a hole very easily out of a solid cube. An example of CSG being used outdoors is applying the CSG difference operator to subtract cubes from a building shape. This could be used when the user needs to carve out indented windows. In Figure 2 part 1a and 2a, the user places a cube at a distance, and then drags it sideways until it enters the building shape. Alternatively, in Figure 2 part 1b and 2b, the cube is pushed into the surface of the building (similar to a cookie cutter), and requiring closer access to the building. As the cube is being positioned by the user, the CSG difference operator is interactively calculated and displayed to the user. Infinite planes are normally limited to producing only convex shapes, but using CSG techniques allows us to produce more complex concave shapes very intuitively.

AR Working Planes Techniques

This section describes a series of CAAD techniques based on AR working planes (Piekarski & Thomas, 2004). The previous techniques are capable of placing prefabricated objects and capturing bounding boxes for large objects, but detailed modelling is not provided. Using AR working planes and a 2D input device, the user can specify much more intricate details to create realistic 3D models.

Projection Carving

The projection carving technique modifies existing objects by projecting points against surfaces and then cutting away extrusions to produce new highly concave shapes. This technique provides the ability to construct features such as zig-zag roofs and holes that are

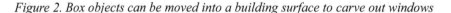

Figure 2. Box objects can be moved into a building surface to carve out windows

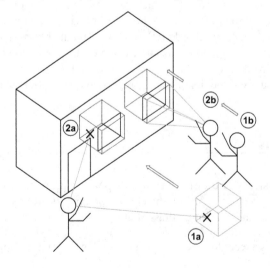

Figure 3. AR working planes are used to specify vertices and are projected along the surface normal for carving the object's roof

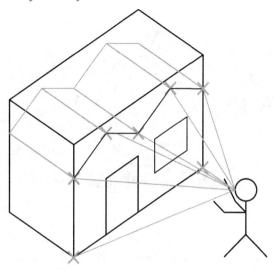

difficult or impossible to model using previously described techniques. Figure 3 depicts an example of how this technique can be used to carve two peaked roofs onto a building model. These building models may have been created using infinite planes and projection carving can be used to restrict the infinite roof to a finite volume. The AR working plane is created relative to a polygon that has been selected by the user. The object that contains the polygon is then used as the input for the upcoming carving operation. The user then creates vertices along the surface of the AR working plane and these are connected together to form a 2D concave outline. This outline is then extruded along the surface normal of the working plane and used as an input tool for a CSG difference carving operation.

The projection is performed using orthogonal extrusion from the AR working plane, and is position invariant so points can be entered from any location in front of the polygon. This enables the user to cut a flat roof on a 100 metre high building while standing at ground level and looking up. If the cursor was used to carve the object directly like a laser beam, the system would produce pyramid-shaped extrusions. For some buildings, the user may only desire to create a flat roof or a single slope, and by creating only one point the system will create a horizontal cutting plane, and with two points a diagonal cutting plane is created. More than two points implies the user wishes to cut with an outline and so it must be fully specified as in Figure 3. The CSG operation can be switched from difference to intersect if desired, with the effect being that the user can cut holes or split an object into separate parts instead of carving the outside. Used in this form, orthogonal extrusion is limited to carving operations that can be seen in a silhouette representation—other features such as indentations that are not visible from the side can not be captured with this technique. Some of these limitations can be overcome by limiting the depth of the extrusion used for carving. By using a small fixed value or controlling it by moving the body forward or backward, the extrusion can be controlled by the user and used for features such as windows or doors.

Figure 4. AR views of an infinite planes building with sloped roof being interactively carved

Figure 4 depicts the projection carving operation on a box that has been edited to match the shape of a building with a pitched roof. A second example demonstrating this technique is a small automobile being modelled outdoors in Figure 5. In both cases, a larger volume is placed down and the user then intersects points against the box surface to define the silhouette. Each frame in Figure 5 shows the process of specifying the solid region that approximates the car in the physical world. The object can then be carved along any of the other faces to further refine the model until it suits the user's requirements.

Projection Colouring

Once a building has been created, the user may desire to place windows, doors, and other extra details onto the model. While it may be possible to draw these details onto a texture map (which cannot be zoomed arbitrarily), or to place extra polygons outside the building to represent these (covering the original building), the building model itself remains untouched. If these new polygons are removed or manipulated, the original solid object remains since the changes are only superficial. A more desirable scenario is that polygons of a different colour are actually cut into the subdivided surface of an object, so that if they are deleted it is possible to see features inside the object that were previously concealed. I have named this technique projection colouring, and using similar steps as projection carving, vertices are projected against an AR working plane created relative to the surface and then connected into an outline. Instead of carving away the outline, the surface is subdivided and the colour of the outlined polygon is modified. The newly coloured polygons may then be deleted or manipulated freely by the user if desired. For example, a window and door can be cut out, with the door then openable using a rotation. Individual manipulation would not be possible with only the surface texture being modified.

Figure 5. AR frames of an automobile being carving from a box, with markers placed at each corner indicating the silhouette of the object

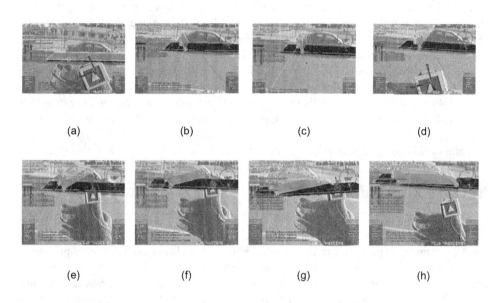

(a)   (b)   (c)   (d)

(e)   (f)   (g)   (h)

Figure 6. (a) AR view of surface of revolution tree with markers on AR working plane (b) VR view of the final surface of revolution tree model as a solid shape

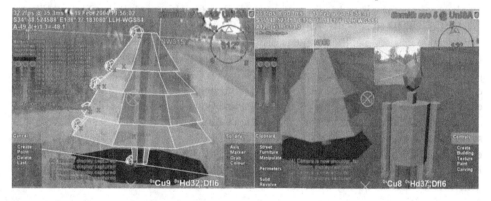

Surface of Revolution

When working outdoors and modelling natural features such as trees and artificial features such as fountains, box-shaped objects are usually poor approximations to use. In an attempt to model these objects, surface of revolution techniques (as used in many desktop CAD systems) have been used to capture geometry that is rotated about an axis. The user starts by creating an AR working plane in the environment, with the most intuitive way being to sight toward the central trunk of the tree and project the AR working plane along the view direction. The user then projects vertices onto the AR working plane, defining one-half of the outline of the object. After specifying the vertices along the axis of rotation, the system generates a solid object by rotating the outline around the axis. Figure 6 shows an example where the vertices of a tree have been specified with a preview shape generated, along with the final shape from an external VR view. This technique generates good results when modelling natural objects such as pine trees that are highly symmetrical about the trunk. For trees that grow with deformities and other non-symmetrical features this technique may not generate suitable approximations. To improve the approximation, previously described carving techniques may be applied to refine the model until the user is satisfied with the object.

Texture Map Capture

When implementing live AR video overlay, the system can automatically match up images from the camera to polygons in the scene. Captured models are normally only presented using a single colour and texture maps increase the realism for users without having to add extra polygons for detail. To perform texture map capture, the user stands at a location where the texture for an object's polygon is clearly visible to the camera. The user selects the polygon to activate capture mode and the system projects the polygon vertices onto the AR video overlay to map the still image as a texture. The user repeats this operation for each polygon until the object is completely textured.

The best results for this technique are obtained when the object is fully visible and fills as much of the HMD as possible. Also, keeping the surface perpendicular to the user's viewing direction ensures that the texture is distorted as little as possible. Although techniques for capturing textures of 3D models have been described previously, this has not been performed in a mobile outdoor AR environment. Previously discussed work by Debevec et al. implemented the capture of 3D models from photographs and extracted textures for each facet (Debevec et al., 1996). Lee, Hirota, and State also implemented the capture of textures in AR but with surfaces being modelled within arm's reach using a wand, with the system automatically capturing textures when video frames were deemed suitable (Lee et al., 2001). The video stream used with mobile AR suffers from problems with motion blur and tracker registration, and having the user choose the moment to capture the texture generates the highest quality models.

User Interface

The user interface is made up of three components: a pointer based on the tracking of the thumbs with a set of gloves worn by the user, a command entry system where the user's fingers interact with a menu for performing actions, and an AR display that presents information back to the user. The display for the interface is fixed to the HMD's screen and presents up

Figure 7. Each finger maps to a displayed menu option, the user selects one by pressing the appropriate finger against the thumb

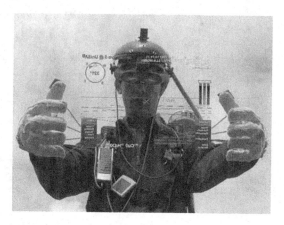

to ten possible commands as menu options at any one time. Eight of these commands are mapped to the fingers as depicted in Figure 7, and the user activates a command by pressing the appropriate finger against the thumb. When an option is selected, the menu refreshes with the next set of options that are available. Ok and cancel operations are activated by pressing the fingers into the palm of the appropriate hand and are indicated in the topmost boxes of the menu. The interaction cursors are specified using fiducial markers placed on the tips of the thumbs, as shown in Figure 4 and Figure 5. With the use of vision tracking for cursor position, and metallic pads for finger press detection, it is possible to control the user interface in the harsh environmental conditions experienced outdoors. As discussed previously, a 2D input device is required to specify 3D points using the AR working planes techniques. This user interface provides the necessary 2D cursor to support this, as well as the command entry capability to control the various techniques described in this chapter.

External Viewpoints

Our user interface is typically operated in an immersive mode where virtual objects are registered with the physical world. This view is intuitive because it is similar to how the user normally experiences the physical world. This view may cause problems in situations where very large objects such as buildings may exceed the field of view of the display, objects may be too distant to clearly view, or other objects may be occluding an object of interest. The immersive view restricts the user if it is impractical or impossible for the user to move to a new viewing position. In these cases, it is more useful to work in an external VR style view such as orbital view (Koller, Mine, & Hudson, 1996), where the user sees the virtual world from an external perspective. The advantages of external views are also discussed by Brooks, who mentions that users find a local map of the world useful to show where they are, what they are looking at, and to build a mental model for navigation (Brooks, 1988).

Figure 8. (a) Top down view with aerial photography to improve situational awareness, (b) orbital view centred on the user showing building under construction

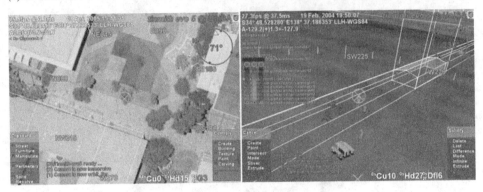

In the external views included in this chapter, the ground and sky are both rendered using texture maps so that the user understands they are looking at a fully virtual view and are no longer immersive. Since the external view is designed to be used while wearing the HMD outdoors, the body of the user is shown in the centre of the display and motion about the physical world is updated in real-time. Top down views, such as that shown in Figure 8(a), provide an aerial perspective of the area, with the display being fixed in north up mode or rotating freely according to the user's current view direction. In this example, an aerial photograph has been used instead of a grass texture to provide additional situational awareness. Orbital views such as that shown in Figure 6(b) and Figure 8(b) link all 3DOFs of head rotation to orbiting motions at a fixed distance around the user. These external views are generally only used while stationary because the physical world is completely blocked out and the user may not be able to safely move. The user is able to adjust the camera view using body position or head rotation (as discussed previously) but not hand gestures, and can freely switch between immersive and a number of pre-programmed external views using menu commands.

Collaborative Modelling Scenario

While a number of techniques can perform the modelling of simple and useful shapes, the true power of CAAD is expressed when techniques are iteratively combined to produce more complicated real-world shapes. Furthermore, the usefulness of a system is enhanced when models can be collaboratively viewed by others at the same time. Customers, architects, and developers both onsite and at remote locations could work together to design buildings and landscapes. A user with a mobile AR system would walk outside to an empty piece of land to create a landscape to preview and perhaps construct in the future. The user creates the outline of the building using infinite planes and then carves out the roof of the building. Doors and windows are then added to the surface of the object. To finish off the model, the outline of a swimming pool can be added, and various street furniture accessories such as tables and chairs are added. Within 10-15 minutes, the user has created a simple model that they can iteratively adjust until they are happy with it.

Using the distributed nature of the Tinmith-evo5 software architecture (Piekarski & Thomas, 2003), indoor users can be connected so they can monitor the progress of the modelling operation on large fixed indoor displays. Using wireless 802.11 networks, the state of the remote system is sent indoors along with two-way voice data so the users can discuss the operation in progress. State information includes the full scene graph and tracking information, so the indoor display is able to reproduce any part of the outdoor system's state as required. The only current limitation is that live video is not streamed over the network due to bandwidth limitations. The indoor users could be remote experts such as architects or developers, observing the design that the customer wants and making comments in real-time. At the completion of the design, the indoor users can extract the model as VRML and then convert it into a proper set of building plans for construction.

Operational Performance

The CAAD techniques rely on the position and orientation sensors for all tracking, and so increasing the accuracy of these devices will produce improved results and affect the minimum model size that can be properly captured. Errors from each sensor have different effects on the captured models since one is measured as a distance and the other as an angle. Systems such as OSGAR (Coelho, MacIntyre, & Julier, 2004) attempt to model these errors for the registration of information, dynamically adjusting the display depending on the sensor errors. However, when rendering the AR display during 3D modelling, results are also affected not only by the errors in the current tracker data, but also those from the capture process. The position sensor used in these examples is a Trimble Ag132 GPS, with an accuracy of better than 50 centimetres and working reliably amongst small buildings and light tree cover. For orientation, an InterSense IntertiaCube2 hybrid magnetic and inertial sensor is used, although the tracking is unreliable when there are magnetic distortions present in the environment or when the user is moving quickly.

When modelling a new object, the accuracy of projection-based techniques is dependant on the user's current location and the direction they are looking. For the highest accuracy, it is desirable to be as close to the object as possible, minimising the distance the projection can stray from the desired direction caused by angular errors in the orientation sensor. When viewing an existing virtual object, the registration errors with the physical world caused by the GPS will be the most accurate when viewed from a distance due to perspective, while standing very close to an object will cause these errors to be more noticeable. For registration errors caused by the InertiaCube2, these remain constant on the display at all distances due to their angular nature.

Conclusion

This chapter has presented my novel CAAD techniques, designed to support the capture and creation of 3D models in outdoor environments using AR. CAAD takes advantage of the presence of the user's body, AR working planes, landmark alignment, CSG operations, and iterative refinement to perform modelling tasks with mobile AR systems. When used in an AR environment, users can capture the geometry of objects that are orders of magnitude larger than themselves without breaking AR registration or having to touch the object directly. These modelling techniques are intuitive and support iterative refinement for detail in areas that require it with AR providing real-time feedback to the user. While existing techniques are available for the capture of physical world objects, these still have limitations and also cannot be used to create models that do not physically exist. The CAAD techniques were field tested using a number of examples to show how they may be applied to real world problems. By discussing insights gained from these examples, I have identified areas for improvement that currently cause accuracy problems.

References

Azuma, R., Baillot, Y., Behringer, R., Feiner, S., Julier, S., & MacIntyre, B. (2001, November). Recent advances in augmented reality. *IEEE Computer Graphics and Applications, 21*(6), 34-47.

Baillot, Y., Brown, D., & Julier, S. (2001, October). Authoring of physical models using mobile computers. In *Proceedings of the 5th International Symposium on Wearable Computers*, Zurich, Switzerland (pp. 39-46).

Bowman, D. (1996). *Conceptual design space: Beyond walk-through to immersive design* (pp. 225-236). New York: John Wiley & Sons.

Brooks, F. P. (1988, May). Grasping reality through illusion: Interactive graphics serving science. In *Proceedings of the Conference on Human Factors in Computing Systems*, Washington, DC (pp. 1-11).

Brooks, F. P. (1999). What's real about virtual reality? *IEEE Computer Graphics and Applications, 19*(6), 16-27.

Coelho, E. M., MacIntyre, B., & Julier, S. J. (2004, October). OSGAR: A scene graph with uncertain transformations. In *Proceedings of the 3rd International Symposium on Mixed and Augmented Reality,* Arlington, VA.

Cutting, J. E., & Vishton, P. M. (1995). *Perceiving layout and knowing distances: The integration, relative potency, and contextual use of different information about depth* (pp. 69-117). San Diego, CA: Academic Press.

Debevec, P. E., Taylor, C. J., & Malik, J. (1996, August). Modeling and rendering architecture from photographs: A hybrid geometry- and image-based approach. In *Proceedings of the International Conference on Computer Graphics and Interactive Techniques*, New Orleans, LA (pp. 11-20).

Koller, D. R., Mine, M. R., & Hudson, S. E. (1996, November). Head-tracked orbital viewing: An interaction technique for immersive virtual environments. In *Proceedings of the 9th Annual Symposium on User Interface Software and Technology*, Seattle, WA (pp. 81-82).

Lee, J., Hirota, G., & State, A. (2001, March). Modeling real objects using video see-through augmented reality. In *Proceedings of the 2nd International Symposium on Mixed Reality*, Yokohama, Japan (pp. 19-26).

Mine, M., Brooks, F. P., & Sequin, C. H. (1997, August). Moving objects in space: Exploiting proprioception in virtual-environment interaction. In *Proceedings of the ACM SIGGRAPH 1997*, Los Angeles (pp. 19-26).

Piekarski, W., & Thomas, B. H. (2003, May). Interactive augmented reality techniques for construction at a distance of 3D geometry. In *Proceedings of the 7th International Workshop on Immersive Projection Technology / 9th Eurographics Workshop on Virtual Environments,* Zurich, Switzerland.

Piekarski, W., & Thomas, B. H. (2003, October). An object-oriented software architecture for 3D mixed reality applications. In *Proceedings of the 2nd International Symposium on Mixed and Augmented Reality,* Tokyo, Japan.

Piekarski, W., & Thomas, B. H. (2004, October). Augmented reality working planes: A foundation for action and construction at a distance. In *Proceedings of the 3rd International Symposium on Mixed and Augmented Reality,* Arlington, VA.

Pierce, J. S., Forsberg, A., Conway, M. J., Hong, S., Zeleznik, R., & Mine, M. R. (1997, April). Image plane interaction techniques in 3D immersive environments. In *Proceedings of the Symposium on Interactive 3D Graphics*, Providence, RI (pp. 39-43).

Stoakley, R., Conway, M. J., & Pausch, R. (1995, May). Virtual reality on a WIM: Interactive worlds in miniature. In *Proceedings of the Conference on Human Factors in Computing Systems*, Denver, CO (pp. 265-272).

Chapter X

The Evolution of a Framework for Mixed Reality Experiences

Charles E. Hughes, University of Central Florida, USA

Christopher B. Stapleton, Simiosys LLC, USA

Matthew R. O'Connor, University of Central Florida, USA

Abstract

This chapter describes the evolution of a software system specifically designed to support the creation and delivery of mixed reality (MR) experiences. We first describe some of the attributes required of such a system. We then present a series of MR experiences that we have developed over the last four years, with companion sections on lessons learned and lessons applied. We conclude with several sample scripts that one might write to create experiences within the current version of this system. The authors' goals are to show the readers the unique challenges in developing an MR system for multimodal, multi-sensory experiences and to demonstrate how developing MR applications informs the evolution of such a framework. "Making Memories of a Lifetime," (Chapter XVI), is the creative content companion piece.

Introduction

Mixed reality (MR) presents unique challenges in its requirement to seamlessly integrate interacting virtual objects, audio landscapes, visual presentations, haptic feedback, and show-control devices with real world objects such as human participants, props, and physical settings. In this chapter, we describe the evolution of our MR framework. The key connections between each section are the lessons we learned along the way while developing ever more complex and diverse applications of MR. We also emphasize the system's flexibility in its design (components can be distributed or aggregated as appropriate for a given scenario's needs); its provisions for all modes of MR (ranging from physical reality to augmented reality to augmented virtuality to pure virtual reality); its support for diverse modes of experiencing MR (ranging from video-see through head-mounted displays to vision domes to desktop systems, and from unaltered physical environments to theatrical sets to unidirectional retro-reflective "caves"); its openness (all components not developed in our lab are from the open source community); its modularity (its plug-in architecture can accommodate other network protocols, new physics engines, new user interfaces, new interaction devices, new authoring interfaces and new AI components); and its adaptability (we added the concept of story-based rendering in one evening). Our framework has been field-tested with installations for entertainment, free-choice learning, training, and cognitive rehabilitation. Each such application has revealed strengths and exposed weaknesses that informed our evolving design and implementation, and influenced our program of basic research.

The central component of the MR framework is the MR story engine (SE), a container for software agents (actors): one for every user, virtual object and real object that interacts with other agents; one for communication with the underlying system; zero or more to maintain the story line; and zero or more to support abstractions. The software agents manage the

Figure 1. The integration of engines and devices in the MR framework (©2006 Media Convergence Laboratory/UCF, used with permission)

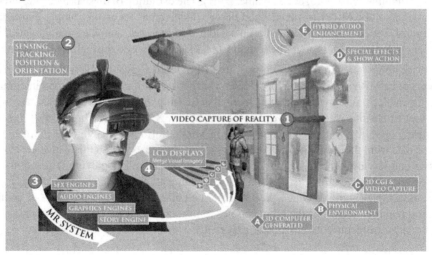

semantics of the story in that their states and behaviors determine much of what a user sees, hears, and feels.

The SE allows for a wide range of functionality through its object-based scripting language. Language features include prototype-based object-oriented programming, real-time binding of variables (the names that reference variables can be created at run-time) and dynamic array sizes (that's the scheme for dynamic memory allocation). At run-time, agents in the SE can interact with interdependent engines (such as graphics and audio), and read/activate sensors and actuators (such as tracking and special effects devices). The SE provides an integrated physics engine, a pluggable interface for auxiliary physics engines and other autonomous behaviors, a protocol for graphical user interfaces, and both an abstraction and a network-based protocol for interaction devices. See Figure 1 for a visual depiction of the integration of some of these components. In this, the (1) video see-through HMD captures the real world scene. This captured imagery is then augmented based on (2) the user's orientation and position as sensed through tracking and (3) the states/behaviors of the agents as directed by the story engine and carried out by the graphics, audio, and SFX (special effects) engines. The user's experience is then provided through (A/B/C) visual and (E) auditory landscapes, and via (D) special effects.

To set our MR framework in context, we first discuss the Canon MR system and our needs to extend it. We then present examples of some experiences we have developed and how each influenced our system's evolution. The end result is a system that can support experiences as diverse as interactive story-telling, collaborative design, technology demonstrations, games, education, training, and rehabilitation.

CANON's MRPlatform

Our first MR system was built around Canon's work in mixed reality. The Canon team, under the direction of Hideyuki Tamura, had already developed several influential experiences, including AR^2 Hockey (Ohshima, Satoh, Yamamoto, & Tamura, 1998), AquaGuantlet (Tamura, 2001), Contact Water (Murakami, Morita, Okuno, Shimoyama, & Yonezawa, 2001), and others (Tamura, Yamamoto, & Katayama, 2001). The evolution of these projects resulted in the creation of the MRPlatform API and library (Uchiyama, Takemoto, Satoh, Yamamoto, & Tamura, 2002). This is a Linux-based system that captures, analyzes, manipulates, and delivers video, as seen through the Canon COASTAR video see-through HMD's cameras.

As revolutionary as Canon's system was, its API focused almost exclusively on the visual aspects of an MR experience and provided no scenario creation support beyond integration with OpenGL (http://opengl.org) and Open Inventor (http://oss.sgi.com/projects/inventor/). Our first extensions were to create story, audio, and SFX engines, each written in Java for platform portability. In this context, the Canon MRPlatform handled video capture and acquired data from the hardware tracker. Our graphics engine extended this with a set of C++ classes and services for integrating virtual and real content and displaying these composite scenes. To support engine distribution and communication, we developed a low latency network protocol through which the story engine could function as the center of control, sending requests to each of the other engines to trigger the visual, auditory and special effects events that contributed to an MR experience.

MR Experiences

We briefly describe four MR experiences: MR Time Portal, MR Sea Creatures, MR Kitchen, and MR MOUT (Hughes, Stapleton, Hughes, & Smith, 2005a). The various versions of MR MOUT, developed through six iterations, most accurately reflect the evolution of our system. However, since that evolution both influenced and was influenced by the other applications, we describe its final iteration last. In all cases, we discuss lessons learned and lessons applied, using these to motivate the evolution of our software systems.

MR Time Portal

MR Time Portal, publicly shown at SIGGRAPH 2003, was the first widely seen experience we developed that involved complex 3D models with rich animations and a non-trivial story line. Its goal was to immerse participants within a story, with some people at the center of the action, and others at the periphery. Figure 2a is a scene from an animatic[1] we produced that helped us to test story elements while still in VR mode. Figure 2b shows the full MR with one person on the right wearing an HMD in order to be embedded in the experience and two people at a vision dome on the left observing the experience from the perspective of an unseen second participant. In essence, this is an MR version of a theme park experience employing those venues' notion of divers (the ones who get in the action), swimmers (those who influence the action), and waders (those who observe from afar) (Stapleton & Hughes, 2003, 2005).

Our Evolving Story Engine

In 2003, our story engine was based on the concept of Java objects holding the states and primitive behaviors of actors, each having an associated finite state machine (Coppin, 2004) that controlled the manner in which these behaviors were invoked based on stimuli such

Figure 2. MR Time Portal: Experiential movie trailer: (a) animatic and (b) mixed (©2006 Media Convergence Laboratory/UCF, used with permission)

as timed events, GUI inputs, and interactions with other actors. Most actors reflected the virtual and active real objects of the MR world, but some existed to play the roles of story directors, encouraging players in directions deemed most supportive of the underlying story. For instance, MR time portal contained actors associated with a back-story movie; the portal through which threats to our world arose; various pieces of background scenery; each robotic threat; each friendly portal guard; a futuristic physical weapon; a ray tracing beam to make it easier to aim the gun; a number of virtual explosions; the lighting rig above the exhibit area; several abstract objects operating as story directors; and, of course, the real persons who were experiencing this world. Each of these actors had optional peers in our graphics engine, audio engine(s), and special effects engine. The reason these are optional is that, at one extreme, abstract actors have no sensory peers, at the other extreme, robotic threats have visual representations, audio presentations that are synchronized in time and place with the visuals, and special effects when the robots hit the ground (a bass shaker vibrates the floor under the shooter); and in between are things like the lighting rig that has only a special effects peer.

An actor component, when added to the authoring system, had a set of core behaviors based on its class. An Actor class sat at the top of this hierarchy providing the most common default behaviors and abstract methods for required behaviors for which no defaults exist. A finite state machine, consisting of states and transitions, was the primary means of expressing an actor's behavior. Each transition emanated from a state, had a set of trigger mechanisms (events) that enabled the transition, a set of actions that were started when the transition was selected, and a new state that was entered as a consequence of carrying out the transition. A state could have many transitions, some of which had overlapping conditions. If multiple transitions were simultaneously enabled, one was selected randomly. The probability of selecting a particular transition could be increased by repeating a single transition many times (the cost was just one object handle per additional copy). States and transitions could have associated listeners causing transitions to be enabled or conditions to be set for other actors.

Lessons Learned and Lessons Applied

In order to stay within the time constraints of completing time portal in the few months before SIGGRAPH 2003, we retained one part of our existing closed system, Canon's MRPlatform, and added another, Granny 3D (http://www.radgametools.com/gramain.htm), which provides capabilities that allowed us to smoothly transition between animations (e.g., from running to kneeling down). The problem with each of these is that the experiences created by them could not be distributed due to the proprietary nature of Canon's API and the licensing costs of Granny 3D.

By this time, we had developed our own audio engine, MRAudio, and a soundscape authoring system, SoundDesigner. Both of these were based on OpenAL with EAX extensions (http://www.openal.org). This new audio suite allowed us to place sounds in 3D space using OpenAL's model of sources whose attached sound buffers are capable of being heard by a single listener based on that person's position and orientation relative to those of the sound source. While suitable for most dramatic effects, this version still did not meet our goals of total control of individual speakers. That feature was deferred to our next release of the audio suite.

This version of our system used two protocols for communication between the story and other engines. TCP/IP was used for communication to the graphics engine(s), and multi-cast UDP was used for communication to audio and SFX engine(s). We did this with the belief that missing a sound like a gun shot was acceptable, but missing a command such as starting an animation was not. Later tests showed that we got very little gain in performance out our use of UDP and that our primary network problem was congestion due to the manner in which we shared positional and orientation data.

Perhaps the biggest overarching lesson we learned from the development of time portal was the near impossibility of succeeding on such a complex project without having a well thought-out production pipeline in place (Hughes et al., 2005).

MR Sea Creatures Experience

MR Sea Creatures is described in detail elsewhere (Hughes et al., 2005). Here we just note that it takes place in the Orlando Science Center's DinoDigs exhibit, augmented with Cretaceous sea life that appears to swim around the pillars of the hall (Figure 3) (Hughes et al., 2005). The visitor is able to navigate a Rover through the ocean environment to explore the reptiles and plant life. The viewing window of the Rover is what the visitor sees in the heads-up display. Thus, this application brings together physical reality, augmented reality, and virtual reality in a single experience.

Tension is greatly enhanced by integrating the audio with the visual experience. Achieving this effect is partially technical—one needs to control the soundscape through a sophisticated delivery system, but the technical does nothing without the capture and/or synthesis of the "right" sounds. To capture turbulent underwater sounds, we made a custom-designed "XY" mount to position four hydrophones, enabling us to capture four discrete channels of audio

Figure 3. MR sea creatures: Free choice learning at Orlando Science Center (©2006 Media Convergence Laboratory/UCF, used with permission)

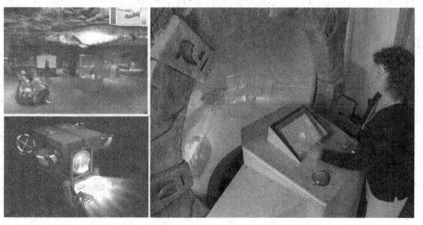

for surround sound play back (Hughes, 2005). Ocean ambience was captured at New Smyrna Beach, Florida using a multi-channel mobile recording unit. The turbulence created by crashing waves made for a realism that reflects the violent seas of the Cretaceous period.

Lessons Learned and Lessons Applied

While the interface worked well with gamers and children in the middle school years (12-14), younger children (4-11) tended to consume the experience and adults were confused by the interface unless taught by their children (Hughes et al., 2005). This clearly demonstrated the need to support multiple interfaces that can be tailored to different audiences.

A big winner in this experience was the audio, reflecting lessons learned in MR time portal and various aspects of MR MOUT (to be discussed later). While Sea Creatures did not have as rigid positioning requirements for audio as some of our other applications, given that the experience was restricted to the dome, it was our first public use of our new audio engine, built using PortAudio (Bencina & Burk, 2001). One aspect that distinguishes it from other audio engines is its support for dynamic delivery based on user-specified speaker constraints. This feature is extremely useful for public access areas like science centers where speaker placement constraints may change from time to time, and rarely are reproducible in the laboratory in which the development first occurs.

The visual aspects of this experience tested our graphics engine that is now based on OpenSceneGraph (http://www.openscenegraph.org/), and the Character Animation Library (http://cal3d.sourceforge.net/), a skeletal-based 3d character animation library written in C++. The change to Cal3d removed the last vestige of dependence on proprietary software (Granny3D), while giving up none of the features, such as occlusion models with or without blue-screens, or the scalable performance we had previously achieved.

Sea Creatures was also successful in that it demonstrated the flexibility of our system, allowing us to swap out the HMD for an observer camera and dome; build an experience with multiple virtual views as well as a mixed reality view; run unattended for days; support interacting groups of participants, continuing the model started in Time Portal; embed the experience into its environment, masking the technology; have the appeal of a video game and the lasting memory of a theme park, while delivering relevant information and experiences; and be capable of being persistent (we could capture and replay people's interactions).

MR Kitchen Experience

The goal of the MR Kitchen was to demonstrate the use of MR in simulating a cognitively impaired person's home environment for purposes of helping that individual regain some portion of independence. More broadly, the goal was to experiment with the use of MR as a human experience modeler—an environment that can capture and replicate human experiences in some context. Here the experience was making breakfast and the context was the individual's home kitchen (Fidopiastis et al., 2005).

Experience Capture starts by recording the spatial, audio, and visual aspects of an environment. This is done at the actual site being modeled (or a close approximation) so we can accurately reproduce the space and its multi-sensory signature. To accomplish this we employ a 3D laser scanner (Riegl LMS-Z420i), a light capture device (Point Grey Ladybug™ camera), and various means of acoustical capture (Holophone™ H2 Pro, stereo microphones on grids, transducers to pick up vibrations and sounds in micro environments, and even hydrophones for underwater soundscapes). Once captured, models of this real environment can be used to augment a real setting or to serve as a virtual setting to be augmented by real objects. This MR setting immerses a user within a multi-modal hybrid of real and virtual that is dynamically controlled and augmented with spatially registered visual, auditory, and haptic cues.

For our MR Kitchen experiment, we went to the home of a person who had recently suffered traumatic brain injury due to an aneurism. Spending about two hours there, we "captured" his kitchen (see bottom right monitor of Figure 4 for an image of him in his home kitchen).

This capture included a point cloud, textures, and the lighting signature of the kitchen and its surrounds (audio was not used for the experiment). We then built parts of the real kitchen out of plywood to match the same dimensions and location of critical objects (pantry, silverware drawers, etc.). We purchased a refrigerator, cupboard doors, a coffee maker, and toaster oven, and borrowed common items (cups, utensils, and favorite cereal). Figure 4 shows two participants in this kitchen. The screen on the left shows the view from the man on the right. Notice that the real objects are present, however, the textures of the counter and doors are the same as in the subject's home.

All aspects of the subject's movement and his interaction with objects and the human therapist are captured by our system as seen in the center monitor of Figure 4. This capture includes a detailed map of the subject's movement and head orientation, allowing for analysis and

Figure 4. MR kitchen: Cognitive rehabilitation—demonstrates real and mixed views, captured movement data for one participant, and subject's home kitchen (©2006 Media Convergence Laboratory/UCF, used with permission)

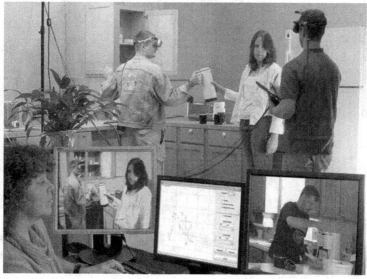

replay. Additionally, cameras can be positioned to capture any number of observer viewpoints of his activities and those of his therapist. Replaying the experience allows viewing events from multiple perspectives and with appropriate augmentation (e.g., data on the user's response times and measured stress levels).

Lessons Learned and Lessons Applied

The recorded activities of our participant showed dramatic improvement in his accessing needed items (bowl, spoon, milk, and cereal) over a five-session training period. This provides anecdotal evidence that MR is an effective means for helping in the rehabilitation of an adult who has suffered brain injury. Transfer of learning from the MR environment to his home environment was evidenced in decreased time spent on task, decreased number of location errors, and decreased wandering behavior. The after action review, supported by experience capture/replay from multiple points of view, including that of the participant, was an essential contribution.

MR MOUT Experiences

The MR MOUT (military operations in urban terrain) test bed is a training simulation that recreates urban façades to represent a 360-degree mini MOUT site. Tracking employs the

Figure 5. MR MOUT: Military training—demonstrates observer views (mixed and virtual) with a direct view of real world containing MR participant (©2006 Media Convergence Laboratory/UCF, used with permission)

Intersense IS-900 acoustical/inertial hybrid system. The tracked area contains virtual people (friends, foes, and neutrals), real props (crates, doors, and a swinging gate), a realistic tracked rifle, real lights, and building façades. Standing inside the mini MOUT creates the sense of reality faced by a dismounted soldier who is open to attack on all sides and from high up.

Using a combination of blue screen technology and occlusion models, the real and virtual elements are layered and blended into a rich visual environment. The trainee has the ability to move around the courtyard and hide behind objects with real and virtual players popping out from portals to engage in close-combat battle. The most effective and powerful result of this mixed reality training is the fact that the virtual characters can occupy the same complex terrain as the trainees. The trainees can literally play hide and seek with virtual foes, thereby leveraging the compelling nature of passive haptics.

Figure 5 shows the mini MOUT from the observer station. In the middle, to the right of the observer, you can see the participant with HMD and rifle. That person's view is shown on the screen mostly blocked by the observer; the other three views are from an observer camera (middle right) and two virtual characters (lower right and top center). Notice the crates in the view on the middle right side. The models that match these physical assets are rendered invisibly, providing appropriate occlusion (they clip the rendered images of characters that they would partially or totally occlude in the real world). Special effects complete the creation of a realistic combat scenario where the real world around the trainee feels physically responsive. This is done using the SFX engine to control lights, smoke from explosions, and other types of on/off or modulated actions. The system can react to the trainee based on position, orientation, or actions performed with a gun that is tracked and whose trigger and reload mechanism are sensed. For example, the lights on the buildings can be shot out (we use a simple ray casting auxiliary physics engine that returns a list sorted by distance of all intersected objects), resulting in audio feedback (the gunshot and shattered glass sounds) and physical world visual changes (the real lights go out).

With all the compelling visual and haptic effects, one's hearing and training can provide a competitive edge, due to a heightened acoustical situational awareness (Hughes, Thropp, Holmquist, & Moshell, 2004). You can't see or feel through walls, around corners or behind your head. However, your ears can perceive activity where you cannot see it. In urban combat where a response to a threat is measured in seconds, realistic audio representation is vital to creating a combat simulation and to training soldiers in basic tactics. Standard 3D audio with earphones shuts out critical real-world sounds, such as a companion's voice or a radio call. The typical surround audio is still two-dimensional (x and z axis) with audio assets designed for a desktop video game that tend to flatten the acoustical capture. Our system allows audio to be synchronized temporally and spatially, leading to an immersive experience.

Lessons Learned and Lessons Applied

Most of the lessons learned during the various versions of MR MOUT have already been discussed in previous sections. One requirement very specific to MOUT was its demand for long-term hands-off deployment. While the science center had this characteristic, we were able to enter the center at night to do fine-tuning, and the experiment was for only three weeks. In contrast, MOUT is inaccessible for longer periods of time, is never available at night, and has far more restricted access since entrance to and operation in the Army facility requires clearances that we didn't have. MOUT was also the place where we first needed and developed 360 degree audio whose position and orientation cannot be delivered to just one listener, but rather must be precisely associated with dynamically changing 3d positions (within the constraints of speaker placements).

The Current MR Framework

The current incarnation of our framework utilizes an XML scripting language, based on the concepts of interacting agents, behaviors, guards, and state information. This separates the scriptwriters from the internals of the engine, while providing them a meaningful and effective context in which to encode simple, direct behaviors (O'Connor & Hughes, 2005). The reorganization of the system prompted the development of other supporting engines, dubbed auxiliary physics engines (APEs). These engines are responsible for tasks such as path-finding and ray-casting, since our revised architecture attempts to make distinct and clear the tasks of each engine.

The philosophy of a distributed system was key to the construction of this framework. The story engine is the hub, providing scriptwriters access to any presentation requirements they need. For complex cases, our XML-based script language allows one to escape into a special sub-language, dubbed the advanced scripting language, or ASL. The ASL provides the ability to code behaviors using C-style programming constructs. Such constructs include loops, conditionals, basic arithmetic, and assignment operations.

The script defines a set of *agents*, each of which generally embodies some character the user may interact with (directly or indirectly). Agents are defined in terms of behaviors, which include actions, triggers, and reflexes, and a set of state variables that define an agent's current state. Each behavior can perform several tasks when called, such as state modification and the transmission of commands to the presentation engines. Thus, agents are the fundamental building blocks of the system. The ability for agents to communicate with each another allows for a "world-direct" representation to be built: you define a set of agents in terms of how you want them to act around each other, rather than such actions being a side-effect of a more program-like structure.

The graphics and audio engines understand the same basic set of commands. This allows the script-writer to easily generate worlds that offer visual and audio stimulation. Each engine also has a set of commands unique to its particular functionality (e.g., audio clips can be looped and visual models can have associated animations).

The SFX engine utilizes the DMX protocol, but control over it originates from the story engine through a series of commands, most of which are defined by loadable "DMX scripts." These scripts are direct control specifications that offer a set of basic functions (typically setting a device to a value between 0 and 255 meaning off to fully on and anything in between). These primitives are hooked together to form complex DMX events.

In our older versions of the system, agent information, such as position and orientation, was managed by the graphics engine. This required the story engine to request regular updates, thus causing network congestion when the number of agents was high. The current incarnation of the system does away with this, and now all physics simulation is performed by the story engine. The data is transmitted as a binary stream, encapsulated in a cross-platform and cross-language format. The data stream is denoted the "control stream," as it controls the position, orientation, velocities and accelerations of agents. A given control stream is broken up into numbered channels, one channel for each agent (channel numbers are automatically assigned to agents and are accessible through the reserved state variable name *channel*). This enables us to transmit only a subset of the data, usually only that which has changed since the last transmission. The system scales remarkably well.

Many of the distributed capabilities not only involve the major engines, but also a set of utility servers. One type of utility server, the auxiliary physics engine, was referenced earlier. Two APEs were developed for our projects: one to control path finding on a walk-mesh, and another to manage ray-casting in a complex 3D universe. These engines plug in at runtime, and simply serve the requests of agents.

Another utility server is the sensor server. This basically abstracts data from position and orientation sensors into data streams, which are then transmitted across a network to interested clients. This allows any number of agents to utilize the data. The data stream is transmitted via TCP/IP for reliability purposes. The data format follows that of the story engine's control stream data. Thus, to a graphics or audio engine, it is immaterial where control data comes from; a given agent's control may be governed by the user's own movements, or that of a simulated entity's. The sensor server also enables us to record user movement, a vital piece of information for after-action review (a military training term, but equally important for rehabilitation applications such as MR Kitchen) and cognitive experimentation.

The ability to define a set of behaviors to be reused in several scripts came to life in the "script component" architecture. This architecture allows "component" files to be written by the script-writer, and then included in any number of scripts. Behaviors or entire agents can be scripted, and consequently included, into the main script. This also means that difficult-to-code behaviors and algorithms can be written once and used repeatedly, without having to perform copy-and-paste operations or rename a vast number of states and agents. The Story Engine allows object-oriented capabilities such as prototype-based inheritance and delegation to make coding agents reasonably straightforward and simple.

A final and rather recent innovation to the architecture was that of a remote system interface. Originally designed as an interface to allow remote (over-the-network) access to agent state information for display on a graphical user interface, the Remote GUI protocol also provides a way to transmit information back to the story engine. It is, in effect, a back door into the virtual world controlled by a given script, whereby agent command and control can be affected by a purely remote, alien program. We recently took advantage of this capability to link our system to DISAF (dismounted infantry semi-automated forces), an AI system that provides behaviors used in many distributed interactive systems (DIS) applications.

Used for its original purpose, the remote GUI protocol and program architecture allows graphical interfaces to be defined by a simple XML file. The file specifies graphical components to be used, as well as options for each component that link it to agents and states in the script. An example of this would be to display the number of times a particular agent was encountered by the user. A simple state variable in the agent itself would keep track, and changes to that information would be retrieved and displayed by the remote GUI. This approach is amenable to a drag-and-drop approach for creating such GUIs, something we will do in the next release of the software.

Figure 6. Trivial rifle agent (©2006 Media Convergence Laboratory/UCF, used with permission)

```
<agent name="rifle" type="model">
        <init>
                <gfxcommand>system make rifle as model</gfxcommand>
                <gfxcommand>rifle set model MOUT3_props.M4</gfxcommand>
                <gfxcommand>rifle set control 2@SensorServer:4095</gfxcommand>
                <gfxcommand>world add agent rifle </gfxcommand>
                <gfxcommand>world show rifle </gfxcommand>
                <gfxcommand>world set mode occlude for agent rifle </gfxcommand>
                <audcommand>system make rifle as model</audcommand>
                <audcommand>rifle set control 2@SensorServer:4095</audcommand>
                <audcommand>SurroundChannel show rifle </audcommand>
        </init>
        <stateset>
                <int name="ammo">30</int>
                <int name="buzzer">0</time>
        </stateset>
        <action name="fire">
                <case name="haveAmmo">
                        <guard state="ammo"> <gt>0</gt> </guard>
                        <result state="ammo"> <subt>1</subt> </result>
                        <audcommand>gun play MOUT3_audio.rifleshot</audcommand>
                </case>
                <case name="noAmmo">
                        <guard state="ammo"> <eq>0</eq> </guard>
                        <guard state="buzzer"> <lt>8</lt> </guard>
                        <result state="buzzer"> <add>1</add> </result>
                        <devcommand device="HapticVest" channel={@buzzer}>255</devcommand>
                </case>
        </action>
        <action name="reload">
                <case name="always">
                        <result state="ammo"> <set>30</set> </result>
                        <result state="buzzer"> <set>0</set> </result>
                        <audcommand>rifle play MOUT3_audio.reload</audcommand>
                        <asl>
                                <![CDATA[
                                        for(i = 0; i < 8; i += 1)
                                                <devcommand device="HapticVest" channel="{@i}">0</devcommand>
                                ]]>
                        </asl>
                </case>
        </action>
</agent>
```

Sample Scripts

Figure 6 is a snippet of script associated with a rifle that is tracked separately from the user's position and orientation. This shows the "init" script that is called when the agent is initially loaded by the SE and two actions, "fire" and "reload." The "fire" message is sent by the SYSTEM object when the trigger is pulled (SYSTEM can provide callbacks for all external events); the "reload" is sent when the magazine reload mechanism is pulled back and released. In this simple case, most commands are messages to the Graphics or Audio Engines or a device called the haptic vest. These are denoted by the tags <gfxcommand>, <audcommand>, and <devcommand device="HapticVest" channel=...>, respectively.

The rifle agent maintains state for the physical rifle. This includes ammunition remaining and the next buzzer on the haptic vest to be enabled, plus position and orientation, state variables that are inherited by any agent that is associated with type "model." The actual rendered model here is an occlusion model for an M4, kept in the props folder for the MOUT3 (Military Operations in Urban Terrain Version 3) experience; the audio is in the corresponding audio folder. By occlusion model, we mean that, when the rifle is shown, it is actually rendered invisibly, but its presence results in occlusion (partial or total) of virtual objects that it would occlude were it rendered visibly. The effect is that the real rifle appears to visually occlude virtual objects whose line of sight is blocked from the user. This is extremely important in retaining the suspension of disbelief needed to accept that the real and virtual share the same space.

The most complex statements in "init" are the ones that tie the rifle model's position and orientation to the actual rifle. This is achieved by "rifle set control 2@SensorServer:4095" causing the rifle's control information to come from logical stream 2 at TCP/IP port 4095 on a node named SensorServer. The node name can be anything that resolves to an IP address, including "localhost" if the sensor server is on the same node as the SE. Typically this is done symbolically, allowing changes to be done via configuration files or even through a GUI. The first stream on the sensor server port is dedicated to the first user and the second to that person's rifle. Other streams can be associated with other sensors including those for additional users and additional interaction devices.

You will note that the "show" commands for the rifle differ between the graphics and audio engines. The "world show" and "world set mode occlude for agent rifle" commands for graphics place the rifle in the collection of objects that will be rendered invisibly, thus creating the desired occlusion effect. The "SurroundChannel show rifle" command tells the audio engine that it should use the speakers in the SurroundChannel collection to accurately deliver the sounds associated with the rifle to the current position of the rifle, as specified by the sensor server. Where appropriate sounds can be associated with fixed channels (e.g., the sounds delivered through a headset would be played on the channels connected to that head set, not on the speakers set up in the environment).

The first action (behavior) of this rifle is to "fire." As previously noted, this communiqué (message) is sent when the trigger is depressed. This behavior has two cases. The first is enabled when its one guard, ammo>0, is true. It results in ammo being decremented by one and a sound clip, rifleshot, being played as if produced at the position of the gun. The second is enabled when its guards, ammo=0 and buzzer<8, are true. This means the user tried to shoot with no ammunition remaining. When this first occurs, we set an actuator on the haptic vest to give the person a slight buzzing sensation in the front of the left shoulder. If the user tries to shoot again without reloading, the next actuator is turned on, giving a buzzing sensation on the front of the right shoulder. All in all, we have actuators at eight points, four in the front and four in the back. Once all are turned on, pulling the trigger does nothing else because the case is now disabled (buzzer=8).

The only way for a user to stop the haptic vest from buzzing is to reload the ammunition magazine. When this is done, ammo gets reset to 30, buzzer gets reset to 0, a sound is played to simulate the loading of the magazine, and all the channels of the vest are deactivated (set to 0). The deactivation could be done by a series of eight results, but ASL's support for iteration makes this easier. The tags <asl<![CDATA[escape to ASL and C syntax, allowing us to write a typical "for loop." The only oddity here is the surrounding of buzzer, {@buzzer}. The reason for this is that buzzer by itself would be interpreted as the string "buzzer" not the value stored in buzzer, whereas @buzzer is the value. The surrounding braces demarcate the start and end of such an evaluation, allowing new strings to be dynamically formed, such as with buzz{@buzzer}on, which would become the name buzz3on if buzzer=3. This ability to dynamically create names can lead to very compact but potentially cryptic code. It, as well as many other language features, are constantly being evaluated. Fortunately, our remote interface allows us to attach behaviors created in any language so long as the new API implements our communication protocol.

Demonstrating all the features of the scripting language would consume another chapter, so we direct the reader to http://mcl.ucf.edu/software/MRSS/docs/StoryEngine/ at which detailed descriptions can be found. For now, we just note that our system supports blue-screening just by the command:

```
<gfxcommand hold="n">world set mask on for agent {@SELF}</gfxcommand>
```

to turn on blue screening (the character's rendering appears only if in front of a blue screen background), and:

```
<gfxcommand hold="n">world set mask off for agent {@SELF}</gfxcommand>
```

Figure 7. Regions and blue-screening (©2006 Media Convergence Laboratory/UCF, used with permission)

```
<scene>
        <region name="OfficeBuilding" c1="-1000 3000 0" c2="1000 4000 4000">
                <action name="ENTERED">
                        <case>
                                <communique signal="maskOn" target="{@ARGS.SOURCE}"/>
                        </case>
                </action>
                <action name="EXITED">
                        <case>
                                <communique signal="maskOff" target="{@ARGS.SOURCE}"/>
                        </case>
                </action>
        </region>
</scene>
```

to turn it off. As this is often used in conjunction with a character entering and exiting a building (inside, use blue screen; outside, do not), regions within the scene can be used to trigger messages to agents telling them when they make such transitions. As an example, the scene in Figure 7 has one region. If any object (denoted by being the SOURCE field of the argument ARGS) enters this region {-1000 to 1000 east to west (one meter in each direction from the center)}, {3000 to 9999 north to south (basically anything three meters or beyond in the north end))} and {0 to 4000 in the vertical (ground to four meters high)}, then the object will be blue-screened. Once it exits this region it will stop using the blue screen and thus be rendered unclipped, except where occluded. Note that regions can exist for reasons other than blue-screening, e.g., to cause a character to fall if it enters a region that represents a hole in the ground.

Conclusion

This chapter describes the evolution of one specific system for authoring and delivering mixed reality experiences. We make no specific claims about its comparative benefits over other systems such as AMIRE (Traskback, 2004), MX Toolkit (Dias, Monteiro, Santos, Silvestre, & Bastos, 2003), Tinmith-evo5 (Piekarski & Thomas, 2003), and DELTA3D (http://www. delta3d.org). Rather, our goal is to note the challenges we faced creating complex MR experiences and, within this context, to describe our means of addressing these issues.

As in any project that is coping with an evolving technology, we must sometimes provide solutions using existing and new technologies (e.g., solving clipping problems with blue screens and then employing unidirectional retro-reflective material in contexts that require the dramatic effects of changing real light). Other times we need to develop new scientific results, especially in the algorithmic area as in addressing realistic illumination and associated shading and shadowing properties in interactive time (Konttinen, Hughes, & Pattanaik, 2005). Yet other times we must create new artistic conventions to deal with issues not easy solved by technology or science (e.g., taking advantage of people's expectations in audio landscapes) (Hughes et al., 2004).

We believe that the most important properties of the framework we evolved are its use of open software, its protocols for delivering a scalable distributed solution, and its flexible plug-in architecture. In general, flexibility in all aspects of the system has been the key to our success and is helping us to move forward with new capabilities, such as a bidding system for story-based rendering.

In its present form, our framework still requires scripts to be written or at least reused to create a new experience. Our goal (dream) is to be able to use our experience capture capabilities to evolve the behaviors of virtual characters in accordance with actions performed by human participants, as well as those of other successful virtual characters. For instance, in a training environment, the actions of an expert at room clearing could be used to train virtual SWAT team members by example. In a rehabilitation setting, the actions of a patient could be used as a model for those of a virtual patient that is, in turn, used to train a student therapist in the same context. Of course, this is a rather lofty goal, and just making authoring more intuitive, even with drag-and-drop, would help.

The MR framework described here is a system that is intended to generate, deploy, capture, analyze and synthesize an interactive story. Whether these stories are designed to train, teach, sell or entertain is immaterial. The point is that we drive an MR experience by generating a world within, on top, beneath, and around the real world and real senses that we live in. Our goals for this framework and for mixed reality in general are bounded only by our temporal imagination. Tomorrow, we will conceive of new applications of MR, leading to new requirements that continue to guide the evolution of our system and place new demands on our creativity.

Acknowledgments

The research reported here is in participation with the Research in Augmented and Virtual Environments (RAVES) supported by the Naval Research Laboratory (NRL) VR LAB. The MR MOUT effort is funded by the U.S. Army's Science and Technology Objective (STO) Embedded Training for Dismounted Soldier (ETDS) at the Research, Development, and Engineering Command (RDECOM). Special thanks are due to the Mixed Reality Laboratory, Canon Inc., for their generous support and technical assistance. Major contributions were made to this effort by artists Scott Malo, Shane Taber, and Theo Quarles, artist and scriptwriter Nathan Selikoff, audio designer/engineer Darin Hughes, experience designer Eileen Smith, and computer scientists Nick Beato and Scott Vogelpohl.

References

Bencina, R., & Burk, P. (2001, September 18-20). PortAudio: An open source cross platform Audio API. In *Proceedings of International Computer Music Conference (ICMC 2001)*, Havana, Cuba.

Coppin, B. (2004). *Artificial intelligence illuminated.* Sudbury, MA: Jones and Bartlett Publishers.

Cruz-Neira, C., Sandin, D. J., DeFanti, T. A., Kenyon, R., & Hart, J. C. (1992). The CAVE: Audio visual experience automatic virtual environment. *Communications of the ACM, 35*(6), 64-72.

Dias, J. M. S., Monteiro, L., Santos, P., Silvestre, R., & Bastos, R. (2003, October 7). Developing and authoring mixed reality with MX toolkit. In *Proceedings of the IEEE International Augmented Reality Toolkit Workshop* (pp. 18-26).

Fidopiastis, C. M., Stapleton, C. B., Whiteside, J. D., Hughes, C. E., Fiore, S. M., Martin, G. A., Rolland J. P., & Smith, E. M. (2005, September 19-21). Human experience modeler: Context driven cognitive retraining and narrative threads. In *Proceedings of the 4th International Workshop on Virtual Rehabilitation (IWVR2005)*, Catalina Island, CA.

Hughes, C. E., & Stapleton, C. B. (2005, July 22-27). The shared imagination: Creative collaboration in augmented virtuality. In *Proceedings of Human Computer Interaction International 2005 (HCII2005)*, Las Vegas, NV.

Hughes, C. E., Stapleton, C. B., Hughes, D. E., & Smith E. (2005). Mixed reality in education, entertainment and training: An interdisciplinary approach. *IEEE Computer Graphics and Applications, 26*(6), 24-30.

Hughes, D. E. (2005, July 22-27). Defining an audio pipeline for mixed reality. In *Proceedings of Human Computer Interaction International 2005 (HCII2005)*, Las Vegas, NV.

Hughes, D. E., Thropp, J., Holmquist J., & Moshell, J. M. (2004, November 29-December 2). Spatial perception and expectation: factors in acoustical awareness for MOUT training. In *Proceedings of the 24th Army Science Conference (ASC 2004)*, Orlando, FL.

Konttinen, J., Hughes, C. E., & Pattanaik, S. N. (2005). The future of mixed reality: Issues in illumination and shadows. *Journal of Defense Modeling and Simulation, 2*(1), 51-59.

Murakami, T., Morita, K., Okuno, Y., Shimoyama, T., & Yonezawa, H. (2001, March 14-15). Contact water. In *Proceedings of International Symposium on Mixed Reality (ISMR 2001)*, Yokohama, Japan (p. 215).

O'Connor M., & Hughes, C. E. (2005, January 23-27). Authoring and delivering mixed reality experiences. In *Proceedings of 2005 International Conference on Human-Computer Interface Advances in Modeling and Simulation (SIMCHI'05)* (pp. 33-39). New Orleans, LA.

Ohshima, T., Satoh, K., Yamamoto, H., & Tamura, H. (1998, March 14-18). AR2 Hockey: A case study of collaborative augmented reality. In *Proceedings of the Virtual Reality Annual international Symposium (VRAIS 1998)*, Washington, DC (pp. 268).

Piekarski, W., & Thomas, B. H. (2003, October 7-10). An object-oriented software architecture for 3D mixed reality applications. In *Proceedings of the 2nd IEEE and ACM International Symposium on Mixed and Augmented Reality (ISMAR 2003)* (pp. 247-256).

Stapleton, C. B., & Hughes, C. E. (2003). Interactive imagination: Tapping the emotions through interactive story for compelling simulations. *IEEE Computer Graphics and Applications, 24*(5), 11-15.

Stapleton, C. B., & Hughes, C. E. (2005, January 23-27). Mixed reality and experiential movie trailers: combining emotions and immersion to innovate entertainment marketing. In *Proceedings of 2005 International Conference on Human-Computer Interface Advances in Modeling and Simulation (SIMCHI'05)* New Orleans, LA (pp. 40-48).

Stapleton, C. B., & Hughes, C. E. (2006). Believing is seeing. *IEEE Computer Graphics and Applications, 27*(1), 88-93.

Tamura, H. (2001, March 14-15). Overview and final results of the MR project. In *Proceedings of International Symposium on Mixed Reality (ISMR 2001)*, Yokohama, Japan (pp. 97-104).

Tamura, H., Yamamoto, H., & Katayama, A. (2001). Mixed reality: Future dreams seen at the border between real and virtual worlds. *IEEE Computer Graphics and Applications, 21*(6), 64-70.

Traskback, M. (2004, September 26-29). Toward a usable mixed reality authoring tool. In *Proceedings of the 2004 IEEE Symposium on Visual Languages and Human Centric Computing* (pp. 160-162).

Uchiyama, S., Takemoto, K., Satoh, K., Yamamoto, H., & Tamura, H. (2002, September 30-October 1). MR platform: A basic body on which mixed reality applications are built. In *Proceedings of the IEEE and ACM International Symposium on Mixed and Augmented Reality (ISMAR 2002)* (pp. 246-256). Darmstadt, Germany.

USITT. (1990). *DMX512/1990 & AMX192 Standards*. Syracuse, NY: United States Institute for Theatre Technology, Inc.

Endnote

[1]   An animatic is a simple visual rendering of the story from a single point-of-view. Its purpose is to communicate the vision of the creative team. This allows the art director, audio producer, and lead programmer to effectively exchange ideas and determine each team's focus.

Section III:

Interface Design and Evaluation of Augmented Reality Applications

Chapter XI

Lessons Learned in Designing Ubiquitous Augmented Reality User Interfaces

Christian Sandor, Technische Universität München, Germany

Gudrun Klinker, Technische Universität München, Germany

Abstract

Ubiquitous augmented reality (UAR) is an emerging human-computer interaction technology, arising from the convergence of augmented reality and ubiquitous computing. In UAR, visualizations can augment the real world with digital information. Interactions can follow a tangible metaphor. Both should adapt according to the user's context and are distributed on a possibly changing set of devices. Current research problems for user interfaces in UAR are software infrastructures, authoring tools, and a supporting design process. We present case studies of how we have used a systematic design space analysis to carefully narrow the amount of available design options. The next step in our approach is to use interactive, possibly immersive tools to support interdisciplinary brainstorming sessions. Several tools are presented. We conclude by summarizing the lessons we have learned while applying our method.

Introduction

In recent years, a number of prototypical demonstrators have shown that augmented reality has the potential to improve manual work processes as much as desktop computers and office tools have improved administrative work (Azuma et al., 2001; Ong & Nee, 2004). Yet, it seems that the "classical concept" of augmented reality is not enough (see also http://www.ismar05.org/IAR). Stakeholders in industry and medicine are reluctant to adopt it wholeheartedly due to current limitations of head-mounted display technology and due to the overall dangers involved in overwhelming a user's view of the real world with virtual information. It is more likely that moderate amounts of augmented reality will be integrated into a more general interaction environment with many displays and devices, involving tangible, immersive, wearable, and hybrid concepts of ubiquitous and wearable computing. We call this emerging paradigm ubiquitous augmented reality (UAR) (MacWilliams, 2005; Sandor, 2005; Sandor & Klinker, 2005).

It is not yet clear which UAR-based human-computer interaction techniques will be most suitable for users to simultaneously work within an environment that combines real and virtual elements. Their success is influenced by a large number of design parameters. The overall design space is vast and difficult to understand.

In Munich, we have worked on a number of applications for manufacturing, medicine, architecture, exterior construction, sports, and entertainment (a complete list of projects can be found at http://ar.in.tum.de/Chair/ProjectsOverview). Although many of these projects were designed in the short-term context of one semester student courses or theses, they provided insight into different aspects of design options, illustrating trade-offs for a number of design parameters. In this chapter, we propose a systematic approach toward identifying, exploring, and selecting design parameters at the example of three of our projects, PAARTI (Echtler et al., 2003), FataMorgana (Klinker et al., 2002), and a monitoring tool (Kulas, Sandor, & Klinker, 2004).

Using a systematic approach of enumerating and exploring a defined space of design options is useful, yet not always feasible. In many cases, the dimensionality of the design space is not known a-priori but rather has to be determined as part of the design process. To cover the variety of aspects involved in finding an acceptable solution for a given application scenario, experts with diverse backgrounds (computer science, sensing and display technologies, human factors, psychology, and the application domain) have to collaborate. Due to the highly immersive nature of UAR-based user interfaces, it is difficult for these experts to evaluate the impact of various design options without trying them. Authoring tools and an interactively configurable framework are needed to help experts quickly set up approximate demonstrators of novel concepts, similar to "back-of-the-envelope" calculations and sketches. We have explored how to provide such first-step support to teams of user interface designers (Sandor, 2005). In this chapter, we report on lessons learned on generating authoring tools and a framework for immersive user interfaces for UAR scenarios.

By reading this chapter, readers should understand the rationale and the concepts for defining a scheme of different classes of design considerations that need to be taken into account when designing UAR-based interfaces. Readers should see how, for classes with finite numbers of design considerations, systematic approaches can be used to analyze such design options. For less well-defined application scenarios, the chapter presents authoring tools and a framework for exploring interaction concepts. Finally, a report on lessons learned from implementing such tools and from discussing them within expert teams of user interface designers is intended to provide an indication of progress made thus far and next steps to be taken.

Background

In this section, we provide an overview of the current use of UAR-related interaction techniques and general approaches toward systematizing the exploration of design options.

User Interface Techniques for Ubiquitous Augmented Reality

User interfaces in UAR are inspired by related fields, such as virtual reality (VR) (Bowman, Kruijff, LaViola, & Poupyrev, 2004), attentive user interfaces (AUIs) (Vertegaal, 2003), and tangible user interfaces (TUIs) (Ishii & Ullmer, 1997). Several interaction techniques for VR have been adapted to UAR: for example the World-in-Miniature (Bell, Höllerer, & Feiner, 2002), pinch gloves for system control (Piekarski, 2002), and a flexible pointer to grasp virtual objects that are beyond arm's reach (Olwal & Feiner, 2003). The core idea of TUIs is to use everyday items as input and output simultaneously. This idea has also been applied to UAR (Kato, Billinghurst, Poupyrev, Tetsutani, & Tachibana, 2001; Klinker, Stricker, & Reiners, 1999; MacWilliams et al., 2003). Ideas from AUIs have been used in UAR interfaces by using head tracking (Olwal, Benko, & Feiner, 2003) and eye tracking (Novak, Sandor, & Klinker, 2004).

Implementing New Interaction Techniques

To develop new interaction techniques and visualizations for UAR, several software infrastructures have been created to simplify the development of new interaction techniques by programmers: distributed frameworks, dataflow architectures, user interface management systems, scene graph-based frameworks, a variety of class libraries, and finally scripting languages. A detailed discussion can be found in Sandor (2005).

For novice users, several desktop tools for authoring augmented reality content have been developed: PowerSpace (Haringer & Regenbrecht, 2002), DART (MacIntyre, Gandy, Dow, & Bolter, 2004), and MARS (Güven & Feiner, 2003). Several systems exist that follow an immersive authoring approach (Lee, Nelles, Billinghurst, & Kim, 2004; Poupyrev et al., 2001). Piekarski describes a mobile augmented reality system that can be used to capture the geometries of real objects (Piekarski, 2002). Several hybrid authoring approaches combine immersive authoring with desktop authoring (Olwal & Feiner, 2004; Zauner, Haller, Brandl, & Hartmann, 2003).

Design Optimization for
High-Dimensional Design Spaces

One of the most difficult issues in designing novel interaction techniques for UAR is the wealth of criteria that are potentially involved in finding an optimal solution. We divide such criteria into three classes: criteria pertaining to the task(s) that need to be executed, the knowledge and skills of the user, and the current state-of-the-art of technology. Figure 1 illustrates the classes and their relationships.

Classes of Design Criteria

- **Task-specific criteria** are related to the requirements of specified tasks in an application. According to principles of *software engineering*, they are determined from scenarios and use cases, taking the environmental setting and the required technical quality into account. Yet, they may change over time due to changing work processes, which may indirectly depend on evolving technology.

- **System-specific criteria** are defined by the state-of-the art of *engineering-related parameters* of sensing and display devices and computer systems. Due to evolving technology, these criteria have to be continuously re-evaluated, resulting in ever-changing optimal system configurations (Klinker et al., 1999).

- **User-specific criteria** depend on ergonomic issues and the cultural background of users—*human factors* and *anthropology*. They describe current working conditions, habits (working culture), and educational background, as well as specific user-related restrictions.

Criteria Reduction through Inter-Class Constraints

Finding an overall optimal system that works perfectly with respect to all criteria seems to be impossible. We have thus adopted the approach of selecting specific criteria of one or two classes to impose constraints on design options in other classes. In this section, we analyze the relationship between the classes of criteria from user-, system-, and task-centric specifications. Later we illustrate the exploitation of such constraints in specific examples.

The relationships between *task and system* requirements are described by the edge linking the task and system nodes in Figure 1. From the *task*-perspective, they are described as the *functional and non-functional* requirements of software systems. From the *system*-perspective, they need to be matched with the currently available technical options. Trade-offs must be made to obtain pragmatically implementable solutions—with an eye toward upcoming requirements and technical developments. Later, we will present an example of casting such trade-offs.

The relationships between *task and user* requirements are described by the edge linking the task and user nodes in Figure 1. This case does not involve any considerations of currently available technology. Thus, options that are discussed here should hold true now, as well

Figure 1. Design criteria classified according to tasks, systems, and users

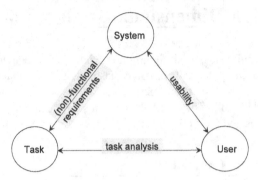

as 100 years ago or 100 years in the future. They are analyzed by disciplines such as *task analysis* and *system ergonomics* (Bubb, 1993). Yet, they can provide significant constraints upon today's technically achievable system configurations. We will present an example of analyzing how a user (car designer) physically behaves with respect to a number of tasks geared toward analyzing and comparing different automotive designs.

The relationships between system and user are described by the edge linking the system and user nodes in Figure 1. From the *user*-perspective, they are described as *usability* criteria, evaluating how users perform, given a specific technical system–in comparison to other technical options. From the *system*-perspective, they describe user requirements that need to be satisfied with currently available technical means. Later, we show an example of how a specific technical device can be evaluated with respect to specific physical user skills in using such a device.

Dealing with Ill-Defined Design Spaces

By applying inter-class constraints on a user interface, the design space can often be reduced considerably. The next step in our proposed design process is to explore the reduced design space with interactive tools that encourage collaboration. In this section, we first give the rationale for our interactive tools. Then, we proceed by highlighting the problems that occur when using this approach. Finally, we give an outlook of how we elaborate on these concepts within this chapter.

To further explore the design space, collaboration between researchers with different backgrounds is imperative to yield a solution that is well balanced according to our three main classes: user, task, and system. Thinking about this problem led to the invention of a new development process: Jam Sessions. The name Jam Sessions was inspired by the spontaneous collaboration of Jazz musicians that is also named Jam Sessions. However, in our case we collaborate on user interface elements, instead of music. In Jam Sessions, development takes place at system runtime, next to a running system. This allows playful exploration of user interface ideas. Our experience with Jam Sessions was first presented in (MacWilliams et al., 2003); we have already discussed these from a software engineering (MacWilliams, 2005) and user interface (Sandor, 2005) perspective.

To support this development process, interactive tools for novices are an important ingredient, since they foster the interdisciplinary collaboration with other researchers. Desirable would be a set of generic tools that can be applied in all Jam Sessions—independent of the user interface to be developed. Although we have achieved this for programmers, for novices this is yet an unsolved problem. We go in line with several other research tools that allow modifying only a quite limited amount of user interface functionality. Since these tools are customized toward the user interface that has to be built, most projects require writing new tools. Thus, a sophisticated software infrastructure that quickly allows building new tools is very useful.

The final section of this chapter describes a complex user interface that we have designed in Jam Sessions. Additionally, we first describe briefly our software infrastructure and elaborate on the tools that we have created for this project.

Projects Using Inter-Class Constraints

This section presents three examples of analyzing design options by exploring inter-class constraints.

PAARTI

In the PAARTI project (practical applications of augmented reality in technical integration), we have developed an intelligent welding gun with BMW that is now being used on a regular basis to weld studs in the prototype production of cars (Echtler et al., 2003). It exemplifies the systematic exploitation of constraints between task and system criteria.

The **task** was to assist welders in positioning the tip of a welding gun with very high precision at some hundred predefined welding locations on a car body. The main **system** design issue was to find an immersive solution with maximal precision. An AR-based system would need a display (D), a tracking sensor (S), and some markers (M) that needed to be installed in the environment on the user or on the welding gun in a manner that would yield maximal precision. As a fourth option, we considered the case that one of the objects (esp.: markers) would not be necessary at all. The result was the definition of a 3-dimensional design space, $S \times M \times D$, with each dimension spanning a range of four options. In total, there were $4^3 = 64$ solutions that needed to be considered.

According to an analysis of all options, the highest precision could be achieved by using an outside-in tracking arrangement with sensors placed in the welding environment and markers attached to the welding gun. A small display was attached to the welding gun. The

Figure 2. Part of the design space for the intelligent welding gun (Reprinted with permission of Springer Science and Business Media, Echtler et al., 2003, Figures 17.6, 17.7, and 17.8)

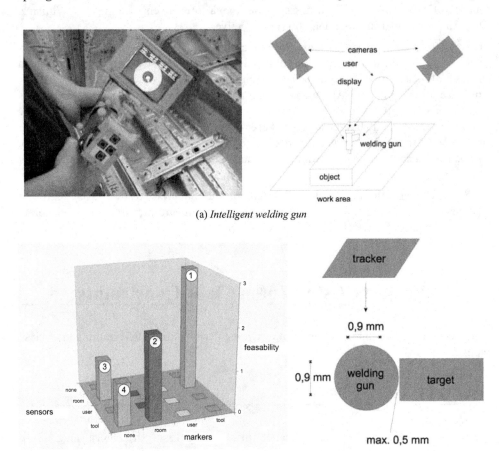

(a) *Intelligent welding gun*

(b) *Display attached to the welding gun*

visualization used a notch and bead metaphor of real guns, consisting of several concentric rings. A sphere was positioned three-dimensionally at the next welding location. Welders were requested to capture the sphere within the concentric rings by moving the gun (and the display) to the appropriate location (see Figure 2(a)).

The left diagram of Figure 2(b) shows the optimal setup. The center diagram of Figure 2(b) indicates the design space of $S \times M = 16$ options of placing markers and sensors in the environment, with the fixed display dimension D of placing the display on the welding gun. The right diagram presents the analysis pertaining to the achievable precision for this setup. This setup clearly outperforms the classical AR-arrangement involving a head-mounted display (Echtler et al., 2003).

FataMorgana

In the FataMorgana project, we have developed an AR-based prototypical demonstrator for designers at BMW, helping them compare real mock-ups of new car designs with virtual models (Klinker et al., 2002). The rationale for building this system was that, although the importance of digital car models is increasing, designers have not yet committed whole-heartedly to a VR-based approach but rather prefer relying on physical mock-ups. One of the reasons may be that special viewing arrangements such as projection walls do not permit people to view the digital models within a real environment. AR can help alleviate this problem by placing virtual cars next to real (mock-up) cars.

Here we present this project as an example of a systematic analysis of the relationships between tasks and user actions. The underlying thesis is that users (designers) behave in specific ways in order to achieve tasks. If a system is expected to support users in achieving their tasks, it has to be designed to function well within the range of typical actions performed by the user. To this end, we have subdivided the task in a set of different approaches and asked a designer to act out each of these tasks within the real car presentation environment. We recorded the designer's motions with a camera that was attached to his head (Figure 3).

- **Turning:** The car designer remains in a fixed location and looks at the car rotating on a turn table.
- **Overview:** The car designer performs an overview evaluation of the car, by walking around and turning his head to change the lighting conditions.
- **Detail:** The car designer focuses on a specific detail of the car, such as a character line on the side of the car or the shape of the front spoiler.
- **Discuss:** The car designer discusses the car under evaluation with a colleague.

Figure 3. Five different tasks resulting in different user head motions (© 2002 IEEE, Klinker et al., 2002)

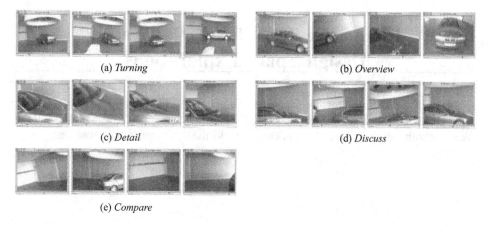

(a) *Turning*   (b) *Overview*

(c) *Detail*   (d) *Discuss*

(e) *Compare*

- **Compare:** The car designer compares two cars, for example, an existing car and a new design.

For each scenario, we determined the typical angular range of head rotations, as well as the range of positional changes. Combined with a projection of the field of view onto the environment, this gave us an indication how markers had to be laid out in the room in order to guarantee that enough of them were clearly visible during all user actions.

Monitoring Tool for Determining Usage Patterns of Novel Interaction Techniques

We have developed a monitoring tool (Kulas et al., 2004) to evaluate the usability of novel input techniques and devices. The monitoring tool allows us to systematically analyze relationships between *user* and *system* criteria, analyzing whether a system is well tailored to the physiological and cognitive skills of its users.

We have used the monitoring tool to evaluate the usability of a novel input device called *TouchGlove* that was developed at Columbia University (Blasko & Feiner, 2002). It consists of a touch-sensitive plate (similar to a touchpad in a laptop) that is attached to the center of a user's palm. It is sensitive to single-finger input, measuring 2D location and pressure. In the evaluation setup, we have compared two techniques of using the TouchGlove to select items from a menu. In the first case, users were asked to make a linear gesture with their fingertip on the TouchGlove to select items from a regular pull-down menu. In the second case, the TouchGlove was combined with a gyroscope to select items from a pie menu. Users were asked to rotate their hands around their wrists, generating only a tapping signal on the touchpad to signal start and end of the gesture rotating the pie menu.

During a usability evaluation, the user is placed at a suitable distance from a usability engineer. The engineer enters observations into a usability logging system and also monitors what the user actually sees on screen. Simultaneously, he also monitors real-time visualizations of measured usability data. The tool provides immediate feedback during an interactive tryout session, thereby supporting Jam Sessions.

Interactive Tools for Collaborative Design Space Explorations

This section presents our tools for supporting Jam Sessions. First, we give a brief overview of our tools. Second, we present an interdisciplinary research project, CAR, which uses them. We close with a description of the underlying real-time development environment.

Overview of Tools

To support Jam Sessions, we have created a toolbox of lightweight and flexible tools. They form the basic building blocks which user interface development teams can use to generate, experience, and test their novel interaction techniques.

The tools use AR, TUI, and WIMP interaction paradigms and are designed to support a number of tasks. The first task focuses on *monitoring the user*. The second task involves the *configuration of dataflow networks*. UAR systems need to communicate in real-time with many sensing and display devices, requiring a distributed system approach. A dataflow network connects such devices and components. We provide tools that allow modifying these dataflow graphs during runtime. Another task is related to the *adjustment of dialog control*, i.e., the control of the high-level behaviour of a user interface. Tools that enable developers to specify dialog control quickly speed up the development process significantly. The final task involves the creation of *context-aware animations*. Conventional animations have *time* as the only parameter that changes the appearance of graphical elements. However, for mobile systems a variety of research projects (e.g., a context-aware World-in-Miniature [Bell et al., 2002]) have explored animations that change their appearance according to *context*.

We have developed six tools, T1–T6, in support of these tasks. T1 collects and evaluates usability data during system runtime. T2 uses an augmented reality visualization to shows a user's visual focus of attention in a combination of head and eye tracking (Novak et al.,

Figure 4. Classification of implemented tools. Development tasks are addressed with tools that use different user interface paradigms

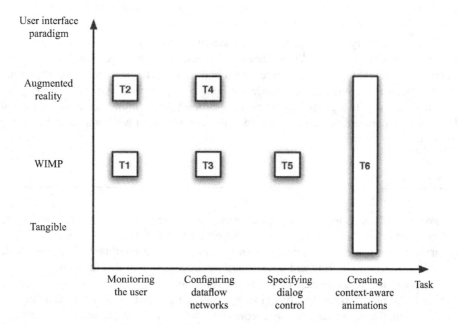

2004) (see Figure 9). T3 is a graphical editor, *DIVE* to adjust dataflow networks (MacWilliams et al., 2003; Pustka, 2003) (see Figure 10[a]). T4 is an immersive visual programming environment (Sandor, Olwal, Bell, & Feiner, 2005). T5 is a User Interface Controller Editor, UIC, to graphically specify dialog control by composing Petri nets (Hilliges, Sandor, & Klinker, 2004) (see Figure 10(b)). T6 is a collection of tools to experiment with context-aware mobile augmented reality user interfaces.

Figure 4 classifies our tools with respect to the user interface paradigms they employ and the tasks they address (Sandor, 2005). It shows that we sometimes developed several tools, addressing the same task, using different interaction paradigms. This reflects our goal of exploring and comparing design options for our own tools as much as for the interaction techniques that will be developed with them.

CAR

CAR is an industry-sponsored multi-disciplinary project to investigate issues pertaining to the design of augmented reality user interfaces in cars. CAR has used most of the tools T1-T6 to investigate several user interface questions.

Motivation

In CAR, we have investigated a variety of questions: How can information be presented efficiently across several displays that can be found in a modern car (e.g., the dashboard, the board computer, and heads-up displays (HUDs))? How can we prevent that information displayed in a HUD is blocking the driver's view in crucial situations? Since a wealth of input modalities can be used by a car driver (tactile, speech, head and hand gestures, eye motion), which modalities should be used for which tasks?

In a multi-disciplinary UI design team, we have discussed, for example, how to present a navigation map on a HUD. Where should it be placed? How large should it be? What level of detail should it provide? Should it be a two-dimensional map or a tilted view onto a three-dimensional environmental model (WIM)? If so, which viewing angle should be selected? Will the angle, as well as the position of the WIM and the size and zoom factor adapt to sensor parameters, such as the current position of the car while approaching a critical traffic area in a town?

Physical Setup

We have set up a simulator for studying car navigation metaphors in traffic scenes (Figure 5). It consists of two separate areas: a simulation control area (large table with a tracked toy car) and a simulation experience area (person sitting at the small table with a movable computer monitor in the front and a stationary large projection screen in the back). In the simulation control area, members of the design team can move one or more toy cars on the city map to simulate traffic situations, thereby controlling a traffic simulator via a tangible object. The simulation experience area represents the cockpit of a car and the driver. The

Figure 5. Physical setup

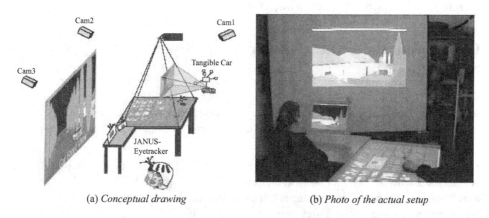

(a) *Conceptual drawing*   (b) *Photo of the actual setup*

picture projected on the large screen in the front displays the view a driver would have when sitting in the toy car. The monitor in front of the driver provides a mock-up for the visualizations to be displayed in a HUD. Further monitors can be added at run-time, if more than one view is needed.

The room is equipped with an outside-in optical tracking system (http://www.ar-tracking. de). The cameras track the toy car, the computer monitor, and the user (simulating a car driver). Each tracked object is equipped with a marker consisting of a rigid, three-dimensional arrangement of reflective spheres.

Information is presented on several devices and surfaces in the room: A projector at the ceiling projects a bird's eye view of a city onto the large, stationary table on the right. Another projector presents the current, egocentric view of a virtual car driver sitting in the toy car on the large screen at the front wall. A third, location-dependent visualization of the driving scenario is shown on the mobile computer monitor—our substitute for a HUD.

Figure 6. Discussion of user interface options for car navigation in a design team

(a)   (b)

The system provides tools for a team of design experts with diverse backgrounds to jointly explore various options to present a map (Figure 6).

Controlling the Context-Aware Adjustment of a Navigation Map

It is not yet clear how navigational aids are best presented within a driver's field of view. In the CAR project, we have experimented with various options of placing and orienting a map in a HUD.

Figure 7 shows how our system provides designers with a tangible object—a plate—that is correlated with the *orientation* (tilt) and *zoom* of a 3D map on the HUD. When the user moves the tangible plane, the 3D map is turned and zoomed accordingly on the HUD. Figure 6(a) shows a member of the design team experiment with different map orientations.

The *position* and *size* of a map in a HUD may have to depend on various parameters that depend on the driving context, such as the current position of the car relative to its destination, the driver's viewing direction, and immanent dangers in the environment. Interface designers need to explore schemes for the display system to automatically adapt to context parameters. Figure 8 shows an interactive sketching tool for designers to describe functional

Figure 7. Tangible interaction for adjustment of a three-dimensional map

Figure 8. Sketching the context visualization function: (a) Staircase function; (b) linear function

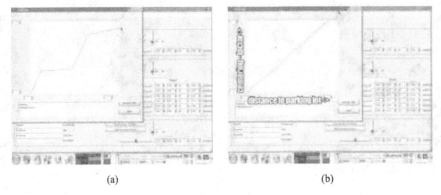

(a)   (b)

dependencies between context parameters and display options. Figure 9 shows first steps toward using tracked head and eye motions to provide a context-dependent interaction scheme (Novak et al., 2004). Figure 6(a) shows the head and eye tracking device. We are in the process of analyzing context-dependent information presentation further. First user studies of selected issues are presented in Tönnis, Sandor, Klinker, Lange, and Bubb (2005).

Real-Time Development Environment for Interaction Design

The tools presented in earlier sections were geared toward the immediate use by non-programming user interface experts. They mainly address the customization of a set of functionalities and filters, linking context measurements to information presentation schemes. In order to add new functionality to a system, the development team must also be able to modify the underlying network of components, and its dataflow scheme. Tools T3 and T5 provide such support.

All system configuration tools are based on DWARF (distributed wearable augmented reality framework) (Bauer et al., 2001) and AVANTGUARDE (Sandor, 2005; Sandor & Klinker, 2005). DWARF is the underlying infrastructure that connects a set of distributed components. AVANTGUARDE is composed of DWARF components that address the specific requirements for user interfaces in UAR.

DWARF's interactive visualization environment (MacWilliams et al., 2003) (tool T3, Figure 10[a]) enables developers to monitor and modify the dataflow network of distributed components. However, since this requires substantial knowledge of DWARF and distributed programming, novices have difficulties to use this tool.

The core component of AVANTGUARDE is a Petri net-based dialog control management system (Hilliges et al., 2004) (Tool T5, Figure 10[b]). We have developed a visual programming environment that eases the modification of the Petri nets (and accordingly the user interface) during system runtime. However, it is still too difficult to use for non-programming design experts, since understanding Petri nets requires knowledge in computer science.

Figure 9. Attentive user interface, visualizing a driver's eye and head motions: (a) The DWARF's Interface Visualization Environment for managing distributed components; (b) The User Interface Controller for specifying dialog control

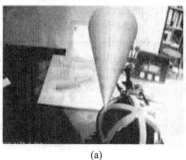 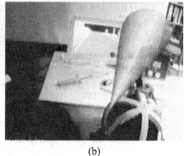

(a)   (b)

Figure 10. Tools for programmers used in CAR: (a) The DWARF's interactive visualization environment for managing distributed components; (b) the user interface controller for specifying dialog control

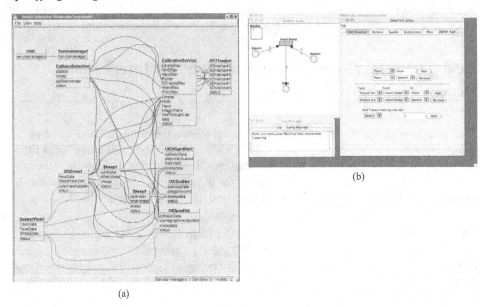

(a)

(b)

Conclusion

In PAARTI and FataMorgana, we have learned that the reduction of criteria through inter-class constraints is a valuable approach for designing user interfaces. The crucial issue of this method is to determine the most important constraints by talking with domain experts. The subsequent systematic design space exploration is straightforward.

We have presented an example for the inter-class constraint of user and system: the evaluation of the TouchGlove input device. In this project, we have observed the importance of immediate feedback through interactive tools. Our first prototype of the TouchGlove had a loose contact. While we conducted the usability study with the first user, we immediately spotted the problem and solved it. This saved us a lot of valuable time.

Our tool-based approach for further design space explorations has been applied successfully in several projects. The idea of providing user interface developers with a toolbox of flexible, lightweight tools seems feasible. However, one problem has to be pointed out: when creating a variety of tools, a supporting real-time development environment is imperative. Otherwise, too much development time has to be allocated to tool creation—leaving little time for the actual use of the tools. In this respect, we have successfully built our tools on top of DWARF and AVANTGUARDE.

The combination of tools with different user interface paradigms turned out to be a valuable idea. We have made two important observations: first, there seems to be a trade-off between ease of use for a tool and the complexity of results that can be accomplished with it. WIMP tools can be used to model more complex interactions, whereas ease of use is greater with tools that have a tangible user interface or an augmented reality user interface. Second, the combination of tools with different paradigms opens new possibilities of interaction design that would not be possible with tools employing a single paradigm. Interaction designers are typically not fluent in complex programming tasks, so their involvement with easy to use tools yields important benefits.

Ideally, it would be enough to create one generic tool that novices can use to explore the design space of UAR user interfaces. Our first prototype toward this goal has been published in Sandor et al. (2005).

This tool seems to be very easy to use, as it employs only direct manipulation of real world objects—no conventional programming is required at all. However, the ceiling of the tool (i.e., what can be achieved with it) is quite low, since our system supports only a fixed, and very limited number of operations. We are exploring how we can extend it to allow users to specify new operations at runtime. While we anticipate using programming-by-demonstration to address a carefully planned universe of possibilities, supporting arbitrary operations through demonstration and generalization is an open problem.

The CAR project also showed us that for design space explorations, rapid prototyping is more important than realism for finding new interaction techniques. Though, for the thorough evaluation of these new concepts, formal usability studies within a realistic environment are still necessary. We have conducted a first study in this respect (Tönnis et al., 2005).

References

Azuma, R., Baillot, Y., Behringer, R., Feiner, S., Julier, S., & MacIntyre, B. (2001). Recent advances in augmented reality. *IEEE Computer Graphics and Applications*, *21*(6), 34-47.

Bauer, M., Brügge, B., Klinker, G., MacWilliams, A., Reicher, T., Riss, S., et al. (2001). Design of a component-based augmented reality framework. In *ISAR '01: Proceedings of the International Symposium on Augmented Reality* (pp. 45-54). New York.

Bell, B., Höllerer, T., & Feiner, S. (2002). An annotated situation-awareness aid for augmented reality. In *UIST '02: Proceedings of the 15th Annual ACM Symposium on User interface Software and Technology* (pp. 213-216). Paris: ACM Press.

Blasko, G., & Feiner, S. (2002). A menu interface for wearable computing. In *ISWC '02: Proceedings of the 6th IEEE International Symposium on Wearable Computers* (pp. 164-165).

Bowman, D. A., Kruijff, E., LaViola, J. J., & Poupyrev, I. (2004). *3D user interfaces: Theory and practice*. Redwood City, CA: Addison Wesley Longman Publishing Co.

Bubb, H. (1993). Systemergonomische Gestaltung. In H. Schmidtke (Ed.), *Ergonomie* (1st ed., pp. 390-420). München, Germany: Carl Hanser.

Echtler, F., Sturm, F., Kindermann, K., Klinker, G., Stilla, J., Trilk, J., et al. (2003). The intelligent welding gun: Augmented reality for experimental vehicle construction. In

S. Ong & A. Nee (Eds.), *Virtual and augmented reality applications in manufacturing.* London: Springer Verlag.

Güven, S., & Feiner, S. (2003). A hypermedia authoring tool for augmented and virtual reality. *New Review of Hypermedia, 9*(1), 89-116.

Haringer, M., & Regenbrecht, H. (2002). A pragmatic approach to augmented reality authoring. In *ISMAR '02: Proceedings of the IEEE and ACM International Symposium on Mixed and Augmented Reality*, Darmstadt, Germany (pp. 237-245).

Hilliges, O., Sandor, C., & Klinker, G. (2004). A lightweight approach for experimenting with tangible interaction metaphors. In *MU3I '04: Proceedings of the International Workshop on Multi-user and Ubiquitous User Interfaces*, Funchal, Madeira, Spain.

Ishii, H., & Ullmer, B. (1997). Tangible bits: Towards seamless interfaces between people, bits, and atoms. In *CHI '97: Proceedings of the SIGCHI Conference on Human Factors in Computing Systems*. Atlanta, GA: ACM.

Kato, H., Billinghurst, M., Poupyrev, I., Tetsutani, N., & Tachibana, K. (2001). Tangible augmented reality for human computer interaction. In *Proceedings of Nicograph 2001,* Nagoya, Japan.

Klinker, G., Dutoit, A., Bauer, M., Bayer, J., Novak, V., & Matzke, D. (2002). Fata Morgana: A presentation system for product design. In *ISMAR '02: Proceedings of the IEEE and ACM International Symposium on Mixed and Augmented Reality*, Darmstadt, Germany.

Klinker, G., Stricker, D., & Reiners, D. (1999). Augmented reality: A balancing act between high quality and real-time constraints. In *ISMR '99: Proceedings of the 1st International Symposium on Mixed Reality*, Yokohama, Japan (pp. 325-346).

Kulas, C., Sandor, C., & Klinker, G. (2004). Towards a development methodology for augmented reality user interfaces. In *MIXER '04: Proceedings of the International Workshop Exploring the Design and Engineering of Mixed Reality Systems,* Funchal, Madeira, Spain.

Lee, G. A., Nelles, C., Billinghurst, M., & Kim, G. J. (2004). Immersive authoring of tangible augmented reality applications. In *ISMAR '04: Proceedings of the IEEE and ACM International Symposium on Mixed and Augmented Reality* (pp. 172-181). Arlington, VA: IEEE Computer Society.

MacIntyre, B., Gandy, M., Dow, S., & Bolter, J. D. (2004). Dart: A toolkit for rapid design exploration of augmented reality experiences. In *UIST '04: Proceedings of the 17th Annual ACM Symposium on User Interface Software and Technology*, Santa Fe, NM (pp. 197-206).

MacWilliams, A. (2005). *A decentralized adaptive architecture for ubiquitous augmented reality systems.* PhD thesis, Technische Universität München, Germany.

MacWilliams, A., Sandor, C., Wagner, M., Bauer, M., Klinker, G., & Brügge, B. (2003). Herding sheep: Live system development for distributed augmented reality. In *ISMAR '03: Proceedings of the IEEE and ACM International Symposium on Mixed and Augmented Reality*, Tokyo, Japan (pp. 123-132).

Novak, V., Sandor, C., & Klinker, G. (2004). An AR workbench for experimenting with attentive user interfaces. In *ISMAR '04: Proceedings of IEEE and ACM International Symposium on Mixed and Augmented Reality*, Arlington, VA (pp. 284-285).

Olwal, A., Benko, H., & Feiner, S. (2003). SenseShapes: Using statistical geometry for object selection in a multimodal augmented reality system. In *ISMAR '03: Proceedings of the 2nd IEEE and ACM International Symposium on Mixed and Augmented Reality* (pp. 300-301). Washington, DC: IEEE Computer Society.

Olwal, A., & Feiner, S. (2003). The flexible pointer–An interaction technique for selection in augmented and virtual reality. In *UIST '03: Proceedings of the 24th Annual ACM Symposium on User Interface Software and Technology*, Vancouver, BC (pp. 81-82).

Olwal, A., & Feiner, S. (2004). Unit: Modular development of distributed interaction techniques for highly interactive user interfaces. In *GRAPHITE '04: International Conference on Computer Graphics and Interactive Techniques* (pp. 131-138). Singapore: ACM Press.

Ong, S., & Nee, A. (2004). *Virtual and augmented reality applications in manufacturing*. London: Springer Verlag.

Piekarski, W. (2002). *Interactive 3D modelling in outdoor augmented reality worlds*. PhD thesis, University of South Australia.

Poupyrev, I., Tan, D. S., Billinghurst, M., Kato, H., Regenbrecht, H., & Tetsutani, N. (2001). Tiles: A mixed reality authoring interface. In *INTERACT '01: The 7th Conference on Human-Computer Interaction*, Tokyo, Japan (pp. 334-341).

Pustka, D. (2003). *Visualizing distributed systems of dynamically cooperating services*. Unpublished master's thesis, Technische Universität München.

Sandor, C. (2005). *A software toolkit and authoring tools for user interfaces in ubiquitous augmented reality*. PhD thesis, Technische Universität München, Germany.

Sandor, C., & Klinker, G. (2005). A rapid prototyping software infrastructure for user interfaces in ubiquitous augmented reality. *Personal Ubiquitous Computing, 9*(3), 169-185.

Sandor, C., Olwal, A., Bell, B., & Feiner, S. (2005). Immersive mixed-reality configuration of hybrid user interfaces. In *ISMAR '05: Proceedings of IEEE and ACM International Symposium on Mixed and Augmented Reality*, Vienna, Austria.

Tönnis, M., Sandor, C., Klinker, G., Lange, C., & Bubb, H. (2005). Experimental evaluation of an augmented reality visualization for directing a car driver's attention. In *ISMAR '05: Proceedings of IEEE and ACM International Symposium on Mixed and Augmented Reality*, Vienna, Austria.

Vertegaal, R. (2003). Attentive user interfaces. *Communications of ACM, Special Issue on Attentive User Interfaces, 46*(3).

Zauner, J., Haller, M., Brandl, A., & Hartmann, W. (2003). Authoring of a mixed reality assembly instructor for hierarchical structures. In *ISMAR '03: Proceedings of the IEEE and ACM International Symposium on Mixed and Augmented Reality*, Tokyo, Japan (pp. 237-246).

Chapter XII

Human Communication in Collaborative Augmented Reality Systems

Kiyoshi Kiyokawa, Osaka University, Japan

Abstract

The main goal of this chapter is to give characteristics, evaluation methodologies, and research examples of collaborative augmented reality (AR) systems from a perspective of human-to-human communication. The chapter introduces classifications of conventional and 3D collaborative systems as well as typical characteristics and application examples of collaborative AR systems. Next, it discusses design considerations of collaborative AR systems from a perspective of human communication and then discusses evaluation methodologies of human communication behaviors. The next section discusses a variety of collaborative AR systems with regard to display devices used. Finally, the chapter gives conclusion with future directions. This will be a good starting point to learn existing collaborative AR systems, their advantages and limitations. This chapter will also contribute to the selection of appropriate hardware configurations and software designs of a collaborative AR system for given conditions.

Introduction

The fundamental elements of augmented reality, such as head tracking and display hardware technologies, have matured sufficiently such that reasonably working AR systems are being produced in many application domains. An increasing number of researchers are therefore studying the human issues relating to AR, especially the impact of AR on human behaviors. The more computers become invisible and transparent to users, the more important this problem becomes. As an introduction to the following discussion, this section introduces fundamental issues related to collaborative AR systems.

Categories of Conventional Collaborative Systems

Since the advent of computers, networked computers have been used to support collaboration. In the 1960s and 1970s, however, computers were mostly used to exchange single-user activity among multiple workers. People gradually recognized the importance of the need for understanding how people work in a group and how technology could affect it. In 1984, Cashman and Grief organized a workshop on this issue and coined the term computer supported cooperative work (CSCW) to describe this common interest (Grudin, 1994). Since then, CSCW and groupware have been intensively investigated.

Collaborative systems are commonly classified into four types in two dimensions as shown in Table 1 (Rodden, 1991). One dimension is the form of interaction, and the other is the geographical nature of the users. Regarding the form of interaction, some tasks such as brainstorming require group members to cooperate in a synchronous manner, whereas other tasks such as group authoring mainly require independent activities followed by asynchronous discussion. Therefore, collaborative systems are either synchronous or asynchronous. On the other hand, regarding the geographical nature of the users, group members may be either distributed over the network (remote collaboration) or co-located in the same room (co-located collaboration). In the majority of AR systems, synchronous collaboration is supported in a co-located arrangement.

Augmented Reality as a Media for Collaboration Support

Characteristics of collaborative augmented reality systems are better understood by comparing those with networked virtual reality (VR) systems in a context of 3D collaboration. Table 2 shows a classification of 3D collaboration. Studies on networked virtual environ-

Table 1. A classification of collaborative systems

	Synchronous	Asynchronous
Co-located	e.g., Face-to-face meeting	e.g., Co-authoring
Remote	e.g., Video conferencing	e.g., E-mail

Table 2. A classification of 3D collaboration

	Real	Synthetic
Co-located	Real world activity	Augmented Reality
Remote	Telepresence	Virtual Reality

ments (NVEs) or shared virtual environments (SVEs) have begun in the 1980's. SIMNET developed by DARPA (U.S. Defense Advanced Research Projects Agency) was one of the first deployments in this regard. NVEs and SVEs support spatial activities and interactions among participants in a similar way as in the real world. As VR inherently implies that the synthetic environment is isolated from the real environment, NVEs are normally classified as remote systems even if the participants are co-located in the same room in the real environment. Although most of NVEs are synchronous systems, they can support asynchronous activities by providing, for example, a messaging system in the virtual environment.

Augmented reality technology has also been explored for years as another media to enhance collaboration. Figure 1 and Table 3 show a few typical applications and examples of

Figure 1. Typical collaborative AR systems: (a) Education (Image courtesy of Hannes Kaufmann, Vienna University of Technology); (b) 3D modeling (Image taken from Kiyokawa, Takemura, & Yokoya, 2000, © 2000 IEEE, used with permission); (c) archaeology (Image courtesy of Hrvoje Benko, Edward Ishak, & Steven Feiner, Columbia University); (d) disaster planning (Image taken from Kiyokawa et al., 2001, © 2001 IEEE, used with permission); (e) indoor entertainment (Image taken from Tamura, Yamamoto, & Katayama, 2001, © 2001 IEEE, used with permission); and (f) outdoor entertainment (Image courtesy of Adrian Cheok, Mixed Reality Lab, Nanyang Technological University of Singapore)

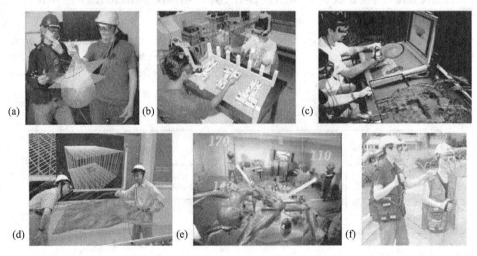

Table 3. Typical applications and examples of collaborative AR systems

Application domain	Research examples	See also
Education	(Kaufmann & Schmalstieg, 2003)	Figure 1(a)
3D Modeling	(Kiyokawa, Takemura, & Yokoya, 2000)	Figure 1(b)
Automobile Design	(Regenbrecht, Wagner, & Baratoff, 2002)	
Urban Planning	(Broll et al., 2004)	
Archaeology	(Benko, Ishak, & Feiner, 2004)	Figure 1(c)
Disaster Planning	(Kiyokawa, Niimi, Ebina, & Ohno, 2001)	Figure 1(d)
Remote Instruction	(Ogawa, Kiyokawa, & Takemura, 2005)	Figure 8
Indoor Entertainment	(Ohshima, Satoh, Yamamoto, & Tamura, 1998, 1999)	Figure 1(e)
Outdoor Entertainment	(Cheok et al., 2003)	Figure 1(f)

collaborative AR systems. As Ishii, Kobayashi, and Arita point out (Ishii et al., 1994), seamlessness is a key characteristic of successful CSCW interfaces. Collaboration in collaborative AR systems is supported by the seamless nature of those interfaces. That is, co-located AR interfaces do not separate the communication space from the task space, and allow users to interact with virtual content as well as familiar real objects.

Taking advantage of this nature, most collaborative AR systems support co-located collaboration, rather than remote collaboration. For example, in the Studierstube project, co-located users can see each other and the virtual images between them at the same time in the real world (Schmalstieg, Fuhrmann, Szalavari, & Gervautz, 1996). Similarly, the AR2 Hockey interface allows two users to play a version of the game of air hockey where the puck is a virtual object (Ohshima, Satoh, Yamamoto, & Tamura, 1998). In both cases, users are able to easily collaborate with each other and interact with the virtual content at the same time. On the other hand, some collaborative AR systems support remote collaboration by using telepresence techniques (Hiura, Tojo, & Inokuchi, 2003; Kurata, Sakata, Kourogi, Kuzuoka, & Billinghurst, 2004; Ogawa, Kiyokawa, & Takemura, 2005). In these systems, a user observes the remote environment whereas the remote user performs target tasks in the real environment with the observer's support in a manner of AR.

Design Considerations of Collaborative AR Systems

This section deals with a number of design considerations of collaborative AR systems from a perspective of human communication. Issues discussed here will provide good insights when designing a collaborative AR system.

Workspace Arrangement

Task and Communication Spaces

To share information, tables, white boards, or large screen displays are typically used in cooperative work. When a shared workspace is a screen on the wall, participants cannot see each other's faces and gestures while paying attention to shared information on the wall. In this setup, they cannot see information on the wall either while seeing each other. On the other hand, when participants sit around a table facing each other, it is easy to communicate by exchanging non-verbal communication cues such as facial expressions, poses, gestures and viewing directions. These cues play great roles in communication to attract attention. Attentions from non-verbal information are referred to as awareness. With respect to awareness, it is useful to use a table-type screen (Ishii et al., 2002; Rekimoto & Saitoh, 1999; Streitz et al., 1999).

In this context, AR displays are even more suitable for supporting face-to-face collaboration than tabletop interfaces, since they are normally capable of showing imagery between participants in midair. When the shared information appears in the middle of participants, they can see the partners and the information at the same time, and collaboration efficiency is improved. At least, co-located AR interfaces have been proven to support awareness better than shared virtual environments. For example, Kiyokawa, Takemura, and Yokoya report that the collaborative AR interfaces transmit gaze cues better than an immersive virtual environment (Kiyokawa, et al., 1998) does. Billinghurst, Weghorst, and Furness (1998) report that users perform better on a task in a collaborative AR interface than when completing the same task in an immersive virtual environment. Billinghurst, Belcher, Gupta, and Kiyokawa (2003) also report that communication behaviors exhibited in HMD-based co-located AR interfaces are more similar to those in the real face-to-face collaboration than those in wall-screen based collaboration.

Kiyokawa et al. (2002) explored how the separation between the task space and the communication space affected collaboration. They found that by presenting the shared information in midair between two participants, the communication between them became more natural, social, and easier compared with conventional wall-screen and tabletop-screen configurations. Being able to see the partner all of the time, participants were motivated to involve each other by pointing gestures and initiatory utterances. Participants also made less clarification and made more laughter. Placing the task space between users in space is useful for natural communication. Whenever possible, face-to-face arrangements should be considered.

Figure 2. A tabletop collaborative system (Nakashima, Machida, Kiyokawa, & Takemura, 2005)

Personal and Public Workspaces

When information is shared by multiple participants, it is important that the entire workspace be divided into a shared workspace and a number of personal workspaces. A shared workspace is always accessible by all users, encouraging discussion in collaboration. On the other hand, personal workspaces placed near the shared workspace are said to have an important role in terms of independent activity and collaboration efficiency (Streitz et al., 1999). In addition, a personal workspace should be provided in a way that each participant can easily access and process information in it. For example, Nakashima et al. (2005) developed a collaboration system using the IllusionHole (Figure 2). This system is specifically designed for integration of personal and shared workspaces. This system provides a number of standard Windows desktop environments as personal workspaces, as well as a single shared workspace with a dedicated graphical user interface. In the shared workspace, 2D and 3D objects can be constructed and manipulated. In personal workspaces, users can simultaneously access existing applications and data, and exchange information between personal and shared workspaces.

When separating the entire workspace into the shared and personal ones, information filtering techniques are of importance as well for independent activity and for securing privacy (Benko, Ishak, & Feiner, 2004; Höllerer, Feiner, Hallaway, & Bell, 2001).

Awareness Support

Real World Visibility

Stereo goggles and see-through head mounted displays hinder viewing of the real environment in terms of reduced brightness and field of view. Video see-through HMDs further degrade the real world visibility in terms of resolution, small depth-of-field, low dynamic range, color purity, and latency. Those headsets will restrict periphery vision as well. Poor visibility of the real world degrades awareness among participants. With those headsets, collaborators will recognize other users' activity less often and less accurately than with naked eyes (Billinghurst et al., 2003). Whenever appropriate, possibility of using non goggle-type display devices should be considered. Note that workspace arrangement also affects visibility of other users significantly as previously discussed.

Recovery of Gaze Awareness

Among a variety of non-verbal communication cues, gaze awareness is one of the strongest. By watching partners' eyes, collaborators easily notice what they are paying attention to. Among display devices used for collaborative AR systems, video see-through HMDs disable gaze awareness. To recover natural appearance of the wearer's eyes, Miyasato (1998) developed the Eye-Through HMD. In this HMD, video images of the user's eyes captured by a pair of miniature cameras embedded in the headset are presented on a pair of miniature displays attached outside of it. As another way of recovering gaze information, Takemura and Ohta (2002) overlaid a realistic computer generated face model of the user onto his or her real face using an eye-tracking device.

Optical see-through HMDs allow direct observation of users' eyes through the semi-transparent optical combiner. However, the synthetic imagery shown to a user is also reflected and visible to other users (small, reversed images appear around the user's pupils). To eliminate the reflection, polarized filters could be used to cancel it out. As another problem, eye regions are darkened due to the optical combiner. This problem can be improved by using recent optical elements such as holographic optical elements (HOEs) and light-guide optical elements (LOEs).

Enhancement of Gaze Awareness

By taking advantage of nature of augmented reality technologies, gaze awareness could also be "augmented" or enhanced by overlaying artificial clues of gaze directions in the real environment. The simplest way of achieving this is to render a line segment (a viewing line) from the center of the eyes toward his or her face direction (Kiyokawa, Takemura, & Yokoya, 1998, see Figure 3). By looking at the viewing line, participants are able to recognize one's rough viewing direction even when his or her face is out of view. Different entities such as cones, viewing frustums and virtual spotlights can be used in place of line segments (Dyck & Gutwin, 2002; Mogilev, Kiyokawa, Billinghurst, & Pair, 2002). Rendering viewing frustums help understanding of visible regions of other participants (Figure 5, right). Eye-tracking devices improve accuracy and interactivity of viewing direction (Novak, Sandor, & Klinker, 2004). In addition, the observed virtual object can be highlighted by calculating intersection. The same effect for a real object will require real-time tracking of the object.

Tateno, Takemura, and Ohta (2005) proposed a unique approach to enhance gaze awareness. In this approach, computer generated eyes are overlaid on the HMD not only to recover gaze awareness but also to enhance it, by introducing eye-drawing techniques commonly

Figure 3. Seamless transition between shared AR and shared VR workspaces

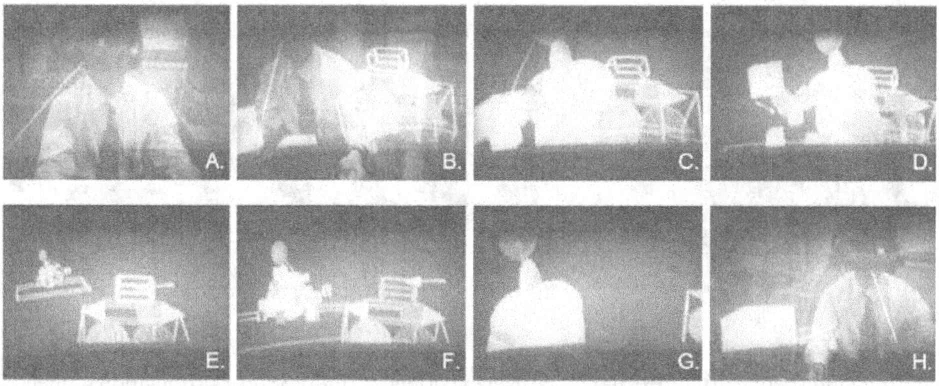

used in comic strips. By doing this, they achieved better user preference and recognition accuracy in viewing direction.

Seamless Integration of Different Environments

Registration Accuracy

Collaboration is performed relying on common understandings about shared information. In this sense, registration error must be minimized to share synthetic information in the same reference frame among participants. With erroneous registration, the same virtual object will appear at different positions to different users in the real environment. As registration error increases, pointing gestures to virtual objects will become less effective. On the contrary, registration accuracy is not a crucial problem in shared virtual environments compared to collaborative AR systems.

Transition between Augmented and Virtual Environments

Collaborative AR systems and shared VR systems are complementary to each other in terms of natural awareness support and flexibility in spatial configurations. One of the advantages of SVEs is that they can support free control over users' viewpoints and scaling factors in their individual reference frames. Flexibility in spatial relationships helps parallel activities in 3D collaboration (Leigh et al., 1996). For example, having exactly the same viewpoints among participants is impossible in the real world; however, such a configuration in a SVE has been proved helpful for some sort of spatial tasks (Takemura & Kishino, 1992). However, due to poor awareness of remote participants and communication latency, participants in a SVE often face significant difficulty in recognizing what partners are doing.

A number of collaborative AR systems including SeamlessDesign (Kiyokawa et al., 2000, see Figure 1b) and MagicBook (Billinghurst et al., 2001) support both AR and VR workspaces,

Figure 4. A virtual room observed from two users' respective viewpoints (Images taken from Kiyokawa, Takemura, & Yokoya, 2000, © 2000 IEEE, used with permission)

and transition between them to maximize user experience. Figure 3 shows a transition sequence of a user's view captured through an optical see-through HMD (MediaMask from Olympus) by a miniature camera attached in a dummy head. At first, the user observes the real partner (A). As he translates his location using the navigation widget (B), his partner becomes a CG avatar (C) and their reference frames become independent from each other (D, E). For instance, Figures 4 shows a situation where two users are examining the same virtual room from different viewpoints and scaling factors. When he selects a 'home-position' button on the widget (F), his reference frame automatically changes back to the original (real) one (G) with a smooth animation, and the CG avatar is replaced by the real partner again (H). Whenever appropriate, a SVE is worth introducing with a transition mechanism.

Compatibility with Conventional Computing Environments

Compatibility with a conventional desktop environment is an important issue in designing collaborative systems. In a typical face-to-face meeting, each participant brings one's own laptop computer as a personal workspace. Each participant knows how to best utilize it in collaboration. On the other hand, AR systems often try to fully replace conventional interfaces with new ones. However, as AR systems become more common, seamless integration of AR and conventional interfaces must be exploited. Several attempts have been made to seamlessly integrate a conventional desktop graphical user interface (GUI) with a shared screen (Mantei, 1988; Nakashima et al., 2005; Rekimoto & Saitoh, 1999; Stefik et al., 1987; Streitz et al., 1999). Some studies have developed a set of dedicated interaction techniques for shared information on the table (Shen, Vernier, Forlines, & Ringel, 2004). Some collaborative AR systems also try to integrate conventional computer environments into 3D workspace (Butz, Höllerer, Feiner, MacIntyre, & Beshers, 1999; Regenbrecht, Wagner, & Baratoff, 2002).

Evaluation of Human Communication Behaviors

Remote collaboration with conventional communication media such as videoconferencing has been extensively studied, but there have been few user studies on collaborative AR systems, and particularly communication behaviors with such technologies. This section introduces typical metrics applicable to the studies on human communication behaviors in collaborative AR systems.

Human Communication in Mediated Environments

A number of researchers have studied the influence of verbal cues on the communication process. These include cues such as the presence or absence of speech, explicit words, pauses, paraverbals, and prosodics or intonation. For example, Orestrom (1983) identifies five linguistic features that operate as conversational turn-yielding signals: rise and fall in pitch, completion of a syntactic sequence, completion of a semantic sequence, loudness, and silent pauses.

In addition to verbal messages, 55% of communication messages are in the form of visual cues such as gaze, gesture, and body language (Walsh, 1992). Gaze plays an important role in face-to-face collaboration by providing visual feedback, regulating the flow of conversation, communicating emotions, and relationships (Kendon, 1967). Argyle finds that in face-to-face conversation 60% of the time one participant is gazing at the other, while for 30% of the time both participants are engaged in mutual gaze (Argyle, 1967). Finally, humans are capable of producing a wide range of gestures that aid in face-to-face collaboration.

Real objects and interactions with the real world can also play an important role in face-to-face collaboration. Garfinkel (1967), and Mehan and Wood (1975) all report that people use the resources of the real world to establish shared understanding. Minneman and Harrison (1996) show that real objects are more than just a source of information, they are also the constituents of the collaborative activity, create reference frames for communication and alter the dynamics of interaction, especially in multi-participant settings.

The various cues presented in face-to-face collaboration can be organized according to the different communication channels used. In unmediated face-to-face collaboration there are essentially three channels available (see Table 4):

- **Audio:** The various audio signals produced by the person.
- **Visual:** The various visual cues that can be produced by a person.

Table 4. Cues supported by different channels

Audio	Visual	Environmental
Speech	Gaze	Object Manipulation
Paralinguistic	Gesture	Writing/Drawing
Paraverbals	Face Expression	Spatial Relationships
Prosodics	Body Position	Object Presence
Intonation		

- **Environmental:** The interactions of the person with the surrounding real world.

In technologically mediated collaboration, each of these cues may or may not be transmitted between the collaborators. The ability of different communications media to support different communication cues is related to the affordance of the media (Gaver, 1992). For example, although face-to-face collaboration and video conferencing both enable the transmission of visual cues, the visual affordances in each case are very different; it is difficult for users to separate non-verbal communication cues from the background in video conferencing (Heath & Luff, 1992).

Co-located users collaborating on separate workstations do not perform as well as they would if they were huddled around a single machine (Inkpen, 1997). However, screen-based collaboration is different from face-to-face collaboration. When people face each other, the space between them is used for sharing communication cues. However, when users are collaborating in front of a screen their attention is often focused on the screen space. The task space is part of the screen space, and is separate from the interpersonal communication space. As Fussell, Kraut, and Siegel point out, having a shared visual space positively affects collaboration (Fussell et al., 2000).

Shared AR interfaces allow users to see each other at the same time as virtual objects, merging the task and communication spaces. So collaborative AR interfaces should allow people to share the same verbal and non-verbal cues used in unmediated face-to-face collaboration. Thus, users of a collaborative AR interface should exhibit the same communication behaviors as in unmediated face-to-face collaboration.

Human Communication Metrics

In order to be able to understand the impact of AR technologies it is necessary to arrive at methods for evaluating collaborative interfaces. Researchers such as Monk, McCarthy, Watts, and Daly-Jones (1996) argue that a multidimensional approach is needed. Here introduced are performance, process, and perceptual measures.

Performance Measures

Performance measures are those that measure a task outcome, such as the time it took to finish. However, task outcome time is often a poor measure of the effect on communication of different technologies. Indeed, in many telecommunication experiments there were no performance differences between mediated conditions (Williams, 1977). This may be because subjects try to protect the primary task of getting the work done (McCarthy & Monk, 1994), with increased workload or subjective cost, a factor not measured by performance-oriented studies. Performance measures often contribute only to provide a gross measure of the difference between communication conditions.

Process Measures

Process measures are objective measures that capture the process of collaboration. These are extracted from transcriptions of video recordings and notes made during the collabora-

Table 5. Examples of process measures

Process Measures	Research Examples
Frequency of conversational turns	(Daly-Jones, Monk, & Watts, 1998; O'Conaill & Whittaker, 1997; O'Malley, Langton, Anderson, Doherty-Sneddon, & Bruce, 1996)
Incidence of overlapping speech	(Daly-Jones et al., 1998; O'Conaill et al., 1997; Sellen, 1995)
Number of interruptions	(Boyle, Anderson, & Newlands, 1994; O'Conaill & Whittaker, 1997)
Turn Completions	(Tang & Isaacs, 1992)
Backchannels	(O'Conaill & Whittaker, 1997)

tive task. With the right process measures, considerable differences between technology conditions can be found. Measures that have been found to be significantly different across technology conditions are shown in Table 5. Gesture and non-verbal behaviors can also be analyzed for characteristic features. For example, Bekker, Olson, and Olson (Bekker et al., 1995) categorize gestures exhibited in a face-to-face design task.

Perceptual Measures

Perceptual measures (or subjective measures) are based entirely on the users' perception of their experience using the collaborative interface. The typical method for gathering subjective data is to have users fill out a survey questionnaire. Daly-Jones provides a set of questions that have been found to be sensitive to the differences in mediating technology (Daly-Jones et al., 1998). These questions refer to interpersonal awareness, ease of communication, and the suitability of the communication mode for the experimental task. These are usually answered on a scale of Disagree to Agree. Typical questions include "I was very aware of my conversational partner." and "I could readily tell when my partner was concentrating."

Collaborative Augmented Reality System

In this section, a number of existing collaborative AR systems are discussed from a perspective of human communication. The section introduces co-located systems with regard to display devices employed and then introduces two types of remote systems: symmetric and asymmetric.

Co-Located Systems

A number of different display devices have been used for co-located 3D collaboration. Each display has different pros and cons from a perspective of collaboration support as summarized in Table 6. Specifically, Table 6 deals with eight types of display devices: volumetric displays, the IllusionHole (Kitamura, Konishi, Yamamoto, & Kishino, 2001), the Virtual Showcase

Table 6. Characteristics of display devices with regard to collaboration support

Collaboration-related Issues \\ Type of display	# of user	Real view	Accessibility to image	Location of synthetic imagery	Visuo-pro-prio-ceptive consistency
	Scalability	Gaze interaction /periphery awareness	Pointing to synthetic information	Application domains, workspace layout	pointing gesture, gaze interaction
Volumetric Display	Inf	Naked	Impossible	Limited volume	Very good
IllusionHole	~4	Goggle	Possible	Limited volume	Good
Virtual Showcase	~4	Goggle	Impossible	Limited volume	Good
Optical STHMD	Inf	Goggle	Possible	Free	Good
Video STHMD	Inf	Goggle	Possible	Free	Good
Projective HMD	Inf	Goggle	Possible	Retroref. surfs.	Good
Handheld video ST	Inf	Naked	Possible	Free	Not good
Projection-based AR	Inf	Naked	Possible	Surface (2D img.)	Good (2D img.)

Table 6. continued

	Virtual over real	Real over virtual
Collaboration -related Issues 〵 Type of display	Application domains, workspace layout (e.g. virtual objects appear in midair)	Application domains, availability of physical tools (e.g. pointing virtual objects by a finger)
Volumetric Display	No	Yes (only outside the display)
IllusionHole	No	Yes
VirtualShowcase	Yes (pattern light source)	Yes (phantom objects)
Optical STHMD	No (visible but semi-transparent)	Yes (phantom objects)
Video STHMD	Yes (phantom objects)	Yes (phantom objects)
Projective HMD	Yes (block by retroref. objects)	Yes
Handheld video ST	Yes (phantom objects)	Yes (phantom objects)
Projection-based AR	Limited (merged pattern)	Yes (phantom objects)

(Bimber, Frohlich, Schmalstieg, & Encarnacao, 2001), optical see-through head mounted displays (STHMDs), video see-through head mounted displays, projective HMDs (or head mounted projective displays (HMPDs)), handheld displays coupled with video see-through capability, and projection-based AR displays. Table 6 also deals with seven issues related to collaboration support; number of available users, real scene visibility, accessibility to the synthetic imagery, available location for synthetic imagery, visuo-proprioceptive consistency, capabilities of overlaps between the virtual and the real imagery (virtual over real, and real over virtual).

Volumetric Displays

Volumetric displays present true 3D imagery without the need for a pair of glasses for an arbitrary number of observers at the same time. User interfaces using a volumetric display, therefore, inherently support multiple users, at least for observation (Balakrishnan, Fitzmaurice, & Kurtenbach, 2001). In this sense, volumetric displays can support 3D collaborative activity. As volumetric displays normally make use of an afterimage effect with a moving screen, it is impossible to reach the synthetic imagery by hand and to present an opaque imagery (Actuality Systems, 2001; Soltan, Trias, Dahlke, Lasher, & McDonald, 1995). However, volumetric displays are normally not considered as AR displays, as the synthetic imagery is difficult to be merged with the real environment. Although hologram is another common approach to produce true 3D imagery, real-time rendering of computer-generated hologram is still a tough problem with current technology.

Multiplexed Stereoscopic Displays

Conventional stereoscopic displays, composed of a pair of stereo glasses and a projection screen, are originally intended for a single user. Coupled with head-tracking facility, stereoscopic displays support dynamic 3D image viewing. If the viewpoint of the user is different from that of rendering, the rendered image appears distorted and skewed. For this reason, multi-user support has been difficult to achieve. Recently, however, attempts have been made to tackle this problem by using time- or space-multiplexed projection techniques. For example, Agrawala et al. (1997) developed a two-user stereo projection system by doubling the cycle of stereo shuttering so that only one out of four images (left and right images for two users) is visible at a time. On the other hand, the Virtual Showcase (Bimber et al., 2001) and the IllusionHole (Kitamura et al., 2001) are examples of space-multiplexed multi-user displays. These devices render multiple images from multi-users' respective viewpoints and separate them to corresponding users by using mirrors or a masking plate. With these displays, 3D imagery can be shared in the middle of multiple participants, allowing a face-to-face arrangement. Practical number of available users is limited up to around four.

Head Mounted Displays

Most collaborative AR systems employ HMDs as their display devices. AR interfaces using HMDs allow virtual objects to be shown at arbitrary locations, such as in midair between participants (Kiyokawa et al., 2000; Ohshima et al., 1998; Schmalstieg et al., 1996). Another advantage of HMD-based interfaces is that they have the potential capability of showing correct occlusion phenomena between virtual and real scenes. The ability of true occlusion not only expands application domains significantly, but also improves collaboration experience. For example, to be able to point to a virtual object, the user's finger needs to be overlaid on the object. On the other hand, to be able to present a virtual object among users, a virtual object needs to be overlaid on users behind. With a video see-through HMD and proper depth information of a real scene, virtual objects can cover further real objects, and be covered by closer real objects (Kanbara, Okuma, Takemura, & Yokoya, 2000; Kato & Billinghurst, 1999).

However, the video see-through approach degrades the quality of the real scene dramatically and inevitably introduces system latency. Users often feel the captured real image is something like a television or video game image and the sense of presence is severely damaged. Stereo depth cues are not available with biocular video see-through HMDs (the same image to the both eyes). On the other hand, an optical see-through display keeps the intrinsic quality of the real scene. However, in optical see-through displays, virtual images often appear as semi-transparent ghost images due to the optical combiner. Kiyokawa's prototypical display tackles this problem, however, it is bulky and heavy for casual use (Kiyokawa et al., 2003).

Kiyokawa et al. (2002) explored how the visual condition of a HMD affected collaboration. They compared four conditions: optical see-through, biocular video see-through, stereo video see-through, and immersive (VR). They found that the optical case produced the fastest average time and the least number of miscommunications. Generally, the more difficult it was to use non-verbal communication cues, the more subjects resorted to speech cues to compensate. Subjects also felt the optical case was the easiest to tell where their partner was looking or pointing. When the virtual scene is well registered to the real world, optical see-through approach is the best in order for natural and smooth communication. The stereo video see-through interface was more favored by subjects than the biocular condition. The stereo condition also reduced the need for extra pointing gestures and positional phrases compared to the biocular condition.

Projective HMDs are promising for collaboration, because they do not require eyepieces that may be obstacles for gaze interaction, and because they can theoretically support wide field of view up to 120 degrees. To the author's knowledge, however, there is no report on comparison between projective HMDs and other display devices from a perspective of human communication.

Handheld Devices

A number of studies have explored how handheld displays can be used for viewing AR content, such as TransVision (Rekimoto, 1996), NaviCam (Rekimoto & Nagao, 1995), mPARD (Regenbrecht & Specht, 2000), and AR Pad (Mogilev et al., 2002, see Figure 5). These systems employ a miniature camera on the back of a small display to support for video see-through AR. Handheld AR displays can also be used as a tool for supporting co-located collaborative AR. Several users can sit around a common workspace each with a handheld display to look at the same content. Unlike most HMD-based systems, handheld systems are unencumbering, allowing users to see each other's eye gaze and facial expressions. Thus, handheld displays do not obstruct the non-verbal cues. The AR Pad also supports mutual understanding of spatial relationship among users by presenting partners' viewing frustums (Figure 5, right).

Billinghurst et al. (2003) compared handheld systems with video see-through HMD systems. They found that awareness among users is better exchanged with handheld devices than with video see-through HMDs because of better real world visibility. However, users with handheld devices needed to be positioned further from the workspace to acquire enough field of view than with HMDs. This is mainly due to the large offset between the camera and the user. Cell phone based collaborative AR systems have not yet been studied deeply.

Figure 5. AR Pad (Mogilev et al., 2002)

Non-Stereo Projection-Based Systems

Recently, projection-based AR systems have been intensively explored. As opposed to stereo projection, non-stereo projection-based AR systems do not require cumbersome goggles and they can support arbitrary number of users in exchange for giving up 3D content. Some non-stereo projection-based AR systems are intended for supporting collaboration including Augmented Surfaces (Rekimoto & Saitoh, 1999) and Illuminating Clay (Piper, Ratti, & Ishii, 2002). Registration error among participants is eliminated, as the projected imagery is on the surface of the real world. As long as 2D content satisfies the task requirements, non-stereo projection-based AR systems offer a good solution.

Figure 6. An AR videoconferencing (Image courtesy of Mark Billinghurst, Hit Lab NZ)

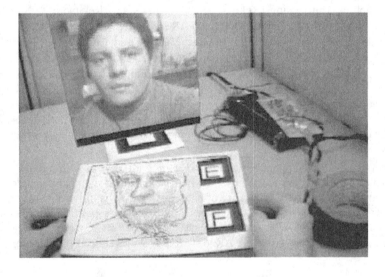

Figure 7. A telepresence system

Remote Systems

As discussed earlier, some collaborative AR systems support remote collaboration over the network. AR-supported remote collaboration can be classified into two types; symmetric and asymmetric. Symmetric systems support remote face-to-face collaboration by presenting a single reproduced environment. They virtually connect different locations in the real environment. Asymmetric systems, on the other hand, are normally used when there is a specific task to perform at one of the user locations, whereas other users observe and solve the task cooperatively over the network. In this case, every user often shares the same viewpoint.

Symmetric Systems

Attempts have been made for years to improve spatial cues and gaze interaction in video conferencing systems. For example, Hydra preserves spatial cues such as head turning by arranging multiple displays side-by-side (Sellen, Buxton, & Arnott, 1992). ClearBoard-2 supports eye contact by carefully designing camera layouts (Ishii & Kobayashi, 1992). HMD-based AR systems are advantageous over conventional video conferencing systems, as they allow video images to be positioned at an arbitrary location in an arbitrary scale regardless of physical geometry constraints (Billinghurst & Kato, 2002, see Figure 6). However, with 2D video images, it often becomes difficult for users to recognize spatial gestures such as pointing. Being unable to control viewpoint of the 2D image is also disadvantageous for human communication.

To preserve 3D information, multi-user 3D telecommunication systems have been studied for years (Kishino et al., 1993). Many of those systems aim at reproducing a realistic virtual environment from measurement of the real environment. For example, Ogi, Yamada, Tamagawa, Kano, and Hirose (2001) developed a 2.5 D video avatar system. Yoshikawa, Machida, Kiyokawa, and Takemura (2004) developed a 3D telepresence system using a set of real-time range finders (see Figure 7). Such systems are considered as augmented virtuality (AV) systems on the Milgram's reality-virtuality continuum. 3D telecommunication systems allow free viewpoint control and realistic, stereo representation of participants, and

Figure 8. A remote instruction system (Image taken from Ogawa, Kiyokawa, & Takemura, 2005, © 2005 IEEE, used with permission)

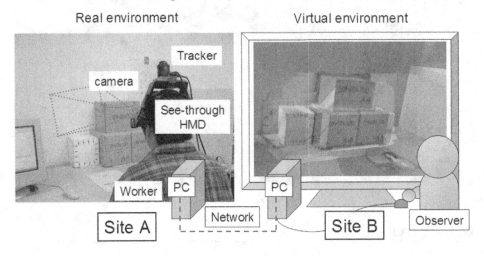

facilitate exchanging of non-verbal communication cues. Real-time 3D geometry acquisition is, however, still erroneous and/or costly with current technology.

Asymmetric Systems

Asymmetric remote collaboration systems have been used for, for example, remote surveillance and remote instruction. Asymmetric systems can be simply implemented by using a user-worn camera (Kuzuoka, 1992; Mann, 2000). By watching the remote live video, observers can recognize the situation around the cameraman. However, viewpoints of the participants are forced to be identical in such a setup. On the other hand, some systems support free viewpoint control over the remote environment. Kurata et al. (2004) used a shoulder-mounted remote control camera to allow the remote observer to change the camera direction on demand. Hiura et al. (2003) developed a projection-based AR system. In their system, 3D geometry of the task space is acquired on demand, and the stroke instructions drawn on the rendered task space is overlaid onto the real task space using pre-calibrated projectors. Ogawa et al. (2005) developed an AR remote instruction system that has the advantages of both the video-based and model-based approaches (see Figure 8). By using video projection onto a static 3D geometry, a remote observer is able to see the realistic virtual environment from any viewpoint whose texture information is updated in real-time.

Conclusion

Billinghurst and Kato (2002) identify following four properties of AR techniques that contribute to explore different types of collaborative interfaces:

- The ability to enhance reality.
- Seamless interaction between real and virtual environments.
- The presence of spatial cues for co-located and remote collaboration.
- The ability to support multi-scale collaboration.

Compared to other communication media such as video conferencing and networked VR, however, collaborative AR systems are still at their infant stage. Especially, display technologies must be progressed further for AR technology to be widely accepted as a standard medium for collaboration.

As shown in Table 6, there is no ideal display device for collaboration support. Therefore, a display device or a combination of different display devices needs to be chosen to best satisfy the task requirements. For example, combining HMDs and a projection-based AR system solves both privacy issues in personal workspaces and registration error in the shared workspace. For naturally exchanging gaze and face expression, HOE-based and LOE-based HMDs appear promising. Considering their accessibility and increasing capability, cell phone-based collaborative AR systems should be explored in detail. Other technologies such as wearable and ubiquitous computing should also be explored to couple with AR technology.

Though a number of useful insights have been given by recent studies, much more formal user studies must be conducted to investigate the technical impact of AR technology on human communication. For example, differences of the impacts in gender, age, number of participants should be explored to choose a right configuration for a given condition. Other metrics such as physiological measures may be useful for analyzing collaboration activity in deeper detail.

References

Actuality Systems Website. (2001). Retrieved from http://www.actuality-systems.com/

Agrawala, M., et al. (1997). The two-user responsive workbench: support for collaboration through individual views of a shared space. In *Proceedings of the ACM SIGGRAPH '97* (pp. 327-332).

Argyle, M. (1967). *The psychology of interpersonal behavior*. London: Penguin Books.

Balakrishnan, R, Fitzmaurice, G. W., & Kurtenbach, G. (2001). User interfaces for volumetric displays. *IEEE Computer, 34*(3), 37-45.

Bekker, M. M., Olson, J. S., & Olson G. M. (1995). Analysis of gestures in face-to-face design teams provides guidance for how to use groupware in design. In *Proceedings of the Symposium on Designing Interactive Systems* (pp. 157-166).

Benko, H., Ishak, E. W., & Feiner, S. (2004). Collaborative mixed reality visualization of an archaeological excavation. In *Proceedings of ISMAR 2004* (pp. 132-140).

Billinghurst, M., Belcher, D., Gupta, A., & Kiyokawa, K. (2003). Communication behaviors in co-located collaborative AR interfaces. *International Journal of Human Computer Interaction (IJHCI)*, *16*(3), 395-423.

Billinghurst, M., & Kato, H. (2002). Collaborative augmented reality. *Communications of the ACM*, *45*(7), 64-70.

Billinghurst, M., Kato, H., & Poupyrev, I. (2001). The MagicBook—moving seamlessly between reality and virtuality. *IEEE Computer Graphics and Applications*, *21*(3), 6-8.

Billinghurst, M., Weghorst, S., & Furness, T. (1998). Shared space: An augmented reality approach for computer supported cooperative work. In *Virtual Reality: Research, Development, and Application*.

Bimber, O., Frohlich, B., Schmalstieg, D., & Encarnacao, L. M. (2001). The virtual showcase. *IEEE Computer Graphics & Applications*, *21*(6), 48-55.

Boyle, E., Anderson, A., & Newlands, A. (1994). The effects of eye contact on dialogue and performance in a co-operative problem solving task. *Language and Speech*, *37*(1), 1-20.

Broll, W., Lindt, I., Ohlenburg, J., Wittkamper, M., Yuan, C., Novotny, T., Schieck, A. F., Mottram, C., & Strothmann, A. (2004). ARTHUR: A collaborative augmented environment for architectural design and urban planning. *Journal of Virtual Reality and Broadcasting*, *1*.

Butz, A., Höllerer, T., Feiner, S., MacIntyre, B., & Beshers, C. (1999). Enveloping computers and users in a collaborative 3D augmented reality. In *Proceedings of IWAR '99* (pp. 35-44).

Cheok, A. D., Fong, S. W., Goh, K. H., Yang, X., Liu, W., & Farzbiz, F. (2003). Human Pacman: A sensing-based mobile entertainment system with ubiquitous computing and tangible interaction. In *Proceedings of the 2nd Workshop on Network and System Support for Games* (pp. 106-117).

Daly-Jones, O., Monk, A., & Watts, L. (1998). Some advantages of video conferencing over high-quality audio conferencing: Fluency and awareness of attentional focus. *International Journal of Human-Computer Studies*, *49*, 21-58.

Dyck, J., & Gutwin, C. (2002). Groupspace: A 3D workspace supporting user awareness. In *Proceedings of CHI 2002 Extended Abstracts* (pp. 502-503).

Fussell, S. R., Kraut, R., & Siegel, J. (2000). Coordination of communication: Effects of shared visual context on collaborative work. In *Proceedings of CSCW 2000* (pp. 21-30).

Garfinkel, H. (1967). *Studies in ethnomethodology*. Englewood Cliffs, NJ: Prentice-Hall.

Gaver, W. (1992). The affordances of media spaces for collaboration. In *Proceedings of CSCW 1992* (pp. 17-24).

Grudin, J. (1994). CSCW: History and Focus. *IEEE Computer*, *27*(5), 19-26.

Heath, C., & Luff, P. (1992). Media space and communicative asymmetries: Preliminary observations of video-mediated interaction. *Human-Computer Interaction*, *7*, 315-346.

Hiura, S., Tojo, K., & Inokuchi, S. (2003). 3-D tele-direction Interface using video projector. In *Proceedings of ACM SIGGRAPH 2003*.

Höllerer, T., Feiner, S., Hallaway, D., & Bell, B. (2001). user interface management techniques for collaborative mobile augmented reality. *Computers and Graphics*, *25*(5), 799-810.

Inkpen, K. (1997). *Adapting the human computer interface to support collaborative learning environments for children*. PhD Dissertation, Dept. of Computer Science, University of British Columbia.

Ishii, H., & Kobayashi, M. (1992). ClearBoard: A seamless medium for shared drawing and conversation with eye contact. In *Proceedings of CHI 1992* (pp. 525-532).

Ishii, H., Kobayashi, M., & Arita, K. (1994). Iterative design of seamless collaboration media. *Communications of the ACM (CACM) (Special Issue on Internet Technology)*, *37*(8), 83-97.

Ishii, H., Underkoffler, J., Chak, D., Piper, B., Joseph, E., B., Yeung, L., & Kanji, Z. (2002). Augmented urban planning workbench: Overlaying drawings, physical models and digital simulation. In *Proceedings of ISMAR 2002* (pp. 203-211).

Kanbara, M., Okuma, T., Takemura, H., & Yokoya, N. (2000). A stereoscopic video see-through augmented reality system based on real-time vision-based registration. In *Proceedings of the IEEE VR 2000* (pp. 255-262).

Kato, H., & Billinghurst, M. (1999). Marker tracking and HMD calibration for a video-based augmented reality conferencing system. In *Proceedings of the IEEE & ACM IWAR '99* (pp. 85-94).

Kaufmann, H., & Schmalstieg, D. (2003). Mathematics and geometry education with collaborative augmented reality. *Computers & Graphics*, *27*(3), 339-345.

Kendon, A. (1967). Some functions of gaze direction in social interaction. *Acta Psychologica, 32*, 1-25.

Kishino, F., et al. (1993). Virtual space teleconferencing system—real time detection and reproduction of 3-D human images. In *Proceedings HCI International '93* (pp. 669-674).

Kitamura, Y., Konishi, T., Yamamoto, S., & Kishino, F. (2001). Interactive stereoscopic display for three or more users. In *Proceedings of the ACM SIGGRAPH 2001* (pp. 231-239).

Kiyokawa, K., Billinghurst, M., Campbell, B., & Woods, E. (2003). An occlusion-capable optical see-through head mount display for supporting co-located collaboration. In *Proceedings of ISMAR 2003* (pp. 133-141).

Kiyokawa, K., Billinghurst, M., Hayes, S. E., Gupta, A., Sannohe, Y., & Kato, H. (2002). communication behaviors of co-located users in collaborative AR interfaces. In *Proceedings of ISMAR 2002* (pp. 139-148).

Kiyokawa, K., Niimi, M., Ebina, T., & Ohno, H. (2001). MR2 (MR Square): A mixed-reality meeting room. In *Proceedings of ISAR 2001* (pp. 169-170).

Kiyokawa, K., Takemura, H., & Yokoya, N. (2000). SeamlessDesign for 3D object creation. *IEEE MultiMedia*, *7*(1), 22-33.

Kiyokawa, K., Takemura, H., & Yokoya, N. (1998). Collaborative immersive workspace through a shared augmented environment. In *Proceedings of SPIE '99* (Vol. 3517, pp. 2-13).

Kurata, T., Sakata, N., Kourogi, M., Kuzuoka, H., & Billinghurst, M. (2002). Remote collaboration using a shoulder-worn active camera/laser. In *Proceedings of IEEE ISWC 2004* (pp. 62-69).

Kuzuoka, H. (1992). Spatial workspace collaboration: A shared view video support system for remote collaboration capability. In *Proceedings of ACM CHI 1992* (pp. 533-540).

Leigh, J., et al. (1996). Multi-perspective collaborative design in persistent networked virtual environments. In *Proceedings of IEEE VRAIS 1996* (pp. 253-260).

Mann, S. (2000). Telepointer: Hands-free completely self contained wearable visual augmented reality without headwear and without any infrastructure reliance. In *Proceedings of IEEE ISWC 2000* (pp. 177-178).

Mantei, M. (1988). Capturing the capture concepts: A case study in the design of computer-supported meeting environments. In *Proceedings of CSCW '88* (pp. 257-270).

McCarthy, J., & Monk, A. (1994). Measuring the quality of computer-mediated communication. *Behavior & Information Technology, 13*(5), 311-319.

Mehan, H., & Wood, H. (1975). *The reality of ethnomethodology*. John Wiley & Sons.

Minneman, S., & Harrison, S. (1996). A bike in hand: A study of 3-D objects in design. In N. Cross, H., Christiaans, & K. Dorst (Eds.), *Analyzing design activity*. J. Wiley.

Miyasato, T. (1998). An eye-through HMD for augmented reality in face-to-face communication. In *Proceedings of IEEE ROMAN 1998*.

Mogilev, D., Kiyokawa, K., Billinghurst, M., & Pair, J. (2002). AR Pad: An interface for face-to-face AR collaboration. In *Proceedings of CHI 2002 Extended Abstracts* (pp. 654-655).

Monk, A. F., McCarthy, J., Watts, L., & Daly-Jones, O. (1996). Measures of process. In P. J. Thomas (Ed.), *CSCW requirements and evaluation* (pp. 125-139). Springer-Verlag.

Nakashima, K., Machida, T., Kiyokawa, K., & Takemura, H. (2005). A 2D-3D integrated environment for cooperative work. In *Proceedings of VRST 2005* (pp. 16-22).

Novak, V., Sandor, C., & Klinker, G. (2004). An AR workbench for experimenting with attentive user interfaces. In *Proceedings of ISMAR 2004* (pp. 284-285).

O'Conaill, B., & Whittaker, S. (1997). Characterizing, predicting, and measuring video-mediated communication: A conversational approach. In K. Finn, A. Sellen, & S. Wilbur (Eds.), *Video mediated communication*, LEA.

Ogawa, T., Kiyokawa, K., & Takemura, H. (2005). A hybrid image-based and model-based telepresence system using two-pass video projection onto a 3D scene model. In *Proceedings of the IEEE ISMAR 2005* (pp. 202-203).

Ogi, T., Yamada, T., Tamagawa, K., Kano, M., & Hirose, M. (2001). Immersive telecommunication using stereo video avatar. In *Proceedings of IEEE VR 2001* (pp. 45-51).

Ohshima, T., Satoh, K., Yamamoto, H., & Tamura, H. (1998). AR2 hockey: A case study of collaborative augmented reality. In *Proceedings IEEE VRAIS '98* (pp. 268-275).

Ohshima, T., Satoh, K., Yamamoto, H., & Tamura, H. (1999). RV-border guards: A multi-player entertainment in mixed reality space. In *Proceedings of IWAR 1999*.

O'Malley, C., Langton, S., Anderson, A., Doherty-Sneddon, G., & Bruce, V. (1996). A comparison of face-to-face and video-mediated interaction. *Interacting with Computers*, *8*(2), 177-192.

Orestrom, B. (1983). *Turn-taking in English conversation*. Chartwell-Bratt, Bromley, Kent.

Piper, B., Ratti, C., & Ishii, H. (2002). Illuminating clay: A 3-D tangible interface for landscape analysis. In *Proceedings of SIGCHI* (pp. 355-362).

Regenbrecht, H., & Specht, R. (2000). A mobile passive augmented reality device. In *Proceedings of the International Symposium on Augmented Reality (ISAR 2000)* (pp. 81-84). IEEE Press.

Regenbrecht, H., Wagner, M., & Baratoff, G. (2002). MagicMeeting: A collaborative tangible augmented reality system. *Virtual Reality: Systems, Development and Applications*, *6*(3), 151-166.

Rekimoto, J. (1996). TransVision: A hand-held augmented reality system for collaborative design. In *Proceedings of Virtual Systems and Multi-Media (VSMM '96)*.

Rekimoto, J., & Nagao, K. (1995). The world through the computer: Computer augmented interaction with real world environments. In *Proceedings of User Interface Software and Technology (UIST '95)*.

Rekimoto, J., & Saitoh, M. (1999). Augmented surfaces: A spatially continuous workspace for hybrid computing environments. In *Proceedings of CHI '99* (pp. 378-385).

Rodden, T. (1991). A survey of CSCW systems. *Interacting with Computers*, *3*(3), 319-353.

Schmalstieg, D., Fuhrmann, A., Szalavari, Z., & Gervautz, M. (1996). Studierstube: An environment for collaboration in augmented reality. In *Proceedings of the CVE '96 Workshop*.

Sellen, A. (1995). Remote conversations: The effects of mediating talk with technology. *Human Computer Interaction*, *10*(4), 401-444.

Sellen, A., Buxton, B., & Arnott, J. (1992). Using spatial cues to improve videoconferencing. In *Proceedings of CHI 1992* (pp. 651-652).

Shen, C., Vernier, F. D., Forlines, C., & Ringel, M. (2004). DiamondSpin: An extensible toolkit for around-the-table interaction. In *Proceedings of CHI 2004* (pp. 167-174).

Soltan, P., Trias, J., Dahlke, W., Lasher, M., & McDonald, M. (1995). Laser-based 3D volumetric display system: Second generation. In *Interactive technology and the new paradigm for technology* (pp. 349-358). IOP Press.

Stefik, M., Foster, G., Bobrow, D. G., Kahn, K., Lanning, S., & Suchman, L. (1987). Beyond the chalkboard: Computer support for collaboration and problem solving in meetings. *Communications of the ACM*, *30*(1), 32-47.

Streitz, N. A., Geisler, J., Holmer, T., Konomi, S., Muller-Tomfelde, C., Reischl, W., Rexroth, P., Seitz, P., & Steinmetz, R. (1999). i-LAND: An interactive landscape for creativity and innovation. In *Proceedings of CHI '99* (pp. 120-127).

Takemura, H., & Kishino, F. (1992). Cooperative work environment using virtual workspace. In *Proceedings of CSCW 1992* (pp. 226-232).

Takemura, M., & Ohta, Y. (2002). Diminishing head-mounted display for shared mixed reality. In *Proceedings of ISMAR 2002* (pp. 149-156).

Tamura, T., Yamamoto, H. & Katayama, A. (2001). Mixed Reality: Future Dreams Seen at the Border between Real and Virtual Worlds. *IEEE Computer Graphics and Applications, 21*(6), 64-70

Tang, J., & Isaacs, E. (1992). *Why do users like video? Studies of multimedia-supported collaboration* (Tech. Rep. No. SMLI TR-92-5). Sun Microsystems Laboratories.

Tateno, K., Takemura, M., & Ohta, Y. (2005). Enhanced eyes for better gaze-awareness in collaborative mixed reality. In *Proceedings of ISMAR 2005* (pp. 100-103).

Walsh, J. (1992). *Personal video: A reality.* ITCA Teleconferencing Yearbook.

Williams, E. (1977). Experimental comparison of face-to-face and mediated communication: A review. *Psychological Bulletin, 84*(5), 963-976.

Yoshikawa, K., Machida, T., Kiyokawa, K., & Takemura, H. (2004). A high presence shared space communication system using 2D background and 3D avatar. In *Proceedings of IEEE SAINT 2004* (pp. 50-55).

Chapter XIII

Interaction Design for Tangible Augmented Reality Applications

Gun A. Lee, Electronics and Telecommunications Research Institute, Korea

Gerard J. Kim, Korea University, Korea

Mark Billinghurst, Human Interface Technology Laboratory, New Zealand

Abstract

This chapter describes designing interaction methods for tangible augmented reality (AR) applications. First, we describe the concept of a tangible augmented reality interface and review its various successful applications, focusing on their interaction designs. Next, we classify and consolidate these interaction methods into common tasks and interaction schemes. Finally, we present general design guidelines for interaction methods in tangible AR applications. The authors hope that these guidelines will help developers design interaction methods for tangible AR applications in a more structured and efficient way, and bring tangible AR interfaces closer to our daily lives with further research.

Introduction

The first augmented reality (AR) scene was created nearly forty years ago by Ivan Sutherland (1965) with a wire frame cube generated by computer graphics on a see-through head mounted display (HMD). Computer graphics have advanced tremendously since then. For instance, real-time photorealistic renderings of complex objects are now possible, and instead of using a mechanical head tracker like Sutherland, there are now a wide variety of commercially available sensors such as electromagnetic, ultrasonic, computer vision based, and inertial systems.

In recent years, interaction methods for AR have become a very active area of research. Various interaction techniques have been developed, including those adopted from other related areas such as virtual reality (Kiyokawa, Takemura, & Yokoya, 1999; Schmalstieg, Fuhrmann, & Hesina, 2000), 2D desktop user interfaces, and wearable computing. One promising direction is to explore the use of physical objects to interact with virtual content. Ishii popularized this with the concept of the tangible user interface (TUI) (Ishii & Ullmer, 1997) in which physical objects were used to manipulate digital data.

The TUI metaphor can be effectively applied to AR interfaces as well. Kato, Billinghurst, Poupyrev, Imamoto, and Tachibana referred to this concept as the 'tangible augmented reality' (Kato et al., 2000). In a tangible AR interface, the visual display of the AR content is coupled to a tangible object. Thus, tangible AR interfaces are those in which (Billinghurst, Grasset, & Looser, 2005):

- Each virtual object is registered to a physical object, and
- The user interacts with virtual objects by manipulating physical objects.

For instance, with a tangible AR interface, users can handle physical "records" to manipulate virtual music, or flip over real book pages to see different virtual scenes from a storybook.

Figure 1. Example of tangible augmented reality interface

Tangible AR interfaces provide intuitive and effective manipulation of virtual objects by taking advantage of the immediacy and familiarity of physical objects in our everyday life.

Figure 1 shows a simple application of the tangible AR interface. The user wears a video see-through (Azuma, 1997) HMD which has a video camera attached in front of it. When the user looks at a real book page through the display, one can see a virtual object (e.g., a yacht) popping out from it. As the virtual yacht is registered to the physical book page, the user can move and rotate the virtual yacht by simply moving the book.

While TUI offers great advantages in interacting within an AR scene, there are no specific guidelines to as how to design a tangible interface for a given AR application. Despite some recent progresses in interaction modeling (Bowman, Kruijff, LaViola, & Poupyrev, 2001), finding the best interaction method for a given AR application usually requires costly and time-consuming development and usability testing.

In this chapter, we review the interaction designs of a number of representative tangible AR applications, and develop several guidelines in designing interaction methods for tangible AR applications.

Background

The basic goal of designing an interface is to "map user input onto computer output using an appropriate interaction metaphor" (Billinghurst et al., 2005, p. 17). In Tangible AR interfaces, the user inputs are from physical objects, while the computer outputs are virtual objects. A physical object and a virtual object are combined into an augmented object by mapping their inputs and outputs. The mapping between these two entities (physical and virtual objects) involves updating virtual object properties according to physical object behaviors (see Figure 2).

In many tangible AR applications, a virtual object is visualized at the same position and orientation as its physical counterpart, thus forming *direct mapping* of properties (position and orientation) between them. Although this is natural for direct 3D manipulation, direct mappings may not always be the best solution. For instance, a snap-to-grid function is an *indirect mapping* in which the position of a virtual object is attracted to discrete grid points.

In tangible AR applications, most of the mappings occur between a virtual object and its physical object counterpart. Usually virtual objects appear as if they are anchored to a *paired* physical object. If this mapping is unchanged within the application, we refer to this

Figure 2. Interface design as a mapping

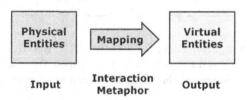

Figure 3. Spectrum of relationship between the physical interface and the target interaction object in terms of the similarity in their tangible property (e.g., shape)

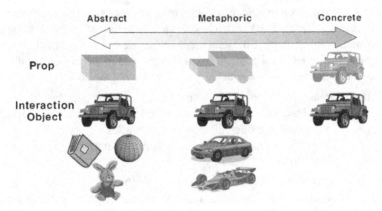

as *static pairing*. However, the pairing might change dynamically (*dynamic pairing*) for some applications. For instance, the user may hold a real paddle that is used to pick up and manipulate a variety of different virtual models, so the real virtual object pairing changes dynamically.

In providing TUI, it is desirable to match the physical (or tangible) properties (e.g., shape, weight, texture, etc.) of the interaction prop (physical object) to the target interaction object (virtual object) as much as possible. However, on the other hand, if the match is too exact, then the prop can represent only few virtual objects. Figure 3 shows the spectrum of the relationship between the physical and virtual objects in terms of their similarity in physical properties. While abstract props can represent anything, the tangible feel is reduced with non-exactly matched shape. A metaphorically designed prop can represent a class of virtual objects, while it looses concrete representations.

Survey: Tangible Applications

In this section, we review some successful tangible AR applications and examine their interaction designs. We will later attempt to consolidate the various interaction methods into general design guidelines.

MagicBook

The MagicBook (Billinghurst, Kato, & Poupyrev, 2001) is a real storybook with specially marked pages that is viewed through a hand held display (see Figure 1). The display consists of a small LCD display on a handle with a video camera attached in front of it. When the user looks at the book through the display, he or she can see a 3D virtual object/scene popping out of the book pages. The virtual objects are visually registered to the book page, so the user can easily move and rotate the virtual scene by manipulating the physical book. The user can also turn the real pages of the Magic Book to see different virtual scenes.

MagicLenses

MagicLenses (Looser, Billinghurst, & Cockburn, 2004) allows the user to see multiple virtual datasets at the same time. While the basic display configuration is similar to that of the MagicBook, the MagicLens interface has an additional hand held prop which represents a reading glass. Looking through the glass, the interface shows different representations of the virtual object. For instance, Figure 4 shows how the MagicLens can be used to look inside a virtual human body.

Shared Space

In the Shared Space interface (Billinghurst, Poupyrev, Kato, & May, 2000), multiple users play a card matching game in a shared (i.e., multi-user) AR environment. On the table in front of the users, there are cards placed face down. As the user picks up a card and turns it over, he or she can see different virtual objects on each card, through a see-through HMD. When two cards with matching virtual objects are placed side by side, an animation is triggered. For instance, when the card with an alien is placed next to the UFO, the alien appears to fly around the earth.

Figure 4. MagicLenses

Augmented Groove

The augmented groove application (Poupyrev et al., 2001) shows how a tangible AR approach can be used for controlling electronic music. In this interface, users stand in front of a projection screen, which shows a live video taken from the camera facing down from the ceiling. On the desk, there is a shelf of LP records from which the user can select one. Each record is associated with a different music clip and the music starts to play when the LP record is shown to the camera. Users are also able to see a virtual 3D widget on the LP record, visualized on the front display. This virtual widget works as a controller for modifying the music. Users can apply different modulations to the music (such as pitch, amplitude, and cut-off frequency filters) by manipulating the LP record in 3D space (e.g., raising it up and down, or tilting it).

MagiPlanet

The MagiPlanet from Human Interface Technology Laboratory New Zealand (HITLabNZ, http://www.hitlabnz.org) is an interactive AR system that helps users to learn about the solar system. The users of the MagiPlanet application stands in front of a desk with a set of cards each named after the planets in the solar system. Users can see the 3D models of each planet registered to the card by looking through a hand held display (see Figure 5). On the desk, the orbit of each planet is drawn with a blank square on which the cards should be placed. When the user places all of the planets in the correct order, a complete virtual solar system appears with animation.

Augmented Chemistry

In the augmented chemistry (Fjeld & Voegtli, 2002) application, users can learn the basics about chemical elements from an AR book. The user can select virtual elements from the book with a paddle-like prop and compose complex molecular models by adding the selected

Figure 5. MagiPlanet

elements onto each other. Users can manipulate (or rotate) the molecular model built on the platform pad by rotating a cube shaped prop. The workspace is configured in a style of a workbench (showing the mirrored live video of the tabletop on the screen in front), so the conventional 2D graphical user interface is easily integrated for system commands.

Tangible Hypermedia

Sinclair, Martinez, Millard, and Weal (2002) presented what was called a tangible hyperme-dia, a tangible AR-based information system in which virtual annotations were controlled by the context associated with the tangible interface. In their prototype system, the spatial relationships and movement of the markers were used for various interactive features. For instance, bringing a card with a pile of labels close to a virtual object and imitating a sprin-kling gesture added labels to the object. Users could also shake off the labels attached to a virtual object by shaking the object itself. By using different cards with different sets of labels and contexts, users were able to browse through a huge amount of information linked to a virtual object in interest.

Tiles

Tiles (Poupyrev et al., 2002) was a tangible AR system for fast design of aircraft cockpits. Users attached different virtual instruments to real tiles and placed them on a whiteboard to test their configuration. Most of the functions were invoked by placing a pair of tiles side by side. Users could make a copy of an instrument on another tile by placing an empty tile next to it. Similarly, users could also copy instruments from the menu book by placing an empty tile next to it. There were also several special tiles with virtual objects representing different operations, such as delete or help, which could be applied to adjacent tiles.

VOMAR

The VOMAR interface (Kato et al., 2000) provided more generic scene construction func-tionalities, demonstrated in a furniture layout interior design application. In this system, the user used a paddle like prop and made gestures with it for 3D manipulation of virtual objects. For instance, one could pick up an object by placing the paddle beneath the object, and place it by dropping it on a desired position. The user could also delete objects by hit-ting or throwing them away.

Virtual Studio

The virtual studio (Grasset, Gascuel, & Schmalstieg, 2003) is a tangible AR workspace that allows users to modify visual appearances of real world objects. With magnetically tracked real tools and a palette, users can paint on a surface of real objects or add geometri-cal objects registered to the real object. Users can virtually paint a real object by touching

Figure 6. iaTAR: Immersive authoring tool for tangible AR interfaces

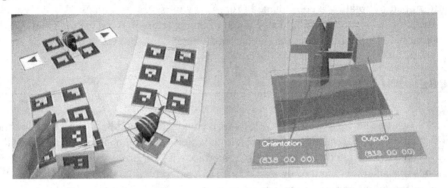

a virtual color on the real palette with a real brush and brushing the object surface with it. Similarly, users can also choose simple geometrical objects from the palette to add it into the augmented scene.

iaTAR

The iaTAR system (Lee, Nelles, Billinghurst, & Kim, 2004a) was an immersive authoring tool for tangible AR content. In this system, a cube shaped manipulator prop (see Figure 6) was used for manipulating virtual objects in 3D space. In addition to constructing a virtual scene, users could also add simple behaviors to virtual objects. For this purpose, iaTAR provided an interface, named inspector pads, for forming and modifying dataflow graphs between Tangible AR interface entities (i.e., physical and virtual objects). For instance, users could make a virtual fan spin around by connecting its orientation property to another virtual abstract object representing a motorized rotational motion.

Tasks and Common Interaction Schemes in Tangible Applications

Although we have only looked at a small subset of tangible AR applications that have been developed, we can readily see that there are commonalities in terms of the subtasks performed and specific interaction styles. Bowman et al. (2001) has carried out systematic research on 3D interaction techniques in the context of virtual reality systems. He suggested that general 3D tasks in virtual environments can be viewed as compositions of primitive tasks, such as object selection, object manipulation, navigation, and system control. A similar observation can be made about tangible AR applications. We take a closer look at the tangible AR interfaces in terms of these primitive tasks and characterize tangible AR interfaces to them.

Viewpoint Control (Navigation)

Since tangible AR environments are based in the real world environment, there can be three main configurations for viewpoint control deeply related to the display configuration of the system: mobile, fixed, and tele-mobile.

The viewpoint control is *mobile* when the virtual viewpoint is identical to the user's physical viewpoint. This can be achieved by tracking the user's viewpoint and using see-through displays (usually head mounted) or spatial augmented reality display techniques (Bimber & Raskar, 2005; Raskar, Welch, & Chen, 1999). In this case, users can freely change their viewpoint just as they do in their every day lives, by moving their head. In comparison, the viewpoint is *fixed* for a workbench style display configuration (as is in the Augmented Groove application). In this case, users see from the viewpoint of a fixed camera, carefully placed to cover the whole workspace. Although users are not able to change the augmented view, they are still able to freely look around the real world directly, and the interaction space (usually a table) is placed just in front of them. Besides, with a workbench style display configuration the camera still can be mobile (e.g., held in the user's hand), forming a monitor-based AR configuration (Azuma, 1997). In this case, the movement of the camera is usually not coupled to the motion of the user's eye; hence, we refer to it as *tele-mobile* situation.

Each configuration has its own advantages and disadvantages. The mobile configuration is the most natural; although field of view and resolutions can be limited with head mounted displays. On the other hand, with the fixed and tele-mobile view configurations the actual viewpoint and the viewpoint to the AR scene do not coincide. In a fixed view configuration, the camera is usually placed in front, looking towards the user. Thus, the resulting image is a mirrored image, creating a flip in the perceived direction. Therefore, the fixed and tele-mobile configurations require users to reinterpret the spatial configuration due to different reference frames between the view coordinate and the manipulation point. Although sacrificing viewpoint controllability, the fixed configuration has the advantage that users do not need to wear any devices. The tele-mobile configuration restores viewpoint controllability by dedicating one hand for the viewpoint control, but this makes difficult to support bimanual interactions. Overall, in contrast to the immersive VR case, viewpoint control in a Tangible AR environment is mostly limited to physical movements without many alternatives.

3D Spatial Manipulation

Spatial manipulation is perhaps the most frequent interaction task in 3D spaces. Bowman and Hodges (1999) divided 3D spatial manipulation into three subtasks; selection, manipulation and release.

Selection and Release

Selecting an object of interest is the most basic interaction task. Usually, selection is done by pointing to an object, such as is with a cursor/pointer in 2D GUI environments or a virtual hand (or ray) in an immersive virtual environment. For this purpose, users need to use a physical interface (such as a mouse or a tracking sensor) to move the virtual pointer over the objects they want to select and interact with. Thus, the action is carried out indirectly.

However, in a tangible augmented reality environment, the selection can be accomplished more directly. When each virtual object has its own physical counterpart, selecting a virtual object happens implicitly when the user picks up the physical object that it is paired with. In this case, both selection and other interactions, such as 3D manipulation, occur at the same time. For instance, in the shared space application (Billinghurst et al., 2000), users pick up a card with a virtual object which they are interested in, as they start to move it.

In Tangible AR applications where virtual objects and their counterpart physical objects are paired dynamically, explicit interaction methods are necessary for selection, as it is within virtual environments. For example, selecting a virtual instrument in Tiles (Poupyrev et al., 2002) is done by placing an empty tile next to another tile with the virtual instrument. In the VOMAR application, Kato et al. (2000) introduces a tangible AR version of a 3D mouse cursor represented in a paddle form. Users can place the paddle under a piece of virtual furniture they want to pick up, and once the virtual furniture is selected (appears on the paddle) they are able to move it to another place. In iaTAR (Lee et al., 2004a), the user points to an object with a virtual ray which is emitted from a physical prop—such as a box or a pad—held in his or her hand.

Selection tasks in tangible AR applications mostly occur within arms reach of the user (because it is a direct interaction). It is well known that provision of binocular stereoscopy is important for correct depth perception and efficient close range interaction. Thus, without binocular stereoscopy, users can often get frustrated in carrying out object selection tasks because the proprioceptive and visual senses do not coincide. Once the selection is made, the difficulty seems to ease as the hand-eye coordination is much better with the object in hand. Many AR applications only use monoscopic displays (e.g., for reasons of cost), thus it would be beneficial to provide artificial depth cues to aid the selection process (such as shadow and limited occlusion information). However providing correct artificial cues in a mixed reality environment is difficult in general, because it requires a correct understanding of the physical environment.

After the selected object is used, it must be released. Statically paired objects do not need explicit releasing; virtual objects are released from the user's hand as soon as the user drops the corresponding physical objects. However, in dynamically paired cases, explicit interaction methods are needed for triggering the release. In iaTAR, virtual objects are released from the cube manipulator when the manipulator cube is invisible to the camera. Thus, users just need to hide the cube with their fingers when they want to release the selected object. In VOMAR, users need to tilt the paddle so that the selected object slides off into the virtual scene.

Manipulation

Object manipulation in 3D spaces refers to changing the 6 degree-of-freedom pose (i.e., position and orientation) of an object. As with selection, direct manipulation is the most natural interaction method for object manipulation. In many cases of virtual reality systems, this is usually implemented through tracking the user's hand (using data gloves and tracking sensors). On the contrast, in a tangible AR interface, this is accomplished by tracking the interaction objects. The real objects act as surrogates for manipulation of virtual objects, and users can manipulate virtual objects by manipulating their corresponding real objects.

Most typically, the physical motion applied to the surrogate is directly mapped to the virtual object. However, non-direct mappings (distorted and multiplexed mappings) are also useful in some cases. In the *distorted mapping* case, the source property values are altered, according to specific rules, before they are mapped to the target. For example, a snap-to-grid function where the virtual object position is attracted to the virtual grid's crossing points. In iaTAR, the distorted mapping is used for separating controls during manipulation. When a virtual object is selected by the cube manipulator, its position is fixed relative to the cube center at the moment it was selected, while it is rotated in-place. That is, the virtual object center, instead of the center of the cube manipulator, acts as the center of rotation. This is useful for changing orientation independently from translation, otherwise the position would change when rotating the selected object. In the *multiplexed mapping* case, object properties are controlled by separate input objects. For instance, in augmented chemistry, the orientation of the molecular model is controlled with the cube manipulator, while its position is anchored on the platform pad. This is especially useful for the fixed view configuration, since the position of the model is kept at the best viewing location, while users can still rotate the molecule.

Sometimes, object poses are decided through complex calculations, so that the manipulation can appear as physically realistic as possible. For instance, in VOMAR, users can not only pick up and drop an object to a desired position, but can push it with the paddle. Moreover, virtual furniture acts as if it was affected by gravity and friction, falling and dragging on the floor when there are no supporting objects beneath. Applying such physical rules adds to the intuitiveness of the interface.

Event Generation and System Command

While the three primitive tasks (viewpoint control, selection, and manipulation) are the most prevalent subtasks in any tangible AR applications, applications also require additional interactive features for triggering events. In particular, system commands that do not have any 3D connotation are also often needed.

Location and Pose Based

One popular form of event generation is by using a particular spatial configuration of multiple objects; when objects are brought together, or at a certain orientation and location, an event is triggered, such as an animation (Shared Space, MagiPlanet), object selection or deletion (Tiles), or making a connection among object attributes (see Figure 7).

Figure 7. A Tangible AR puzzle calculator: A data flow graph for calculating a mathematical expression is made by connecting puzzle pieces with mathematical entities

Gestures with Props

Gestures are movements made to express emotions or information and are often made using objects (props). While physical objects decide the outer appearance of an interface, gestures specify how to use them. Thus, different gestures can be made for different tasks while using the same object. For instance, knives are not only used for cutting, but also for spreading jam on bread. Gestures and objects can be combined for natural and intuitive interface for generating various types of events in tangible AR environments.

In VOMAR, users can do different tasks by performing different gestures with the paddle interface. Users can pick up an object by scooping it up, or release it by tilting the paddle to make it slide into the virtual scene. Shaking the paddle throws away the selected object and the paddle becomes empty. Pushing objects with the paddle makes them slide over the floor, while users can also delete objects by hitting them. The iaTAR application uses tilting gestures for selecting an item from a list of object attributes (see Figure 8). The sprinkling action in the Tangible Hypermedia controls the amount of annotation.

The downside of using special interaction objects and gestures is that sometimes people might have different ideas in terms of what the object is supposed to do. If there are many special tasks needed to be done, the user can be overwhelmed both mentally and physically

Figure 8. Tilting gestures for selecting an item from property list in iaTAR

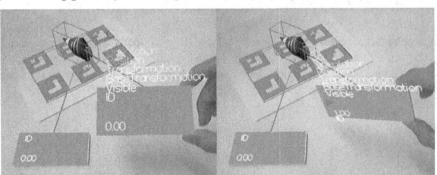

(too many interface handles). A right balance must be maintained between making objects multipurpose or special. Using familiar objects like a book (MagicBook), LP record (Augmented Groove), trash can (iaTAR, Tiles), or magnifying lens (MagicLenses) allow users to easily understand the functionality and usage of the interface.

2D Interactions

Although tangible augmented reality interfaces are 3D by nature, 2D interactions are unavoidable, especially for triggering events and system commands that are not space related. System commands are usually best handled using a 2D metaphor due to user's familiarity with the 2D desktop interface. The most naive approach for implementing 2D input is using the conventional 2D interaction devices within the AR environment. For instance, in the augmented chemistry application, users are provided with a mouse and 2D graphical user interface overlaid on the AR scene. In addition, by using it, users can save or load the chemical composite built. This works well with a fixed view case where the configuration is similar to that of a desktop environment.

However, in the mobile view case other techniques are needed. Dias et al. (2003) proposed to use screen space interaction with a 2D projected 3D pointers that moves along with the Magic Ring interface (a tracking marker worn as a ring). Although this approach was good enough for providing a 2D pointing method on the screen space, displaying 2D GUIs on the screen space might cause a depth perception mismatch with stereoscopic visualization. This is one of the reasons why world stabilized 2D GUIs are needed where users interact with a two-dimensional surface embedded within the 3D augmented reality environment. 2D GUI registered on tangible surfaces could be used together with conventional 2D input devices (Geiger, Oppermann, & Reimann 2003), but this might not be suitable in some cases, such as in a mobile environment.

McDonald and Roth (2003) proposed using bare hands for interacting with 2D GUIs registered on a tracking marker surface. They used computer vision techniques for detecting users' hands on the surface, and let the users point on the 2D GUIs with their fingers. Combined with gesture recognition, users can also give commands while they touch 2D GUI elements. Other various gesture based interaction methods used in the descendants of the digital desk interface (Wellner, 1993) would provide good references to this topic.

An alternative approach to computer vision-based gesture recognition is based on observing that most of tangible AR applications use tracking systems with multiple markers. The occlusion-based interaction method (Lee, Billinghurst, & Kim, 2004) is an easy and simple method for 2D interactions using occlusions. In this case, a set of markers placed with a predefined spatial relationship is used for tracking rigid body physical objects. When a subset of these markers are invisible while they are supposed to be in the view, the system considers them occluded, and triggers proper interaction events. Figure 9 shows using this method for interacting with a Tangible AR calculator and a tic-tac-toe game.

Developing special devices with buttons and switches might be an alternative choice when available. For instance, in the MagicBook interface, the user holds a handheld display which also has buttons on its handle. Recently, handheld devices, such as PDAs and smart phones, are concerned as next generation tangible AR platforms (Möhring, Lessig, & Bimber,

Figure 9. Occlusion-based Interaction with calculator and tic-tac-toe game

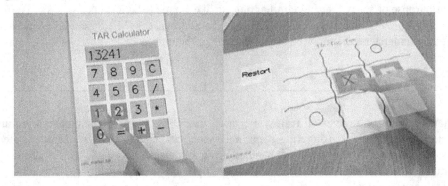

2004). In such cases, 2D interfaces are already available on the device itself (e.g., buttons, scroll wheels, and touch screens) and tangible AR applications could also take advantage of these.

Summary

So far, we have examined some of the important application tasks and various interaction methods that have been proposed for those tasks. This information is useful as guidelines for designing tangible AR interfaces. Table 1 summarizes the main surveyed results.

Table 1. Common tasks in Tangible AR applications and their interaction designs

Tasks	Interaction design	Comments
Viewpoint Control (Navigation)	mobile	most natural, limited field of view
	fixed	hands and head free, fixed view
	tele-mobile	free viewpoint control, space mismatch
Selection and re-lease	pick up with bare hands	statically paired case
	using props	dynamically paired case, 3D pointer

Table 1. continued

3D manipulation	direct mapping		most natural
	distorted mapping		handy (e.g., snap-to-grip)
	multiplexed mapping		isolated control
Event generation & system command	location and pose based		distance, specific spatial configuration
	gestures with props		easy to learn, confusing when too many
	2D interaction	keyboard & mouse	familiar, good for fixed view case
		pointing with bare hands	natural, slow, less haptic feedback
		special devices	need extra hardware

Design Guidelines

In this section, we describe common guidelines for designing tangible AR interfaces. First, we start with general guidelines that originate from natural characteristics of tangible AR interfaces. Next, we describe guidelines for dealing with problems that developers could encounter often during implementation.

General Guidelines

Tangible augmented reality environments are more than virtual environments with a live real world video backdrop. Allowing the users to see the real world and letting them to use physical objects to interact with virtual entities provide extremely intuitive interaction designs. These support types of interaction that are usually uneasy or even unthinkable with immersive virtual environments, although they also cause limitations due to their physical nature.

Using Metaphors from Every Day Life

Since tangible AR applications are located in a real environment, it is useful to design interfaces similar to those in our everyday lives. This not only preserves consistency between the real and virtual worlds, but also makes it easier to learn and use the interface. Thus, many tangible AR applications use familiar real world metaphors as an interaction method.

We use various objects dedicated to specific tasks in the real world, such as pens to write with, or files to organize papers. Similarly, it is useful to design the AR interface and interaction objects to resemble those used for a similar purpose in the real world. LP records used in the augmented groove and a real brush in the virtual studio are good examples.

Introducing physical rules to interaction design also helps to build natural and intuitive interfaces. For example, the VOMAR application uses the illusion of gravitational force. It is common that objects fall when there is no supporting underneath. Thus, users can easily learn that they can push a bookshelf to the border of the desk in order to drop it onto the floor.

Taking Advantage from Parallel Activities

With tangible AR interfaces, users interact with the interface using their bare hands. They do not need to wear special tracking devices, which makes users feel more natural and comfortable while manipulating objects in 3D space. In addition, since there are no requirements for wearing sensors, users can hold and manipulate objects freely and naturally using both of their hands. This also supports natural collaboration between multiple participants, such as it is in the Shared Space (Billinghurst et al., 2000) and Tiles (Poupyrev et al., 2002) applications.

Adding multiple interaction objects is another way to utilize parallel activities. Since users are able to manipulate multiple objects at the same time, it is useful to make copies of interfaces to allow parallel interactions. For instance, in iaTAR, users can use multiple cube manipulator props to record synchronized motions of multiple virtual objects.

Guidelines for Dealing with Implementation Problems

Due to physical and technical limitations, interaction problems can occur during implementation of Tangible AR applications. Here we present useful guidelines to deal with some of these.

Using Timers to Prevent Unintentional Operations

While individual interaction methods might work nicely in isolation, in an application with many interactive features, unintentional operations can be triggered while performing other actions. For instance, to release objects in iaTAR, the user hides the props; however, there are cases where the user hides the props by accident causing false actions. This is particularly apparent when there are many props to be used. The users of the Tiles system experienced a similar situation; when there are many tiles to be manipulated with, it is easy to misplace them and accidentally place a tile next to another, triggering false activities. One of the best methods to prevent such unintentional operations is to use timers. In both iaTAR and the Tiles systems, users need to perform an action for a certain period of time, confirming that they mean to do it. In addition, using timers provides chances to cancel mistaken operations.

Setting the Interaction Volume According to the Users' Physical Limits

Problems might also occur due to the user's physical limitations. For instance, in iaTAR, users need to bring inspector pads near enough to their eyes to make the property list appear. In this case, if the threshold distance is too near, users might not be able to see the long list very well. Thus, the distance must be decided properly according to the users' viewing limits. Similarly, in the augmented groove application, the height limit must be decided according to the users' reach, so that they could change the music pitch by raising up the record high enough.

Securing Tracking Losses

The volume of the tracking system is another important factor that should be considered for deciding the space where the interaction can be performed. When using ultrasonic or magnetic sensors, the tracking volume is bound to the source of tracking signal and a tracking target gets lost when it travels too far from the source. With vision-based tracking techniques, the tracking volume is limited to the field of view of the camera. In most cases, tracking also relies on the same camera that provides the real world view to the user and hence tracking can get easily lost while moving the viewpoint.

Moreover, for computer vision or ultrasonic sensor based systems, tracking also gets lost when the target is occluded by other objects (e.g., the users' hands). This can occur when users hold augmented objects to manipulate them and cover up tracking targets. To prevent such cases, the basic remedy is to secure enough white space so that users would not cover the tracking markers (or sensors) while they grab the object. For example, with the paddle in VOMAR, the tracking marker is placed far from the handle that the users hold on to. Besides, when objects are mostly placed on a table, glass tables could also be useful for preventing occlusions by placing a tracking camera underneath the table and placing tracking markers on the bottom of the objects (Ulbricht & Schmalstieg, 2003).

In vision-based tracking systems, besides adding more tracking cameras and enlarging the marker size, introducing more tracking markers is another way to reduce tracking losses. When multiple tracking markers are attached on a rigid body object, the pose of one marker can be inferred from that of another by knowing their pre-defined spatial relationships. Hence, the tracking would not get lost even though some of the markers are not tracked successfully. The cube shaped manipulator used in augmented chemistry and iaTAR applications make use of such approach. This method is well supported in computer vision based tracking libraries, such as the ARToolKit (http://www.hitl.washington.edu/artoolkit).

Tracking loss can make interaction difficult, but might also cause false alarms. To prevent such problems, designers must consider the case when interaction objects get lost for tracking. For instance, in the puzzle calculator application (see Figure 7), the connection status between two puzzle pieces are only updated when both of them are visible (tracked successfully). Otherwise, the connection can get broken improperly when one of those are out of view since the calculation of the spatial relationship is not correct anymore. Hence, developers must carefully treat hidden objects, especially when implementing interaction methods using spatial relationships.

Considering Limitations in Visualization

When visualizing virtual objects in AR systems, the occlusion problem is often encountered. Occlusion is one of the factors that make users feel depth in an image and can be correctly represented between virtual objects using computer graphics techniques, such as using z-buffers. However, when virtual objects are superimposed on the real world view, they tend to always occlude real objects even when the real objects are nearer to the user's viewpoint. This is mainly due to having no depth information of the real world scene. Breen, Whitaker, Rose, and Tuceryan (1996) proposed two representative methods to solve this problem. One is using 3D models of the real objects and the other is acquiring a depth map from the real world scene. With the first method, the depth information can be acquired in real-time by projecting virtual models of the real objects (a.k.a. ghosts). However, this requires 3D models of the real world objects to be prepared in advance. When such models are not available, depth information can also be reconstructed from video images using computer vision techniques. Though recent advanced researches showed real-time performance from a contour-based stereo matching method (Hayashi, Kato, & Nishida, 2005), this still requires heavy computation and stereoscopic camera setups which are not widely available yet. As an alternative, some Tangible AR applications try to partially solve this problem by making the virtual image semi-transparent (see Figure 9). Although it still does not show an augmented scene with correct occlusion, this helps users a lot while interacting since they can see their hands.

Another thing to consider while designing visualizations is the amount of information available. Due to technical limitations, most video cameras have a narrow field of view, and this causes restrictions in amount of objects that can be viewed together. For instance, when designing interaction methods using two or more real objects (as in the Shared Space), the size of the object must be adjusted so that it is big enough for reliable tracking and handling, and small enough to have all the necessary objects within the view at the same time.

Conclusion

In this chapter, we reviewed the tangible AR interface metaphor and some applications of its use to find typical subtasks and common interaction methods for them. For each of these interaction methods, we assessed their advantages and possible shortcomings. Finally, we have proposed some further guidelines in terms of the overall application-level interaction design also considering the implementation issues. Despite interaction limitations of tangible

AR interfaces and less than perfect tracking/sensing/recognition and display technologies, tangible AR interfaces provide rich interactivity with virtual objects by introducing physical objects as the main medium of interaction. There are a multitude of possible applications for the tangible AR approach as demonstrated by the number of successful interfaces in education, training, gaming, and engineering. Further research will bring tangible AR closer to our daily lives, especially through next generation mobile multimedia and communication devices.

References

Azuma, R. (1997). A survey of augmented reality. *Presence: Teleoperators and Virtual Environments, 6*(4), 355-385.

Billinghurst, M., Grasset, R., & Looser, J. (2005). Designing augmented reality interfaces. *Computer Graphics, the SIGGRAPH Quarterly Newsletter, 39*(1), 17-22.

Billinghurst, M., Kato, H., & Poupyrev, I. (2001). The MagicBook—moving seamlessly between reality and virtuality. *IEEE Computer Graphics and Applications, 21*(3), 6-8.

Billinghurst, M., Poupyrev, I., Kato, H., & May, R. (2000, July 30-August 2). Mixing realities in shared space: An augmented reality interface for collaborative computing. In *Proceedings of IEEE International Conference on Multimedia and Expo (ICME 2000)*, New York (pp. 1641-1644).

Bimber, O., & Raskar, R. (2005). *Spatial augmented reality: Merging real and virtual worlds*. A K Peters.

Bowman, D., & Hodges, L. (1999). Formalizing the design, evaluation, and application of interaction techniques for immersive virtual environments. *The Journal of Visual Languages and Computing, 10*(1), 37-53.

Bowman, D., Kruijff, E., LaViola, J., & Poupyrev, I. (2001). An introduction to 3D user interface design. *Presence: Teleoperators and Virtual Environments, 10*(1), 96-108.

Breen, D., Whitaker, R., Rose, E., & Tuceryan, M. (1996). Interactive occlusion and automatic object placement for augmented reality. *Computer Graphics Forum, 15*(3), 11-22.

Dias, J., Santos, P., Nande, P., Barata, N., Correia, A., & Bastos, R. (2003, October 7). In your hand computing: Tangible interfaces for mixed reality. In *Proceedings CD of 2nd IEEE International Augmented Reality Toolkit Workshop (ART'03)*, Tokyo, Japan.

Fjeld, M., & Voegtli, B. (2002, September 30-October 1). Augmented chemistry: An interactive educational workbench. In *Proceedings of the IEEE and ACM International Symposium on Mixed and Augmented Reality (ISMAR'02)*, Darmstadt, Germany (pp. 259-260).

Geiger, C., Oppermann, L., & Reimann, C. (2003, October 7). 3D-registered interaction-surfaces in augmented reality space. In *Proceedings CD of 2nd IEEE International Augmented Reality Toolkit Workshop (ART'03)*, Tokyo, Japan.

Grasset, R., Gascuel, J., & Schmalstieg, D. (2005, October 7-10). Interactive mediated reality. In *Proceedings of the International Symposium on Mixed and Augmented Reality (ISMAR'03),* Tokyo, Japan (pp. 302-303).

Hayashi, K., Kato, H., & Nishida, S. (2005, December 5-8). Occlusion detection of real objects using contour based stereo matching. In *Proceedings of 15th International Conference on Artificial Reality and Telexistence (ICAT2005),* Christchurch, New Zealand (pp. 180-186).

Ishii, H., & Ullmer, B. (1997, March 22-27). Tangible bits: Towards seamless interfaces between people, bits, and atoms. In *Proceedings of the SIGCHI Conference on Human Factors in Computing Systems (CHI'97),* Atlanta, GA (pp. 234-241).

Kato, H., Billinghurst, M., Poupyrev, I., Imamoto, K., & Tachibana, K. (2000, October 5-6). Virtual object manipulation on a table-top AR environment. In *Proceedings of the IEEE and ACM International Symposium on Augmented Reality (ISAR 2000),* Munich, Germany (pp. 111-119).

Kiyokawa, K., Takemura, H., & Yokoya, N. (1999). A collaboration supporting technique by integrating a shared virtual reality and a shared augmented reality. In *Proceedings of the IEEE International Conference on Systems, Man, and Cybernetics (SMC'99),* Tokyo, Japan (Vol. 4, pp. 48-53).

Lee, G. A., Billinghurst, M., & Kim, G. J. (2004b, June 16-18). Occlusion based interaction methods for tangible augmented reality environments. In *Proceedings of ACM SIG-GRAPH International Conference on Virtual-Reality Continuum and its Applications in Industry (VRCAI 2004),* NTU, Singapore (pp. 419-426).

Lee, G. A., Nelles, C., Billinghurst, M., & Kim, G. J. (2004a, November 2-5). immersive authoring of tangible augmented reality applications. In *Proceedings of IEEE and ACM International Symposium on Mixed and Augmented Reality (ISMAR'04),* Arlington, VA (pp. 172-181).

Looser, J., Billinghurst, M., & Cockburn, A. (2004, June 15-18). Through the looking glass: The use of lenses as an interface tool for Augmented Reality interfaces. In *Proceedings of the 2nd International Conference on Computer Graphics and Interactive Techniques in Australasia and SouthEast Asia (Graphite 2004)* (pp. 204-211). New York; Singapore: ACM Press.

McDonald, C., & Roth, G. (2003). Replacing a mouse with hand gesture in a plane-based augmented reality system. In *Proceedings of 16th International Conference on Vision Interface,* Halifax, Canada.

Möhring, M., Lessig, C., & Bimber, O. (2004, November 2-5). Video see-through AR on consumer cell-phones. In *Proceedings of IEEE and ACM International Symposium on Mixed and Augmented Reality (ISMAR'04),* Arlington, VA (pp. 252-253).

Poupyrev, I., Berry, R., Billinghurst, M., Kato, H., Nakao, K., Baldwin, L., & Kurumisawa, J. (2001). Augmented reality interface for electronic music performance. In *Proceedings of the 9th International Conference on Human-Computer Interaction (HCI International 2001)* (pp. 805-808).

Poupyrev, I., Tan, D. S., Billinghurst, M., Kato, H., Regenbrecht, H., & Tetsutani, N. (2002). Developing a generic augmented reality interface. *IEEE Computer, 35*(3), 44-50.

Raskar, R., Welch, G., & Chen, W. (1999, October 20-21). Table-top spatially-augmented reality: Bringing physical models to life with projected imagery. In *Proceedings of the 2nd International IEEE Workshop on Augmented Reality (IWAR '99),* San Francisco (pp. 64-71).

Schmalstieg, D., Fuhrmann, A., & Hesina, G. (2000, October 5-6). Bridging multiple user interface dimensions with augmented reality. In *Proceedings of the IEEE and ACM International Symposium on Augmented Reality (ISAR 2000),* Munich, Germany (pp. 20-29).

Sinclair, P., Martinez, K., Millard, D., & Weal, M. (2002, June 11-15). Links in the palm of your hand: tangible hypermedia using augmented reality. In *Proceedings of the 13th ACM Conference on Hypertext and Hypermedia (HT2002),* College Park, MD (pp. 127-136).

Sutherland, I. (1965). The ultimate display. *International Federation of Information Processing, 2*, 506-508.

Ulbricht, C., & Schmalstieg, D. (2003, September 8-10). Tangible augmented reality for computer games. In *Proceedings of the 3rd IASTED International Conference on Visualization, Imaging, and Image Processing (VIIP2003),* Benalmadena, Spain (pp. 950-954).

Wellner, P. (1993). Interacting with paper on the digital desk. *Communications of the ACM 36*(7), 87-96.

Section IV:

Case Studies of Augmented Reality Applications

Chapter XIV

Industrial Augmented Reality Applications

Holger Regenbrecht, University of Otago, New Zealand

Abstract

This chapter explains and illustrates the terminology and the different types of industrial augmented reality (IAR) applications according to their purpose and degree of maturity. Augmented reality is well on its way to becoming a valuable application tool in industry. Certain stages in research and development are required to get there, namely demonstration systems, prototype systems, and productive systems. We discuss the progress made within these requirements, with illustrating examples, and conclude with some lessons learned while implementing augmented reality in an industrial context. The information presented here provides valuable insights into the underlying principles and issues associated with augmented reality applications. We hope that this chapter becomes a useful resource for all individuals who research or develop augmented reality tools.

Introduction:
Augmented Reality in an Industrial Context

Bringing research results out of the laboratory and into an industrial context is always a challenge. If this process eventually leads to success on the market, it is usually called innovation.

Innovations in the technological area of augmented reality are rare. It has to be considered that research and development (R&D) is still in its early days. However, academic and industry partners both agree that there is huge potential for the technology in a broad variety of applications. As a result, various attempts to bring R&D and "real world use" of AR together have been made and are still top of the list for potential innovations.

Reviewing the research literature in augmented reality over the last couple of years leads to the impression that there are a variety of applications in the field. In contrast, having a look at the industrial and commercial market AR applications are barely found. Because of the maturity of AR applications we rather opt for more precise descriptions of projects presented.

We introduce a classification approach identifying demonstration systems, prototype systems, and productive systems as the main types of AR systems. Each of these types has its own advantages and disadvantages and all of them are necessary to establish AR as an enabling technology. Criteria and a discussion of characteristics are given to identify the appropriate type. The different types and conglomerates of types are illustrated with practical examples and are discussed in detail.

We will start with highlighting the background of industrial AR applications followed by the approach to define the term IAR applications.

Then we propose three main categories on a maturity continuum, illustrate these categories with a variety of examples from international IAR R&D. Based on these classifications we will illustrate and discuss in detail three of our own projects.

Finally, we will conclude with some lessons learned from our experience to give some advice or guideline for industrial AR research and development.

Background: Reported Industrial AR Applications

There are three driving forces in any industrial context, which lead to the introduction of new technologies: cost reduction, speed-up of processes, and quality improvement. If one can bring the appropriate information, to the right place, at the right time all three forces can be addressed. Augmented reality seems to be an ideal candidate in almost any contexts. It lies in the very nature of AR to be applied within the current working context (e.g., the assembly line) and to deliver accurate, useful, and up-to-date information (e.g., the number and representation of the next product part to be assembled). This will eventually lead to shorter production times, less training effort, reduction of errors, and finally to lower production costs.

But, why is it so difficult to implement AR technology in an industrial context? We believe that the maturity of the contributing technologies (tracking, displays, content generation, wearable computing, etc.) does not suit the demanding industrial environment conditions yet regarding robustness, reliability, quality, and practical experience. But, we also believe, that it is very close to being applied successfully in a broad range of fields.

It can be said that the application of augmented reality in an industrial context started with Boeing's wire bundle assembly project in the early '90's (see Mizell, 2001). The wiring for each individual airplane to be built is unique. Therefore, the wire bundles needed to be pre-configured in a workshop beforehand according to plans displayed on large boards in huge numbers. The display of the wiring paths for this very manual task of forming bundles at the boards seemed to be a promising area for the application of AR technology: the wire plans are augmented directly onto the board using an optical see-through head-worn display. Even if this application did not make it into the real production process for various, mainly organizational reasons, the wire bundle assembly still stays as the first prototype example for industrial AR.

This project was followed by several smaller projects until the end of the last century. While numerous academic projects evolved in the following years, industrial augmented reality (IAR) applications are still rare. In some cases, AR technology was applied successfully in certain use cases. For instance in supporting welding processes (Echtler et al., 2003), where the welding helmet itself is used to overlay information and to ease the visibility of the welding point and seam.

To date there have been two major initiatives for AR innovation. The Mixed Reality Systems Laboratory in Japan, with its focus set on the development of mixed reality prototype applications comprising hardware and software, has demonstrated the potential for the real-world use of AR (see Tamura, Yamamoto, & Katayama, 2001). The success of this project led to the release of the mixed reality platform, a comprehensive toolkit consisting of display, tracking, and AR software technology.

The other initiative has been the German project "ARVIKA" lead by Siemens, which included the majority of the manufacturing industry in the country as well as selected partners in academia, and small and medium enterprises (see Friedrich, 2004). The focus here was on the application of AR in the fields of design, production, and servicing.

There is noticeable progress in the application of all kind of augmented reality technology in a broad scope of fields. For instance, the use of projection-based augmented reality in the context of museum exhibitions by Froehlich et al. (2005), where a permanent installation at a German exhibition clearly shows the reliable use of AR technology. Another example being the use of head-mounted display based AR technology in the education of students at TU Vienna reported by Kauffmann (2005) with major benefits for students in understanding complex geometric properties by applying interactive techniques.

The European Commission currently supports a variety of projects related to augmented reality in its framework programs (Badique, 2005), which is a strong indicator for the importance of the dissemination of this technology.

In the realm of industrial augmented reality applications, Navab (2004) identified design, commissioning, manufacturing, quality control, training, monitoring and control, and service and maintenance as main application field for augmented reality and gives guidance based on own experiences made. Navab emphasizes the need for "killer applications" to progress further the research and development in IAR applications. He, for instance, overlays images, drawings, and virtual models onto the geometry of plant equipment, in particular industrial pipelines with high accuracy.

All projects encountered serious problems regarding the instrumentation of the industrial site with tracking equipment to track the user's position and orientation, several calibration issues, and the robustness, ergonomics, and fidelity of the AR display technology, among others.

All these initiatives brought forward various prototypes and demonstrated applications and have therefore been valuable in progressing the field of AR. The lessons learned in these projects have had a strong influence on the direction of AR R&D worldwide.

Definition and Scope of IAR Applications

The term "industrial augmented reality applications" is used in the literature in a very broad context. As far as we have reviewed the related work there is no clear definition of the term used nor its scope.

Definition

We will address this problem by giving a preliminary definition, dividing the term into its components "industrial," "AR," and "applications":

"Industrial" refers in one way or another to the organized activity of making goods and services for sale and therefore, differentiates itself from things such as entertainment, medicine, or education.

"Augmented reality" has often been defined in various ways. Either a more conceptual point of view has been taken (which could also include very different media and even dreaming) or emphasis has been placed on a technological point of view, which often refers to the display or tracking devices used (ranging from context activated information display on a personal digital assistant to projection systems applied to real world geometries). In this article, we will rely on a definition from Azuma et al. (2001) which is widely acknowledged and can serve as a benchmark for what AR includes and excludes: "we define an AR system to have the following properties:

- Combines real and virtual objects in a real environment;
- Runs interactively, and in real time; and
- Registers (aligns) real and virtual objects with each other."

The most difficult part in trying to give a precise definition for IAR applications lies in the last word: for what is an application? Can one talk about an application if the system presented is running on a computer and is not only described with formulas? Then again, can one talk about applications if and only if there is a market success of such a system?

It is often confusing for the reader to decide whether the system is applicable in his or her targeted context based on the descriptions given. To overcome this problem, we provide a simple classification system on a maturity continuum. Before we describe this classification, we will define industrial AR applications in the following way:

Industrial augmented reality applications are systems to be used in a product lifecycle process utilizing the concept of spatially aligned and interactive overlay of computer generated information in a working context.

With this definition, there is still sufficient room to define the kind of application, which we characterize in the following section.

AR Applications Maturity Continuum

Reviewing the recent literature on AR applications regarding their maturity or applicability is a difficult task. We are introducing a classification system that places three main types of applications on a continuum of maturity and innovative character: demonstration systems, prototype systems, and productive systems (see Figure 1).

The main characteristics of a *demonstration system* can be outlined as follows:

• It has to be novel or unique in some way. This is the strongest benefit and the biggest challenge. If the system is demonstrating existing technologies or approaches only, it is

Figure 1. Types and maturity of applications

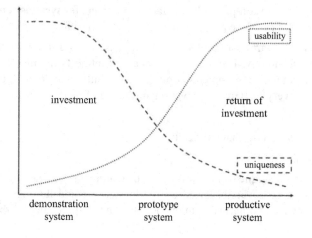

probably not worth to be published or reported and therefore will probably be rejected by most publication bodies for good reason. While a productive system has to have a unique selling proposition, a demonstration system has to have a unique research or invention proposition. An excellent example for a unique demonstration system is the introduction of tabletop marker-based Augmented Reality by Kato, Billinghurst, Poupyrev, Imamoto, and Tachibana (2000). The main purpose is to explain concepts and ideas.

- It focuses on a single or *few aspects* to be shown in comparison to the provision of a comprehensive application solution. It shows the benefits of the technology rather than of the real use case.

- It is often a prerequisite to approach or convince customers and users. Highlighting some central aspects demonstration systems motivate customers to invest further into augmented reality research or development. Potential future users can benefit from demonstration systems in getting their first idea about possible use cases. Because these systems do not actually solve a real world problem it is mainly up to the user to imagine possible application scenarios, which can be a very contributing factor because it involves users from the very beginning. It is a required, first step in the innovation process.

- It is not targeted for real users. The developer or presenter is the user of the system. That's why almost no documentation is needed.

- Hardly ever will it be replicated: The demonstration system is a dedicated, proprietary solution and should not serve as a technological basis for further development. It has a short life cycle regarding usage and development.

- The provision of prepared data/content is sufficient. It is neither required nor reasonable to invest much time and effort into the integration of existing real world content. Rather information out of a possible actual working context are taken as a basis for the preparation of a convincing demonstration scenario.

- It is applied in a laboratory-like, demonstration-friendly environment that can be the place where the system was developed or a conference, exhibition or fair.

- These types of applications require investment and will not provide immediate return on investment.

- It does not have to comply with any standards (except for systems demonstrating standards) and does not need to fit into existing organizational or workflow processes.

- The main targets are customers and technologists, who are going to introduce or implement AR technology. The needs of users are of interest only insofar as the customer understands them. This statement might look a little paradoxical, but it reflects the (sometimes very) different motivation and scope of work of customers and users.

A *prototype system* can be characterized:

- It has to show unique or new properties or features in comparison to existing products or solutions. Mainly based on the knowledge and findings of demonstration systems (own and others) the uniqueness lies in the application of these findings in a "close-to-real-use" context. It is a required step before a potential productive system development.

- Therefore the focus is set on an application scenario and work context rather than on the technology itself.

- It involves (few) real users and with this allows for first usability investigations.

- Because the developer or presenter is no longer the only user, some documentation and self-explanatory user interfaces are needed.

- Requires a certain (often underestimated) amount of development time

- It is used and applied more often than a demonstration system and has to be *robust* in its core functionality.

- Makes use of and integrates real-world data, even if as example data sets only.

- It has to comply with existing work processes in those aspects to be investigated.

- It can be used in the laboratory or another technology-friendly environment. For instance, a prototype system is installed first at one work place in a plant, where it does not interfere with the existing workflow, and where the environmental conditions are safe and controllable.

- The prototype tests concepts in a real context.

- The targets are customers and users, because real users are confronted with the system. But still, the customers (e.g., the management) have to be convinced to invest further into AR technology.

Finally, a *productive system* can be described in brief with the following:

- It addresses real users, which are very often unknown. While in the process of prototype testing a face-to-face contact between developers and users is given and needed, here the system will be delivered to users never seen before.

Figure 2. Relation between types of applications

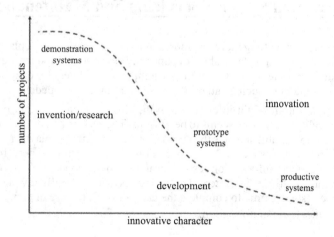

- Therefore, documentation and well-designed and tested user interfaces are essential.
- It has to be integrated into existing data chains and working processes.
- It has to be robust and reliable.
- It is applied in the "field," often in very harsh environments (see description of example)
- It has to be profitable; this is the main reason for a product. There has to be a market.
- The use of standards (technological, organizational) is mandatory and it has to fit into the technological environment (operating systems, middle-ware, hardware, network infrastructure, data interfaces, GUI guidelines...)
- Acceptance is a key issue; the main targets are the users.

Given the characteristics previously described, it is obvious that (1) only a small number of AR projects will comply with the requirements of a productive system as the main result of the innovation process and that (2) we need a huge number of demonstration and prototype systems as a prerequisite for successful innovation. This is illustrated in Figure 2.

Illustrating Examples

To make our classification approach a bit more tangible, we will show with three of our own projects the commonalities and differences in the types of AR applications. We chose our own projects because (1) we have in-depth knowledge about these and (2) it is easier to highlight flaws in our own work than that of others in the field where only their reported descriptions are available.

We will describe in detail one example for each of the three types. These application examples are part of Regenbrecht, Baratoff, and Wilke (2005).

Demonstration System: Servicing and Maintenance

Today's products are getting more and more complex. The days when a plan of the electrical circuits of a car fit onto one large sheet of paper have long gone. Modern high-tech cars now require a database system and state of the art computer equipment for electric and electronic diagnosis. A printout of such a database is as thick as an encyclopedia.

How can one bring the right information to the right place at the right time? The use of augmented reality technology seems to be obvious. The service personnel is equipped with a (wearable) computer unit and gets the appropriate information displayed next to or overlaid onto the object being inspected. Not only can this do away with the need for a paper schematic, but a far richer information resource can be provided via online access to dedicated information and multi-media content. The promise is to increase effectiveness (fewer errors) and efficiency (shorter time to complete the task) through the use of context-sensitive, up-to-date, and media-rich information.

All major manufacturing enterprises are thinking about how to make use of AR technology in their maintenance and servicing areas. The more complex the product is, the greater the potential benefit of AR.

For the diagnosis of maintenance and repair tasks, modern cars provide a system interface (mostly via a plug-like connector). While this interface allows for very fast and precise analysis of the state of the engine, the accompanying information is still found on a dedicated PC or on printouts. Hence, the object to which the diagnosis is applied (part of the engine) and the resulting data yielded by the diagnosis are spatially separated. AR has the potential to close this gap, enabling the diagnosis results to be displayed right in immediate proximity to the engine.

There are many important questions that must be considered, however, what kind of information is useful and should it be represented? What are the technological alternatives available for solving this? If the data is very complex, as it often is, where and how do you place the information at the engine?

These were the issues we had to address when implementing a demonstration system for a real Mercedes-Benz (8 cyl. SL) engine. A head-mounted display solution connected to a portable PC (alternatively, a notebook computer) was chosen. The tracking of the user's position and orientation was done by using a marker-based approach. In this case, markers were attached to a U-shaped object, which was placed into a certain location at the engine. The use of multiple markers at well-defined positions provided us with reasonably precise tracking.

The following data types were presented (see Figure 3): (1) Maintenance and repair instructions taken from the garage information system, represented as textual and pictorial information in space. (2) Pre-recorded video instructions in the form of a "virtual TV set" placed at a fixed position in space. (3) 3D models with predetermined animated sequences as overlays. (4) A video/audio link to an expert technician as an example of remote technical assistance displayed with the TV set approach.

While the choice of computer and display technology is straightforward, taking into account such matters as cost, quality of design, and reliability, the information provision is a bigger challenge due to various key factors. (a) The appropriate information has to be selected automatically out of the existing information system (normally text and graphics with ref-

Figure 3. Maintenance demonstration system

erences to 3D models), (b) the user interaction has to be supported in an easy-to-use way, (c) new multi-media content (esp. video and 3D models) has to be created and edited, and finally (d) the multi-media information has to be brought into a spatial relationship with the object (engine). This entire authoring process is subject to research and development (see Haringer & Regenbrecht, 2002) and clearly deserves stronger attention.

Although the application scenario looks obvious and straightforward, the developed system is not ready for actual use yet. It can very well serve for the presentation of the concept behind and the application potential. Hundreds of potential customers and users have seen the demonstration system at the laboratory and at exhibitions and are now able to validate the applicability in their working contexts. The feedback of the potential customers led to the following main findings.

The use of a head-mounted display (HMD) cannot be recommended at this stage of the maturity of the technology. Tracking fidelity, calibration issues, and display resolution and fidelity are the main reasons for this. While it is possible in certain cases to apply a HMD in a different context (e.g., display of context-activated 2D information, see productive system example next), 3D, registered overlay has to be implemented in a different way.

The use of the inexpensive marker tracking is not suitable for such a real-world application yet, because (a) the instrumentation of the environment (markers at or around the engine) is unacceptable and (b) the reliability and accuracy of this tracking method is not sufficient in a garage workshop context.

The authoring process is far from being comprehensive (see previous).

Nevertheless, this demonstration system clearly shows the benefits and limitations of the idea and the technology that led to follow-up projects with a shifted focus.

Demonstration and Prototype System: Visualization of Volume and Surface Data in Airplane Cabins

This application allows the interpretation of computational fluid dynamics (CFD) data within a real airplane cabin (Regenbrecht & Jacobsen, 2002). The information is displayed as volumetric data in the form of voxels. The setup demonstrates the combined visualization of four domains: video see-through, VR data, phantom model, and voxel data, as shown in Figure 4.

Non-visible physical properties of a real or simulated environment can become visible using VR technology. In our case, climate conditions within the cabin of an Airbus airplane are displayed as spatially distributed voxel data. These data represent air temperature, velocity, or pressure. The physical values are coded with different colors using 3D texture mechanisms available in rendering hardware today.

One main problem in interpreting such volumetric data is the loss of relationship to the real environment, for which the data sets were originally computed. Using AR technology, the volumetric data can be spatially aligned with the real world for appropriate interpretation. Furthermore, missing parts of the real environment, like seats not yet placed and compartments not yet built in, can be visualized.

Figure 4. Principle of combined display of VR, phantom, voxel models, and video

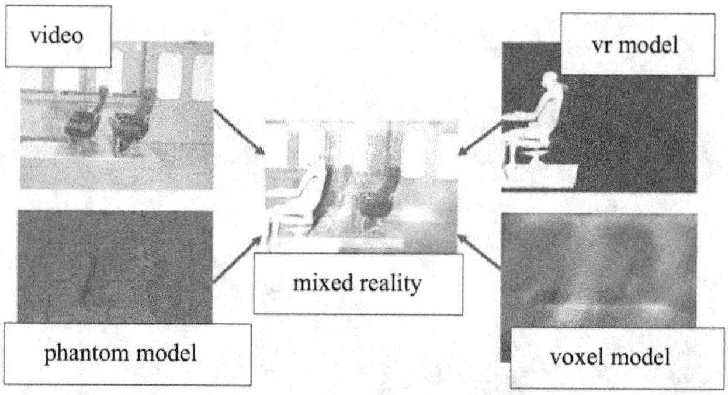

video

vr model

mixed reality

phantom model

voxel model

Finally, we used a phantom model of parts of the real environment, in our case of the seats, to render the hybrid scene with the correct occlusion relations between real and virtual world.

We incrementally implemented three versions of the system: (1) a demonstration system located in our laboratory (Figure 5a), (2) a second mobile demonstration system with a scaled-down model for presentation and teaching purposes (Figure 5b), and a prototype system implemented at the customers site (Figure 7).

In both demonstration setups (Figure 5a and b), the user wears a head-mounted display with a mini camera attached to it. The main difference is the tracking system used. Setup (1) tracks the user's head with an A.R.T. Dtrack system (ART 2003) with very high quality. This system tracks retro-reflective markers within the environment by self-flashing infrared cameras. The main disadvantage is the need to place fixed cameras (in our setup three of them)

Figure 5. (a) Mockup of real-size cabin, (b) miniature cabin model

(a)

Figure 5. continued

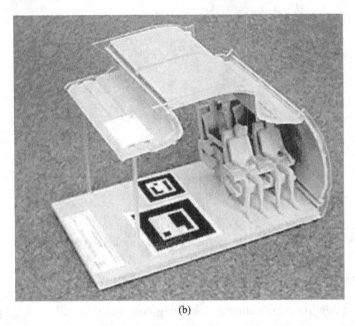

(b)

within the real environment, which is not suitable for the application in a real airplane cabin. Setup (2) uses a marker-based tracking approach described in this chapter. This tracking is not as accurate but more flexible. The markers are detected using the video camera already mounted to the HMD. HMD and the camera are connected to a standard PC equipped with a graphics board capable of generating 3D textures.

The application allows all model domains to be switched on or off, and appropriate files to be loaded. The virtual-to-real-world calibration (i.e., the positioning of the virtual models in the real world coordinate system) is done in a pre-processing step using a special calibration tool. All data sets (CFD, VR, phantom) are pre-computed and respectively pre-modelled.

After the implementation of these two demonstration systems, we have developed a prototype system to be transferred to the customer's factory plant. To do so, we have extended the miniature mock-up system to a real-world sized tracking approach. As in the engine example previously mentioned, it was not possible to instrument the environment (airplane cabin) permanently with markers. We opted for a solution where markers were temporarily placed within the cabin using self-adhesive markers. To do so, we have researched and developed a semi-automatic self-calibration system that computes the geometric relation between these temporarily placed markers (Baratoff, Neubeck, & Regenbrecht, 2002).

The whole system, including all hardware components needed (PC, helmet with HMD and camera, video-splitter, controllers, battery operated power supply, self-adhesive markers, interaction device), is integrated into a portable unit (flight attendant trolley, see Figure 6). It has been transferred to its final destination at Airbus Industries in Hamburg, Germany. In each session, the engineer rolls this unit into the airplane cabin, attaches markers to the environment, and calibrates the coordinate systems. After these preparatory steps, he can

Figure 6. Final AR system integrated into trolley

visually interpret the CFD data in its relation to the real world. Finally, he removes the markers and leaves the cabin.

Because we were using a virtual reality system as a basis for the AR system, the solution can be used for digital mock-up displays as well. Even elements of the cabin that have not yet been built in can be visualized in 3D with this system. Interestingly enough this is now what this system is primarily used for at the customer's site.

Figure 7. Prototype system in use at customer's site

This prototype system is ready to use, but more design and engineering is needed to prepare it for long-term use. The HMD needs to be more robust and ergonomically designed, the update rate and robustness of the tracking system has to be improved, and access to CFD and 3D model data has to be improved.

On the other hand, the system has reached a stage of maturity, which allows for usability studies as well as for actual engineering tasks. Once the initial prototype test phase is completed, decisions can be made on whether a final productive system will be developed.

Productive System Example: Picking

Whoever comes into a large manufacturing or production shop floor will immediately realize the difficulty in introducing any kind of sensitive equipment to such an environment. By their very nature these environments are crowded with workers and/or robots, are noisy, mostly tidy but dirty, have very little wasted space (no room for extras), and are a scene of endless activity.

Given the requirement to provide a value-adding augmented reality application, the identification of a suitable workplace is very hard. AR technology at this stage of maturity is far from being robust enough to be applied to the whole manufacturing process. Together with internal and external specialists (ar-solutions.de, shared-reality.com) we have identified some application scenarios where AR could be applied successfully and could gain a reasonable return on investment.

In two German car manufacturing plants, we were investigating applications for the use of AR technology with the potential to provide the benefits previously mentioned. The working process of "picking," present at all assembly line manufacturing locations, was chosen as an initial test case for the widespread use of AR.

Picking in this case refers to the manufacturing process where an employee picks car parts out of storage according to a sequentially numbered list of parts written on paper, puts these parts into a cart, brings the cart to the next process location for later just-in-time assembly, and confirms this action on the paper list.

The main shortcomings of this procedure are: (1) the list of items to pick is locally separated from the storage location to be picked from, this results in unnecessary travel between the cart and the storage shelf, (2) the confirmation of picked parts is done on paper and therefore error-prone, and (3) incorrectly reading the list (e.g., reading the wrong row) can also lead to errors.

There are two main technologies which attempt to address these issues: (1) A so called "pick-by-light" system, where lamps on the storage shelf indicate which part to pick next (including a confirmation button), this technology is not applicable in our scenario because the system has to be reinstalled every time the storage arrangement is changed according to new assembly line needs. (2) A "pick-by-voice" system instructs the worker using audible instructions via a headset. Confirmation is also done using voice commands. This system has not been accepted by a majority of workers for ergonomic reasons.

This task however looks like a promising candidate for the use of AR. The paper list can be transformed into electronic information brought to the worker on a head-worn display, and confirmation can be provided electronically enabling greater integration into the entire logistic process. This approach is presented here.

A further motivating factor in selecting this task is that, if one can successfully introduce AR supported picking into a given manufacturing environment, (1) the resulting system can easily be modified and deployed into almost any environment where picking takes place (not limited to car manufacturing, but also applicable in dispatch and other fields), and (2) that the proof-of-concept of AR in picking will serve as an enabler for the introduction of AR into other processes (e.g., in assembly or servicing).

After conducting a comprehensive requirement analysis (not presented here for reasons of brevity) together with our supplier experts (ar-solutions.de and shared-reality.com), we have implemented the entire introduction process in an industrial case study. This was also conducted in close partnership with our customers and end-users with extended periods spent on site.

Here we focus on the process of data delivery and handling, the technology chosen, and the integration of the system into the existing working processes.

Data Delivery

The logistics of a just-in-time assembly line is very complex and has to be robust and failure free. The process we found at the car manufacturing plant was highly optimized and, with regard to the electronic data provision, without having had a single error in seven years! Any intervention in this process was going to be considered cautiously for good reason. Therefore, "non-invasive" data integration was the only option.

For picking, the existing process can be described briefly as follows: A control system governed by the pace of the assembly line selects, compiles, and provides a "selective assembly task." This is sent to the appropriate printer within the picking storage area. Multiple tasks are put onto one sheet of paper that is retrieved from the printer by the worker. After the completion of each picking task, confirmation that this task has been completed is made by writing a checkmark on the sheet. All sheets from a shift are collected and checked.

In the case where clarification is required and for specialized assembly tasks, additional information is needed in the form of drawings or textual descriptions. This is rarely used in the picking process, but is often used in assembly processes on the production line.

After much consideration, a data delivery solution was developed where a virtual printer was implemented and controlled in exactly the same way as the real printer. With this approach, we (1) ensured that the actual current data are sent and (2) enables paper and AR to be used in parallel, which is needed for the initial introduction phase and doubles as a fallback in the case of malfunction of the AR system.

We implemented tailored software on a dedicated PC networked to the production system, which presents itself to the rest of the system as a printer. Figure 8 shows an example of the user interface of an AR client. The information displayed is reduced to necessary information only, with options for additional requests. The interface is operated by buttons only and (in this example) makes use of different colors and font sizes to ensure effective information delivery.

Figure 8. Example of display content

At this stage of the project, we have not done any optimization of the sequence in which data is presented. The data is presented in the same temporal and content order as on the paper. The only difference is the layout and amount of information shown at once. In a later step, it might be advisable to optimize the sequence according to part type, location in the storage facility, or even on a user's individual preferences.

Wearable Technology

If one wants to support a given workflow with new technology, the technology itself should really be of help and must not disturb or distract the attention of the user. In our case, the AR technology and interface should be as unobtrusive as possible and should not require massive instrumentation of the environment or worker.

We considered various display and computer technologies for use within our scenario, like tracked video-see-through head-mounted displays, head-mounted or environment mounted projectors, and displays on the cart or within the storage environment. Eventually two systems remained worth considering, the first being a combination of a MicroOptical display unit and a personal digital assistant (PDA) and the second, a Microvision Nomad Expert Technician System consisting of a head-worn display unit connected to a Nomad wearable computer (see Figure 9).

Both systems include integrated wireless LAN (WLAN), work with lightweight head-worn displays, the computer units can be worn on a belt and are battery-operated.

The MicroOptical display unit was attached to standard safety glasses. Workers are obliged to wear these glasses while working. The PDA was integrated into an industrial housing with customized buttons for operating the unit mounted and interfaced to the PDA. A high capacity battery was used instead of the standard one. The Microvision display unit was attached to a baseball cap (see Figure 9 bottom left).

The pros and cons of each system can be summarized as follows: Both systems were robust enough to be suitable for the picking task environment. The housings and components used

Figure 9. Displays and wearable computer units of technologies chosen

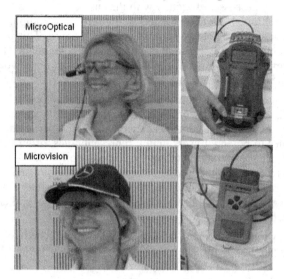

already do, or will soon, comply with industry requirements for the near future. Although not extensively tested yet, both computer units as well as the display units were acceptably comfortable to wear, though we recognize there is room for improvement.

The main issue is the display technology. The MicroOptical system blocks parts of the user's sight. Even though this is only a small portion of the entire field of view, it is disturbing and concerns the customers. The Microvision system allows for optical see-through and therefore blocks only those parts of the environment where the actual information is displayed. Unfortunately, a psychological aspect comes into play with the Microvision system. Because the image is provided by applying a laser beam to the retina of the user, an acceptance barrier has to be broken first before one can introduce the display.

To be worn for a full working day (a shift), a wearable AR system has to operate continuously for about eight hours. Because of the high-capacity battery used in the MicroOptical/PDA system, this can be achieved easily. The Microvision system on the other hand, when operated together with the WLAN, has to be recharged after less than 4 hours. If no extra battery option is available, more than one system per worker and shift has to be provided including a transparent, continuous, and seamless information provision/hand-over.

The user interface has to be robust, easy-to-use, and must not require fine motor-movements to control, like mouse cursor movements. For this reason, the use of a button-only interface is advisable. This can be implemented with both systems. The lack of colors with the Microvision system can be substituted with a careful interface design.

Process Integration

The readiness to invest into augmented reality technology for a customer presupposes the provision of return on investment (ROI) estimates by the AR technologists. In our case, the customer was already given a report by an external supplier on the ROI of AR introduction into certain assembly processes. Together with the customer experts and our suppliers (ar-solutions.de and TU Munich) we double-checked this report and computed new ROI numbers for the picking task as it had not been considered in the report. This provided the base for our presentation to the management and eventually led to the financial and organizational support for this implementation study. Without any ROI figures it would have been very difficult to start the project on a serious level.

A necessary next step was to establish a close working relationship with the customers. We had to identify their current work processes, their needs, expectations, and ascertain their attitudes toward new technologies in general and AR in particular. We presented pilot prototype examples to potential users, union representatives, group leaders, and occupational health and safety experts (including the company physician). We found the various customer groups receptive to the new technology and willing to support the introductory process and its eventual deployment. Later on an informal user interview study was carried out to get an idea of the potential level of acceptance within the worker community and it was actually very high.

Last but not least, we established an ongoing communication schedule with the technicians and IT experts within the enterprise whose support was critical to the AR project in providing data and infrastructure assistance.

Compared to state-of-the-art augmented reality research projects our approach is a very humble one from a technological and invention point of view:

- We are using commercially available, off-the-shelf components with little modification.
- We display two-dimensional information only.
- This overlaid information consists of text and some graphics only.
- The user is neither located, nor tracked, nor registered within the environment.
- The tangible user interface is reduced to button-clicks.
- The task to be supported is very simple by nature.
- All information for task completion is available.

It becomes apparent that the focus of effort with a productive system compared to demonstration and prototype systems shifts from the introduction of new and unique solutions to process and data integration and robustness and reliability. We have neither developed new hardware nor have we invented new algorithms. The main challenge was the analysis of the requirements and the implementation of a seamless integrated solution.

Conclusion

We have briefly introduced augmented reality projects applied in the automotive and aerospace industries. As previously shown, there are many technical and organizational issues to be resolved before one can apply AR in the field. Besides the application-specific issues addressed, some general guidelines can already be drawn from the experience we have gained. Even those may not represent empirical evidence; we think some humble suggestions can be made here that have value for anyone who wants to apply AR in an industrial context.

Data Integration

Firstly, the effort required to incorporate real-world data into the AR application is often seriously underestimated. Most demonstration scenarios work pretty well with (manually) pre-configured and specially prepared data sets. When it comes to the first real data trial, however, the systems mostly tend to fail. This is usually either because of the quantity of data needed, or the complexity and historic diversity of the data. One could probably argue that the data delivery and preparation falls outside the realm of AR research, but nobody else better understands the data interface than the team of end-users and AR researchers involved in the project. The early consideration of real-world data sets is crucial for the successful final deployment of the system.

If the existing data cannot be used right away, a dedicated workflow and tools (especially authoring tools) need to be developed for successful process integration.

Acceptance

AR technology and research has not yet reached a level of maturity that allows for a wide-spread deployment "from scratch." The initial application fields need to be identified very carefully with key persons in innovator roles. These persons should work together with the researcher as close as possible, should know the application field very well, and should be widely accepted among their colleagues to serve as a point of multiplication for later dissemination. If one cannot find such a person who fully accepts the approach and is willing and able to drive it to success, the entire project will probably fail. Furthermore, the integration of many parties in the early process of the project (managers, company physician, union representatives etc.) is laborious but worthwhile. Additionally, usability studies with representative subjects should be a part of every application project.

Finally, if one has the opportunity to choose between different application scenarios, the preference should be given to single-user, single-location, and single-task settings. There is a far greater chance of success if your AR system is setup in an "island" environment compared with, for example, trying to equip hundreds of workers with wearable AR systems.

Simplicity

Albert Einstein once said: "Keep it simple, but not simpler!" This is very true for industrial AR projects. From the researcher's point of view, the best solution found might not be the one with the highest level of originality or novelty, but imagine if the users realize later on that there was a simpler, more elegant solution for their problem. The disappointment will probably put an end to future cooperation. It is advisable therefore to provide a simple, but accepted solution first and to build on it for advanced versions at a later time.

The maturity of AR display and tracking technology, in particular, seldom allows for the use of the most advanced and most recent systems available. One has to consider all alternatives available. Choosing the most accepted and robust one is always better than offering the latest "bleeding-edge" technology.

Added Value

At the beginning of a planned project, consideration of factors like cost, quality, time, and knowledge obtainment helps and often enables the project to get started. Even if the figures are "educated guesses," estimates of the value added and sometimes even a return on investment appraisal are widely expected. Indeed, this is not the core competence of an AR researcher, but it is to be expected that the researcher will be concerned with these issues. Preferably, one can find experts in the field of industrial economics to provide appropriate data or estimates.

Demonstrators and Prototypes

As shown in the first part of this chapter, a huge number of convincing demonstration and prototype systems are needed before a productive system can be developed and introduced. From our experience, these systems should avoid "pretending" to be productive systems. Rather the knowledge gained with these systems will probably lead to much better and productive solutions.

All types of applications are actually needed for successful innovation in the field of industrial augmented reality.

In a mid-term perspective, augmented reality is on its way to become a productive tool in industry. The spectrum of application fields is very wide and early applications of the technology have already demonstrated its value. A comprehensive, multi-disciplinary approach to future research and development conducted in partnership with potential users will bring about the increased use of AR.

Acknowledgments

We would like to thank G. Baratoff, W. Wilke, T. Alt, M. Dittmann, M. Duthweiler, S. Jacobsen, B. Kounovsky, W. Krauss, B. Luehr, U. Munzert, C. Ott, M. Wagner, B. Westerburg, H. Schmidt, and R. Specht for their contributions to the projects, E. Badiqué for his kind contribution of pointers to European activities, and A. Richter for her help with the manuscript.

References

Azuma, R., Baillot, Y., Behringer, R., Feiner, S., Julier, S., & MacIntyre, B. (2001). Recent advances in augmented reality. *IEEE Computer Graphics and Applications*, 34-47.

Badiqué, E. (2005). *IST projects related to industrial applications of augmented reality.* Personal e-mail communication.

Baratoff, G., & Regenbrecht, H. (2004). Developing and applying AR technology in design, production, service, and training. In S. K. Ong & A. Y. C. Nee (Eds.), *Virtual and augmented reality applications in manufacturing* (pp. 207-236). London: Springer.

Baratoff, G., Neubeck, A., & Regenbrecht, H. (2002, September 30-October 1). Interactive multi-marker calibration for augmented reality applications. In *Proceedings of ISMAR 2002*, Darmstadt, Germany. IEEE.

Echtler, F., Sturm, F., Kindermann, K., Klinker, G., Stilla, J., Trilk, J., & Najafi, H. (2003). The intelligent welding gun: Augmented reality for experimental vehicle construction. In S. K. Ong & A. Y. C. Nee (Eds.), *Virtual and augmented reality applications in manufacturing*. London: Springer.

Friedrich, W. (2004). ARVIKA: *Augmented Reality für Entwicklung, Produktion und Service* (Augmented reality for design, production, and servicing). Erlangen, Germany: Publicis MCD Verlag.

Froehlich, B. (2005). *The virtual showcase*. Retrieved from http://typo3.medien.uni-weimar. de/index.php?id=91

Haringer, M., & Regenbrecht, H. (2002, September 30-October 1). A pragmatic approach to augmented reality authoring. In *Proceedings of ISMAR 2002*, Darmstadt, Germany. IEEE.

Kato, H., Billinghurst, M., Poupyrev, I., Imamoto, K., & Tachibana, K. (2000). Virtual object manipulation on a tabletop AR environment. In *Proceedings of ISAR 2001*, Munich, Germany.

Kauffmann, H. (2005). *Geometry education with augmented reality*. Unpublished dissertation at TU Vienna.

Mizell, D. (2001). Boeing's wire bundle assembly project. In Barfield & Caudell (Eds.), *Fundamentals of wearable computers and augmented reality* (pp. 447-467). NJ: Lawrence Erlbaum & Associates.

Navab, N. (2004, May/June). Developing killer apps for industrial augmented reality. *IEEE Computer Graphics and Applications*, 16-20.

Poupyrev, I., Tan, D. S., Billinghurst, M., Kato, H., Regenbrecht, H., & Tetsutani, N. (2002). Developing a generic augmented-reality interface. *IEEE Computer, 35*(3), 44-50.

Regenbrecht, H., & Jacobsen, S. (2002). Augmentation of volumetric data in an airplane cabin. In *Proceedings of the IEEE Augmented Reality Toolkit Workshop*, Darmstadt, Germany.

Regenbrecht, H., Baratoff, G., & Wilke, W. (2005). Augmented reality projects in automotive and aerospace industry. *IEEE Computer Graphics and Application*.

Regenbrecht, H., Wagner, M., & Baratoff, G. (2002). MagicMeeting: A collaborative tangible augmented reality system. *Virtual Reality: Systems, Development, and Applications, 6*(3), 151-166.

Tamura, H., Yamamoto, H., & Katayama, A. (2001). Mixed reality: Future dreams seen at the border between real and virtual worlds. *Computer Graphics and Applications, 21*(6), 64-70.

Chapter XV

Creating Augmented Virtual Environments

Ulrich Neumann, University of Southern California, USA

Suya You, University of Southern California, USA

Abstract

An augmented reality fuses computer graphics onto images or direct views of a scene. In a new alternative augmentation approach, a real scene is captured as video imagery from one or more cameras, and these images are used to augment a corresponding 3D scene model or virtual environment. This arrangement is termed an augmented virtual environment (AVE) and it produces a powerful visualization of the dynamic activities observed by cameras. This chapter describes the AVE concept and the major technologies needed to realize such systems.

Introduction

Most augmented realities fuse computer graphics onto images or direct views of a scene. This chapter describes an alternative augmentation scenario that offers unique capabilities and challenges. In this alternate form of augmented reality, a real scene is captured as video imagery from one or more cameras and these images augment a corresponding 3D scene model or virtual environment. This arrangement is termed an augmented virtual environment (AVE) and it produces a powerful visualization of dynamic activities occurring over wide and occluded areas (Figure 1).

This chapter describes the AVE concept and its benefits. In addition, the chapter details solutions to the major technologies needed to realize such systems as well some technical barriers that are yet to be overcome.

Figure 1. An AVE visualization is created by projecting camera images (a-e) onto 3D models (f) to produce arbitrary views (g, h), in this example, for an area in Washington, DC

Background

The AVE concept is a variation of augmented reality (AR), in which the user's view of the real world scene is not tied to their physical presence. Rather, the user's view is freely modified, as in a virtual environment, and their perception of the real world scene arises from viewing multiple camera images projected in the 3D model. This concept of using a virtual environment for viewing imagery from cameras has its roots in several research areas, including texture projection, camera pose calibration, 3D modeling, and virtual environments.

The fusion of images or video in the context of 3D models has a long history in computer graphics, computer vision, and telecommunications. The following represent much of the earliest research that has some clear relation to the AVE concept. Dorsey, Sillion, and Greenberg (1991, pp. 41-50) present methods and applications for simulating projected textures for the theater stage sets. This is perhaps the earliest work that contemplates the projection of imagery onto 3D models, rather than the more common mapping of textures onto a surface through an explicit parameterization. Segal, Korobkin, Widenfelt, Foran, and Haeberli (1992, pp. 249-252) formalizes the notion of projective image textures and provides the mathematical framework in the context of efficient graphics-hardware implementation. Bajura, Fuchs, and Ohbuchi (1992, pp. 203-210) presents the concept of a video-see-through AR system and the idea of a 3D polygonal surface embedded in the virtual world with real-time video mapped onto it. State (1996, pp. 439-446) also presents 3D polygons with live video and a volumetric rendering of stored past video. Debevec, Taylor, and Malik (1996, pp. 11-20) presents 3D building models and the use of multiple projected texture images to produce view-dependent texture rendering. Simsarian and Åkesson (1997) introduce the notion of projecting live video of real-world objects onto their virtual world counterparts for enhancing the reality of remote scene comprehension. Weinhous and Devarajan (1997, pp. 325-365) presents the texture projection process in the context of modeling buildings and terrain. Dorbie (1997) presents OpenGL implementations of projective textures and occlusion processing. Spann and Kaufman (2000) present methods of calibrated image projection onto 3D building models to produce realistic scene models.

The work of Karl-Petter Åkesson is really the beginning of the complete AVE concept. In his Master's Thesis (1998), Åkesson presents his vision of how "...to create augmented virtual worlds in an automatic way with textures generated from real world images." This idea is presented in the context of tele-surveillance where video cameras capture a scene, and remote observation is enabled by projecting the images onto a virtual 3D scene model of the scene. In 1999 (p. 11-18), Åkesson and Simsarian also describes how white-board tele-collaboration and remote robotic tele-operation are facilitated by video projection onto 3D scene models. Sequeira, Bovisio, and Gonçalves (1999, pp. 661-666) describe the use of internet video with a Web-based AVE system for video surveillance. This work also highlights the importance of scene modeling fidelity and the scene-comprehension benefits of the AVE visualization.

The previous research exemplifies the variety of ways that have been developed to combine images, video, and 3D models for the purpose of augmenting human perception of the world. Three specific examples, *Augmented Virtuality* (Åkesson, 1998), *Reality Portals* (Åkesson et al., 1999, pp. 11-18), and *Augmented Reality in Multi-Camera Surveillance* (Sequeira et al., 1999, pp. 661-666), form the inception of what we now term an *augmented virtual environment* (AVE), in which video images are projected onto corresponding 3D models of a scene. The result provides a viewer with both the spatial context of the 3D scene model and the dynamic activities captured by the video images. The argued and evident benefit of rendering the video images in the context of the 3D models is the aid in human comprehension of the events and the entire scene. Specifically, the activities observed by fixed or moving video cameras become more easily understood in relation to each other when the images are presented by AVE methods in the context of the surrounding scene that has been modeled. These three pioneering publications describe many aspects of creating an AVE system, including the use of multiple cameras, camera calibration, dynamic model updates, user or automated view control, the use of recorded or real-time video, and tagging objects with labels or icons.

AVE Technologies and Challenges

The next and main section of this chapter surveys the components needed and approaches available for creating AVE visualizations. Before proceeding with these details, a table of system components is presented to provide a framework for introducing the main technologies and challenges.

Video Acquisition

The video cameras determine the bounds and coverage of the scene view. Multiple cameras are needed to adequately cover the scene and any specific areas of interest. An overlap

Table 1. System components

System Components	Technical Challenges
Video Acquisition	cameras, transmission network, computer interface
Video Projection	decode, texture transfer, projection, hidden surfaces
Projection Calibration	pose calibration for stationary and moving cameras
3D Scene Modeling	data acquisition and model refinement
Moving Objects	object tracking, dynamic modeling, and rapid modeling

between camera views is helpful to ensure that there are no gaps in coverage. Projection distortion is minimized if the camera views are in line with the likely user viewing directions. Projection distortions are also minimized by placing clusters of cameras at similar locations or on similar sides of an observed scene. Roof level cameras often provide better coverage and lower projection distortion than ground level cameras.

Regardless of camera locations, the video streams must be gathered and interfaced to the computer. Technical solutions to this range widely. In simplest form, analog video is routed from cameras via coax cables that connect to video digitizer interfaces in the host computer. While this simple solution is suitable for up to three or four cameras, it does not scale well. There are limits to how many digitizers are supported by any host computer, both in terms of physical interface slots and in terms of how much bandwidth is available within the computer I/O and memory buses to accept this data.

As a design example, consider that a single uncompressed 720x480-color image in 24-bit RGB format requires 1 MByte. At 15 Hz frame rates, a sustained bandwidth of 15 MB/s is required to transfer a camera stream from the interface to memory or to the graphics card. Different resolutions or frame rates impact these figures proportionally.

The simple coax/digitizer approach does not scale to sixteen cameras, for example, where current PCs do not support sufficient IO slots, and the required 240 MB/sec I/O bandwidth far exceeds 32-bit PCI bus capabilities.

An alternative solution is the use of network video cameras that stream compressed video over IP networks. This approach can simplify video routing, since it does not require separate coax cables for each camera. More importantly, the interface problem is diminished since the cameras can share one or more high-speed (100Mb/s or 1Gb/s) IP interfaces. A good quality MJPG compressed stream for a single camera is 60 KBytes/image, meaning that one camera stream consumes 7.2 Mb/s on the network. Therefore, about 10 cameras can reasonably share a single 100Mb/s interface, or 100 cameras can share a 1Gb/s interface. These figures improve if the image size or compression quality is reduced, or if more aggressive MPEG compression methods are employed. The use of network video technology is a clear solution to the video acquisition, routing, and interface problem (Figure 2).

Figure 2. Video acquisition with an IP camera network

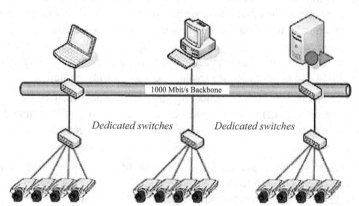

Video Processing: Decode, Texture Transfer

The drawback of network video is the need for decoding the compressed video streams. Decoding is a potential bottleneck, but video decoding is a common problem in multimedia applications and therefore a number of solutions are available. An Intel IPP library performance report (2003) shows that a 3.06 GHz Pentium 4 can decode an MJPEG image of size 720x480 in under 0.01 secs. Therefore, a CPU can decode over 100 fps, or 6.7 camera streams. A dual CPU system is therefore needed to decode ten full camera streams with about 50% of a CPU still available for the application. If we use MPEG-2 cameras, the IPP library performance increases to 310 fps, or over 20 camera streams per CPU.

Once video frames are available in memory, they must still be transferred to the graphics card for use in texture projection. Fortunately, the peak AGP 8x bus bandwidth of 2.1 GB/s can support up to 140 camera streams. In practice, transfers for RGB texture of size 720x480 take about 1.4 ms, with the AGPx8 interface capable of supporting up to 47 camera streams. Increased performance is feasible with PCI Express x16.

Video Texture Projection

Projecting imagery onto a 3D model is effectively performed through a projective texture mapping method. Although the technique was originally proposed only for shadow and lighting effects (Segal et al., 1992, pp. 249-252), researchers later found it extremely useful in various areas of computer graphics, image-based rendering, and visualization.

A projective texture mapping models the process of perspective image projection by casting the lines of projected light onto objects using the camera position as the projection center. The projection of an image I onto a scene is the inverse of the corresponding camera transformation. Given an arbitrary eye-view transformation V_e to create image J, the mapping between I and J is determined once a scene surface and projection camera pose V_c are specified. In practice, as each scene surface (triangle) is rendered for image J, the texture coordinates t of image I are computed and applied as a texture to the surface, as shown in Figure 3.

From a practical point of view, the value of the projective texture mapping lies in the way that texture coordinates are assigned to model surface points automatically during the rendering process. By dynamically updating the texture scene image and the camera pose, the projection onto the scene geometry dynamically "paints" the acquired images onto the model. The projection parameters are analogous to cameras parameters; the view transforms and view volume clip planes can be modified for dynamic control during rendering.

There are several steps involved in projecting streams of video imagery onto 3D models: (1) video texture upload; (2) visibility and occlusion processing; (3) compute projection parameters; and (4) texture rendering. These steps in the projection algorithm are summarized next.

Initially, the video imagery and camera pose data (position and orientation) are available in memory buffers and converted to the formats required for texturing and projection. Video frames are tagged with time, internal camera parameters, and camera pose.

Figure 3. Camera projection and eye-viewpoint geometry

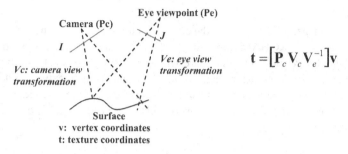

$$t = \left[P_c V_c V_e^{-1} \right] v$$

The projection transformations are constructed for each camera, and applied in sequence during the rendering process to produce multiple projections onto the same model.

Simply applying a texture projection to the entire scene model will produce textures on all surfaces that fall within the camera projection frustum. Visibility information is needed to modulate the projection process and several techniques are available. For example, stenciled shadow volumes and shadow mapping (Dorbie, 1997) will compute visibility information. Occluded portions of the model are omitted from the projection process, thereby keeping their original colors and reducing the rendering time.

The texture coordinates are automatically computed and assigned to model surface points in the rendering process. However, the texture must be clipped to the projection frustum specified by the camera parameters. Texture color can blend with or overwrite exiting color information.

The projection algorithm is summarized as pseudo code below with corresponding section numbers that provide additional detail.

for each frame

> *Upload video (3.3.1)*
>
> *Move video into texture memory*
>
> *if (projection camera moved)*
>
>> *Perform occlusion processing (3.3.2), and texture setup (3.3.3)*
>
> *Render whole scene (lit, texture)*
>
> *Enable blending*
>
> *for each projection camera*
>
>> *Enable video texture and automatic texture generation (3.3.4)*

Configure register combiner or pixel shader (3.3.4)

Render (unlit, non-texture) visible polygon set (3.3.4)

> *Disable blending*

Video Texture Upload

Decoded video images are loaded into the center of a texture buffer using OpenGL function *glTexSubImage2D*. An RGBA texture buffer is allocated and bound of size video_width+2 by video_height+2 (round up to the nearest power of two). This sets the buffer's alpha channel to one for the video texture region and allows at least one texture border pixel with zero alpha value. The alpha channel is used later for blending the live video streams with the existing scene and ensuring that regions outside of the camera frustum are not affected during texture projection.

Visibility and Occlusion Processing

A visibility calculation is necessary from the viewpoint of each projection-camera. To achieve real-time projection of multiple cameras, a culling and depth-map shadow process is employed. A depth-map shadow algorithm is supported by many high performance graphics cards. The depth map is generated by rendering the scene from the projection-camera pose. This depth information is then compared to the interpolated texture depth coordinate used for perspective division. The resulting visibility mask is used to determine partial visibility of the visible-set triangles for each projection-camera and to filter partially hidden triangles in the texture-blending stage.

Instead of a brute-force re-rendering of the entire scene for each video-projection texture-rendering pass, a list of visible polygons is created for each projection camera. This overcomes the scalability problem that would otherwise require rendering the entire scene $N+1$ times for N projection cameras. This approach is optimal if the projection cameras are static, since off-line processing can be employed to determine an exact visibility set (Cohen-Or, Chrysanthou, Silva, & Durand, 2003, pp. 412-431). Dynamic projection-cameras require run-time visibility-set determination that may be approximate (Roden & Parberry, 2005, p. 3). In general, a visible-set of polygons is produced in three phases:

1.   Test if an object (e.g., geometry node in *VRML*) bounding box intersects with the projection-camera frustum.

2.   Clear the depth buffer, enable *OcclusionQueryNV* extensions, and render each object visible in the projection-camera frustum, producing a complete depth map of the scene from the perspective of the projection-camera.

3.   Test individual triangles in visible objects to see if they pass an occlusion query test.

Once the visible set R_i is found for each projection camera i, the complexity of rendering a scene of D triangles with N projection cameras becomes: $\mathbf{O}(D + \sum R_i)$ (i = 1...N)

Compute Projection Parameters

The projection transformation is based on the inverse of the calibrated camera transformation. High-performance graphics cards support real-time projective texture mapping in hardware with OpenGL texture coordinate generation.

It is noteworthy that the OpenGL projective texture mapping is not a real projective projection. The mathematics of OpenGL projective texture mapping actually produces dual projections. One is along the camera view direction, and another is in the opposite direction, producing a reverse projection. The sign of the component q of the generated texture coordinates is negative behind the projector, inverting the texture image of the reverse projection. The programmer must manage the negative projection in the application. Setting an appropriate near clip-plane can prevent the reverse projection, and far clip-plane can be added to control how far video textures are projected. Furthermore, since the allocated texture-buffer size is larger than the video width/height by at least two-pixels, the projected video is smaller than the projection-camera frustum, requiring offset and scaling.

Texture Rendering

The final appearance of video texture rendering depends on many factors, including the input video quality, texture blending between the projection areas, and the geometry of the eye and projection-camera frustums. Due to the two frusta involved in texture projection, there may be portions of the textured image that require extreme anisotropic filter kernels, extreme minification, and extreme magnification, all within the same image. A developer has to consider those factors in designing the camera views and tuning the system. Recent graphics hardware offers register-combiner and pixel-shader features that optimize these rendering processes.

Camera Calibration and Tracking

One of the key challenges in creating an AVE is to maintain accurate registration between the 3D scene model and projected images. When projected, the camera image must align with the corresponding 3D positions and orientations of the scene model. This calibration requirement is identical to that of a conventional video-see-through AR system. The alignment between the real and virtual scene elements depends on accurately calibrating the sensor pose, relative to either the environment or a defined inertial reference.

Assuming the scene model is accurate, and the cameras are fixed, an off-line process can determine correspondences of image features to model features and compute the camera pose. This is a traditional camera calibration problem, and there are many approaches that have been developed in the photogrammetry and computer vision communities (Brown, 1971, pp. 855-866; Faig, 1975, pp. 1479-1486; Faugeras & Toscani, 1986, pp. 15-20; Tsai, 1986, pp. 364-374; Wang, 1992, pp. 161-175). Camera calibration often involves two steps. First, a mathematical camera model is built to approximate the mechanical and optical behaviors of the sensor; then the parameters of the model are estimated (Ito, 1991, pp. 321-335). There are several camera models to choose from, depending on the desired accuracy. The simplest models are based on linear transformations or ideal pinhole projections that omit models of lens distortion (Hall, Tio, McPherson, & Sadjadi, 1982, pp. 42-54). Given a set of corresponding model and image points (*Pm, Pi*); a camera can be modeled by means of a linear transformation $\mathbf{M}$, that is, $\mathbf{P_i} = \mathbf{M} \cdot \mathbf{P_m}$.

The linear camera model is simple and its parameters are relatively easy to estimate. However, a model of the camera optical system is needed to obtain greater precision by compensating for lens distortions. A more realistic camera model employs a non-linear model with four parameters, two of which are intrinsic parameters representing the effective focal length and principle point of the optics and sensor system. The remaining two parameters embody the extrinsic pose (position and orientation) of the camera in relation to the scene. These four parameters are often augmented with additional parameters that model mechanical distortion effects such as sensor skew, anisotropic scale, and radial lens distortions. These factors are explicit parameters in the photogrammetric collinearity equations. Since the equations are nonlinear, it is important to have reasonable approximations for the unknown parameters for a well-conditioned estimation (Faugeras, Luong, & Maybank, 1992, pp. 321-334).

The camera model parameters are estimated by optimal estimation techniques. While four corresponding features are sufficient to estimate the linear camera model, in practice additional features produce a more-robust estimation with tolerance for feature detection and 3D model inaccuracies. Least-squares techniques are often employed to resolve over-determined parametric equations, and multi-pass statistical techniques are used to improve estimate accuracy (Fischler & Bolles, 1981, pp. 381-395). Often, an initial calibration is obtained by using the linear model approximation, and an iterative refinement optimizes the solution. One of the most popular multi-pass calibration methods is the Tsai camera calibration method (1986, pp. 364-374), which is suitable for a wide range of application since it deals with coplanar and non-coplanar points. This method also allows for separate calibration of intrinsic and extrinsic parameters, which is particularly useful since it offers the option of fixing the intrinsic parameters of the camera, once known, and thereafter only estimating pose.

The ability to steer a camera's viewing direction is useful in AVE systems since it extends the scene coverage of single camera. Pan, tilt, zoom (PTZ) cameras offer dynamic control of their view direction and focal length. Use of such cameras implies that three degrees of freedom (3DOF) must be calibrated dynamically. In fact, changes to focal length (zoom) generally impact other intrinsic parameters such as the principle point and lens distortion; however dynamic calibration of those parameters is often ignored. Generally, pan and tilt changes also modify the camera position, however, this position change is often a small and ignored. A general approach to the PTZ calibration problem involves placing known moving targets in the environment, while tracking a pre-defined path of the target motions to estimate the camera transforms (Thrun, Fox, & Burgard, 1998, pp. 253-271). A vision-based tracking method or motion sensor can be used for target tracking. While this approach automatically calibrates a PTZ camera, the requirement for accurate tracking is a severe constraint that makes this approach difficult to implement in general applications.

An alternative solution to the PTZ problem is to use a "scenario-driven" PTZ camera control mechanism. The application scenario is analyzed and each PTZ camera location is calibrated and assumed fixed. A set of preset view-directions and zoom settings are created for each camera and calibrated as fixed views. These presets are often associated with anticipated scene activity or sensors that inform the system to automatically switch to a corresponding preset PTZ and viewpoint. Each PTZ camera preset is calibrated with the stationary calibration approach and the results are saved as a *lookup table* that represents the available PTZ views of the scene and their relationships to sensor signals. At runtime, the system consults the lookup table to select optimal PTZ views based on sensor status or operator view control. This approach is flexible and scales linearly in the number of PTZ cameras and the average number of preset views per camera.

Cameras can also be freely moving on robotic or manned platforms. In such cases, high-performance dynamic camera-calibration and tracking is required to report the complete 6DOF pose of a camera as well as any changes to its intrinsic parameters. Unconstrained camera tracking is challenging, especially in unconstrained outdoor scenes. Several tracking methods have been developed including active-target, passive-target, and hybrid approaches. Active-target systems incorporate powered signal emitters and sensors placed in a prepared and calibrated environment. Examples of such systems use magnetic, optical, radio, laser, and acoustic signals. Passive-target systems use ambient or naturally occurring signals. Examples include compasses sensing the Earth's field, inertial systems sensing physical phenomena created by linear acceleration and angular motion, and vision systems sensing intentional landmarks or natural features. Hybrid tracking methods attempt to compensate for the shortcomings of any single technology by using multiple measurements to produce robust results. Hybrid system examples include active-target magnetic and passive-target vision in State (1996, pp. 429-438), inertial sensors and active-target vision are combined in Azuma et al. (2001, pp. 34-47), inertial and natural-feature vision tracking approach are combined in You, Neumann, and Azuma (1999, pp. 36-42) and Jiang, You, and Neumann (2004, pp. 3-10). The fusion approach is based on the SFM (structure from motion) algorithm, in which approximate feature motion is derived from the inertial measurement, and vision feature tracking corrects and refines these estimates in the image domain. Furthermore, the inertial data aids vision tracking by reducing the feature-search space and providing tolerance to interruptions.

3D Modeling: Acquisition and Refinement

Modeling is crucial for AVE visualizations. The model acts as the projection surface for all video images and provides the context for understanding the relationships between images. As such, common errors in modeling may clearly reveal the differences between the actual scene images and the corresponding models of the scene (Figure 4). For example, buildings are often constructed with flat-wall surfaces at right angles and symmetric roof structures, so models should also adhere to such constraints to minimize the differences and artifacts that become visible under image projection. One view is that the modeling system should enforce and preserve such constraints to minimize artifacts in AVE visualizations.

Methods such as Haala and Brenner (1997) pursue an automated method for creating 3D models from both 2D ground plans (CAD or GIS) data and 3D airborne LiDAR data. A constrained interactive method (You, Hu, Neumann, & Fox, 2003, pp. 579-588) uses only

Figure 4. A simple building model created from LiDAR data (left) shows artifacts under image projection, a constrained model built from that same data (right) shows fewer artifacts; the lines illustrate the projection frustum in both images

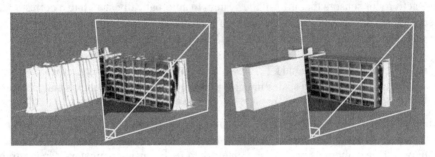

airborne LiDAR data. The latter does not depend upon the availability of CAD or GIS data and argues that a human in the loop is an essential part of modeling.

The method of You et al. (2003, pp. 579-588) allows a user to select 3D primitives such as a plane, ridged plane pair, cuboid, polyhedron, wedge, cylinder, sphere, ellipsoid, and superquadric to 3D scan data (Figure 5). While shape fitting is common (Wilczkowiak, Boyer, & Sturm, 2002, pp. 221-237), the You method speeds the process and optimizes the resulting models for use with texture projection by enforcing the constraints that are common in building construction. Coincidently, these constraints are related to the ways people express and represent building structure. The interactive modeling process takes this into account. Building structures are often represented and expressed in hierarchies of geometric primitives. For example, one can describe a simple building as having four outer walls, a peaked roof, and an extruded entry. Unspoken, but equally important is the notion that the walls are vertical, meet at right angles, and the roof is symmetric. The You fitting system makes these inferences based on simple descriptions that users input, and then automatically computes the best possible constrained fit to the LiDAR data.

A ground plan is used in Haala, Brenner, and Anders (pp. 339-346) to describe the entire footprint of a building, thereby limiting the complexity of the modeled structure. The interactive approach allows users to define a series of connected parts of a building, rather than the entire structure at once, thereby allowing the creation of arbitrarily complex buildings. As users select a series of primitives, constraints are applied automatically to ensure a completely connected and seamless model. All constraints can be overruled by users, but as defaults, they greatly speed the process of model building.

Fitting constrained cuboids or spheres to range data is more accurate than simple plane finding. The problem of determining unconstrained plane edges is described in Haala et al. (1997). The fitting of constrained primitives determines the best constrained edges that fit the scan data without the need for 2D CAD or GIS data. The constraints of symmetry and alignment with wall orientations are useful inferences for fitting roof structure. Since users can override the constraints, arbitrary structures are also possible.

Figure 5. A complex model is created by fitting multiple constrained primitives, including spheres and symmetric roof-peak structures, to LiDAR data

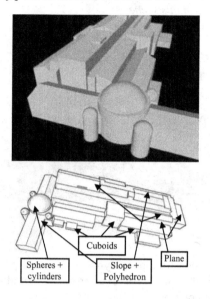

Moving Objects: Tracking, Dynamic Modeling, and Rapid Modeling

The 3D scene model in an AVE visualization will generally not include all the scene details a camera image captures. Models of such details can greatly enhance the visualization and reduce projection distortions. For example, fences, utility poles, people, cars, and vegetation are commonly missing in 3D scene models created from LiDAR or aerial images. Limited LiDAR resolution does not capture utility poles and aerial images only see vegetation cano-pies. However these and other static scene elements are often clearly visible from ground or building-level imagery that can be used to model them, if only approximately and manually. A different problem arises, however, when moving objects are in the scene. For example, people and cars are often objects of interest in AVE visualizations, yet they are transient and therefore impractical to model a-priori.

If no special treatment is afforded dynamic objects, they are simply projected onto the scene model as part of a video image. For example, cars are projected onto the road surface and people are projected onto sidewalks and building walls (Figure 6). Under such projection, distortions arise as the eye-viewpoint moves away from the viewpoint of the camera(s) observing the real scene. Such distortions are localized, so the overall scene comprehension is not lost, however, these distortions can be minimized.

Ideally, a complete 3D model of the moving object should be computed and placed where the video will project the object's texture on it. Such models are difficult to compute in real time for moving people and cars, however, there are examples of work in progress.

Figure 6. A scene viewed from near the real camera viewpoint (left) shows minimal distortions, while a different eye-viewpoint (right) reveals distortions of dynamic or unmodeled objects (people/cars/poles) in this scene

A complete real time 3D reconstruction of dynamic models is produced in Kanade, Tanaka, Oda, Yoshida, and Kano (1996, pp. 671-676) using a custom multiple-sensor and computing system. Likewise, an array of sensors is employed to produce dynamic 3D models in CMU (1999). These systems produce approximate models that are suitable for AVE visualizations, but their acquisition requirements are impractical for most environments in terms of the number of cameras needed and constraints on their locations.

Another approach is to rapidly construct and position approximate models. Most simply, a polygon acts as an approximate model when positioned to track the projected object through the scene (Sebe, You, & Neumann, 2004, 2005, pp. 82-93). Estimating a 3D model from a single image is ill-posed due to loss of information during projection. However, a simple model can be inferred using knowledge of the scene.

First, a background image is estimated by a sliding temporal-window average (Sebe et al., 2004). Such background estimation allows for slow lighting changes. Dynamic objects are detected by background subtraction, a threshold, and morphological filtering. A connected component process then produces a labeled object, and its convex hull is computed.

Once an object is detected, its color properties, size, and motion vectors are computed and the objects are matched or tracked in future frames. Tracking is formalized as a generalized combinatorial assignment problem (Sebe, 2005, pp. 82-93). In general, this an NP-hard problem, however, a successful approximation can be made in $O(n^3)$ complexity, where n is the number of objects in the scene. A resemblance matrix encodes the similarity between currently tracked objects and newly detected objects.

$$f(i,j) = \frac{\dfrac{4*Int(O_i,O_j)}{S_i+S_j}\left(\dfrac{\sqrt{S_i*S_j}}{S_i+S_j} + 2\lambda\dfrac{\sqrt{\|V_i\|*\|V_j\|}}{\|V_i\|+\|V_j\|}*\left(\dfrac{\vec{V_i}\bullet\vec{V_j}}{\|V_i\|*\|V_j\|}+1\right)\right)}{1+\lambda}$$

Figure 7. A convex hull computed for a tracked vehicle: (a) Polygon models placed in the 3D scene to display projections of moving objects (b, c)

(a)   (b)   (c)

This function compares the size (S_i, S_j), shape (O_i, O_j), and motion vectors (V_i, V_j) of objects as a measure of resemblance. Object are classified into one of the following modes: Appear, Disappear, Track, Split, and Merge. A mode likelihood matrix is calculated for every object for every mode. The optimal overall classification is computed with a modified multiple-hypothesis tracking method.

Tacked objects are assumed to rest on the ground plane. A ray from the bottom of an object is backprojected onto the scene model. The intersection of a ray with the ground plane is the 3D location for a 2D polygon with the shape of the object's convex hull. This approximation works well when the objects have little depth variance compared to their distance to the camera (Figure 7).

For higher quality models and near views of moving objects, a part-based modeling approach is employed (Sebe, 2005, pp. 143-146). Similar to the constrained fitting approach used for buildings, the part-based method creates high quality models of specific classes of objects, in this case vehicles. The current method is semi-automatic and requires users to provide 10-20 mouse clicks of key features to create 3D models from single images. If these features were detected automatically, the model could be created in mere seconds (Leung, 2004).

The part-based approach fits a generic car model to different vehicle images. Proper design of the parts and their constraints allows rapid modeling of many types of vehicles, including SUVs, minivans, and sedans, from single images. During modeling, visible portions of the vehicle texture are recovered. Model surfaces that are neither visible nor inferred by symmetry are assigned an estimated color of the vehicle.

User input facilitates fitting by dragging on the parts of a pose-aligned wire frame model (Figure 8). The algorithm estimates the best 3D movement of model parts based on their constraints. Changes to one part of the vehicle are distributed to other parts through connectivity and symmetry constraints and a scattered data interpolation. The distribution of part changes to other parts prevents gaps in the model and speeds up the interaction process. Examples of vehicle models created with this method are shown in Figure 9.

Modeled vehicles can be tracked in video using a model-aided tracker to estimate the pose and location changes of the vehicle in the scene. The 3D model patches are tracked by matching their 2D projections on the image. Tracked 3D models are animated in the 3D scene and viewed from an arbitrary viewpoint (Figure 10).

Figure 8. The part-based modeling process fits a generic model to an image of a desired vehicle

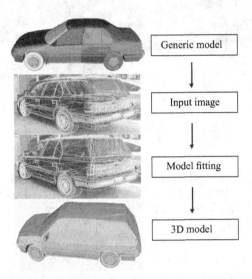

Figure 9. Examples of varied car models created with part-based approach

Open Problems

AVE technology is rapidly maturing and initial deployments have already occurred for commercial and government installations. However, the technology is still in it its first generations and there are significant opportunities for improvements (Neumann, You, Hu, Jiang, & Sebe, 2004, pp. 222-233).

Figure 10. Tracked car movement in video (a, b) and novel viewpoints of textured and animated 3D cars rendered into the scene model (c, d)

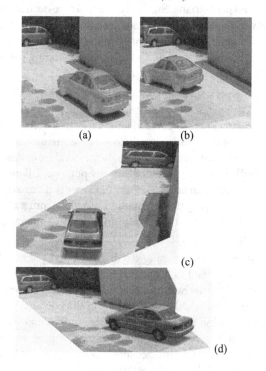

(a)   (b)

(c)

(d)

Dynamic models are still difficult to compute in real time. Fast and robust algorithms are needed for detecting and tracking the silhouettes of moving objects. An automated 3D modeling or reconstruction of moving objects from multiple images or range sensors is desirable. This is a long-term area of research and further advances are needed.

Tools for rapidly modeling 3D static scene elements are often focused on buildings and large-scale scene structures (Pollefeys, Koch, Vergauwen, & Gool, 1999, pp. 14-23). Much can be gleaned from the methods employed in the fields of photogrammetry and GIS (geographic information systems). However, while tools exist for modeling terrain and buildings, they can be made smarter, more accurate, and more automated. Algorithms are needed to deal with partial visibility or occlusion of sensors (Allen et al., 2003, pp. 32-41). Tools that use common cameras as sensors can make modeling more broadly accessible (Gibson, Hubbold, Cook, & Howard, 2003, pp. 293-301). Tools are needed to facilitate fusion of data from multiple sensors and modalities, such as aerial LiDAR and ground images (Hu, You, & Neumann, 2003, pp. 62-69). Modeling tools need to facilitate the inclusion of smaller but important structures such as utility poles, sidewalk curbs, vegetation, fences, awnings, etc. Overall, current modeling capabilities are far from practical for modeling entire cities at the detail level desired for AVE visualizations.

The acquisition and mapping of static textures onto large-scale models is a serious current problem. While large image sequences can be obtained from aerial or ground vehicles, algorithms are needed to solve many outstanding problems in the use of such imagery. Automatic methods are needed for mapping such large image collections to 3D models. Images taken from a single viewpoint or moment in time need methods for the removal of foreground occlusions such as cars and pedestrians. Similarly, methods are needed for merging multiple images from different vantage points (and times) in order to capture textures for high-rise or heavily occluded structures. The alignment of texture and geometry may disagree and methods for optimally refining the models and the image mapping parameters are needed.

Video management for hundreds and thousands of cameras is a crucial problem for scaling AVE capabilities to large areas such as industrial centers, defense facilities, and government complexes. Clearly, an AVE system only needs to access and process video imagery that will be visible in the output image. Therefore, the visible sets associated with each camera can be used to cull the video streams to ensure that only the visible streams are processed. Graphics algorithms, currently used to cull and manage polygon rendering based on visibility, are likely candidates for application or adaptation for this purpose. Likewise, network stream management becomes an issue with large numbers of cameras. The network community has developed algorithms for managing the distribution of video from a few sources to a large number of users. AVE requires new, but related, methods that manage the distribution of video from large numbers of camera sources to a relatively small group of users.

An integrated AVE system merges existing databases of geospatial information. For example, data that is currently viewed in 2D GIS systems would benefit from 3D models and video augmentation. Maps, internal building data, addresses, travel routes, zoning, property records, and utility information could all be viewed in the context of 3D models and live video that provides confirmation about area activities, traffic, and work in progress. The connection of such data sources requires an interface for mapping and filtering the data for semantic meaning. Manual and automatic geospatial queries need to be feasible. Once data is available, its placement, visibility, and occlusions within the scene need to be managed (Bell, Feiner, & Höllerer, 2001, pp. 101-110).

Video decode and texture projection improvements are needed to scale to higher numbers of camera streams. Such improvements are needed in the graphics systems and recent history indicates that progress in that area will continue. Texture upload performance could be improved by hardware video decoding and scaling to varied resolutions. Alternately, decoders that output images in S3TC DXT1 compressed texture format would reduce texture size by a factor of six. The depth map read back performance is a bottleneck that could be solved by implementing the new OpenGL multiple render target API that binds depth maps to texture directly without read back. The last phase in visible set identification is time consuming since it involves an occlusion query for each triangle. An algorithm that takes advantage of spatial coherence and geometric topology could minimize the number of occlusion queries. Graphics cards now support N multiple concurrent textures, so the whole scene could be rendered exactly once, as long as no single triangle has more than N video cameras projected on it. Lastly, the register combiner mechanism for blending textures could be replaced by GLSL which is a cross-vendor standard.

Conclusion

In conclusion, it is instructive to consider an integrated application to illustrate the potential benefits and utility of AVE technology in wide-area situational awareness and surveillance. This system offers a unique solution for monitoring, assessment, and response support for security and management personnel. Traditional monitoring and surveillance systems display camera images on separate windows/screens, the AVE system provides a high-level view of the entire scene including 3D geospatial models of the structures and terrain, static aerial and terrestrial imagery, real-time video imagery, and dynamic sensor alarm status–all on one screen, and from arbitrary viewpoints. This section explores the system design and capabilities needed to produce an integrated AVE system for real-time situation awareness. Figure 11 depicts the architecture of the system and the six major functional modules.

Data Acquisition and Interface Module

This module interfaces to different sensors and messages including dynamic or static imagery, 2D/3D geospatial measurements, electronic security sensors, abstract and symbolic datasets, and system control commands and messages. Dynamic data such as real-time video streams, security sensor status messages, and control messages from/to other devices modules are communicated via the TCP/IP network. Static information such as pre-loaded aerial or terrestrial images, 2D/3D geospatial models, and symbolic abstract data is loaded directly to the system from databases or servers and can be updated when necessary or accessed from external data sources via the network. Control and data are exchanged in XML format over TCP/IP, allowing for a general bi-directional communication mechanism. For

Figure 11. Integrated AVE system architecture

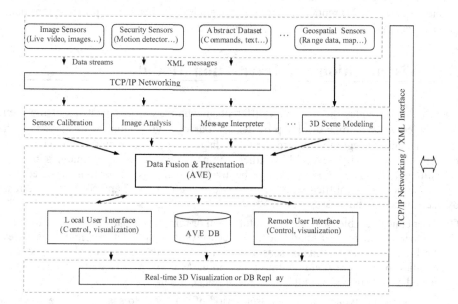

example, a sensor system can issue commands that direct the AVE system to focus on a region of interest or alarm zone.

Data Processing and Analysis Module

This module incorporates a variety of tools to model, process, and analyze real-time or recorded data to facilitate data fusion, scene understanding, and visualization. For example, an integrated camera calibration system employs the scene model, detected or selected features, and an error minimization system to facilitate accurate and robust camera calibration. The geometry modeling module incorporates a semi-automatic modeling system to rapidly create new 3D scene models or dynamic refinements and updates from new sensor data. The dynamic event analysis and modeling system incorporates automatic analysis of imagery and other sensor data for detecting, tracking, and modeling of dynamic objects (people or vehicles). The analysis produces locations and tracked paths of the moving objects in the 3D scene. Shape models are created for use as dynamic models that can be animated in the 3D scene to minimize viewpoint distortions. Furthermore, the data processing module also interprets the messages or commands received over the TCP/IP network from external sensor devices and systems. While an AVE visualization system can operate in a stand-alone configuration, it is more likely to operate as part of an existing security and command systems. In addition, the command interpreter provides the capability for remote control and data sharing with multiple distributed users and display systems.

Data Fusion Module

This is the core graphics module that combines all manner of models, images, videos, and data in the real-time 3D rendering. This component is described by the prior sections detailing the video-texture projection and rendering methods.

Data Visualization and Interaction Module

This module provides the user with different viewpoints and perspectives of the scene. A small iconic scene map display provides a "gods-eye" view along with a rectangle that shows the current region visible in the main display. The main display window presents the arbitrary scene view selected by either a human operator or an automated subsystem. A traditional 2D image window can also be invoked to display one or more selected video streams as conventional tiled images. These views are integrated and controlled manually by users or command messages.

Operator control enables a system operator (local or remote) to manually control the viewpoint. Operators also can set and selects preset views for display at any time. Preset views can be linked to video events or sensor alarms so that when events or alarms occur, the system flies to the corresponding preset viewpoint. Multiple events/alarms are placed in a queue and a list is provided to the operator to select among them.

System control is invoked after a pre-set period of inactivity to scan or fly the viewpoint over a preset path. An event or alarm automatically reverts control to the preset view of the event or alarm, following a smooth transition between the current and preset views to maintain an overall sense of scene comprehension.

A temporal display mode enables users to assess and analyze any prior events observed in the scene. The system records all signals to a time stamped database, including all images, tracked paths, and dynamic events or alarms. An operator can manipulate time with a slider interface. Once a prior time is selected, a freeze-frame, normal, or accelerated playback commences and the user is free to modify the view to explore the scene of interest. In many cases, this capability is important to understand what transpired prior to an alarm or to cause an alarm.

In summary, the AVE based system offers many powerful integrated capabilities. This approach to visualizing events and activities over a wide-area provides a new level of real-time situational awareness and scene comprehension (You & Neumann, 2005, pp. 713-724). AVE is the enabling technology for a new generation of monitoring and surveillance systems that employ large numbers of cameras and sensors to convey the activities at complex sites such as military bases, government facilities, airports, rail stations, borders, coastlines, harbors, power plants, and commercial infrastructure.

Acknowledgments

The authors recognize Ismail Oner Sebe for his assistance with the dynamic modeling section, and Kelvin Chung for his assistance with the video acquisition and processing sections. We thank Professor Ram Nevatia and Sung Chun Lee of the IRIS Lab at USC for the site models employed to produce the images of figures 1 and 6. We also recognize all the members of the USC Computer Graphics and Immersive Technology (CGIT) Lab for their contributions.

References

Åkesson, K. P. (1998). *Reality portals.* MS thesis.

Åkesson, K. P., & Simsarian, K. (1999). Reality portals. In *Proceedings of the ACM Symposium on Virtual Reality Software and Technology* (pp. 11-18).

Allen, P. K., Troccoli, A., Smith, B., Murray, S., Stamos, I., & Leordeanu, M. (2003). New methods for digital modeling of historic sites. *IEEE Computer Graphics and Applications, 23*(6), 32-41.

Azuma, R., Baillot, Y., Behringer, R., Feiner, S., Julier, S., & MacIntyre, B. (2001). Recent advances in augmented reality. *IEEE Computer Graphics and Applications, 21*(6), 34-47.

Bajura, M., Fuchs, H., & Ohbuchi, R. (1992). Merging virtual objects with the real world: Seeing ultrasound imagery with the patient. In *Proceedings of the ACM SIGGRAPH Computer Graphics* (pp. 203-210).

Bell, B., Feiner, S., & Höllerer, T. (2001). View management for virtual and augmented reality. In *Proceedings of the ACM Symposium on User Interface Software and Technology (UIST)* (pp. 101-110).

Brown, D. C. (1971). Close-range camera calibration. *Photogrammetric Engineering, 37*(8), 855-866.

CMU. (1999). *Appearance-based virtual view generation of temporally-varying events from multi-camera images in the 3D room* (Computer Science Tech. Rep. No. CMU-CS-99-127).

Cohen-Or, D., Chrysanthou, Y., Silva, C., & Durand, F. (2003). A survey of visibility for walkthrough applications. *IEEE Transactions on Visualization and Computer Graphics, 9*(3), 412-431.

Debevec, P. E., Taylor, C. J., & Malik, J. (1996). Modeling and rendering architecture from photographs: A hybrid geometry and image-based approach. In *Proceedings of the 23rd Annual Conference on Computer Graphics and Interactive Techniques (ACM Siggraph)* (pp. 11-20).

Dorbie, A. (1997). *Silicon Graphics Witches Brew UAV.*

Dorsey, J. O. B., Sillion, F. X., & Greenberg, D. P. (1991). Design and simulation of opera lightening and projection effects. *ACM SIGGRAPH Computer Graphics, Proceedings of the 18th Annual Conference on Computer Graphics and Interactive techniques, 25*(4), 41-50.

Faig, W. (1975). Calibration of close-range photogrammetry systems: Mathematical formulation. *Photogrammetric Engineering and Remote Sensing, 41*(12), 1479-1486.

Faugeras, O., Luong, T., & Maybank, S. (1992). Camera self-calibration: Theory and experiments. In *Proceedings of the European Conference on Computer Vision* (pp. 321-334).

Faugeras, O., & Toscani, G. (1986). The calibration problem for stereo. In *Proceedings of the IEEE Computer Vision and Pattern Recognition* (pp. 15-20).

Fischler, M. A., & Bolles, R. C. (1981). Random sample consensus: A paradigm for model fitting with applications to image analysis and automated cartography. *Communications of the ACM, 24*(6), 381-395.

Gibson, S., Hubbold, R. J., Cook, J., & Howard, T. L. J. (2003). Interactive reconstruction of virtual environments from video sequences. *Computers & Graphics, 27*(2), 293-301.

Haala, N., & Brenner, C. (1997). Generation of 3D city models from airborne laser scanning data. In *Proceedings of the EARSEL Workshop on LIDAR Remote Sensing of Land and Sea.*

Haala, N., Brenner, C., & Anders, K. H. (1998). 3D urban GIS from laser altimeter and 2D map data. In T. Schenk & A. Habib (Eds.), *ISPRS Commission III Symposium on Object Recognition and Scene Classification from Multispectral and Multisensor Pixels* (pp. 339-346).

Hall, E. L., Tio, J. B. K., McPherson, C. A., & Sadjadi, F. A. (1982). Measuring curved surfaces for robot vision. *Computer, 15*(12), 42-54.

Hsu, S., Samarasekera, S., Kumar, R., & Sawhney, H. S. (2000). Pose estimation, model refinement, and enhanced visualization using video. *Computer Vision and Pattern Recognition, 1*, 488-495. Retrieved from http://www.sgi.com/products/software/performer/brew/pdfs/uav.pdf

Hu, J., You, S., & Neumann, U. (2003). Approaches to large-scale urban modeling. *IEEE Computer Graphics and Applications, 23*(6), 62-69.

Intel. (2003). *Performance benchmarks for intel integrated performance primitives.* Retrieved from http://www.intel.com/software/projects/ipp/techtopics/wp_ipp_benchmark.pdf

Ito, M. (1991). Robot vision modeling: Camera modeling and camera calibration. *Advanced Robotics*, 321-335.

Jiang, B., You, S., & Neumann, U. (2004). A robust tracking system for outdoor augmented reality. *IEEE Virtual Reality* (pp. 3-10).

Kanade, T., Tanaka, M., Oda, K., Yoshida, A., & Kano, H. (1996). A video-rate stereo machine and its new applications. In *Proceedings of the 27th International Symposium on Industrial Robots* (pp. 671-676).

Leung, B. (2004). *Component-based car detection in street scene images.* Master's thesis, Massachusetts Institute of Technology.

Neumann, U., You, S., Hu, J., Jiang, B., & Sebe, I. O. (2004). Visualizing reality in an augmented virtual environment. *Presence: Teleoperators and Virtual Environments Journal, 13*(2), 222-233.

Pollefeys, M., Koch, R., Vergauwen, M., & Gool, L. V. (1999). Hand-held acquisition of 3D models with a video camera. In *Proceedings of the 2nd International Conference on 3-D Digital Imaging and Modeling (3DIM'99)* (pp. 14-23).

Roden, T., & Parberry, I. (2005). Portholes and planes: Faster dynamic evaluation of potentially visible sets. *ACM Journal of Computers in Entertainment, 3*(2), 3.

Sebe, I. O., You, S., & Neumann, U. (2004). Dynamic objects modeling and 3D visualization. In *Proceedings of the American Society for Photogrammetry and Remote Sensing (ASPRS) Annual Conference.*

Sebe, I. O., You, S., & Neumann, U. (2005). Globally optimum multiple object tracking. In *Proceedings of the SPIE Defense and Security Symposium, Acquisition, Tracking, and Pointing XIX Conference* (Vol. 5810, pp. 82-93).

Sebe, I. O., You, S., & Neumann, U. (2005). Rapid part-based 3D modeling. In *Proceedings of the ACM Virtual Reality Software and Technology (VRST)* (pp. 143-146).

Segal, M., Korobkin, C., Widenfelt, R. V., Foran, J., & Haeberli, P. (1992). Fast shadows and lighting effects using texture mapping. In *Computer Graphics (SIGGRAPH '92 Proceedings)* (pp. 249-252).

Sequeira, V., Bovisio, E., & Gonçalves J. G. M. (1999).Augmented reality in multi-camera surveillance. In *Proceedings of the 21st ESARDA Symposium on Safeguards and Nuclear Material Management* (pp. 661-666).

Simsarian, K. T., Åkesson, K. P. (1997). Windows on the world: An example of augmented virtuality. *Interfaces: Man-Machine Interaction.*

Spann, J., & Kaufman, K. (2000). Photogrammetry using 3D graphics and projective textures. In *The 19ᵗʰ ISPRS Congress*.

State, A., Hirota, G., Chen, D. T., Garrett, B., & Livingston, M. (1996). Superior augmented reality registration by integrating landmark tracking and magnetic tracking. In *Proceedings of SIGGRAPH'96* (pp. 429-438).

State, A., Livingston, M. A., Garrett, W. F., Hirota, G., Whitton, M. C., Pisano, E. D., & Fuchs, H. (1996). Technologies for augmented reality systems: Realizing ultrasound-guided needle biopsies. In *Proceedings of the 23ʳᵈ Annual Conference on Computer Graphics and Interactive techniques, (ACM Siggraph)* (pp. 439-446).

Thrun, S., Fox, D., & Burgard, W. (1998). A probabilistic approach to concurrent mapping and localization for mobile robots. *Autonomous Robots, 5*(3-4), 253-271.

Tsai, R. Y. (1986). An efficient and accurate camera calibration technique for 3D machine vision. In *Proceedings of IEEE Conference on Computer Vision and Pattern Recognition* (pp. 364-374).

Wang, C. C. (1992). Extrinsic calibration of a vision sensor mounted on a robot. *IEEE Transactions on Robotics and Automation, 8*(2), 161-175.

Weinhaus, F. M., & Devarajan, V. (1997). Texture mapping 3D models of real-world scenes. *ACM Computing Surveys (CSUR), 29*(4), 325-365.

Wilczkowiak, M., Boyer, E., & Sturm, P. (2002). 3D modeling using geometric constraints: A parallelepiped based approach. In *Proceedings of the 7ᵗʰ European Conference on Computer Vision* (Part IV, pp. 221-237).

You, S., & Neumann, U. (2005). V-Sentinel: A novel framework for situational awareness and surveillance. In *Proceedings of SPIE Volume 5778, Sensors, and Command, Control, Communications, and Intelligence (C3I) Technologies for Homeland Security and Homeland Defense IV* (pp. 713-724).

You, S., Hu, J., Neumann, U., & Fox, P. (2003). Urban site modeling from LiDAR. In G. Goos, J. Hartmanis, & J. Van Leeuwen (Eds.), *Proceedings of the 2ⁿᵈ International Workshop on Computer Graphics and Geometric Modeling* (LNCS 2669, pp. 579-588).

You, S., Neumann, U., & Azuma, R. (1999). Orientation tracking for outdoor augmented reality registration. *IEEE Computer Graphics & Applications, 19*(6), 36-42.

Chapter XVI

Making Memories
of a Lifetime

Christopher B. Stapleton, Simiosys LLC, USA

Charles E. Hughes, University of Central Florida, USA

Abstract

This chapter explores how mixed reality (MR) allows the magic of virtuality to escape the confines of the computer and enter our lives to potentially change the way we play, work, train, learn, and even shop. Case studies demonstrate how emerging functional capabilities will depend upon new artistic conventions to spark the imagination, enhance human experience, and lead to subsequent commercial success. The Media Convergence Laboratory at the University of Central Florida is creating a content framework for applying mixed reality to entertainment, education training, and rehabilitation. Utilizing classical concepts of mimesis and state-of-the-art experiential entertainment, new models are examined and evaluated that will shape the next generation MR content. The convergence of story, play, and games become the cornerstones of "Interplay Conventions" that will transform MR technical capabilities into new creative possibilities ("The Evolution of a Framework for Mixed Reality Experiences," Chapter X, is the technical companion piece).

Introduction

Virtuality can simulate worlds with great realism or as far-fetched fantasy, yet it remains a disembodied experience trapped in the box of the computer or venue and echoing the limitation of traditional passive media. The power of mixed and augmented reality expands the dynamics of virtual reality (VR) by fully engaging the physical world (Figure 1).

The more we can effectively melt the boundaries between the realities, the more we can leverage the best of both worlds. Integrating the art and science of mixed reality (MR) enables the power of VR to expand its impact on an unlimited number of human experiences. Its full potential will be realized when we integrate the full imagination into real and virtual worlds using emerging artistic conventions.

Our approach to enhancing human experience through MR focuses on the time-tested conventions of story, game, and free-play that have been shown to appeal to the broadest demographic. However, it is important to distinguish between traditional conventions that transcend media and those that do not adapt to the new functionality of Mixed Reality (Stapleton & Hughes, 2006). As diverse as our case studies are, they all come down to a common denominator—making memories for a lifetime (Hughes, Stapleton, Hughes, & Smith, 2005).

Making memories is the business of entertainment, training, and education. In the case of cognitive rehabilitation, we are tapping existing memories where new ones are hard to create. Making memories is the power of imagination that can change lives (education), save lives (training), provide alternate lives (entertainment), or resurrect lives (rehabilitation). Media employs the expanse of the human imagination to define our culture, inform our understanding, and spark our vision of the future. Imagination is where every medium takes its mimetic[1] form from Aristotle poetics to the latest amusement park simulation ride. For Mixed Reality to reach its full potential, we must think of it "not as a tool, but as a

Figure 1. Concept art for Sea Creatures' Journey. Kids use the Mixed Reality Kiosk to cooperatively operate an underwater vehicle around the Orlando Science Center's Dino Digs fossil exhibit where underwater prehistoric reptiles come alive. (©2006 Media Convergence Laboratory/UCF, used with permission)

medium," as Brenda Laurel did with virtual reality prior to the explosion of the home video games market (Laurel, 1991).

> *"Think of the computer, not as a tool, but as a medium."*
>
> ~ Brenda Laurel

Getting the Genie Out of the Bottle: Applying the Best of All Realities

The magic of media is to make technology disappear. For virtuality to escape the confines of computers, we must look beyond technology to complete the illusion for the audience. Former Disney Imagineer and video game designer, Jesse Schell, describes the role of entertainment as it applies to magic of media, "interactive entertainment creates significant overlap between perception and imagination, allowing the guests to directly manipulate and change the story world." What can we learn from other forms of interactive entertainment in MR applications to engage the imagination? Schell elaborates that "in a good interactive entertainment experience, the guest forgets that the interface exists." In this transparency, imagination is taken for granted when transforming MR from a functional tool to an expressive media form. Transforming MR will take an evolved interactive framework that leverages both new capabilities and traditional forms of interactive entertainment and the imagination. When reviewing Milgram's reality to virtuality continuum diagram (Milgram & Kishino, 1994), imagination is explicitly missing.

Our research objective is to expand the notion of Milgram's mixed reality continuum to include imagination within a mixed fantasy continuum (Stapleton & Hughes, 2003). This effort involves both the creation of a real-time technical framework of a *mixed reality software system* (Hughes et al., 2005) in conjunction with developing a creative content framework of *Interplay Conventions* to transform MR into a compelling and expressive media. To understand more of the technology behind these case studies, refer to the companion chapter, "The Evolution of a Framework for Mixed Reality Experiences." Understanding that there will always be technical limitations to any new capability, we took a fresh perspective to the content framework. Throughout media history, it has been new artistic conventions that have allowed media to overcome the technical limitation and engage the human imagination to fill in where technology leaves off. There are other interactive entertainment forms that seem to transcend new media invention and form the underlying structure from which to create a new MR content framework. How can we integrate traditional interactive entertainment to leverage the emotional engagement of story, the participatory involvement of play and the procedural mechanism of games to help make memories for a lifetime?

Making Memories for a Lifetime

Whether dealing with a traumatic experience or enjoying a Disney classic, our minds are able to capture real or fictional experiences that we may want to or can't help but recall later in life. In producing experiences for entertainment, education, or training, one needs to create a lifetime memory that people can effortlessly recall in order to share with a friend, reach a goal, or even save a life. What are the salient qualities of mixed reality that cannot be achieved with movies, video games, or virtual reality?

Mixed reality media allows us to embed virtuality into the places where we live, work, and play, and thus, influence the physical, social, and emotional aspects of our lives. To introduce this technology, we discuss an entertainment form much older than video games, television, cinema, or the printing press; this is the power and complexity of experiential entertainment handed down from Aristotle's theories of mimesis (imitation of reality and human experience) to modern day theme parks (simulated fantasy). The authors take on the challenge to build the next generation Mixed Reality experience by combining one author's 20 years of experience in designing and producing films, theater, games, and theme parks worldwide with the other's 40 years of experience in designing and building large-scale computer systems. We have partnered with key subject matter experts from each application area to gain insights that help us produce informed solutions.

This chapter will present the case studies as a continuum of development, identifying each project's contribution within its key challenges and lessons learned. They represent a broad enough spectrum to establish and validate many of the emerging "interplay conventions" that will be discussed in later sections.

Case Study: Military Training Simulation

The first and most complex case study was to transform embedded training for dismounted soldiers for the United States (U.S.) Army's Research Development Engineering Command (RDECOM). This effort starts with the hypothesis that future military ground conflicts are most likely to take place in urban terrains. To properly train dismounted infantry in Military Operation in Urban Terrain (MOUT) requires training within a simulation that comes closest to combat reality. This requires creating an extreme situation that presents a richly layered, multi-sensory experience simulating a complex environment (Figure 2).

It requires situational awareness as well as rapid response in all directions, dimensions, and realities to stay alive. Each domain of simulation (virtual, live, or constructive) is critical, but singly cannot achieve the intense physical, cognitive, and emotional intensity of combat reality. Live simulation is compelling, but expensive and laborious to mount. Virtual simulation is dynamic and easily enabled, but provides a limited perspective that is far from a realistic experience. Constructive simulation provides the perspective of the larger theater of military engagement, but traditionally only uses 2D representations with cryptic icons. RDECOM requested a cross-domain solution (mixed reality) that was able to utilize the latest technical developments of MR and the compelling nature of experiential entertainment developed for venues such as theme parks, video games, and extreme sports.

Building an MR application for combat training provided a need and an opportunity to develop tools to simulate scenarios within complex terrains. The end product needed to be more compelling than realistic, leveraging the power of entertainment, not as an end, but as a means. In rendering multiple realities, form, haptics, light, sound, and story are integrated into one MR software system, made up of multiple rendering engines. These

Figure 2. Mixed Reality for Military Operations in Urban Terrain (MR MOUT) concept art merging real and computer generated forces and assets within a physical courtyard (death-trap) surrounded by urban combat terrain with MR views from real and virtual soldiers, observer cameras & combat vehicles. (©2006 Media Convergence Laboratory/UCF, used with permission)

include a graphics engine managing visual objects and geometry; an audio engine providing a hybrid of 3D, surround, point source, and hypersonic audio; and a special effects engine controlling real world elements, similar to the use of show control to actuate devices in a theme park environment. A story engine integrates information from a sensor server; one or more physics engines; zero or more plug-ins (e.g., user interfaces and AI components); and an interactive, non-linear scenario script in order to maintain the state of the scenario and mediate the activities of the three rendering engines. The challenge in producing this system was to develop the technical framework that melts the boundaries between the realities and then develop a content framework for producing compelling experiences that are both interactive and non-linear.

Pioneering use of augmented reality for military operations was achieved by registering location specific data within the physical environment to communicate critical intelligence to the soldier in a hostile environment. At the Naval Research Laboratories, the wearable system called the Battlefield Augmented Reality System (BARS) was tested for operational use within an actual battle (Julier, Baillot, Lanzagorta, Brown, & Rosenblum, 2000). However, in applying similar technology to training, there were additional needs to include the entire spectrum of realities to simulate the intensity and complexity of combat reality. It is the simulation of the battle itself in addition to the communication and coordination with command and fellow soldiers (real or robotic) within a complex and dangerous terrain that requires an extreme form of mixed reality (Malo et al., 2004). Where the video see-through MR HMD would not be suitable for the quick action of real battle due to its resolution, field of view, and frame rate, in a controlled training situation video offered the opportunity to be more convincing by filling in the gaps between the perception of real and virtual reality to provide a seamless mixing of realities.

MR MOUT Facility

In select locations across the country, entire towns are constructed as Military Operations in Urban Terrain (MOUT) sites for the armed forces to practice maneuvers within live simulations. Being heavily instrumented, they are run similar to movie studio backlots with the throughput of soldier training that is similar to theme parks. In a science and technology objective (STO), RDECOM challenged us with enhancing the richness of the live MOUT training experience. In a three-year grant, we integrated art, science, and engineering to experiment with the notion of a cross-domain simulation. Additional work was completed in cooperation with the Naval Research Laboratories at the Virtual Reality Labs (creators of the BARSystem).

In lieu of going out of state and experimenting within a real MOUT site, we created a mini-MOUT within the Science and Technology Training Center (STTC) at the Central Florida Research Park. It was called Mixed Reality for Military Operations in Urban Terrain (MR MOUT). Scenic sets were used temporarily during development (Figure 3). The long-term goal is to be able to develop methods and tools that could be easily deployed to make any site around the world into a cross-domain MOUT site.

Training Experience

The creation of a close-quartered combat training environment involves the design of death traps. Wearing a Canon Video See-Thru, Canon COASTAR™ HMD tracked by an Intersense 900 system, soldiers enter into a courtyard exposed to snipers and aircraft above, and sur-

Figure 3. U.S. Army MR MOUT facility at RDECOM, displaying multiple real, virtual, or augmented views from the operator's panel (left). Trainee observing 3D replay of the scenario with trainer (upper right). Embedded MR security camera capturing alternative views for observation (lower right). (©2006 Media Convergence Laboratory/UCF, used with permission)

rounded by virtual threats hiding in doors and behind crates. Within reach in all directions physical walls, crates, and windows hide potential threats that must be confronted. Each real entity has a corresponding occlusion model that integrates it smoothly with virtual entities, partially occluding them, and being partially occluded by them. Beyond the windows, doors, and over the façades are layers of virtual urban obstructions that strategically block where you can perceive and engage a target or where threats can spot you. The programmed unpredictable behaviors of virtual hostile forces or panicked civilians can come from anywhere in a four block diameter; from the building tops; within roaming vehicles (manned and unmanned); and hidden behind crates and doors. The soldiers must be aware of every potential threat and evaluate their optimal positions and movements with speed, accuracy, and lethality. Hiding behind a crate may be the only way at first to be truly safe.

The use of hybrid chroma-keying provides additional registration accuracy for the layering of real and virtual assets. A two-tiered surround sound system provides 3D ambient and point source simulation without the need to cover the ears with headsets, thereby allowing for interaction with live audio including firearms and communications with peers via radio or in person. The multi-tiered audio allows for the registration of sound in multi-storied buildings critical to a soldier's acoustical situational awareness (Hughes, Thropp, Holmquist, & Moshell, 2004). The reliance on just visual cues can be fatal due to the fact that you cannot see behind your head, around or through walls, but you can hear. When response times can be measured in split seconds, the training of a soldier's acoustical faculties are as important as the visual. Traditional entertainment audio assets and sound systems do not account for the range, subtleties, or depths of realistic acoustical landscapes (Hughes et al., 2005).

Unlike your typical first-person shooter video game where your view, aim, and direction of movement are the same, within MR MOUT you have a dynamic range of movement similar to live training. You have three axes of complex action (viewing, aiming, and moving), which are operating in three different axes simultaneously. Virtual content is no longer confined behind embedded projection screens, nor are you separated, as in a VR HMD, from the physical passive haptics and the tangible interaction with your weapon. Other live soldiers, trainers, or opposing forces can join your space. Integrated with vehicular and constructive simulation, other players working from other simulators can engage your position. Virtual entities can engage and affect real entities and vice versa. The entire training session can be captured, replayed, and evaluated by behind-the-scenes trainers who can leverage multiple views (e.g., taking an observer view or positioning themselves as a virtual terrorist opposing your character) just as one would in a multi-player video game.

Lessons Learned

The MR MOUT project was an ambitious creative leap to what we feel MR should and could be. That is why it is still under development. Yet its evolution constantly feeds our other studies. For MR to work effectively, everything live and inanimate must be tracked and rendered as either a visible or occluding object. This real-time manipulation of data can be captured replayed, and used to analyze and measure performance. This capability has led to our formulating a concept we call human experience modeling that combines the capture, simulation and analysis aspects of a full experience to perform after action review (ARR) and to create novel visualizations of aggregate data that can impact training as either a 3D immersive replay or a visualization of interactions not revealed in the heat of battle. This concept is further explored with the experience called MR Kitchen that uses MR to enhance cognitive rehabilitation.

As we transfer the lessons learned to other applications, the emphasis transfers from technical accuracy and refinement to the ability to tell a good story or play a good game. The power of interactive entertainment cannot be underestimated. However, in serious applications with life and death consequences, it needs to be used as a means and not as an end. Evolving artistic conventions are used more for impact than they are for expression. The value of MR MOUT comes in being able to measure the impact in human performance.

Mixed Fantasy Continuum: Interplay Conventions

Once the technology is incorporated within an integrated system, the creative Interplay Conventions begin to evolve to drive an immersive, interactive, and non-linear scenario both technically and creatively. Where modern conventions of cinema and video games are designed to remove you from reality, there is a need to tap traditions of live theater that have embraced the physical venue in context to the creative content. From the classical theory of mimesis[2] to contemporary video games, it is the author's alchemy of the mind, media and matter that produces the magic of simulation (Figure 4). (I) The **MIND** creates a vision (invento) that is artistically crafted (poiesis) (II) in the form of a **MEDIA** (mimenta) designed to skillfully render (techne) (III) for the reception of the audience as **MATTER** (mimema) and their imagination. (IV) With interactive entertainment, even the level of engagement or causality becomes a spectrum of creativity.

Unlike recorded media, we must also design the causality that builds the audience's invest-ment within the story world (Mott, 2005). In passive media, the performance is from another time and place and the audience merely *absorbs*. In an engaging live theater, the audience presence is *proximate* to the performance and influences the delivery. Theme park rides are active where the audience *participates* even if they are linear. Video games are reactive where one *chooses*, but everything has already been created. Role playing games, on the other hand, are truly interactive where the audience *contributes* to the story. Ultimately, you have experiential where the audience *lives* the experience. Prior to the convergence of real-time simulation, technology limited an artist to one level of causality or another. Now it becomes an entire creative spectrum from which to work with and discover its impact to apply to the procedural interactive story engine.

In driving the MR story engine, it is necessary to be able to create a combat mimema (sin-gular form of mimesis) that could also build a climatic story arc. This required the creative conventions and heuristics of video games combined with techniques of interactive theater and military rules of engagement to achieve the emotional intensity to train and evaluate a soldier's competencies while under pressure. Where story is usually considered passive and linear, we need to author the program with dramatic structure within the dynamic mechanics of a scenario script.

Figure 4. The Mimesis of Mixed Reality shows the relationship between classical theories of Mimesis with Mixed Reality Continuums and the levels of causality used as a foundation for next generation InterPlay Conventions. (©2006 Media Convergence Laboratory/UCF, used with permission)

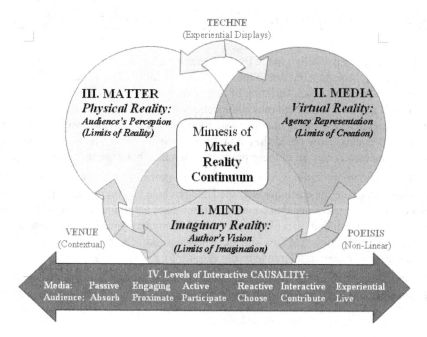

Case Study: Entertainment

Entertainment has defined most of the emerging forms of media technology throughout history by providing an appealing introduction of novel possibilities for an unsuspecting audience. When a new capability like MR emerges, entertainment can be the ultimate qualifying factor in its ability to be applied to other mainstream applications. It is also compelling entertainment content that sparks market demand for the technology and drives the adoption across diverse applications. Unfortunately, entertainment is a reluctant adopter of new technology. This has forced major consumer electronics manufacturers to become entertainment firms to help drive the adoption of new technological products (Sony, Microsoft, Apple, etc.). The easier way to introduce new technology is not to create an entirely new model, but to reinvent an existing model. In this way, you disguise a potentially disruptive technology as an acceptable innovation. Our quest to transform MR into a successful entertainment concept was a "solution looking for a problem." We needed to look for just the right problem to exemplify the unique qualities of MR to mainstream audiences.

With the convenience and economy of online shopping, traditional "bricks and mortar" businesses need to rethink the experience of shopping for their customers to stay competitive. They need to draw customers not only by their selection of goods, but with the entertainment experience of shopping itself, creating what has been coined "retailtainment."

"The more time someone spends in a mall, the more stores they will visit and the more they will buy" (Underhill, 2004). Adapting the advances developed with MR MOUT allows us to bring the extreme experience of a destination theme park to a local mall.

Invention to Innovation: Solution Looking for a Problem

Our partners, experts in retailtainment, Brand Experience Laboratory (http://www.brandexperiencelab.org/), brought a challenge for us to solve with MR. Their client, MGM needed to market their brand and each variation of their franchises in different retail outlets. They needed to sell feature films in the movie theaters, games in the game stores, videos in the video store, merchandise in the merchandising stores, and theme park vacation packages through travel agents. How could they find one vehicle to do all this at the place where customers can actually buy all of these products when they have the propensity to spend?

Naturally, the shopping malls are where theaters and stores exist that sell all forms of entertainment, and where the customer is primed and ready to buy on impulse. The challenge was to construct an experience that could sell all forms of entertainment for all franchises. They requested content that feels like you are in a film; engages you like your favorite video game; and immerses your whole family in the experience like a theme park. This transformed into TimePortal an experiential movie trailer (Figure 5).

As an entertainment company, MGM can spend as much on marketing a film as they do on the production itself. The high-risk, big profit potential is too crucial not to emphasize

Figure 5. Concept art for MR TimePortal, an experiential movie trailer to market MGM entertainment franchises in malls as retailtainment. Multiple levels of interactivity hook diverse participants and increase attendance capacity and through-put. (©2006 Media Convergence Laboratory/UCF, used with permission)

marketing. Most marketing is based on the media where it is distributed. Like new movies, it was in the form of a "movie trailer," a quick synopsis of the story premise presented in the theater to set up expectations to see the film. Yet the emphasis of movie trailers now needs to go beyond just selling films. Even though films only represent a niche market of $10 billion dollars, they drive the entire $100 billion dollar entertainment market. What sells a film needs to also sell videos, music, television, games, merchandise, and amusement attractions. For the movie studio, the investment made in marketing needs to sell the whole franchise, not just the movie. As entertainment companies, studios also need to sell all of their franchises in the form of brand experience marketing.

The Challenge: Retailtainment Experience

To market an entire entertainment franchise within an experiential venue, like a shopping mall, meant that the solution needed to appeal to the entire family (cross-demographic), competing within a highly competitive marketing environment that must demand the attention of the shopper in order to sell the product. With marketing, the first advantage of MR is that novelty sells. However, as just a head mounted experience, it could not draw a majority of the crowds. With only the MR HMDs, the experience would shut out the bystanders capturing only a fraction of the audience. In addition, the operation of placing HMDs on and off guests was too time-consuming and labor intensive to be considered. A new form of display and interaction was needed to address different levels of interaction with a larger amount of peripheral players and spectators.

Levels of Interactivity: Divers, Swimmers, and Waders

The important aspect of experiential entertainment is that not everyone wants the same experience. However, they don't want to feel cheated by making the wrong choice and not getting the best experience that is suited for them. To accommodate a wide variety of needs with the same content, different levels of interactivity and immersion need to be provided. In designing theme parks worldwide, one realizes that there are distinct types of attendees who like different levels of experiences. These levels are known in the industry as swimmers, divers, and waders. The key is to provide each level with the appropriate entertainment value for their investment of time, money, and risk. Divers making up about a fifth of any audience; they will jump right into the center of attention and gear up in the MR HMD. Swimmers would rather participate via the portal view; they are not willing to mess up their hair for the HMD or look silly. Waders just like watch others having a good time. In this case, we needed to make the whole environment come alive with action and special effects.

The content needs to be designed with all three levels of interactivity as options, uncharacteristic of Hollywood style entertainment, where one size fits all. Each level of interactivity operates at different capacity and throughput. Where one diver's experience is typically two minutes, there could be two swimmers interacting during the same time with a peripheral audience of waders equaling two to eight spectators in the same time period.

Lessons Learned

At the 2003 international SIGGRAPH conference's commercial exhibition, the model was tested. It was intended to draw a significant crowd and sustain the anticipated capacity and throughput with interchangeable content (Figure 6).

When the content was not in operation (e.g., during changeover) the crowd immediately dispersed. For an industry where capacity is king, MR is able to expand capacity and throughput as well as provide Web cast of the experience or competition. However, until the MR HMDs are in higher supply and more ruggedly built at a lower cost, the fully designed experience is impractical.

The next challenge was to see if this model could go beyond merely amusing and transfer to more challenging markets and work beyond the novelty and provide a significant functional innovation (Moore, 1991). This made us examine a more economical form of the experience without the use of the HMD. This led us to an even more challenging application for informal education or Edutainment.

Mixing Realty Conventions: Interface to Interplay

It is easy to say you will make an entertainment experience "feel like a film, play like a game, and immerse families like a theme park," but the realities are that the structure of stories,

Figure 6. At the 2003 SIGGRAPH conference, TimePortal showcasing multiple MR displays including Canon's MR HMD and MR Kiosk created with Elumens Vision Domes and Canon fisheye cameras, with magnetic tracking by polhemus FastTrack. (©2006 Media Convergence Laboratory/UCF, used with permission)

games, and free-play are very different forms of entertainment even though they are made up of the same components of emotions and fantasy.

When designing MR experiences, we not only needed to bring story, game, and play together, but needed to leverage each to provide an overall heightened experience (Figure 7). (a) The emotional power (*Pathos*) of the story provides the invitation to draw the audience into the experience and apply their imagination. (b) The irresistible simplicity of play invites physically interaction (*Participatory*). (c) The mixed reality engine gives us the power of game mechanics (*Procedural*) to invite the virtual world of media to integrate with both our physical and imaginary worlds leading to social interactivity. Instead of being distracted by an explicit graphical user "interface" to structure usability, the concept of "interplay" integrates complex environments, relationships, and behavior using story, games, and free-play. Janet Murray (1997) similarly frames the future of interactive narrative in what she calls the *multiform story,* which is composed of the audience's *participation* with the computer's *procedure*, for mediation of the *encyclopedic* ingredients of the story world including its *environmental* navigation of immersion.

Story World: Stories Engaging the Mind with Pathos

The user is motivated in proportion to the ability of the author to make the audience empathetic with the characters (McKee, 1997), so much so that the audience is immersed within

Figure 7. InterPlay Conventions of story, play, and game relating the Mixed Reality Continuum to the pathos, participatory, and procedural aspects computer generated scenarios. (©2006 Media Convergence Laboratory/UCF, used with permission)

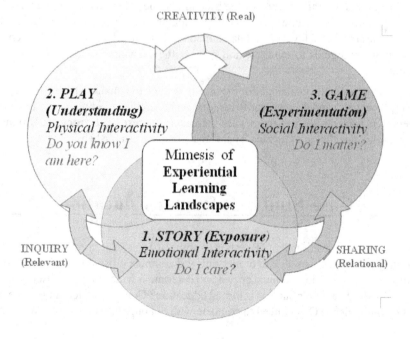

the presence of that character and will be compelled to go wherever or do whatever the author of story directs them to do. The empathy is achieved through emotion. The emotion or *pathos* of the audience is engaged by the story flow that motivates their interplay between intriguing *characters* in context with dynamic *worlds,* and driven by escalating risks in *events* that then help transform the character and achieve an emotional catharsis, or the intent of the author.

Playground: Toys Engaging Matter with Participation

Interactivity is inherently physical. When it asks us to participate, we must act by walking into, triggering effects, or reacting to stimuli. Play interfaces mediate the real world to incorporate *participation* with the virtual and imaginary worlds. Play intuitively engages the entire body and its full range of sensory perception and visceral kinesthetic interaction, just as a playground or a toy does. Where passive media disengages the body in order to work, future interactive media must engage the audience by inviting participation within play (Wirth, 1994).

The structure of free-play involves the *cause* & *effect* that leads to *consequences*. It defines the immediate interaction and exchange that the users employ to understand and participate meaningfully with their surroundings. There are no rules in play, nor are there winners or losers. It drives the curiosity of the users and draws them deeper into the flow of game and story play.

Playing Field: Games Engaging the Media with Procedure

Where play drives the participation of the user and defines the user's interface (UI), something must drive the procedure of the overall computer. The art of game mechanics is used in video games at a basic level of simulated mediation. Game developers use the construct of rules, tools, and goals to motivate and process the exchange between real and virtual behaviors.

Goals are set to prompt a challenge for the user to engage the media. The construct of *rules* is for the player to act and the machine to respond accordingly, providing increasing intensity with persistent and non-linear outcomes and increasing interest. *Tools* are created to empower the user's influence that is motivated by the goals that are established.

Case Study: Informal Education

The strength of an innovation like MR rests in its ability to transfer across diverse applications. For military training, it was able to render rich and complex cross-domain immersion. For entertainment, it was able to draw a crowd and entertain a wide variety of users. But, how will MR transfer to a venue such as informal education? Community learning centers such as the Orlando Science Center need to compete with not only the sophistication of national museums such as the Smithsonian Institution, but with destination theme parks such as Walt Disney World and Universal Studios as well. On a fraction of the budget and a minimum ability to support complex technology, can the use of MR in informal education prove to be as if not more successful as the entertainment or military projects?

Our target application, the Orlando Science Center's Dino Digs exhibit, was not performing up to expectations. Although it is well-designed aesthetically, it became stale over time and unable to change. A cornerstone of the science center when the exhibit first opened five years ago, it showcases large and impressive prehistoric fossil displays. Yet when people come through the doors, it does not take long for them to walk right back out. "There is nothing to do," said one kid, "This is boring, let's go," said another. Although there is plenty to learn on the detailed information plaques, most people do not bother to read them. The center's CEO had few choices to solve this problem. He could leave it as is and lose money, because it would still cost him to staff it, maintain it, heat, cool, and clean it. He could gut the exhibit and start over, but risked the chance of getting complaints about losing a landmark. In addition, the cost to redesign and build a new exhibit took more capital than was available. He could fill the empty space with a rented exhibit, but that venture usually costs as much as it earns. With either choice there is a lot of work and investment without much return. He needed a third option to avoid capital expense of redesign, or rebuilding, but that also increased the educational and entertainment value that would bring more people in, have them stay longer and come back on a regular basis. What could MR do to augment the experience to enhance the educational and entertainment value and draw more attendance? Could the experience draw more people more often with minimal cost and infrastructure, and change the whole economic model for museum redesign? If applied on a larger scale, could it be a model for the whole industry?

MR Sea Creature Learning Experience

As you enter the exhibit called Dino Digs, you are surrounded by prehistoric fossils in an attack position ready to devour you. Prior to incorporating mixed reality, there was little else to do besides read the information panels and play in some sand. The challenge was to spark viewers' interest in order to motivate them to learn more and perhaps even read the plaques to inspire learning back home or in the classroom.

In the expanded exhibit, parents or kids could peer through the MR portal (Figure 8) seeing a live video feed of the museum beyond, augmented with virtual content including a digital docent. These characters, some from live capture and others from computer generated animation, explained or demonstrated the significance of items in the exhibit. After the introduction, the venue was virtually flooded with water as seen through the portal. Prehistoric marine reptile fossils grew muscle and skin and came alive to swim around the exhibit. Users had multiple views from which to interact with the environment. Through the portal, one had a stationary augmented reality view with water and dinosaurs overlaying the exhibit and other guests. Occlusion models allowed for virtual content to flow around exhibit features, moving and disappearing behind and in-between structures. On the user's control panel, a trackball operated a virtual, unmanned underwater vehicle to explore the exhibit space for artifacts. A monitor in the podium displayed a virtual telepresence viewpoint of the underwater vehicle in order to guide the user through the exhibit to find artifacts. This

Figure 8. Users using mixed reality kiosk with content example for Sea Creature's Journey field testing at the Orlando Science Center's Dino Digs exhibit. (©2006 Media Convergence Laboratory/UCF, used with permission)

would occasionally toggle to the laboratory where the paleontologist guided participants from his laboratory. The monitor also contained a heads-up display with readings of health, cargo, research references, and other data. A simulated radar signal identified the spots where interesting artifacts could be found. This encouraged further investigation of the real exhibit to score better on the virtual expedition.

The experience guided participants through the physical exhibits to make the activity that much more realistic. The display provided for activities for participants to work together, enhancing the relational aspects of the experience. The experience revealed that Florida was underwater during the Cretaceous Period when prehistoric reptiles swam the earth. The flooding was not only a dramatic movement for the participants; it also drove home the relevance that the events took place right where viewers were standing.

Validating the Design

During a one-month field study, a third party evaluator from the Text & Technology Doctoral Program at the University of Central Florida observed the exhibit, conducting interviews of the participants concerning the educational and entertainment value of the MR experience. They observed duration of interaction, surveyed the propensity for repeat visits and patronage of similar exhibits. The results showed that younger guests extended their exhibit stay beyond ten minutes and up to 30 minutes, or often until their parents pulled them away. The game encouraged exploration of other parts of the exhibit, typically to become better at the game play (Hughes et al., 2005). The most encouraging observation was how much the imagination of the audience was able to extend beyond the virtuality to areas that had no technology. Some children during the experience chose to pretend to swim through the hall vs. walking.

Figure 9. MR Sea Creature's pilot test results show a significant increase in the entertainment and educational value with increased duration time and likelihood of repeat visit (©2006 Media Convergence/UCF, used with permission)

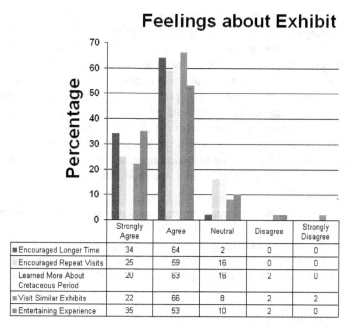

Feelings about Exhibit

	Strongly Agree	Agree	Neutral	Disagree	Strongly Disagree
▪ Encouraged Longer Time	34	64	2	0	0
Encouraged Repeat Visits	25	59	16	0	0
Learned More About Cretaceous Period	20	63	16	2	0
▪ Visit Similar Exhibits	22	66	8	2	2
▪ Entertaining Experience	35	53	10	2	0

Responses

The experience was evaluated for two weeks with more than 500 guests participating in the activity. Evaluations revealed that more than 80% of a random sample of 50 guests surveyed either agreed or strongly agreed that MR enhanced the entertainment experience, added educational value, enticed them to visit similar exhibits, and encouraged extended and repeat play (Figure 9). This means that MR not only provided a better experience for guests, but enhanced the potential economic performance of the exhibit.

Lessons Learned

Mixed reality is able to provide a critical option for museums that allows exhibits to not only keep up with the latest techniques of entertainment in video games, but also incorporate the latest scientific visualization techniques being used regularly by scientists. MR can allow the constantly changing world and advancing scientific knowledge to be directly reflected within learning institutions by having a vehicle to showcase simulated models of actual scientific phenomena drawn from current research. The video see-through technology provides a method to transfer insights from exhibit experiences into the home and classroom. MR expands the value of the unique artifacts of an institution's collections, as well as provides a continuous flow of new content to keep a museum's offerings fresh and relevant. All of this provides means for an industry struggling to survive financially to transform itself so it can compete with the growing amount of leisure activities.

Mixing realities provides a platform for the parent to become an active mentor and inspiration within the learning experience. With your parent being the most important teacher in a child's life, where does the parent learn to be a teacher? What if MR in community-learning centers can become the prime location for parents to learn and play the role of teacher with the help of dynamic augmentation of physical experience? The use of the MR portal allows one-to-one interplay, challenges, and explanations between parent and child. In the traditional exhibit, a parent cannot read information plaques fast enough to either entertain their children or keep up with questions. With the display of passive video, there is no opportunity for the parent to participate within the learning experience. In contrast, with a multi-participant interactive game, the MR learning landscape can be explored together with enough engagement to keep the attention of the child, while allowing enough time for the parent to become the guide.

These results speak to the economic impact. By enhancing the exhibit with augmented reality, museums can keep a valued collection and periodically supply new experiences without any capital improvements. Enhanced games and content can provide added value as a rental facility. The video based technology also allows for unique photo opportunities for guests to purchase at events or email to friends as a promotion.

Interplay Conventions:
Linking Story, Play, and Game into Learning Experiences

The traditional graphical user interface with either virtual content or physical plaques in museums tends to disrupt the playful and active flow of discovery. The distinct and sometimes disruptive inquiry based interaction with multiple-choice answers and fixed branching limits the imaginative play and personal exploration of an experiential venue. With all the types of interaction (physical, social, cognitive) happening at once, the notion of "conversationality" is needed in the next generation of interface interaction. It will need to be more subtle and implemented with more casual interruptions, responsive questions, implicit utterances and peripheral gestures to indicate understanding and propel deeper engagement (Laurel, 1993). The convention of interactive entertainment provides a very intuitive process for this exchange. However, the introduction of entertainment can be controversial when applied to education.

Working with the Communicative Disorders Laboratory at UCF's College of Health and Public Affairs, we started to construct a content framework that sequentially incorporated entertainment structures of story, play, and game as a complete learning engagement. In Figure 10, we have the same underlying story, play, and game interplay diagram as it applies to this learning framework. (1) The emotional impact of story allows us to create a relevant connection to hook the user and answer the prime question, "why should I care?" If the story is successful, the guest's curiosity will be sparked and the audience will begin to inquire. (2) The inquiry validates the success of the story. (3) The set up of a playful

Figure 10. The InterPlay Convention as it is applied to informal education utilizing the use of story, game, and play to engage in physical, emotional, and social interactivity (©2006 Media Convergence Laboratory/UCF, used with permission)

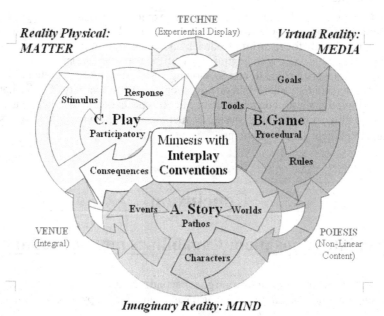

environment that invites users' participation based on their curiosity validates the success of the inquiry. Without the pressures of winning and losing, the user is provided with enough stimulus and response to understand the properties and concepts being presented in the simulation. (4) The play provides the basis for understanding, and if successful, inspires creativity in recombining the learned elements in unique and novel ways. The successful creative process validates the foundational learning from successful play. (5) The play and creativity process is validated when it leads to a higher level of critical thinking where one starts to set up experiments with the elements of games (goals, rules, and tools). (6) Game play naturally brings in the process of sharing with multi-players demonstrating confidence in mastering the subject matter and culminates an experience with social interaction. The process that is driven by the succession of story, play, and game building engagement, and the level of interactivity provides a powerful tool in helping change attitudes in education to increase motivation in learning.

Future Work: Human Experience Modeler

The emphasis on media has been mostly focused on the display and interaction of sensory stimulation. With the extent and precision of tracking and modeling of all the realities and interactions, that data can be captured to a high degree of detail. This captured data can then be replayed, reviewed, and analyzed to rapidly evaluate participant performance. Rapid analysis and replay can significantly improve rehabilitation practices and effectively transfer training into practice.

In pilot tests, we prototyped a multi-purpose human experience modeler for cognitive rehabilitation (Fidopiastis et al., 2005) to explore how mixed reality can capture, replicate, and analyze human behavior for real-time feedback and adaptation to improve human performance (Figure 11). Our work with cognitive scientists, team performance specialists, and human factors engineers has led to our developing a multi-purpose integrated system that has provided understanding and insight on how people perform a variety of tasks, hopefully leading to improved methods and performance in all aspects of life. Applications are now expanding into elite sports training, design & manufacturing, advanced decision support systems, and intelligent security systems.

Conclusion

Invention into Innovation: Capabilities into Possibilities

The transition from invention to innovation goes beyond merely bringing a product to market. It involves applying new technology so that it can change participants' lives. This is even

Figure 11. Human experience modeler capturing, simulating, and analyzing human performance with cognitive rehabilitation for retraining of daily activities for traumatic brain injury patients (©2006 Media Convergence Laboratory/UCF, used with permission)

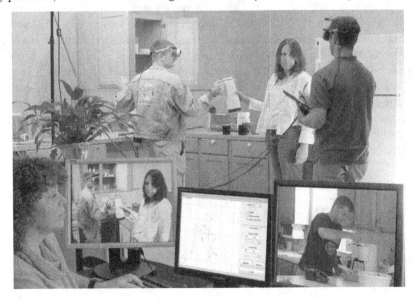

more significant than the invention itself. It transitions technical capabilities into creative possibilities by conducting in-depth development, experimentation and refinement within each application to understand how the invention can be best enhanced and exploited.

The power of mixed and augmented reality in the future will be greater than all existing media forms put together. This is mostly because MR is the convergence of all previous media forms. It involves making creative leaps incorporating ancient traditions and inventing new conventions. We have not yet found an application from which mixed and augmented reality has not been able to benefit.

Acknowledgments

The research reported here was inspired by Dr. Hideyuki Tamura who was able to melt the boundaries between reality and dreams with his pioneering research and his support of our work. Special thanks are due to the Mixed Reality Laboratory, Canon Inc., for their generous support and technical assistance. The research was also in participation with the Research in Augmented and Virtual Environments (RAVES) supported by the Naval Research Laboratory (NRL) VR LAB. The MR MOUT effort is funded by the U.S. Army's Science and Technology Objective (STO) Embedded Training for Dismounted Soldier (ETDS) at the Research, Development, and Engineering Command (RDECOM). Major contributions were made to this effort by artists Scott Malo, Shane Taber, and Theo Quarles, artist, and script writer Nathan Selikoff, audio designer/engineer Darin Hughes, experience designer Eileen Smith, and computer scientists Matthew O'Connor, Nick Beato, and Scott Vogelpohl.

References

Fidopiastis, C. M., Stapleton, C. B., Whiteside, J. D., Hughes, C. E., Fiore, S. M., Martin, G. A., et al. (2005, September 19-21). Human experience modeler: Context driven cognitive retraining and narrative threads. In *Proceedings of 4th International Workshop on Virtual Rehabilitation (IWVR2005)*, Catalina Island, CA.

Glassner, A. (2004). *Interactive storytelling: Techniques for 21st century fiction*. Natick, MA: A. K. Peters Ltd.

Hughes, C. E., Stapleton, C. B., Hughes, D. E., & Smith E. (2005). Mixed reality in education, entertainment, and training: An interdisciplinary approach. *IEEE Computer Graphics and Applications, 26*(6), 24-30.

Hughes, C. E., Stapleton, C. B., Moshell, J. M., Micikevicius, P., Garrity P., & Dumanoir, P. (2002, December 2-5). Challenges & opportunities simulating future combat systems via mixed reality. In *Proceedings of 23rd Army Science Conference (ASC 2002)*, Orlando, FL.

Hughes, D. E., Thropp, J., Holmquist J., & Moshell, J. M. (2004, November 29-December 2). Spatial perception and expectation: Factors in acoustical awareness for MOUT training. In *Proceedings of 24th Army Science Conference (ASC 2004)*, Orlando, FL.

Julier, S., Baillot, Y., Lanzagorta, M., Brown D., & Rosenblum L. (2000, October 9-11). BARS: Battlefield Augmented Reality System. In *Proceedings of the NATO Symposium on Information Processing Techniques for Military Systems*, Istanbul, Turkey.

Laurel, B. (1993). *Computers as theatre*. Boston: Addison-Wesley.

McKee, R. (1997). *Story, substance, structure, style, and the principles of screen writing*. Regan Books, Harper Collins

Milgram, P., & Kishino. A. F. (1994). Taxonomy of mixed reality visual displays. *IEICE Transaction on Information and Systems, E77-D*(12), 1321-1329.

Moore, J. A. (1991, 1999, 2002). *Crossing the chasm: Marketing and selling high-tech products to mainstream customers*. New York: Harper Business.

Mott, D. S. (2005). *Developing participant investment within digital interactive stories*. Honors in the Major Thesis. University of Central Florida.

Murray, J. H. (1997). *Hamlet on the Holodeck: The future of narrative in cyberspace*. New York: Free Press.

O'Connor M., & Hughes, C. E. (2005, January 23-27). Authoring and delivering mixed reality experiences. In *Proceedings of 2005 International Conference on Human-Computer Interface Advances in Modeling and Simulation (SIMCHI'05)* (pp. 33-39). New Orleans, LA.

Sörbom, G. (2002). The classical concept of Mimesis. In P. Smith & C. Wilde (Eds.), *A companion to art theory*.Oxford, UK: Blackwell Publishing.

Stapleton, C. B., & Hughes, C. E. (2003). Interactive imagination: Tapping the emotions through interactive story for compelling simulations. *IEEE Computer Graphics and Applications, 24*(5), 11-15.

Stapleton, C. B., & Hughes, C. E. (2005, January 23-27). Mixed reality and experiential movie trailers: Combining emotions and immersion to innovate entertainment marketing. In *Proceedings of 2005 International Conference on Human-Computer Interface Advances in Modeling and Simulation (SIMCHI'05)*, New Orleans, LA (pp. 40-48).

Stapleton, C. B., & Hughes, C. E. (2006). Believing is seeing. *IEEE Computer Graphics and Applications, 27*(1), 88-93.

Tamura, H., Yamamoto, H., & Katayama, A. (2001). Mixed reality: future dreams seen at the border between real and virtual worlds. *IEEE Computer Graphics and Applications, 21*(6), 64-70.

Underhill, P. (2004). *Call of the mall: The geography of shopping*. New York: Simon & Schuster.

Wirth, J. (1994). *Interactive acting, acting, improvisation, and interactive for audience participatory theater*. Fall Creek, OR: Fall Creek Press.

Endnotes

---

[1]   Reflective or representative of actuality or reality of human experience (derived from Aristotle's concept of mimesis or imitation).www2.cumberlandcollege.edu/acad/english/litcritweb/glossary.htm

[2]   The classical concept of mimesis (Sörbom, 2002) defines the reflective or representative reality of human experience. They distinguished the virtual world as the artistic Media (a painting of Pegasus for instance) that represents both the physical Matter in the real world (a horse and a bird) as well as the vision of the artist (the mythical character). Artistic and technical methods were used to translate this idea from one form or reality to another. The artistic convention of the Mixed Reality author needs to use them to merge realities together.

Chapter XVII

Social and Physical Interactive Paradigms for Mixed Reality Entertainment

Adrian David Cheok, National University of Singapore, Singapore

Abstract

In this chapter, we explore the applications of mixed reality technology for future social and physical entertainment systems. Throughout the case studies that will be presented here, we will show the very broad and significant impacts of mixed reality technology on variety aspects of human interactivity with regards to entertainment. On the technological aspect, the various systems we would be touching on incorporated different technologies ranging from the current mainstream ones such as GPS tracking, Bluetooth, RFID to pioneering researches of vision based tracking, augmented reality, tangible interaction techniques and 3D live mixed reality capture system. We will discuss each project in detail in terms of their motivations and requirements of the particular application domain, their system description and design decisions, as well as their future impacts on the human social and physical entertainment field.

Introduction

Recently more and more people realize that entertainment is a key driver for development of technology. There has been a lot of recent research put in the entertainment industry and it has grown dramatically as a topic of research interest. However, there is still a big gap to achieve physicality, mobility, tangible, social and physical interaction for people's entertainment. The main deficiencies of present entertainment systems is that they make people involved in the play passively and partially due to limited kinds of screen-based interactions imposed by the mouse button or key click (Hall, 1994) and also large lack of social physical interactions between humans and computer entertainment systems.

We believe that social and physical interactions are new paradigms that outline the vision of the next generation of entertainment. Researchers and developers can provide these interactions through employment of technologies such as mixed reality and ubiquitous computing. We have found that those new genres of technology provide much greater degrees of freedom than current entertainment systems, and will describe a resultant development of five novel research prototype systems.

In this chapter, we describe how 3D images and graphical interactions using the principles of mixed reality support the creation of novel ubiquitous computation computing in the developed systems of Magic Land, Human Pacman, Age Invaders. With these systems, there are three main features presented in this chapter. Firstly, the players physically and immersively role-play in the game playing, as if a fantasy computer digital world has merged with the real physical world. Secondly, users can move about freely in the real world whilst maintaining seamless networked social contact with human players in both the real and virtual world. Thirdly, it also explores novel tangible aspects of physical movement and perception, both on the player's environment and on the interaction with the digital world.

The structure of the remaining part of the chapter is as follows: In the following section, we describe some keys of entertainment and previous research works for mixed reality and wearable computer entertainment. Following, we detail new paradigms of social and physical interactive entertainment using mixed reality, ubiquitous computing etc. Finally conclusions are drawn in last section.

Background

Entertainment as an end-product is amusing; as a tool it is powerful. The power of entertainment stretches far beyond venues for amusement (Stapleton, Hughes, & Moshell, 2003). As mentioned before, entertainment is a key driver for development of technology. It is able to excite, motivate, satiate, communicate, and inspire. With powerful functionality of entertainment, it is being applied to all aspects of life from learning, training, designing, communicating and collaborating everywhere. Nowadays, present entertainment focuses the user's attention mainly on computer screens or 2D/3D virtual environments, rather than interactions between humans. Physical and social interaction is constrained, and natural interactions such as gestures, body language and movement, gaze, and physical awareness are lost (Mandryk & Inkpen, 2001).

Today's mainstream entertainment revolves around interactivity. Gone are the days when people were satisfied with passive forms of entertainment as provided by television and cinema. People today enjoy entertainment they can control, and experience in which they are full involved. In fact, not only do they want such entertainment, people want to enjoy it together with family and friends. As shown in a certain survey (Association, 2002), one of the top reasons why game players like to play games is that game playing is a social activity people can enjoy with family and friends. With advancement in networking technology, social gaming has gained popularity since the introduction of networked games (Association, 2002). Networked games overcame the barrier of distance, enabling real people to play against each other over large areas. After all, there is no opponent like a live opponent since no computer model will rival the richness of human interaction (Crawford, 1998). According to a recent study by Nezlek (Nezlek, Richardson, Green, & Schatten-Jones, 2002), enjoyable and responsive interactions increase life satisfaction scores among people. However, there is a big deficiency for network game because people can not have physical interactions between each others. Natural interactions such as behavioral engagement and cognitive states are lost during entertaining. Thus with the power of Mixed Reality providing us with the ability to combine the fantastical worlds of the imagination through virtual reality and seamlessly merge them with the compelling aspects of reality can bring players in physical proximity for interaction and help players regain lost natural interactions because humans enjoy being physically together, and socially interacting with each other (Bowlby, 1983).

Using mixed reality technology in entertainment is an exemple of ubiquitous human media (Dourish, 2001). Thus, we believe that ubiquitous human media is a next generation computing paradigm that involves the elements of ubiquitous computing, tangible interfaces and interaction and social computing for mixed reality entertainment. In this way, it moves the computer interface away from the traditional keyboard and mouse and into the environment, supporting the more social and physical interactive behavior. Furthermore, ubiquitous human media foresees that the future of human-computer interaction will lie in an interface to computing that appears throughout our physical space and time. Thus, humans as physical beings now actually become situated inside the computational world.

The three important research paradigms on which ubiquitous human media is founded, are Weiser's ubiquitous computing (Weiser, 1991), Ishii's tangible bits or "things that thinks" (Ishii & Ullmer 1997), and Suchman's sociological reasoning to problems of interaction (Suchman, 1987). Related research in social and physical mixed reality entertainment can be studied in an overview paper, and due to space constrains, they are not repeated in this chapter (Magerkurth, Engelke, & Memisoglu, 2004). With ubiquitous human media, we present several prototype systems in this chapter to show how people are fully involved in social and physical interactions for entertainment. In the following sections, we will describe these systems in detail.

Magic Land

System Concept and Game Play

Magic Land (Farbiz et al., 2005; Nguyen et al., 2005; Prince et al., 2002) is a mixed reality environment where 3D Live (Prince et al., 2002) captured avatars of humans and 3D computer generated virtual animations play and interact with each other. It demonstrates novel ways for users in real space to interact with virtual objects and virtual collaborators. Using the tangible interaction and the 3D Live human capture system, our system allows users to manipulate the captured 3D humans in a novel manner, such as picking them up and placing them on a desktop, and being able to "drop" a person into a virtual world using users' own hands. This offers a new form of human interaction where one's hands can be used to interact with other players captured in 3D Live models.

After the user is captured inside the system, he or she can go to the interactive room to play with his or her own figure. The interactive room consists of three main components: a menu table, a main interactive table, and five playing cups. On top of these tables and cups are different marker patterns. A four cameras system (ceiling tracking system) is put high above the main interactive table to track the relative position of its markers with the markers of the cups currently put on it. The users view the virtual scenes and/or virtual characters which will be overlaid on these tables and cups via the video-see-through head mount displays (HMD) with the Unibrain cameras mounted in front and looking at the markers. The system obtains images from this Unibrain camera, tracks the marker pattern on these images, calculates the position of the virtual viewpoint, generates a novel view of the captured subject from this viewpoint and then superimposes this generated view to the images obtained from the Unibrain camera and display it on the HMD.

The main interactive table is first overlaid with a digitally created setting, an Asian garden in our case, whereas the cups serve as the containers for the virtual characters and also as tools for users to manipulate them tangibly. There is also a large screen on the wall reflecting the mixed reality view of the first user when he/she uses the HMD. If nobody uses this HMD for 15 seconds, the large screen will change to the virtual reality mode, showing the whole magic land viewed from a very far distant viewpoint.

An example of the tangible interaction on the Main Interactive Table is shown in the Figure 1. Here we can see a user using a cup to tangibly move a virtual panda object (left image) and using another cup to trigger the volcano by putting the character physically near the volcano (right image). Although cables and HMD will constrain the mobility of the user, the user can view the scene from different angles and distances to have full 3D view of scene.

The menu table is where users can select the virtual characters they want to play with. There are two mechanical push buttons on the table corresponding with two types of characters:

Figure 1. Tangible interaction on the nain table: (left) Tangibly picking up the virtual object from the table; (right) trigger of the volcano by placing a cup with virtual boy physically near to the volcano

Figure 2. Menu table: (left) A user using a cup to pick up a virtual object; (right) augmented view seen by users

the human captured 3D LIVE models on the right and VRML models on the left. Users can press the button to change the objects showed on the menu table, and move the empty cup close to this object to pick it up. To empty a cup (trash), users can move this cup close to the virtual bin placed at the middle of the menu table.

In the Figure 2, in the left image, we can see a user using a cup to pick up a virtual object; at the edge of the table closest to the user are two mechanical buttons. In the right image we can see the augmented view seen by this user. The user had selected a dragon previously which is inside the cup.

After picking up a character, users can bring the cup to the main interactive table to play with it. Consequently, there will be many 3D models moving and interacting in a virtual scene on the table, which forms a beautiful virtual world of those small characters. If two characters are close together, they would interact with each other in the pre-defined way. For example, if the dragon comes near to the 3D LIVE captured real human, it will blow fire on the human. This gives an exciting feeling of the tangible merging of real humans with the virtual world.

As an example of the interaction, in the Figure 3, we can see the interaction where the witch who is tangibly moved with the cup turns the 3D Live human character which comes physically close to it into a stone.

Figure 3. Main table: The witch turns the 3D LIVE human which comes close to it into a stone

System Design

As shown in Figure 4 (it is a simple diagram, please check the details in Nguyen et al., 2005), the software system of Magic Land consists of five main parts: 3D live recording, 3D live rendering, main rendering, ceiling camera tracking, and game server. Beside these parts, there is a sound module that produces audio effects including background music and interactive sounds for the whole system. In this system users can record their live model for playback.

Human Pacman

System Overview

Human Pacman (Cheok et al., 2003a, 2003b, 2004) is a novel mixed reality interactive entertainment system that ventures to embed the natural physical world seamless with a fantasy virtual playground by capitalizing on infrastructure provided by mobile computing, Wireless LAN, and ubiquitous computing. We have progressed from the old day's 2D arcade

Figure 4. System setup of Magic Land

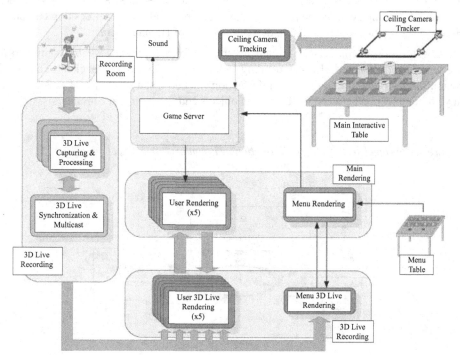

Pacman on screens, with incremental development, to popular 3D game console Pacman, and the recent mobile online Pacman. Finally with our novel Human Pacman, we have a physical role-playing computer fantasy together with real human-social and mobile-gaming that emphasizes on collaboration and competition between players in a wide outdoor physical area that allow natural wide-area human-physical movements.

The main concepts of the game are first given in terms of team collaboration, ultimate game objectives, and the essential nature of the game's playground named Pac-World. The players are assigned to two opposing teams, namely the Pacman team and the ghost team. The former consists of two Pacmen and two Helpers; correspondingly, the latter consists of two ghosts and two helpers. Each Pacman\ghost is in coalition with one helper, promoting collaboration and interaction between the users. As a new character introduced into Human Pacman, helper acts as an intelligence, advisor, and coordinator for her in her quest for achieving her goal. The real-time position of each mobile user is sent periodically to the server through wireless LAN. To enhance the gaming experience for both Pacman and ghost, the players in the physical world with wearable computer are not able to see enemy mobile units. Therefore the helper, who is in VR mode and see all, guides her partner by messaging her with important information. This promotes collaboration and interaction between humans through the internet.

System Design

Human Pacman system features a centralized client-server architecture that is made up of four main entities, namely a central server, and client wearable computers, helper laptops, and Bluetooth embedded objects. Wireless LAN serves as a communication highway between the wearable computers, the helper computers (laptops), and the server desktop computer. Figure 5 shows the top-level system design overview of Human Pacman.

Physical location and players' status updates are sent from the client wearable computers to the server every 10 ms to 21 ms, depending on the processing load on the client. The server maintains up-to-the-minute players' information (location, status, etc.), and presides over any communication between the Bluetooth objects and the wearable computers.

Figure 5. Top-level system overview of Human Pacman

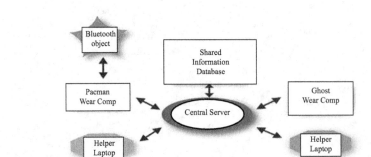

As the main equipment of player, at the heart of the whole wearable computer system is a Desknote A980 system, with a 3GHz processor and a NVidia GeForce4 video card. Twiddler2 acts as handheld keyboard and mouse inputting device for the system. Video input of the surroundings is obtained from USB Web camera and head mounted display (HMD) displays the processed video. Data from the InertiaCube2 (which has been fastened on the HMD) is obtained and used to track the user's head motion with a dynamic accuracy of 3 degrees. RTK GPS/Infrared LED (outdoor/indoor) used to detect the position of player. Bluetooth communication is made with the TDK Bluetooth USB adaptor. A touch-sensor circuit designed and built in our laboratory using capacitive touch sensors QT160 is used to sense the touching of the backpack by the enemy player or the touching of Bluetooth embedded objects by Pacmen.

Game Play

Pacmen and ghosts are now real human players in the real world experiencing mixed computer graphics fantasy-reality provided by using the wearable computers on them. Virtual cookies and actual tangible physical objects (super cookie) are incorporated into the game play to provide novel experiences of seamless transitions between real and virtual worlds. A new character-helper is introduced into this system, each Pacman and ghost will be assigned a partner helper who acts as an intelligence, advisor and coordinator for her in her quest for achieving her goal. Human Pacman follows the game rules of the traditional Pacman game—all players are divided into two teams: Pacman team and ghost team. The Pacman team needs to collect all virtual cookies by walking through them one by one, while ghost team endeavor to catch Pacman before she collect all cookies.

To enhance the gaming experience for both Pacman and ghost, the players in the physical world with wearable computer are not able to see enemy mobile units. Therefore the helper, who is in VR mode and see all, guides her partner by messaging her with important information and thus this promotes collaboration and interaction between human. All physical actions are reflected visually in Pac-World such as virtual cookie collection is reflected through the disappearing of the cookie in both the AR (Pacman) and VR (helper) mode.

In addition, Bluetooth special cookie is provided in this game. Pacman can collect this special cookie by physically picking it up. When Pacman get this special cookie, she achieves one minute of ghost-devouring power. Player can catch her enemy by physically touch her/him. Figure 6 show the overall game flow in Human Pacman.

Age Invaders

Age Invaders (AI) is a novel interactive intergeneration social-physical game which allows the elderly to play harmoniously together with children in physical space while parents can participate in the game play in real time remotely through the internet. With the increase of technology there is a huge gap between youth and elderly culture. Present technology does not often allow the facilitation of family entertainment. Most children greatly enjoy playing computer games from childhood and most of them do not like to take part in more elderly-style games such as chess games or fishing. Parents are often busy at work and may have to travel away from the family on business trips. It is important to put in place a social and physical inter-generational family entertainment system that can connect family members in the home and away from the home.

AI is a novel interactive intergeneration social-physical game that allows the elderly to play harmoniously together with children in physical space while parents can participate in the game play in real time through the internet. This game is based on the popular traditional Space Invader arcade game. The game offers adaptable game parameters to suit the simultaneous gaming of elderly and young. Adjusting game properties automatically compensate for potential elderly disadvantages, for example slower reaction time and slow movement. For example, the rockets of the elderly are faster than those of the children's, and vice-versa. This property is important to sustain the players' interaction and interest in the game. Unlike standard computer games, AI requires and encourages physical body movements rather than constraining the user in front of computer for many hours. It also incorporates puzzle solving games which encourage cognitive stimulating activities for the health benefits of the elderly and young.

AI uses a floor display, which is an unconventional interface for mixed reality entertainment. The key advantage of floor display over HMD or other wearable display is that it does not require the user to wear something bulky and perceive the world through the device and this is an important feature for elderly to participate in augmented reality games. The floor display is very intuitive and provides users with a direct connection to the virtual game world using

Figure 6. The overall game flow of Human Pacman

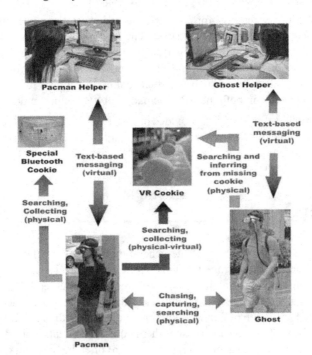

their whole body as the interface. Players can move around the game platform as they would for normal activities without having to adapt to new display interface. In real time, as the players move and shoot rockets or bomb, it will appear that it is physically coming out of their bodies, which gives a real time link between the real world and the virtual world. This will immerse the players into the game and introduce high physicality which is important to sustain the players' interest in the game and encourages them to collaborate actively.

We now describe some of the motivations for Age Invaders: There is a global aging population and increasing generation gap between the grandparents or parents and children. In 1950, just 8% of the world population was aged 60 years or over. By 2005, that proportion had risen to 10% and it is expected to more than double over the next 45 years, reaching 22% in 2050 (World, 2005).

The problem of increasing population of the elderly brings along many socio-economic issues. For example, the elderly require increased health cares for both mental and physical problems. Many of these problems derive from social isolation and lack of activity. Findings from scientific research studies show that playing video games can lead to changes in an individual's pleasure, arousal, dominance, and/or affiliative behavior (Christian, 1978). Furthermore, the elderly enjoy the computer gaming experience (Whitcomb, 2005). Therefore it is a highly positive move to use digital new media to increase elderly happiness, through social interaction, physical activity, and entertainment. Participation in an activity helps elderly to feel better and healthier as they recognize their ability to move and create something which is important to produce a sense of health (Matsuo, Nagasawa, Yoshino, Hiramatsu, & Kurashiki, 2003).

Often a unique bond connects grandparent and grandchildren (Carlson, 1996). Grandparents can have significant impact on their grandchildren's lives in many different ways. They can act as the family historian, mentor, playmate, nurturer, role model, confidante, advocate, advisor, and surrogate parent. The more grandparents and grandchildren are in contact with each other, the more the relationship grows and the more influence grandparents have (Calsson, 1996). As children nowadays are more inclined to play computer games, it is necessary to create a new platform of interactive games so that the elderly and young can play harmoniously together in a physical space and in long run strengthen the inter-generational bond.

System Description

The concept of the Age Invaders game is shown in Figure 7. The children are playing with two grandparents in this interactive physical media space while two parents can join into the game via the internet as virtual players, thus increasing the inter-generational interaction.

The system was designed to track players' positions in real time using RFID embedded in the players' shoes. A large electronic game board made from high resolution LED blocks is where the game will be played on. In real time as players move and shoot using the Bluetooth toy gun, rockets will be shown moving out from the blocks on which they are standing. Players can trigger rockets and bombs to the other players and collect extras to gain or lose score points. Gaining the most points in a set amount of time wins the round.

Bonus items can also be placed and explosions triggered by the virtual players logged in the system through Internet. The virtual players could interact strongly by choosing which

Figure 7. Age Invaders: An inter-generational, social, and physical game

player to help and picking up bonus items for this player. They can also adjust the game parameters (e.g., speed of the rockets) by dragging the slide bar. More importantly, the virtual players can see a real time representation of the physical board space, thus increasing the link between the real and virtual world as shown in Figure 8.

When a player steps on a puzzle, the game enters a "hyperspace" mode where it is specially designed to enhance collaboration between the players. The young players will have to solve the puzzle and the elderly players can help by giving hints. Children will find these games interesting as they are digitally enhanced from the well received puzzle and arcade

Figure 8. 3D virtual player interface linking virtual and real physical game world

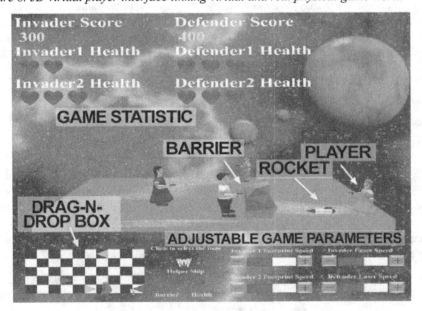

games. These puzzle games also stimulates cognitive activity which is beneficial for the health of the elderly.

The main goals of Age Invaders for the elderly generally focus on four major areas: social, physical, cognitive, and psychological. The social aspect emphasizes family and inter-generational social interaction, sharing and support. The physical aspect attends to the aging individual's need for physical exercise and expression. The cognitive aspect stimulates the mental functioning and improves the elderly adult's mental stimulation. The psychological aspect refers to promoting personal integration, to the expression of emotions, and feelings of self-worth and wellbeing in a family interaction context.

Holistic Overview

Since the beginning of the home computer era in the late 1970s, the term computer entertainment has mostly been used synonymously with computer or console games (Magerkurth et al., 2004). Seven similarities among our various developed research systems come out after similarities analysis. Those seven features for entertainment are very different from traditional computer games which are rather isolated and conservative because even nowadays most games are based on traditional multi-playing and internet connection. This is due to the limitations of the traditional computer interface, such as keyboard, mouse, and screen. We strongly believe that those seven features of our systems domineeringly represent the next generation of entertainment which is social and physical interactive paradigms with mixed reality technology.

The Social Experience

A first and obvious addition to the traditional paradigm is the notion of the social experience. Most of today's computer entertainment titles are multi-playing and draw their attraction between human competition and cooperation. However, since there are limitations of traditional human computer interface, social interaction is still not an integral part of the entertainment experience.

For example, with traditional games, players can not interact with each other in a natural fashion, but communicate each other through computer screen or micro-phone. Also, all actions they play on each other are merely implemented by keyboard, mouse, or joy-controller. Thousands of human interaction such as gestures, physical movement, tangible touch, eye contact is totally lost in the game. However, the problem mentioned above are reduced in the next generation entertainment systems described in this chapter. For instance, in the Human Pacman system, players are physically role-playing the characters of Pacman and the ghost. With wearable computers donned, they use free physical bodily gestures and movements as part of interaction between each person.

The social experience is not just about providing multiplayer experiences where the user's can compete and collaborate with each other, but also have to further augment the strong emotional involvement among the players by introducing direct social face-to-face interactions and new interfaces between the players and the virtual domain which can be found in the systems described in the chapter.

Physical Interaction

Physical interaction allows a psychological insurance that players immerse themselves from the real world to virtual world effectively. Players should keep mental model of the action in real world when they jump into the virtual environment. In traditional game, players use keyboard, mouse or joystick to perform actions in the game, which is not the same as in the real world situation. Physical interaction thus should be fundamental element for the next generation entertainment. Together with the highly dynamic nature of computer simulations, the sensible use of the audio and visual presentation capabilities of entertainment technology has the potential to provide a much more immersive and richer gaming situations than traditional one ever could.

Entertainment such as Human Pacman allowed the compelling aspects of physical which can bring players in physical proximity for interaction and help players regain lost natural interactions. This is of definitive advantage because humans enjoy being physically together, and socially interacting with each other (Bowlby, 1983), and entertainment systems should reflect this compelling need.

We thus propose to the next generation entertainment application which is augmented traditional game with social and physical elements. With social and physical interactive paradigms, the new hybrid application will open a new page for computer entertainment.

Conclusion

In this chapter, it was argued that entertainment is a key driver for development of technology, and it was proposed to use embodied interaction between humans and computation both socially and physically, with the aim of novel interactive computer mixed reality entertainment. Social and physical interactive paradigms for mixed reality involve the elements of ubiquitous computing, tangible interfaces, and interaction, as well as social computing. They bring the opportunity of interaction and entertainment through and with the environment, rather than only on a desktop computer with keyboard and mouse, in addition to incorporating the sociological organization of interactive behavior. Thus, with social and physical interactive paradigms, people can easily play and entertain with each other and computers within real world and virtual world. Essentially, humans as physical beings now actually become situated inside the computational world.

The technical background of social and physical interactive paradigms was discussed, and then research examples where shown where the users had interactions both socially and physically by computing within the physical environment. Moreover, these activities take place in the context of the environment. Using 3D graphical objects, tangible interaction, and 3D sound, it was shown that ubiquitous computing allows the manipulation of objects in physical space to interact with 3D digital information. For these systems, the computer is embedded in the activity in such a way that the user interacts with the environment, and physical objects themselves become the interface.

Acknowledgments

The author wished to greatly thank all the many researchers and students both undergraduate and graduate that were involved in the projects described in the chapter in the Mixed Reality Lab Singapore. In particular, Ta Huynh Duy Nguyen, Tran Cong Thien Qui, Shang Ping Lee, Wei Liu, Khoo Eng Tat, and Xu Ke.

References

Association (2002). *Essential facts about the computer and video game industry*. Retrieved from http://www.theesa.com/files/2005EssentialFacts.pdf

Bowlby, J. (1983). *Attachment and loss (Vol. I: Attachment)*. New York: Basic Books.

Carson, L. (1996). *The essential grandparent*. Deerfield Beach: Health Communications, Inc.

Cheok, A. D., Fong, S. W., Goh, K. H., Yang, X., Liu, W., Farzbiz, F., & Li, Y. (2003a). Human Pacman: A mobile entertainment system with ubiquitous computing and tangible interaction over a wide outdoor area. In *Proceedings of the 5th International Symposium on Human Computer Interaction with Mobile Devices and Service* (pp. 209-223).

Cheok, A. D., Fong, S. W., Goh, K. H., Yang, X., Liu, W., & Farzbiz, F. (2003b). Human Pacman: A sensing-based mobile entertainment system with ubiquitous computing and tangible interaction. In *Proceedings of the NetGames 2nd Workshop on Network and System Support for Games* (pp. 106-117).

Cheok, A. D., Goh, K. H., Liu, W., Farbiz, F., Fong, S. W., Teo, S. L., Li, Y., & Yang, X. (2004). Human Pacman: A mobile, wide-area entertainment system based on physical, social, and ubiquitous computing. *Personal and Ubiquitous Computing, 8*, 71-81.

Christian, H. (1978). An activity analysis of electronic game simulators. *Therapeuticrecreation Journal, 12*, 21-25.

Crawford, C. (1998). Live: What a concept! Networked games. *Digital Illusion*, 241-248.

Dourish, P. (2001, October). *Where the action is: The foundations of embodied interaction*. MIT Press.

Farbiz, F., Cheok, A. D., Wei, L., ZhiYing, Z., Ke, X., Prince, S., et al. (2005, June). Live three-dimensional content for augmented reality. *IEEE Transactions on Multimedia, 7*(3), 514-523.

Hall, W. (1994). Ending the tyranny of the button. *IEE Multimedia* (pp. 60-68).

Ishii, H., & Ullmer, B. (1997). Tangible bits: Towards seamless interfaces between people, bits, and atoms. In *Proceedings of the ACM Conference on Human Factors in Computing Systems* (pp. 234-241).

Magerkurth, C., Engelke, T., & Memisoglu, M. (2004). Augmenting the virtual domain with physical and social elements: Towards a paradigm shift in computer entertainment technology. *Computers in Entertainment, 2*, 12-12.

Mandryk, R. L., & Inkpen, K. M. (2001). Supporting free play in ubiquitous computer games. In *Proceedings of the Workshop on Designing Ubiquitous Computing Games (UbiComp 2001)*.

Matsuo, M., Nagasawa, J., Yoshino, A., Hiramatsu K., & Kurashiki, K. (2003). *Effects of activity participation of the elderly on quality of life*. Yonago Acta.

Nezlek, J. B., Richardson, D. R., Green, L. R., & Schatten-Jones, E. (2002). Psychological well-being and day-to-day social interaction among older adults. *Personal Relationships, 9*, 57-71.

Nguyen, T. H. D., Qui, T. C. T., Xu, K., Cheok, A. D., Teo, S. L., Zhou, Z., Mallawaarachchi, A., Lee, S. P., Liu, W., Teo, H. S., Thang, L. N., Li, Y., & Kato, H. (2005). Real time 3D human capture system for mixed-reality art and entertainment. *IEEE Transactions on Visualization and Computer Graphics, 11*, 706-721.

Prince, S., Cheok, A. D., Farbiz, F., Williamson, T., Johnson, N., Billinghurst, M., & Kato, H. (2002). 3D live: Real time captured content for mixed reality. In *Proceedings of the International Symposium on Mixed and Augmented Reality (ISMAR)* (pp. 7-13).

Stapleton, C. B., Hughes, C. E., & Moshell, J. M. (2003). Mixed fantasy: Exhibition of entertainment research for mixed reality. In *Proceedings of the International Symposium on Mixed and Augmented Reality* (pp. 354-355).

Suchman, L. (1987). *Plans and situated actions: The problem of human-machine communication*. Cambridge: Cambridge University Press.

Weiser, M. (1991). The computer for the twenty-first century. *Scientific American*, 94-104.

Whitcomb, G. R. (1990). Computer games for the elderly. *ACM SIGCAS Computers and Society Archive, 20*(3), 112-115.

World Population Prospects: The 2004 Revision. (2005). *United Nations Department of Economic and Social Affairs' Population Division*.

Chapter XVIII

The Future of Augmented Reality Gaming

Bruce H. Thomas
Wearable Computer Laboratory, University of South Australia, Australia

Abstract

Entertainment systems are one of the successful utilisations of augmented reality technologies to real world applications. This chapter provides my personal insights into the future directions of the use of augmented reality with gaming applications. This chapter explores a number of advances in technologies that may enhance augmented reality gaming. The features for both indoor and outdoor augmented reality are examined in context of their desired attributes for the gaming community. A set of concept games for outdoor augmented reality are presented to highlight novel features of this technology.

Introduction

Augmented reality (AR) in entertainment computing is a well established area of investigation, and may one day prove to be an early "killer app" for this emerging form of technology. AR gaming may well succeed where Virtual Reality gaming had only a limited success. The three features of AR that enable it to support more novel forms of computer games as compared to VR versions games are as follows:

1.   AR only requires a limited amount of the user's field of view to be rendered. The vast majority of the user's view is the physical world, and only the introduced game pieces require computer generated graphics. In VR, the entire visual world (i.e., the virtual world) must be rendered, causing the users to always be left with the feeling of existing in a synthetic world.

2.   The ability to view the physical world allows the users a better sense of where they are and who is around them. Being able to see the physical world allows users to move freely in the combined physical and virtual world with the ability to view and avoid obstacles such as chairs, trees, and other people. The ability to view other people, albeit without being able to view the other person's eyes, is a powerful visual cueing mechanism for collaborative games. For example, aiming a physical ray gun and virtually shooting at someone instead of an avatar is much more personal. Full body cues such as waving one's hand is more naturally supported in an AR environment.

3.   Finally, the physicality of moving in open spaces is appealing to users. The ability to move around in large or small areas allows the users to understand and experience the game at a more primordial level. The ability to physically walk over to a position is more intuitive than the use of keyboard or mouse control.

AR gaming requires additional computer hardware support. In particular, self-contained position and orientation sensors that are rapid to setup and install. AR technologies could be employed in the entertainment industry for theme parks, video arcades, or special purpose arenas (for example paintball or laser tag). This chapter will focus on the home use of AR gaming, as I believe this will have the largest impact for society.

The overall objective of this chapter is to provide an overview of my vision of the future of AR gaming. The chapter starts with an exploration of what advances in technology would enhance AR gaming, and in particular highlighting the required technology advances required to bring this form of game to life. The chapter then goes on to examine indoor AR games in context of their desired attributes for the gaming community. Augmented reality is currently in a number of different form factors based on the following:

1.   Whether it is played indoors or outdoors

2.   The type of display—head mounted displays, handheld displays, or projector-based displays

Some example AR games based on these different form factors will be described to accentuate the properties of this form of gaming. A number of fine examples of the state of the art for the use of AR with gaming and entertainment may be found in the chapters *Mixed Reality for Future Social and Physical Entertainment Systems* and *Making Memories for a Lifetime, Mixed and Augmented Reality Experiences for Entertainment, Education, and Training*. Outdoor AR games are then examined. To show the impact of the use of AR technology, a suite of conceptual games for outdoor AR are presented to draw attention to innovative characteristics of the use of this technology. The chapter finishes with a set of concluding remarks.

Future of Technologies

In this section, a set of well-known outdoor AR problems are outlined and a set of possible technologies to overcome them are postulated.

Standard Outdoor AR Problems

The outdoors is a hostile environment for AR and mobile computer research. There are number of continuing outdoor AR research problems (Azuma, 1999), as most AR investigations tend to be performed indoors in controlled environments. The three areas that are discussed here are head mounted displays (HMD), tracking, and portability.

Current HMD technology is still non-optimal for outdoor AR applications. The field-of-view of current moderately priced HMDs are around $30° \pm 10°$, and this is still only quite narrow considering the very wide angles that the human eye can see. In addition, HMDs have a tendency to have a heavy plastic frame around the lens. This results in the user's peripheral vision being restricted or tunnelled, reducing the overall immersion.

For AR environments to be realistic, a key requirement is that there is accurate and fast tracking in six degrees of freedom. Current technology still is not adequate to perform tracking in an outdoor environment at the required speed and accuracy. Tracking has a propensity to work best in a restricted environment where the conditions are known, and infrastructure can be put in place in advance. In a large outdoor environment, conditions change dynamically and putting infrastructure in place can be difficult.

The mobile nature of outdoor AR gaming also imposes further constraints, such as the overall weight the user may carry. The form factor is very important for the eventual acceptance of games hardware and software. People will desire shrink-wrapped solutions like modern console games (Norman, 1990); therefore the games have to be easy to set up and use.

The following are a number of the well known technology challenges for mobile and wearable computing: electric power, processor power, and communication power. The electric power problem is currently being solved by improved battery technology and the use of less power hungry chips and displays. Future games will, as new games today, require improvement in processing power for computations, graphics, and sensors. New games, such as MMORPG (Massively Multiplayer Online Role-Playing Game), involve increased communication power in both bandwidth and connectivity. These three challenges are being met by current industry developments.

Future Technologies

To really make AR gaming extremely engaging, improved, and less expensive display technologies are required. I will postulate some innovative technologies that could really drive AR gaming into the future. For outdoor use, a very small and portable laser retinal HMD that fits into wire-frame glasses or no glasses at all would be ideal. Laser retinal displays (Kollin, 1993) are one of the few technologies that work well outdoors in full sunlight. Indoor AR gaming could also benefit from the improvements of laser retinal displays. However a revolutionary replacement or augmentation would be the use of very small, portable and bright projectors, approximately the size of a cigarette. These small projectors could be placed around the AR gaming environment or body worn to illuminate the user's surroundings.

To make the presence of game pieces and avatars registered to the physical world in a believable fashion, very high precision and accurate location and orientation sensors are required. These must perform under the following conditions: full coverage of the globe, sub-millimetre accuracy for location, less than a tenth of one degree accuracy for orientation, and with extremely low drift. Current AR rendering provides very poor image quality of the computer generated graphics. Photorealistic rendering of AR images is required to gain the full sense of presence in the augmented world (Grosch, 2005). When an AR game requires the rendered information to be seamlessly integrated with the physical world, photorealistic rendering techniques are required. It is essential all of the previously mentioned technologies be low power, portable, and inexpensive to manufacture.

Indoor AR Gaming

The development of AR games for the indoor home market would most certainly follow the concept of users playing games in one particular location of their home. This would enable the leverage of current tracking technologies. Tracking technologies are more robust and accurate indoors, and the equipment does not suffer from as many environmental concerns. In the most part, these forms of games require only orientation sensing plus very limited or no positional tracking. In these configurations, the people will be tethered to their computers. The following three forms of indoor AR gaming display technologies are examined: immersive head mounted display, spatially immersive display, and tabletop displays.

Immersive HMD

One direction of immersive HMD-based AR games is to develop AR versions of original games. I see this form factor being a new display device attached to existing gaming infrastructure (a game console or existing PC). Because of the static nature of the placement of the gaming infrastructure, the HMD and sensors would be cabled to the infrastructure.

An obvious choice for AR gaming is the ability to make the game more animated. For example, the game of "Wizard's Chess" depicted in the movie *Harry Potter and the Philosopher's Stone* provided graphic animations of chess pieces fighting whenever a piece was captured. The use of AR allows for animated games pieces to interact with each other and the participants of the game. Animation could help with the following features of the game:

1.   Instruction of the game in how to play,

2.   Tactics, and

3.   Current attributes of a playing piece (power level, strength, or abilities).

An interesting feature of AR is that different information may be displayed to different users. In the case of displaying current attributes, private information about a playing piece could be displayed to the user who controls the piece. This private information could include visualisation of potential placement of pieces or future actions.

An example of a "running around the house" style of game is MIND-WARPING (Starner, Leibe, Singletary, & Pair, 2000). This game enables users to see one another, and allows them to virtually shoot each other. This makes for a virtual form of laser tag. This game requires a large instrumented space, as in the case of MIND-WARPING a floor of a computer science building at a university. To play this style of game in someone's home requires a game that is designed of a smaller indoor area. Gandy et al. developed an acting based AR Karaoke game built on top of the DART AR authoring tool (Gandy, 2005). The concept is to play

Figure 1. User's view of AR Karaoke (Used with permission of Maribeth Gandy, Georgia Institute of Technology)

your favourite scene of a movie from inside the movie. The user wears an HMD and acts out a part in the movie scene via voice and movement. The movie is shown to the user in a first person perspective, and the user acts against a pre-recorded scene from the movie. Figure 1 depicts the user's view from an HMD playing AR Karaoke with the movie "Princess Bride." The user's friends can watch the final result of the user's actions. This concept takes the notion of the Eye-Toy® to a new level: a group game in which the players move around in front of their friends instead of in front of a camera. I see group based games that allow people to act *silly* in front of their friends and family as a major new thrust. One possible improvement is placing low cost tracking devices on each of the users to allow them to be draped in virtual costumes. The players can not only act silly but look silly too!

Spatially Immersive Display

Home entertainment centres enhanced with *spatially immersive displays* (SID) will be an interesting entry point for AR. Wrapping the game's visual and sound space around the user would semi-immerse the user in the game. In the near future AR gaming could make use of a number of current technologies. An attractive option over an HMD is to use a SID. A SID is a set of displays that physically surrounds the viewer with a panorama of imagery (Lantz, 1996). A three screen system could easily be setup with one screen in the middle normal to the viewing vector and each side screen 45° to 90° angled in, depending on the visual immersion required. This enables a simple and inexpensive semi-immersive system with lower-cost DLP projector technology[1]. Passive 3D monitors without the need of glasses and laser retinal displays[2] are commercially available. I envision the use of these display technologies in the near future for high-end AR gaming experiences.

An example of a SID based game could be a flight or dog-fighting simulator. The setup is very similar to a commercial flight simulator with project screens where the wind-screens would be located. Looking forward is the wind-screen looking over the nose of the plane. Looking to the left would be out the side window, and to the right would be either the other side window or the co-pilot. Each of the viewpoints for the projections on the screens is slaved to the current virtual view point of the plane. The games would be operated in a normal fashion, but the visual output would be enhanced to allow three separate views from the same user location in the game. This form of AR does not require any tracking. One could easily argue this form of a virtual environment is not AR. I leave it up to the reader to make up their minds on the subject, but it is still an enhanced gaming experience reachable in the very near future.

Players using a SID with games such as first-person-shooter, real time strategy, and puzzle format would have an enhanced situational awareness. A player would operate the game in the normal fashion with the added feature of being able to look over the shoulder to see if someone or something is sneaking up on their side. A problem with the user interface is whether to allow the user to interact with objects on the side screens. In the case of the flight simulator, the front of the plane is the focus of the user input. In these other games, an object on the side screen may require some form on interaction, say shooting it. One possible solution is to force the user to place the desired game object on the front screen to enable them to interact with that object. A second option is to overload the game's input device to allow the fast placing of the side screen view point on to the front screen, in effect rotating the user's view by the amount the screens' are angled in. A third option is to overload the game's input device to switch the screen the game is interacting with. This third option would require the player to rotate their body to face the screen now accepting the input control. These examples provide an indication of how more immersive this form of gaming could be.

Tabletop AR Gaming

The employment of the tabletop as an AR gaming surface provides a number of interesting user interface opportunities for tabletop projected augmented reality entertainment applications. The games may range from extensions to traditional non-computer based games, such as Augmented Reality Chinese Checkers (Cooper et al., 2004) to new games such as Augmented Coliseum (Kojima et al., 2006). There are many advantages to playing games on a computer, rather on a physical board, such as the ability to introduce animation and other multimedia presentations. This animation can do more than add excitement to the game play, it can also aid the players to learn the game and help them to understand invalid moves.

In the case of augmented reality Chinese checkers, AR provides extra functionality to an existing board game. This game is played as a tangle mixed reality game with projector-based AR. The users manipulate cardboard fiducial markers to control the playing space and pieces. Chinese checkers is ideal for a tabletop based AR game because it can be played by up to six players and it has relatively simple rules for a board game.

Augmented coliseum is a special purpose game developed for tabletop AR, which employs small active robots as game pieces. The robots are physically driven around on the tabletop by remote control. The tabletop display (front or rear projected) provides the virtual play-

Figure 2. Augmented coliseum (Used with permission of Professor Masahiko Inami, University of Electro-Communications, Tokyo)

ing space. The AR information indicates virtual barriers, explosions, and gunfire. The game provides a nice blend of virtual and physical interactions. Figure 2 is a photograph of the game in action with two physical robots playing on a front-projected virtual battleground.

Outdoor AR Gaming

The following two forms of outdoor AR gaming are examined: head-down gaming with a handheld display and head-up gaming with an HMD. The sheer nature of these outdoor mobile games requires some form of compact portable computer. Both of these forms of gaming require tracking for location through systems such as GPS and robust orientation sensing.

Outdoor Head-Down Gaming

Outdoor head-down gaming is the presentation of the visual information through a handheld device that augments the world in an indirect manner. Traditionally this has been in a map format that places the user within the virtual environment. The device is independently tracked by position and orientation from the users' body. This enables users to "shoot around the corner." The users' have the following two modes of operation: (1) interacting with the screen head down or (2) moving about looking at the physical world. Players are

Figure 3. (a) (right image) The Real Tournament handset includes inbuilt GPS, electronic trigger and digital Compass, connected to a Compaq iPAQ and team mates via IEEE802.11 or GPRS; (b) (left image) screenshots as seen by a Real Tournament player (Used with permission of Joe Finney, Lancaster University)

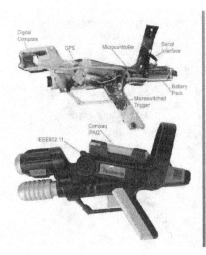

able to move slowly looking at the screen, but to swiftly move, the player would have to look up and pay attention to the physical world. Location-based mobile phone games are an impoverished version of this form of gaming.

The outdoor handheld version of Real Tournament (McCaffery & Finney, 2004; Mitchell et al., 2003) is a good example of this evolving form of game. The players hold a gun-like device and are able walk and turn unencumbered, and these movements in both direction and orientation are simultaneously linked to the physical and virtual worlds. The Real Tournament handset includes inbuilt GPS, electronic trigger, and digital compass, connected to a Compaq iPAQ and the teammates via IEEE802.11 or GPRS (see Figure 3). The gun-like interface provides a good affordance for first-person-shooter style games.

The future of outdoor head-down gaming is following the MMORPG model of gaming. The big advantage of this form factor is the ability of the user to quickly engage and disengage from the game. This mode makes for a socially appropriate game for downtown areas, parks, and general public spaces. Albeit running around with gun-like props would be very disconcerting to the general public. From the user's point of view, the problems of information tunnelling would not go away, but they can be more easily be minimised. *Information tunnelling* is the problem where the user concentrates on the AR information presented to them and ignores the physical world. This form of inattention causes safety problems, such as walking in front of a bus. An additional benefit is that use of HMDs would not be required, and the issues of social weight would be minimised (Toney, Mulley, Thomas, & Piekarski, 2002). The social weight of the device would be lower due to the lower technology apprehension (TA) of a handheld device over an HMD.

Outdoor Head-Up Gaming

The first reported example of an outdoor head-up game is ARQuake, an outdoor AR version of the game Quake (idSoftware, 2000). Figure 4 depicts the user's view from the HMD of

Figure 4. Screenshot of the user's view of ARQuake

the ARQuake game. Notice how the virtual world is overlaid onto the physical world. ARQuake is a first-person perspective application with the following attributes:

1.   The application is situated in the physical world.
2.   The point of view, which the application shows to the user, is completely determined by the position and orientation of the user's head.
3.   Relevant information is displayed as AR information via an HMD.
4.   The user is mobile and able to walk through the information space.
5.   The user interface additionally requires only a simple handheld button device.

In the ARQuake application, the physical world is modelled as a Quake 3D graphical model. The AR information (monsters, weapons, objects of interest) is displayed in spatial context with the physical world. The Quake model of the physical world (walls, ceiling, and floors) is not shown to the user: the HMD allows the user to see the actual wall, ceilings and floors, which ARQuake needs to only model internally. Coincidence of the actual and virtual structures is the key to the game. The AR application models the existing physical outdoor structures as clear objects, and so omission of their rendered image from the display becomes in effect one of the rendering techniques.

Informal evaluation of using AR for game playing indicates people enjoy this environment (Thomas & Piekarski, 2002). There are a number of issues and possible areas of investigation to produce better AR gaming technology, and these are as follows: safety, modelling tools, and the standard set of outdoor AR problems.

Safety

Safety is a major concern operating an AR system in an outdoor setting. While using the HMD with AR information displayed, a user may experience information tunnelling. While operating the AR application, the user could pay more attention to the information on the HMD than the physical world. This may escort the user into dangerous situations, such as placing the user in way of motor car traffic or tripping over an obstacle.

I envision three major ways to tackle this problem. A first method is to have the game necessitate the user to focus on the physical world. Bringing elements of the physical world into the game would help the users focus on the virtual and physical at the same time. In the ARQuake game, the users have to pay attention to the physical buildings, as they occlude monsters and game pieces. This stops users from bumping into walls, but the users are oblivious to hazards not associated with the game. For example the poor tracking of the system could cause game pieces to float onto roads. The desire to acquire a powerful new weapon would entice users to step onto the road. The second method is to contain the user to a safe playing arena. For example, the game could require use of a fenced-in area, such as a cricket oval. This would eradicate a number of possible dangerous elements. The field may be examined for possible loose footing circumstances. The games would then have to be restricted to basically open field arenas. The final method to solve a number of these problems is to design the games to lure people away from dangerous situations. Interesting virtual objects should be placed away from motorways, unsafe footing, and the like.

Modelling Tools

Good tools for building graphical models for outdoor AR games are required. Issues of colour schemes, sizes, and positioning are best determined outdoors (Thomas, Krul, Close, & Piekarski, 2002), while the authoring of the storyline of the game, quest puzzles, and monster attributes may be best determined at a desktop computer.

A particular problem with modelling outdoor AR games is how much of the physical world to model into the game. If a large number of buildings are required, the user must either enter them in themselves or play in a setting that has already been entered. The game needs to be customised for the environment the players are in. For example, not everyone has the same sized cricket oval. Users will need to be able to easily configure the game to their own environment.

The Tinmith-Metro application is designed for the capture of city models (Piekarski & Thomas, 2001). This technique supports the modelling of relatively complex buildings and other large physical structures, and the positioning of prefabricated graphical models of typical community infrastructure and city objects. The user performs these tasks interactively while walking around outdoors with the aid of an AR wearable computer. The user employs hand and head gestures to interact with AR information.

How to Make a Fun Outdoor AR Game?

An appealing feature of outdoor AR games is that movement in the game reflects physical movement (Cheok et al., 2004). The design of games has to reflect this feature, people walk slowly compared with the speed of the characters running in a desktop game. A second smaller feature is to have the restart position of a level close to where a user is physically standing, and not to require the person to walk all the way back to the initial staring point of the playing arena in order to restart the level. Unlike the desktop versions of the games, the users will not be teleported back to the start of a given level. Therefore the games are required to be redesigned to accommodate this feature. Users will want these games to be more like *paintball* and *laser-tag* style games; where they are able to physically move about among a group of users. The users will want the physical game hardware to be lightweight and unobtrusive so people can pretend they are having a real battle. An added feature of AR games is the ability to fight against virtual monsters that cannot exist in a paintball world.

The Wearable Computer Laboratory of the University of South Australia has been performing a quantity of formal and informal testing of the usability and playability issues for AR games and established a number issues for constructing the virtual worlds (Avery, Piekarski, Warren, & Thomas, 2006; Thomas et al., 2002). We have experimented with a number of different field of view (FOV) settings. Setting the FOV in the Quake game to the equivalent as the HMD corrected for the registration of the graphical images, but caused depth perception problems. This FOV difficulty requires further investigation. Minute errors in the tilt orientation of the user's head were quite noticeable. The standard contour of doors and corridors in the Quake worlds are not well suited to ARQuake. ARQuake requires wider corridors and doors that are not so thick. The world feels superior to the user if it is brightly lit. In the Augmented Virtuality and Augmented Reality modes, very dark and black colours (unless used for occlusion purposes) ought to be avoided. These colours give the false impression the physical world is "leaking" into the virtual world. There were a number of particular features we observed:

1. Floating objects succeed quite well in ARQuake.

2. The use of an overhead texture for the sky should be avoided.

3. Users did not enjoy the use of shadows in the virtual worlds.

4. Even with these observations, the users overall enjoyed ARQuake.

Genre of Games for Outdoor AR Gaming

In this section, I explore the following four genres of games set in an outdoor AR context: real time strategy, role playing, sports, and public spaces. I wish to highlight a number of attributes that make these enticing, exciting, and fun modes of gaming playing.

Real Time Strategy

Imagine you slip on an HMD see the battlefield through the eyes of Napoleon and you are leading your troops into battle (Phillips & Piekarski, 2005). Sweeping before you is your army and you must lead and direct them onto victory. You have performed your strategic planning and it is time for actions. As with all planning, a great general must react and adjust during the course of the battle. You direct your troops by issuing commands to your captains through the use of maps, hand signals, and voice commands. The fog of war prevents you from observing the entire battlefield. Situational awareness is gained by what you can see and recognise from the field. You move amongst the battle redirecting forces. The enemy has broken through the battle lines and you are forced to fight hand to hand with the sword that has served you so well. You are victorious through your courage and superior intellect!

Sports Games

Now that you have conquered the world, you wish to climb to the top of the sporting world. Your sword is replaced with a bat or ball, and you become the captain of your favourite sporting team. You are the quarterback of your favourite team and leading them into a different form of battle. As the quarterback, you call the plays from the huddle and take the snap from the center. You fade back and throw a perfect spiral to your wide receiver for a touchdown.

Or for members of the Commonwealth, you face the bowling of the world's fastest cricket bowlers. You could relieve the infamous "body line" series of 1932-1933 and be Don Bradman facing the vicious bowling of the English, as they try to strike "The Don" with deadly fast bowling to the rib cage. The user has to be able to not only bat, but they have to be able to duck or avoid the nasty bowling that is not hittable. A bad stroke of the bat would mean a thick edge and you are caught in the slips, or a solid hit is a boundary for four.

Role Playing Games

In the science fiction novel *Dream Park* by Larry Niven and Steven Barnes, gamers go to a theme park to engage in a multi-day role-playing adventure game. The gamers interact with a number of interfaces in a simulated outdoor environment. These include the following: holographic 3D images, electro-mechanical robotics, human actors, and physical artefacts. The environment is a very large highly instrumented enclosed space. The "game" is controlled by a game master and myriad of technicians. Fantasy creatures and people are created and interacted with to provide a full sensory augmented environment that the players are situated in. I see AR making these forms of gaming experiences possible.

I see role-playing games facilitated by the use of AR. Theme parks are a natural location for such games, but highly portable AR equipment would enable these forms of games in many outdoor spaces. I see two modes of operation for this form gaming, one with a human game master and one with a computer controlled game master. In the case of the latter, the computer would have a very limited or even no knowledge of the playing location. This version of the game would be played in an open space such as a large backyard or playing field.

The use of a human game master opens up a larger set of possibilities for spontaneous gaming situations. The game master, or dungeon master, allows for the unexpected choice of the gamer. As an extreme example, let us examine how a group of friends would create a full role-playing game for a particular location near them, say a favourite forest or park. A number of supporting systems would enable a group of friends to create their own fantasy world with handcrafted characters; this is an important aspect of providing support for this genre of games. The AR gaming interface requires a game master interface that is different from the gamer interface.

I see the phases of the game fall into the following different phases:

1. Game board creation

2. Game creature/artefact creation

3. Character creation

4. Character training

5. Game play over a number of sessions

The first four phases are a combination of the use of traditional indoor workstation technology and outdoor mobile AR technology. In these phases, traditional 3D graphics and CAD like tools may be employed to build the initial rendition of the game and characters.

Once these initial renditions are settled on, the placement in the physical world requires the developer to go out in the field. The mapping of the game pieces to the physical world is essential to the gaming experience. Once the game has been developed, the game is played over a number of occasions.

AR Gaming in Public Spaces

Public spaces such as parks, town squares, or historical locations could provide an interesting backdrop for AR gaming. For example, there are a number of National Battlefield Parks in the United States for both the American Revolution and the Civil War. These battlefield parks are rich in well documented history. These may provide an interesting backdrop to an historical AR game. One particularly interesting set of battles are the First and Second Battle of Bull Run. In the north, these are known as the First and Second Battle of Manassas. The second battle was fought August 30, 1862, and the Confederate's General Robert E. Lee's Army of Northern Virginia defeated the Union's Major General John Pope's Army of Virginia. What make this an interesting location is that the visitors are able to walk over large tracts of land where the armies engaged. A person can stand where the commanders viewed the terrain and made strategic and tactical decisions. AR would be a marvellous technology to allow the visitor to view the battle from these vantage points. Imagine a civil war game that allowed the user to view and direct the battle from these points. This would be truly history coming alive!

Conclusion

The great thing about the future is everyone can predict it, but no one can promise it. The point of this chapter is to provide the reader with a peek into my thinking in the direction of AR gaming of the future. The Wearable Computer Laboratory at the University of South Australia and myself have been investigating AR gaming since 2000, and we have pondered a number of issues, directions, and crazy ideas over that time. The contents of this chapter describe what might happen and what technologies may help with the development of AR gaming, and it is not intended to be a roadmap.

What to take away from this chapter?

1.   There will not be one AR gaming platform. The form factor of AR gaming will be determined by the type of game played.

2.   Games will have to be developed to take into account this new medium of gaming. The genres and fundamental game play may remain the same, but the interaction with the game will be very different.

3.   Games will allow players to move more freely. The physicality is very important to the gaming experience.

4. There will be no one game everyone will play. As with current gaming, everyone's taste is different.

5. AR gaming will allow co-located people to share a gaming experience in a similar fashion to laser tag, chase games, or exploration of new places. The physical sharing and not virtual sharing will be a key new feature of this form of gaming.

Acknowledgments

I wish to acknowledge the following people who have helped shape my views on AR and the use of this technology for gaming: Wayne Piekarski, Aaron Toney, Ben Close, Ben Avery, Ross Smith, Peter Hutterer, Joe Velikovsky, and Greg Macpherson. I would like to thank the School of Computer and Information Science, the University of South Australia, ITEK, and South Australian Film Corporation for their support over the years. I would like to thank Judy Thomas and Andrew Cunningham for proofreading this chapter.

References

Avery, B., Piekarski, W., Warren, J., & Thomas, B. H. (2006). *Evaluation of user satisfaction and learnability for outdoor augmented reality gaming.* Paper presented at the 7th Australasian User Interface Conference (AUIC2006), Hobart, Australia.

Azuma, R. T. (1999). *The challenge of making augmented reality work outdoors.* Paper presented at the 1st International Symposium on Mixed Reality (ISMR99), Yokohama, Japan.

Cheok, A. D., Goh, K. H., Liu, W., Farbiz, F., Fong, S. W., Teo, S. L., Li, Y., & Yang, X. (2004). Human Pacman: A mobile, wide-area entertainment system based on physical, social, and ubiquitous computing. *Personal Ubiquitous Computing, 8*(2), 71-81.

Cooper, N., Keatley, A., Dahlquist, M., Mann, S., Slay, H., Zucco, J., Smith, R., & Thomas, B. H. (2004). Augmented reality Chinese Checkers. In *Proceedings of the 2004 ACM SIGCHI International Conference on Advances in computer entertainment technology* (pp. 117-126). Singapore: ACM Press.

Gandy, B. M., Presti, P., Dow, S., Bolter, J., Yarbrough, B., & O'Rear, N. (2005). *AR karaoke: Acting in your favorite scenes.* Paper presented at the 4th IEEE and ACM International Symposium on Mixed and Augmented Reality, Vienna, Austria.

Grosch, T. (2005). *Differential photon mapping: Consistent augmentation of photographs with correction of all light paths.* Paper presented at the Eurographics 2005, Trinity College, Dublin, Ireland.

idSoftware. (2000). *Quake.* Retrieved May 16th, 2000, from http://www.idsoftware.com/

Kojima, M., Sugimoto, M., Nakamura, A., Tomita, M., Nii, H., & Inami, M. (2006). *Augmented coliseum: An augmented game environment with small vehicles.* Paper presented at the 1st IEEE International Workshop on Horizontal Interactive Human-Computer Systems, 2006. TableTop 2006, Adelaide, Australia.

Kollin, J. S. (1993). *A retinal display for virtual-environment applications*. Paper presented at the Proceedings of Society for Information Display, 1993 International Symposium, Digest of Technical Papers, Playa del Rey, CA.

Lantz, E. (1996). The future of virtual reality: Head mounted displays versus spatially immersive displays (panel) In *Proceedings of the 23rd Annual Conference on Computer Graphics and Interactive Techniques* (pp. 485-486). ACM Press.

McCaffery, D. J., & Finney, J. (2004). The need for real time consistency management in P2P mobile gaming environments. In *Proceedings of the 2004 ACM SIGCHI International Conference on Advances in computer entertainment technology* (pp. 203-211). Singapore: ACM Press.

Mitchell, K., McCaffery, D., Metaxas, G., Finney, J., Schmid, S., & Scott, A. (2003). Six in the city: Introducing real tournament—a mobile IPv6 based context-aware multiplayer game. In *Proceedings of the 2nd Workshop on Network and System Support for Games* (pp. 91-100). Redwood City, CA: ACM Press.

Norman, D. A. (1990). Why the interface doesn't work. In B. Laurel (Ed.), *The art of human-computer interface design*. Reading, MA: Addison-Wesley.

Phillips, K., & Piekarski, W. (2005). *Possession techniques for interaction in real-time strategy augmented reality games*. Paper presented at the ACM SIGCHI International Conference on Advances in Computer Entertainment Technology ACE 2005, Singapore.

Piekarski, W., & Thomas, B. H. (2001). *Tinmith-Metro: New outdoor techniques for creating city models with an augmented reality wearable computer*. Paper presented at the 5th International Symposium on Wearable Computers, Zurich.

Starner, T., Leibe, B., Singletary, B., & Pair, J. (2000). *MIND-WARPING: Towards creating a compelling collaborative augmented reality game*. Paper presented at the Proceedings of the 5th International Conference on Intelligent User Interfaces, New Orleans, LA.

Thomas, B., Krul, N., Close, B., & Piekarski, W. (2002). *Usability and playability issues for ARQuake*. Paper presented at the Special session of International Workshop on Entertainment Computing IWEC2002: Mixed Reality Entertainment Computing, Makuhari, Japan.

Thomas, B. H., & Piekarski, W. (2002). *Making augmented reality outdoor games: Why is it hard?* Paper presented at the Production Process of 3D Computer Graphics Applications—Structures, Roles, and Tools (SIGGRAPH Campfire), Snowbird, UT.

Toney, A., Mulley, B., Thomas, B. H., & Piekarski, W. (2002). *Minimal social weight user interactions for wearable computers in business suits*. Paper presented at the 6th International Symposium on Wearable Computers, Seattle, WA.

Endnotes

[1]   A 800 × 600 SVGA DLP projector are currently under the $(US) 600.00 mark; this was found through http://froogle.google.com/ on the February, 14, 2006.

[2]   http://www.microvision.com/

About the Authors

Michael Haller is a researcher developing innovative computer interfaces that explore how virtual and real worlds can be merged to enhance and improve computer systems. Currently, he is working at the Department of Digital Media of the Upper Austria University of Applied Sciences and responsible for computer graphics, multimedia programming, and augmented reality. He has produced technical publications and his work has been demonstrated at a wide variety of conferences. Furthermore, he is active in several research areas, including augmented and virtual reality, and human computer interfaces. In 2004, he received the Erwin Schroedinger Fellowship Award presented by the Austrian Science Fund for his stay at the HITLabNZ, University of Canterbury (New Zealand) and the CGIT, University of Southern California (USA).

Mark Billinghurst is a researcher developing innovative computer interfaces that explore how virtual and real worlds can be merged. Director of the HIT Lab (New Zealand) at the University of Canterbury, he has produced more than 80 technical publications and presented demonstrations and courses at a wide variety of conferences. He has a PhD from the University of Washington and conducts research in augmented and virtual reality, wearable computing, and conversational interfaces. He has previously worked at ATR Research Labs, British Telecom, and the MIT Media Laboratory. One of his research projects, the MagicBook, was winner of the 2001 Discover Award for best Entertainment Application.

Bruce H. Thomas is the current director of the Wearable Computer Laboratory at the University of South Australia. He is currently a NICTA fellow, CTO of A_RAGE, and a visiting scholar with the Human Interaction Technology Laboratory, University of Washington. He is the inventor of the first outdoor augmented reality game ARQuake. His current research interests include wearable computers, user interfaces, augmented reality, virtual reality, CSCW, and tabletop display interfaces. In addition to his experience at the University of

South Australia, he has run my own computer consultancy company. He was a computer scientist at the National Institute of Standards and Technology, and a software engineer for the Computer Sciences Corporation and the General Electric Company.

***

István Barakonyi is a researcher at the Graz University of Technology, Austria, and a PhD student at the Vienna University of Technology. He obtained a master's degree in computer science at the Budapest University of Technology and Economics. His research interests include augmented reality applications, embodied autonomous agents, affective computing, and human-computer interfaces.

Blaine Bell is a software engineer at Schrödinger in New York City where he focuses on developing visualization and user interface techniques for chemical simulation software used in pharmaceutical and biotechnology research. He received his MS in computer science in 1999, and his PhD in computer science in May 2005, both from Columbia University, USA. His dissertation focused on view management and mobile augmented reality. He received an IBM PhD Fellowship Award and his paper introducing the concept of view management and its applications to virtual and augmented reality won the Best Student Paper Award at the ACM Symposium on User Interface Software and Technology in 2001.

Oliver Bimber is a junior professor for augmented reality at the Bauhaus University Weimar, Germany. He received a PhD in engineering at the Technical University of Darmstadt, Germany. Bimber is co-author of the book "Spatial Augmented Reality" and has lectured several Eurographics and Siggraph courses on this topic. He has invented and developed spatial augmented reality displays, such the virtual showcase and augmented holograms. He serves on the editorial board of the *IEEE Computer* magazine (graphics and multimedia editor). His research interests include next-generation display technologies, as well as enabling real-time rendering and computer vision techniques.

Jay David Bolter is the Wesley chair of new media at the Georgia Institute of Technology, USA. Along with the Augmented Environments Lab at Georgia Tech, he is helping to build augmented reality systems to stage dramatic experiences for entertainment and education. He also wrote several books on hypertext, media theory, and digital design. He received his PhD in classics from the University of Toronto.

Adrian David Cheok is director of the Interaction and Entertainment Research Center, incorporating Mixed Reality Lab, Nanyang Technological University in Singapore. He is associate professor in both the Schools of Computer Engineering and Art, Design, and Media. He has previously worked in real-time systems, soft computing, and embedded computing in Mitsubishi Electric Research Labs (Osaka, Japan) and NUS. He has been working on research covering mixed reality, human-computer interaction, wearable computers and smart spaces, fuzzy systems, embedded systems, power electronics, and multi-modal recognition.

Enylton Machado Coelho graduated with a PhD in computer science from the Georgia Institute of Technology, USA. Coelho's areas of research are augmented reality, visualization, and 3D interaction. He is also interested in how research evolves into innovation and how innovation becomes an end product that can be used on a daily basis.

Matthew R. O'Connor worked as lead software engineer and software designer for the Media Convergence Laboratory from 2003 to 2005. His current work and research interests involve distributed computing and artificial intelligence, specifically in the areas of interacting and cooperating agents, genetic evolution of intelligent agents, scalable scripting systems, and intelligent human/agent interaction. He holds a BS in computer science from the University of Central Florida, USA, from which he is currently pursing his PhD.

Steven Dow is a PhD student in human-centered computing in the College of Computing at the Georgia Institute of Technology. His research interests include design tools, human-computer interaction, ubiquitous computing, mixed reality, and experience design. He has contributed significantly to several mixed reality experiences, including "The Voices of Oakland" audio tour in an historic cemetery in Atlanta and "Augmented Reality Façade" based on the interactive drama created by Mateas and Stern. He received his MS in human-computer interaction from the Georgia Institute of Technology.

Steven Feiner is a professor of computer science at Columbia University, USA, where he directs the Computer Graphics and User Interfaces Laboratory. He received a PhD in computer science from Brown University. His research interests include virtual environments and augmented reality, knowledge-based design of graphics and multimedia, wearable and mobile computing, information visualization, and hypermedia. He is co-author of "Computer Graphics: Principles and Practice and Introduction to Computer Graphics" and over the past few years has served as general chair for the 2004 ACM Symposium on User Interface Software and Technology and program co-chair for the 2003 IEEE International Symposium on Wearable Computers. In 1991, he received an Office of Naval Research Young Investigator Award.

Pascal Fua received an engineering degree from Ecole Polytechnique, Paris, in 1984 and a PhD in computer science from the University of Orsay in 1989. He joined EPFL (Swiss Federal Institute of Technology) in 1996 where he is now a professor in the School of Computer and Communication Science. Before that, he worked at SRI International and at INRIA Sophia-Antipolis as a computer scientist. His research interests include human body modelling from images, optimization-based techniques for image analysis and synthesis, and the use of information theory in the area of model-based vision. He has co-authored more than 100 publications in refereed journals and conferences. He is an associate editor of IEEE journal *Transactions for Pattern Analysis and Machine Intelligence* and has been a program committee member of several major vision conferences.

Maribeth Gandy is a research scientist with the Interactive Media Technology Center at the Georgia Institute of Technology, USA, and a doctoral student there with a focus on augmented reality and HCI. Her other research interests include mobile, wearable, and ubiquitous computing, universal design, and computer audio. She received her MS in computer science and BS in computer engineering from the Georgia Institute of Technology.

Anders Henrysson is a PhD student at the University of Linköping. The topic for his PhD is mobile computer graphics and interaction. Henrysson is fascinated about the possibility of mobile phones to bridge the physical world and the digital domain. In 2004, he did the first port of ARToolKit to the Symbian platform. He sees the camera enabled mobile phone as an ideal platform for Augmented Reality. He is also a member of CUGS, the Swedish National Graduate School in Computer Science.

Charles E. Hughes is professor of electrical engineering and computer science (EECS) and of film and digital media at the University of Central Florida (UCF), USA. He is director of the interdisciplinary Media Convergence Laboratory and of the EECS Mixed Reality Laboratory, and is a member of the EECS Graphics Group. His research interests are in mixed reality, interactive simulation, and models of computation. He has authored or co-authored more than 130 research papers and has been PI or co-PI on more than $5.5M in research grants and contracts. He holds a BA in mathematics from Northeastern University, and MS and PhD degrees in computer science from Penn State University.

Simon Julier is a senior lecturer at the computer science department at the University College London. Before that he worked at the w3D Mixed and Virtual Environments Laboratory at the Naval Research Laboratory, Washington, DC for nine years. He was co-principal investigator on the Battlefield Augmented Reality System (BARS) project, which sought to develop man-wearable mobile augmented reality systems for military applications. He also served as the associate director of the group from 2004 to 2006. He received a DPhil in robotics from the Robotics Research Group, Oxford University, UK. His research interests include mobile augmented reality, data fusion, and virtual reality.

Gerard J. Kim is an associate professor in computer science and engineering at the Pohang University of Science and Technology (POSTECH), one of the top engineering schools in Korea. Prior to joining POSTECH, he had worked as a computer scientist at the National Institute of Standards and Technology (NIST) where he was introduced to the fields of virtual/mixed reality. Since then, he has been conducting research in virtual/mixed reality and human computer interaction with particular focuses on presence, 3D multimodal interaction and VR authoring tools. He has published more than 70 articles on the subject in the leading journals and international conferences such as the Presence, IEEE VR, and ACM VRST. Kim received his bachelor's degree in electrical and computer engineering at the Carnegie Mellon University, and master's and PhD degrees in computer science at the University of Southern California. His personal and lab homepage can be found at www. postech.ac.kr/~gkim and vr.postech.ac.kr.

Kiyoshi Kiyokawa received his MS and PhD in information systems from Nara Institute of Science and Technology in 1996 and 1998, respectively. He was a research fellow of the Japan Society for the Promotion of Science in 1998. He worked for Communications Research Laboratory from 1999 to 2002. He was a visiting researcher at Human Interface Technology Laboratory of the University of Washington from 2001 to 2002. He is currently an associate professor at Cybermedia Center, Osaka University. His research interests include virtual reality, augmented reality, 3D user interface and CSCW. He is a member of IEICE, IPSJ, VRSJ, and ACM.

Gudrun Klinker studied computer science (informatics) at the Friedrich-Alexander Universität Erlangen, Universität Hamburg (Diplom) and Carnegie-Mellon University (PhD) in Pittsburgh, PA, focusing on research topics in computer vision. In 1989, she joined the Cambridge Research laboratory of Digital Equipment Corporation in Boston, MA, working in the visualization group on the development of a reusable tele-collaborative data exploration environment to analyze and visualize 3D and higher-dimensional data in medical and industrial applications. Since 1995, she has been researching various aspects of the newly emerging concept of Augmented Reality, first at the European Computer-industry Research Center, then at the Fraunhofer Institute for Computer Graphics, and since 2000 at the Technical University of Munich. Here, her research focus lies on developing approaches to ubiquitous augmented reality that lend themselves to realistic industrial applications.

Florian Ledermann is a researcher and PhD Student at the Interactive Media Systems Group, Vienna University of Technology, Austria, where he also received his master's degree in "Computer Science and Design." His current research interests include user interface design, usability testing, and content creation for ubiquitous systems.

Gun A. Lee is a researcher at the Electronics and Communications Research Institute (ETRI) in Korea. He has a broad interest in human-computer interfaces, especially in multimodal interactions and virtual/augmented reality interfaces. As a PhD candidate in computer science and engineering at POSTECH (Pohang University of Science and Technology), he has been developing authoring tools for virtual and augmented reality environments. Recently, he has focused his research topics on developing mixed reality interfaces for industrial and entertainment applications.

Vincent Lepetit received engineering and master's degrees in computer science from the ESIAL in 1996. He received his PhD in computer vision in 2001 from the University of Nancy, France, after working in the ISA INRIA team. He then joined the Virtual Reality Lab at EPFL (Swiss Federal Institute of Technology) as a post-doctoral fellow and became a founding member of the Computer Vision Laboratory. He has received several awards in computer vision including the Best Paper Award at CVPR 2005. His research interests include vision-based augmented reality, 3D camera tracking, and object recognition.

Blair MacIntyre is an assistant professor in the College of Computing at the Georgia Institute of Technology. He received BMath and MMath degrees from the University or Waterloo, and an MPhil and PhD from Columbia University. His research focuses on the design and evaluation of augmented and mixed reality systems, and the design of software to support the exploration of interactive environments that mix physical and virtual worlds.

Ulrich Neumann is an associate professor of computer science and electrical engineering at the University of Southern California, USA. He holds an MSEE from SUNY at Buffalo and a computer science PhD from the University of North Carolina at Chapel Hill. His current research relates to immersive environments and virtual humans. He won an NSF CAREER Award in 1995 and the Jr. Faculty Research Award at USC in 1999. Dr. Neumann held the Charles Lee Powell Chair of Computer Science and Electrical Engineering (2000-2005) while he was the director of the Integrated Media Systems Center (IMSC), an NSF Engineering Research Center.

Mark Ollila is a senior lecturer at the University of Linköping with research interests in mobile computer graphics and interaction. During 2003 and 2004, he published several documents for the European Commission on Mobile Entertainment, particularly on Mobile Entertainment Business Models. Dr. Ollila is an industry expert having been involved in the creation of new start up companies and research labs in media and mobile entertainment such as Telcogames Ltd where he is a board member. He sits on the advisory board of GDC Mobile, and on the jury of the IMG Awards. He is a member of the IEEE and ACM.

Wayne Piekarski is the assistant director of the Wearable Computer Lab and senior lecturer in the School of Computer and Information Science at the University of South Australia. He received his PhD in computer science for his dissertation titled "Interactive 3D Modelling in Outdoor Augmented Reality Worlds". Piekarski also has a BE in computer systems engineering. His research interests include mobile outdoor augmented reality systems such as Tinmith, 3D user interfaces and input devices, and computer graphics. For more information, visit http:// www.tinmith.net/wayne.

Holger Regenbrecht is a senior lecturer with the Department of Information Science, University of Otago, Dunedin, New Zealand. His research interests include three-dimensional user interfaces, mixed reality applications, teleconferencing, and embodied interaction. Holger has a doctoral degree from Bauhaus University Weimar, Germany and was working as a principal investigator and research manager for DaimlerChrysler Research and Technology.

Cindy Robertson received her BS in computer engineering from the University of South Carolina and her MS in computer science from the Georgia Institute of Technology. Her research interests lie in creating meaningful augmented reality applications in the face of changing registration error.

Christian Sandor joined Professor Klinker's Augmented Reality research group as a graduate student in 2001. From May to December 2004, he was visiting researcher at Professor Feiner's Computer Graphics and User Interfaces lab at Columbia University, New York. October 2005, he received his PhD from Technische Universiaet Mueunchen. Since November 2005, he has worked as a researcher at Canon's Leading-Edge Technology Development Headquarters in Tokyo. Since current user interfaces hardly match the requirements of today's tasks, he wants to support other researchers in exploring new user interface ideas. He is particularly interested in software and tools that enable these kinds of explorations.

Dieter Schmalstieg is a full professor of virtual reality and computer graphics at Graz University of Technology, Austria, where he directs the "Studierstube" research project on augmented reality. His current research interests are augmented reality, distributed graphics, 3D user interfaces, and ubiquitous computing. He is author and co-author of more than 100 reviewed scientific publications, editorial advisory board member of computers & graphics, member of the steering committee of the IEEE International Symposium on Mixed and Augmented Reality, chair of the EUROGRAPHICS working group on Virtual Environments, and advisor of the K-Plus Competence Center for Virtual Reality and Visualization in Vienna. In 2002, he received the START career award presented by the Austrian Science Fund.

Christopher B. Stapleton, artistic director of the Media Convergence Laboratory, is a faculty member of the University of Central Florida School of Film and Digital Media and the Institute for Simulation and Training. As a 25-year international veteran producer and designer of theme parks, informal education, interactive computer graphics, feature films, and New York theatre, his client list includes Universal Studios, Nickelodeon Recreation, Walt Disney World, Sanrio, IBM, Canon inc., National Science Foundation, and the Department of Defense. He received both his BFA and MFA from the Design Department of the Tisch School of the Arts at New York University. He is currently launching a commercial research company called Simiosys, LLC.

Suya You is a research assistant professor in the Computer Science Department at the University of Southern California (USC). He earned his MSc (1991) and PhD from the Huazhong University of Science and Technology, China (1994). His expertise is in the fundamental and applied aspects of interactive multimodal systems, computer vision, computer graphics, virtual and augmented reality, and advanced human computer interactions. Dr. You is also an investigator in the Integrated Media Systems Center, an NSF Engineering Research Center at USC. He has been developing unique motion tracking, augmented reality, large-scale scene modeling, and 3D visualization techniques, and holds several patents and technology disclosures in those areas. The developed technologies have been licensed to several companies, for example, the special effects house, Rhythm & Hues, has used the developed motion tracking technique successfully for creation of special effects in films such as "X-Men 2," "Daredevil," and "The Cat in the Hat." Dr. You is a member of the ACM, Siggraph, and the IEEE Computing Society, and serves as committee member and reviewer in many conferences and journals.

Index

industrial augmented reality applications
    286, 287
information tunnelling 375
inset window 31
inset windows 29
Integrated Helmet and Display Sighting
    System (IHADSS) 44
intent-based augmentation examples 29
intent-based illustrations 29
inter-class constraints 221
interaction techniques 220
interaction volume 277
interactive 200, 209, 213, 226, 331
interest point detection 7
interface design 263
interface module 324
intermediate image 9
interplay conventions 336
intersect 39
interval tree 118, 127
Invisible Train 93
IP camera network 309
iterative model refinement 184

J

Jam Sessions 226
jitter 9

K

killer applications 285

L

label placement 114, 134, 135
label placer 38
landmarks 2
large expanse, extra perspective (LEEP)
    44
laser-tag 377
latency 26, 56
LCD 92
lens distortion 314
light-guide optical element (LOE) 38, 51,
    242
line-order sweep 126

local descriptor 11
lookup table 315

M

MagicBook 153, 264
Magic Land 354, 357
MagicLenses 265
MagiPlanet 266
main interactive table 355
maintenance demonstration system 291
markers 2
maturity 283, 284, 285, 287, 292, 296,
    301, 302
measuring intensity spreads 77
media 237
mediated environments 245
memories 329
Military Operations in Urban Terrain
    (MOUT) 206, 211, 332, 334
military training simulation 332
mixed fantasy continuum 336
mixed reality (MR) 1, 198, 200, 204,
    207, 213, 214, 330, 352, 353,
    354, 357, 360
Mixed Reality for Military Operations in
    Urban Terrain (MR MOUT) 201,
    206, 333, 334
mixed reality training 207
mobile 269
mobile agent reality systems 181
mobile phone 91, 92, 94, 97, 99, 102
mobile phone augmented reality 90, 95
model-aided tracker 320
modeling errors 26
modelling 181, 183, 194
modularization 141
monitoring tool 219, 226
MR application 7
MR framework 208
MR kitchen 201, 204, 205
MR platform 200
MR Sea Creatures 201
MR Time Portal 201, 338
multi-focal projection 76
multi-focal projection concept 77